JÉRÔME LE ROYER DE LA DAUVERSIÈRE

His Friends and Enemies

(1597 - 1659)

by
Henri Béchard, S.J.

©MCMXCI
Apostolate for Family Consecration
John Paul II Holy Family Center
Box 151
Bloomingdale, Ohio 43910
U.S.A.

Telephone 614-765-4301 or 414-652-2600

AFC Book 323-92

I

Béchard, Henri, S.J.
Jérôme Le Royer de la Dauversière
His Friends and Enemies

ISBN 0-932406-20-3
Library of Congress Catalog Card number 89-082326

Permission for publication granted
Montreal, August 14, 1986
Bernard Carrière, S.J., Provincial

With permission of the Archbishop of Montreal
Most Reverend Paul Grégoire, Prot. No. 8/1986

Printed with ecclesiastical approbation:
Most Reverend Paul Grégoire, Prot. No. 8/1986

JÉRÔME LE ROYER DE LA DAUVERSIÈRE

"Si on veut dire que l'homme est trop peu
pour meriter la communication avec Dieu,
il faut être bien grand pour en juger."

Pascal

*"If one wishes to say that man is too small
to deserve to speak with God,
one must be very big in order to judge him."*

HENRI BÉCHARD, S.J.

Videotape Series on Jérôme Le Royer

The Apostolate for Family Consecration offers a Peace of Heart Forum videotape series to accompany you on your journey through this book on Jérôme Le Royer, *Jérôme Le Royer de la Dauversière: His Friends and Enemies*. The videotapes feature the author of this book, Father Henri Béchard, S.J.; his companion, Father Thomas Egan, S.J., Dr. Burns K. Seeley, and Jerome F. Coniker, founder of the Apostolate for Family Consecration.

We recommend that you set time aside every day to reflectively read this powerful book, and then gather for four weekly meetings with others who are also reading the book, to view two half-hour videotapes and to discuss your insights about the life of this committed family man that had a burning vision.

Video Schedule
First Weekly Gathering: Video #126-1607
> *Program Overview:* A layman's vision, his call to found Montreal and the Religious Hospitallers of St. Joseph.
> *First Week Preview:* St. Joseph and the founding of Montreal.

Second Weekly Gathering: Video #126-1610
> *First Week Review:* The laity's role, prudence, consecration to St. Joseph, more about the founder's experiences.
> *Second Week Preview:* Divine providence; those that helped Jérôme.

Third Weekly Gathering: Video #126-1614
> *Second Week Review:* Missionaries, vows, Jérôme's devotion to St. Joseph, the struggle to obtain funds.
> *Third Week Preview:* Why revelations to a layman?; Ten years left—lost supporters.

Fourth Weekly Gathering: Video #126-1617
> *Third Week Review:* Death of Jerome
> *Program Review:* Three great fruits and how Kateri Tekakwitha's life was affected by Jérôme Le Royer's works.

For the complete set of eight half-hour video programs, simply write to:
Aposotlate for Family Consecration
Box 151
Bloomingdale, OH 43910

or call: 614-765-4301 or 414-652-2600

IV

Jérôme Le Royer
de la Dauversière

His Friends and Enemies

Husband, Father, Founder of Montreal,
Founder of the Religious Hospitallers of St. Joseph,
and Founder of the Holy Family Confraternity.

Jérôme Le Royer sends Mother de Brésoles
and some of the La Fleche Religious Hospitallers
of St. Joseph on their journey to Canada.

Mademoiselle Jeanne Mance, a laywoman,
was the foundress of the Hotel Dieu of Montreal,
Canada, by the approval of Jérôme Le Royer.

DEDICATION

To Reverend Sister Denise Lafond,
Superior General of
the Religious Hospitallers of St. Joseph

To all their members throughout the world
for the 350th anniversary of
their inception on May 15, 1636

And to my confrere,
the Reverend Gérard Lavigne, S.J.,
whose forefather,
Urbain Tessier dit Lavigne,
came to Montreal
with Maisonneuve in 1647

BY THE AUTHOR

J'ai cent ans, L'Eglise Saint-François-Xavier de Caughnawaga,
Ed. du Messager, Montreal, 1946. Out of print.

(English translation of title) *I Am One Hundred Years Old,
The Church of St. Francis Xavier of Caughnawaga*

The Visions of Bernard Francis de Hoyos, S.J., Vantage
Press New York, Washington, Hollywood, 1959. Out of print.

L'Héroïque Indienne Kateri Tekakwitha, Fides, Montreal
and Paris, 1967. 2nd Edition, 1980.

(English translation of title) *The Heroic Indian Maiden
Kateri Tekakwitha*

The Original Caughnawaga Indians, International Publishers', Montreal, 1976.

Founder and Editor of the Quarterlies:
  KATERI, Lily of the Mohawks, 1948-
  KATERI, Lys des Agniers, 1951-

In preparation:

*The Story of Seven Fools: The Missionaries who worked
with Kateri Tekakwitha.*

JÉRÔME LE ROYER DE LA DAUVERSIÈRE

HIS FRIENDS AND ENEMIES

Contents

PART TWO
Hard at Work

PART THREE
Achievement

PREFACE

Although Jérôme Le Royer de la Dauversière was the founder of Montreal and of the Religious Hospitaller Sisters of St. Joseph, who celebrated their 350th anniversary in 1986, he is not well known.

Since the tercentenary of Montreal in 1942, only three lives of this great man have been available: *De La Flèche à Montréal,* a book of less than a hundred pages, prepared by the Compagnie des Associés, Amis de Montréal, first published in France in 1947 and reprinted in 1986; *Monsieur de la Dauversière* by Camille Bertrand, also in 1947, and *Faire Face* by Yvonne Estienne in 1971, translated into English (*Undaunted*) in 1973. These biographies were of considerable value, but it seemed to me that a more searching study had become necessary. It is now my privilege to offer the public *Jérôme Le Royer de la Dauversière: His Friends and Enemies,* which I hope shall help supply this need.

This life of a family man, of a government employee involved in city politics, and of a hospital administrator, relates to our late 20th century, which has been called "the age of the laity."

His efforts resulted in the coming to New France of Monsieur Paul de Chomedey de Maisonneuve, Mademoiselle Jeanne Mance, first full-time lay nurse of North America, Monsieur Louis d'Ailleboust, future governor-general of New France, and his wife, Madame Marie-Barbe de Boullongne, and, not to be forgotten, St. Marguerite Bourgeoys. Besides, this is not his least merit, for at the cost of health and fortune, he sent hardy settlers to the island of Montreal to found a town dedicated to the conversion of the native people to Christianity.

As a result, thanks to the settling of Montreal in 1642,

the Mission of St. Francis Xavier was ready to receive Blessed Kateri Tekakwitha in 1677; the foundation of the Holy Family Association to which Blessed Kateri belonged was established with the cooperation of Mother Moreau de Brésoles, one of Jérôme Le Royer's Sisters; the sight of the Hospital Sisters of St. Joseph tending the patients of the Montreal Hôtel Dieu inspired Blessed Kateri Tekakwitha to pronounce the vow of perpetual virginity.

The achievements of the founder of Montreal and of the Hospital Sisters of St. Joseph were built not only on hard work but also on prayer and penance. His austère penances may shock the modern reader. If the truth be told, they cannot be omitted. Of course, they must be presented in the proper perspective. It would be wrong to blame the Council of Trent for the prevalence of these mortifications in the 17th century and as late as Vatican II, since, as a matter of fact, Christian asceticism is rooted in the Old and New Testaments and the Fathers of the Church.

When Greek philosophy had marked Christian thought, Clement of Alexandria (+222) and his disciple Origen (185-c.254) not only oriented Christian asceticism, they did better it would seem, for they furnished it with a psychological and moral framework.

The protection of virginity in both sexes specially dedicated to God and many forms of religious life rationalized asceticism. Its initial aim was the atonement of past sins, but later on, with St. Bernard and St. Francis of Assisi and the development of devotion to the humanity of Christ, its principal purpose was configuration with the Savior.

Jérôme Le Royer belonged to the 17th century. The fervent Catholics of his day frequently made use of the scourge and the hairshirt. Those who practised asceticism were often blessed with extraordinary vitality. This treatment regularly applied today would lead most of us to an asylum. Old-fashioned asceticism was useful to our ancestors; they could thereby atone for their failings and conform more and more to Christ during His dolorous passion. As for us today, these penances have much less place in our lives since life itself has become an extenuating exercise.

Besides, moderation, which is an integral part of the virtue of temperance, is not always calculated with the same measuring tape. Nowadays the contemporary Christian is very sensitive to whatever is natural or unnatural. He is willing to accept the Savior's Cross, but he doesn't want anything to do with what he considers a contrived holiness. He is willing to ascend Calvary, but on condition that his entire nature, body and soul, enjoy redemption. It was not so formerly.

The La Flèche tax collector's asceticism prepared him for and led him to the mystical life. His experiences were extraordinary, especially for a layman with a family; still they added little to what the history of mysticism in the Church had already recorded. Not surprisingly then, we find Jérôme Le Royer consulting reputed mystics and saints, and working with them to achieve the double mission he had been entrusted with. It is impossible to write an honest life of Le Royer without constantly referring to these servants of God.

Henri Béchard. s.j.

Montreal
November 6, 1986
327th anniversary of the death of
Jérôme Le Royer de la Dauversière

ACKNOWLEDGMENTS

The writer wishes to convey his sincere thanks to those who shared in the preparation of the manuscript of this book: the archivists of the Sisters of St. Joseph in Montreal, Julienne Boisvert and Nicole Bussières as well as Joseph Cossette, S.J., archivist of the French Canadian Province of the Society of Jesus, St. Jérôme, P.Q.; Adrien Pouliot, S.J., regional archivist of the Jesuits, Quebec, P.Q.; Edmond Lamalle, S.J., archivist of the Society of Jesus in Rome; Irénée Noyes, P.S.S., archivist of the French Sulpicians, Paris, France; Bruno Harel, P.S.S., archivist of the French Canadian Sulpicians, Montreal, P.Q.; M. Delafosse, archivist of the Charente-Maritime archives at La Rochelle, France, and August Vachon, archivist of the Public Archives of Canada, Ottawa, Ont.

He also owes a debt of gratitude to the following late history specialists, Maria Mondoux, R.H.S.J., archivist of the Montreal Sisters of St. Joseph; Paul Desjardins, S.J., archivist for the French Canadian Jesuits at the former Collège Ste-Marie, Montreal; Georges Bottereau, S.J., assistant-archivist of the Society of Jesus in Rome, Marie-Claire Daveluy; Maxime Le Grelle, S.J., Brouage, Charente-Maritime, France; Baron de Tretagne, Les Invalides, Paris.

The author is equally indebted to the following who responded to his appeals for information or advice: Jeannine Blanche, R.H.S.J., provincial of the Hospital Sisters of St. Joseph in France; Dr. Lucien Campeau, S.J., of the Université de Montréal; Ellen Davis, R.H.S.J., of the General Administration of the Hospital Sisters of St. Joseph, Montreal; G.M. Dumur, Les Rousses, Jura, France; Wilbord-Christian van Dijk, O.F.M. Cap., provincial librarian of his Order, Paris; Madeleine Faisant, superior of the Hospital Sisters of St. Joseph, La Flèche, France; Jean-Bernard Léveillé of the Documentation Center of St.

Joseph's Oratory, Montreal; Roger Nadeau, S.J., librarian of the Montis Regii Collegium Max. Soc. Jesu Immaculatae Conceptionis of Montreal and Pierre Lebreton, assistant-librarian at the same institution; and Leo McGillivray, Montreal, journalist.

Much of Chapter VI appeared in Montréal, *Artisans, Histoire, Patrimoine*, Société historique de Montréal, Montreal 1979, pp. 11-16, and for the permission to translate into English and reproduce this material, thanks go to Dr. Marcel Cadotte of the Société historique and Fides Publishers of the same city.

Appreciation is extended to the former provincial of the Capuchins of Paris, Father Apollinaire, for the permission to quote from the manuscript biography of Jérôme Le Royer de la Dauversière by Isaïe Boussard, O.F.M. Cap.

Special words of gratitude are due to Marie Baboyant, librarian, at the Historical Section of the Montreal Municipal Library, without whose help this book would not now be ready for the press. In good part, whatever interest *Jérôme Le Royer de la Dauversière: His Friends and Enemies* has for readers, should be attributed to her gracious and intelligent cooperation.

Finally, not to be forgotten is Anita Blier, R.H.S.J., to whom I wish to express my appreciation for having typed my lengthy manuscript with patience and accuracy.

ABBREVIATIONS

AM   Annales de Moulins, ou Histoire de l'institution
de la congrégation des religieuses hospitalières de
Saint-Joseph

ARHSJ Archives des Religieuses Hospitalières de Saint
Joseph, Montréal

ASJCF Archives des Jésuites du Canada français, St.
Jérôme, P.Q.

ASS   Archives de la Compagnie de Saint-Sulpice, Paris

DCB   Dictionary of Canadian Biography

JR   Jesuits Relations and Allied Documents; Travels
and Explorations of the Jesuit missionaries in
New France, 1610-1791

NA   Notions Abrégées sur Jérôme Le Royer de la
Dauversière et Marie de la Ferre, Leur Mission et
les Interventions Surnaturelles qui s'y Rattachent

RPA   Recueil des Pièces Authentiques de l'Histoire de
l'Institut des Religieuses Hospitalières de St.
Joseph

RHAF Revue d'Histoire de l'Amérique Française

RHSJ Religieuses hospitalieres de Saint-Joseph
(Religious Hospitaller Sisters of St. Joseph)

VJLD Vie de Jérôme Le Royer de la Dauversière, by
Isaïe du Breil, O.F.M. Cap.

PART ONE

His Mission

Chapter I

A Child Is Born

ANGLO SAXONS often have the impression that at times Frenchmen express themselves quaintly. If a lover calls his beloved "my little cabbage" in France, no one is surprised. If an irate businessman qualifies a hired hand as a "turkey cock or a gobbler," the employee understands that his employer does not think too highly of his mental capacities.

In the 17th century, the neighboring towns and cities of La Flèche in the Province of Anjou peered at its inhabitants with jaundiced eyes. La Flèche people looked like turkey cocks, they said; they had no more sense than a goose; they were uncouth and their speech was patois![1] These sentiments were summed up in a nasty quatrain,[1] which they muttered in the presence of its townsmen, who, recognizing therein an unwilling compliment to their superiority, were likely to shrug it off with a smile.

At the end of the 16th century, Jérôme Le Royer de la Dauversière, the founder of Montreal and of its Hospital Sisters, was born in this little city, whose origin goes back to the early 11th century, when Comte Jean de Beaugency built his castle on the Loire River.[2] It was a good location renowned for the charm and mildness of its climate, sung by Joachim du Bellay in a sonnet, which to this day, students in France memorize.

La Flèche had already spread out along both sides of its

1

unpretentious waterway flowing through a pleasant dale gracefully rising up to the hills encircling it. Their slopes lush with dull green vineyards yielded excellent wine; and, looking northward, large reaches of tall timber, especially fragrant pine groves, gave promise of a good annual income to their owners.

At the time of Jérôme's birth, March 18, 1597,[3] the country was recuperating from the wars of religion under the rule of Henri IV. With the able assistance of the contemporary poet and literary critic, François de Malherbe, its young intellectuals, who were to nurture and bring to full bloom the great French classical period, were learning to write. St. Francis de Sales was smilingly recalling to his contemporaries that the whole world, my lord and milady, the peasant and the bourgeois as well as the Carthusians in their Charterhouses, were called to the imitation of Christ.

The newborn child's father, Jérôme, was also a native of La Flèche[4] who, as a young man, had first gone to live in the city of Tours. There he worked as collector of poll taxes for the Chapter of the Metropolitan Church of St. Martin, proprietor of seven castle wards in the vicinity of his birthplace. His position plus family ties led him and his wife, Renée Oudin, to settle down in La Flèche.

The earliest of the Le Royer forefathers, whose name history has retained, Jehan,[5] was already established at La Flèche in the late 1400s. Guillaume (or William) his great-grandson, was noted for having served as majordomo to Charles de Bourbon, Duke of Vendôme. Towards 1595, Julien Le Royer, Jérôme's great-grandfather, died at an advanced age. Julien Le Royer had acquired a modest tract of land called La Dauversière, located nine or ten miles outside the city. In turn, his son, Guillaume, Jérôme's grandfather, inherited it. The grandson eventually became its owner and signed Jérôme Le Royer, Master of La Dauversière, in the register of baptisms.[6]

2

Although the young father of twenty-six years did not belong to the aristocracy, he was listed as a nobleman.[7] To be so qualified, it was sufficient to own a small domain free of the obligations imposed on land held by a commoner. He also had the right to a coat of arms. The La Dauversière escutcheon carried "Azure, three cart-wheels; Or, two in chief and one in base."[8] The motto was *Pro fide et patria* (For the faith and the fatherland).

In 1597, the young couple bought a well-built house on what was later known as rue Basse.[9] They were not to remain there very long, for, in December 1603, they felt obliged to sell it to make way for the new presidial court-house. Jérôme was a member of the presidial[10] and it would have been awkward for him not to cooperate. So Jérôme and his wife, Renée, acquired another place on Rue de la Porte St-Germain and moved into it with their three children, René, the eldest, Jérôme, who was six and a half years old, and a daughter named Marguerite.

Jérôme's parents instilled in him a deep love for the Blessed Virgin. It is impossible to imagine them, especially his mother, not leading the three little ones to the shrine of Notre-Dame-du-Chef-du-Pont, erected during the 11th century by the first lord of La Flèche. Its name, Our Lady of the Head of the Bridge, came from its position: the entrance of the chapel opened out on the final arch of the bridge over the Loire River, joining the mainland to the island castle of Comte de Beaugency. As it was dedicated to Mary ever Virgin, the chapel was soon held in high repute and in turn became the cornerstone of the town. Down the years, thousands of pilgrims, not the least of whom were St. Thomas a Becket and St. Louis, king of France, knelt before the statue of their compassionate Queen. When Jérôme first visited the shrine, 15th century and other recent additions nearly gave it the size of the parish church.

3

His childhood resembled that of the lawyers and barristers of his day. In 1608, at the early age of eleven, Jérôme was admitted to the Collège Royal of La Flèche, founded four years before at the Châteauneuf, thanks to the liberality of Henri IV to the Jesuits. As a token of his affection, the king had entrusted them with the home of his progenitors because he thought these religious more competent than others in the education of youth.[11]

Although hardly organized, the new college had quickly gained an enviable reputation. More than 1,200 boys from every corner of Europe were accepted at its inception and the number grew yearly. Among them were René Descartes[12] and François Chauveau, one of Jérôme's future spiritual guides.[13] During the youth's eight or nine years at this institution, young men destined to work as missionaries in the New World were also in attendance, either at the philosophy or theology lectures inaugurated in 1606. Among them were Paul Le Jeune,[14] future superior of the Canadian missions, Barthélemy Vimont,[15] the priest who was to offer the first Mass on the Island of Montreal, and Charles Lalemant,[16] uncle of St. Gabriel, martyr, who was to prove useful to Jérôme Le Royer in carrying out his lifework.

At the end of May 1610, during his second or third year with the Jesuits, Jérôme took part in the public mourning for the founder of the college, His Most Christian Majesty, Henry IV of France and Navarre, who had been stabbed to death by a fanatic named Ravaillac. It is not difficult to imagine the feelings of this boy of thirteen, when the Jesuit Provincial, Ignatius Armand,[17] Peter Coton,[18] and other important members of the Order in France, arrived on Friday, the fourth of June, with their sovereign's heart. They were implementing the late king's wish that it rest in his college of La Flèche as an everlasting reminder of his esteem for the Society of Jesus.[19]

With their teachers, the students of the Royal College,

the Recollect Fathers in their brown homespun robes, representatives from nineteen parishes, and twenty noblemen in deep mourning, their swords adorned with black sword-knots, formed the cortège that met them at the city gate.

Four years later, another event stirred up the students' imagination: the arrival of Fr. Enemond Masse, S.J.,[20] who had spent from 1611 to 1613 in Canada. With what stories of his experiences, this priest, who was one of the first missionaries to work in that distant land, must have regaled his starry-eyed listeners! The taking of the French Mayflower, while it was riding at anchor at St. Sauveur, by Samuel Argall. The death of Brother Gilbert du Thet, S.J., who shot a cannon at the British ship *Treasurer* and was shot down in return. The missionary's meeting with Membertou the Sagamore and other native North Americans . . .

In 1614, Marquis William Fouquet de la Varenne gave a brilliant reception in honor of 13-year-old Louis XIII and the Queen Mother, Marie de Médicis, who were visiting La Flèche.[21] One evening, on the plateau overlooking the Loire, a ballet of 800 flaming torches drew the oohs and ahs of the royal guests and of an enthusiastic public.

Of course, the Royal College welcomed the boy king and his mother with elaborate festivities. They first knelt before the heart of Henry the Great in the college chapel dedicated to St. Louis, where it may still be seen. For their benefit, a drama, *Godefroy of Bouillon*, and other performances were produced by the students.[22] Jérôme, who did not have the makings of an actor, was not given a role, nor did he read any address of welcome to Their Majesties. He did feel the joy and excitement stimulated by the presence of the young monarch, whom all regarded as the ruler of the greatest country in Christendom. Although trouble broke out a few years later between the King and the Queen Mother, which finally ended in open hostility, certainly none of the inhabitants of La Flèche, least of all

Jérôme Le Royer, foresaw it during those exciting days. Did the glitter of pomp and circumstance impress itself on the seventeen-year-old youngster's mind? To some degree, no doubt it did. But his thoughts often turned to God. This penchant was encouraged by the Fathers, who tried "to teach at all times, and not only in class, that it is impossible to be a Christian, if one does not care to draw inspiration from the least of Christ's examples." [23]

Sincere devotion to Mary was advocated as the best manner of living and moving in Christ, and membership in the Sodality of the Blessed Virgin as an excellent means to develop tender, effective love for its patroness.

The Sodality originated in 1563 thanks to the initiative of Jean Leunis, a Jesuit priest.[24] In a short time it spread from Rome to the large and small cities of Europe, and from Europe to India. In the 17th-century colleges of the Society of Jesus, each Sodality was made up of the moral and intellectual elite of the students. This select group rarely consisted of more than one tenth of the entire enrollment. It was considered an honor to be admitted to its ranks. As a student, St. Francis de Sales[25] had been prefect of the Sodality of his college. Tasso, Rubens, Van Dyck, Mozart, Prince de Condé, Maximilian of Bavaria, Volta, Francis de Laval, first Bishop of Quebec, whose jurisdiction extended to nearly all of the continent, most of the Canadian (known in the United States as the North American) Martyrs, and countless other famous men learned as sodalists to love the Queen of Heaven and to serve her well.

Originally there existed only one Sodality at the La Flèche college. After a few years it was divided into four sections: the Sodality for boarders, consecrated to the Assumption of Mary; another for the day-students consecrated to the Immaculate Conception; still another for the gentlemen of the city to her Purification; and, finally, for laborers, tradesmen, and merchants to her Nativity. As a student, Jérôme belonged to the Sodality of the Immaculate Conception,[26] in which he was to receive the spiritual formation that was to make of him "a great servant of Mary," a title which she herself applied to him in later years. In those days, besides prayer, true to its constitutions, the Sodality required that its members help the poor, visit the sick and prisoners, and teach ignorant children the rudiments of the Faith. Thursday, the weekly holiday, often saw the Jesuits with their sodalists, trudging through the poverty-stricken quarters of the city. Jérôme was so taken up by these works of mercy that as a special favor he requested permission to visit the needy on other days also.

When Jérôme reached his middle and late teens, one of his later biographers asserts that he sowed his wild oats.[27] At the age of fifteen and eighteen, it is said he went off to Angers and borrowed important sums of money from a banker. Had he been gambling, a vice to which people of his social standing were often addicted? Or was he involved in a clandestine love affair? Or, more simply, did he get the money to help one of the poor families, perhaps several of them, that he so frequently visited? If Jérôme Le Royer did misbehave, and this is not at all certain, a lifetime of devoted service, not only to the needy of his little city but also to the Amerinds in the distant New World more than made up for it.

Chapter I

Notes

1. (Arthur Melançon, S.J.) *Jérôme Le Royer de la Dauversière et Marie de la Ferre: leurs vies, leurs oeuvres, leur temps.*

Circa, 1935, p. 14. MS, ASJCF, St-Jérôme, Quebec. The quatrain was truly nasty:

Ventre de son et bas de soie,
L'air d'un dindon, l'esprit d'une oie.
Grossier de moeurs et de patois,
Tel est le portrait du Fléchois.

2. (Adolphine Gaudin, R.H.S.J.) *Recueil des pièces authentiques de l'histoire de l'Institut des Religieuses Hospitalières de St-Joseph, fondé à La Flèche en 1636*, Vol. 1, pp. 1-2. MS (photostat), ARHSJ, Montreal. It consists of a series of original manuscript documents related to the foundation of the Hospitaller Sisters of St. Joseph gathered by Sister Adolphine Gaudin. Henceforth we shall indicate this collection with the sigla RPA followed by the related volume and page.

3. *Ibid.*, p. 43.

4. "Acte de vente du Port-Chevaiche du 24 juillet 1597," *Ibid.*, pp. 42-43.

5. Isaïe du Breuil, O.F.M., Cap., (Jules Boussard), *Famille Le Royer*. A four-page typescript written about 1935 and transcribed by Maria Mondoux, R.H.S.J., at the Hôtel-Dieu of La Flèche, on June 6, 1938. MS, ARHSJ, Montreal.

6. Yvonne Estienne, *Undaunted*, Dorval-Montreal, 1973, p. 1.

7. Archange Godbout, O.F.M., "Les livres canadiens," in *Culture*, Vol. 3, No. 3, (Quebec, Sept., 1942), p. 418; Camille Bertrand, *Monsieur de la Dauversière, fondateur de Montréal et des religieuses hospitalières de S. Joseph, 1596-1639*, Montréal, 1947, p. 12. Henceforth: *Monsieur de la Dauversière*.

8

8. Joseph Denais, *Armorial général de l'Anjou d'après les titres et les manuscrits de la Bibliothèque Nationale, des bibliothèques d'Angers, d'Orléans, de La Flèche, etc.*, Vol. 2, Angers, 1885, p. 299; Marie-Claire Daveluy, *La Société de Notre-Dame de Montréal*, 1639-1663. Son histoire, ses membres, son manifeste, Montréal, 1965, p. 96. The same author of "Naissance de Ville-Marie," in *Cahiers de l'Académie canadienne-française*, Vol. 8 (Ville-Marie, "Poème de la Nouvelle-France"), Montréal, (1964), p. 54, mistakenly gives as the La Dauversière coat of arms that of Jean de Lauson, third governor of New France: *"D'azur a trois serpents encerclés d'argent."*

9. *RPA*, Vol. 1, p. 57. Charles Mennétrier, in a letter from La Flèche, to Sister Mondoux, dated April 20, 1953, erroneously asserts that the young couple's home was sold in 1595 and that Jérôme, the founder of Montreal, was probably born in the house on the street of the Ave Maria Nuns.

10. A presidial, formerly a court of justice in certain French cities that did not have a parliament.

11. Excerpt of "Lettre d'Henri IV au cardinal d'Ossat, 1604," RPA, Vol. 2, p. 80; Camille de Rochemonteix, S.J., *Un collège de Jésuites aux XVIIe et XVIIIe siècles*, Vol. 1, *Le collège Henri IV de La Flèche*, Le Mans, 1889, p. 47. Henceforth: *Le collège Henri IV.*

12. Daveluy, *La Société de Notre-Dame de Montréal*, p. 95.

13. *RPA*, Vol. 2, p. 154: Fr. Chauveau was stationed at Collège Henri IV from 1630 to 1636; appointed elsewhere from 1637 to 1638, he was again at La Flèche from 1639 to 1641. In 1642, he was still listed at the Royal College, but with the note, in *missione castrensi* (military chaplain).

14. Jean Bouchard, S.J., *Le R. P. Paul Le Jeune, S.J., et la fondation des missions des Jésuites en Nouvelle-France, 1632-1642. Etude des méthodes missionaires* (Excerpta ex dissertatione ad lauream in Facultate Missiologica Pontificiae Universitatis Gregorianae), Romae, 1958; Léon Pouliot, S.J., art. "Le Jeune, Paul, S.J.," in *Dictionary of Canadian biography*, 1000-1700, Vol. 1, Toronto, 1966, pp. 453-458.

15. Honorius Probost, art. "Vimont, Barthélemy," *DCB*, Vol. 1, p. 665.

16. Léon Pouliot, S.J., art. "Lalemant, Charles," *Ibid.*, Vol. 1, pp. 411-412.

17. Martin, P. Harney, S.J., *The Jesuits in history. The society of Jesus through four centuries*, Chicago, 1962, p. 184.

18. Rochemonteix, *Le collège Henri IV*, Vol. 1, p. 49; *The Jesuit Relations and allied documents, travels and explorations of the Jesuit missionaries in New France, 1610-1791*, edited by Reuben Gold Thwaites, 73 V. in 36, New York, Pageant Books Co., 1959, Vol. 2, p. 306, Note 68. Henceforth: *JR*.

19. *Ibid.*, Vol. 1, p. 38.

20. Léon Pouliot, S.J., *Aventurier de l'Evangile, le père Enemond Masse*, premier missionaire jésuite au Canada, Montréal, 1961, p. 60; Georges Goyau, *Une épopée mystique, les origines religieuse du Canada*, Paris, 1925, p. 26.

21. *RPA*, Vol. 1, p.61.

22. Rochemonteix, *Le collège Henri IV*, Vol. 3, p. 216.

23. *Ibid.*, Vol. 2, pp. 108-110.

24. J(ean) Wicki, S.J., avec la collaboration de R. Dendel, S.J., *Le père Jean Leunis, S.J., (1532-1584) fondateur des congrégations mariales*, Rome, Inst. Hist. S.J., 1951, p. 38.

25. Emile Villaret, S.J., *Les congrégations mariales, Des origines à la suppression de la Compagnie de Jésus (1540-1773)*, Vol. 1, Paris, 1947, p. 92.

26. *Cenomanen*, p. 4; *La Flèche et Montréal, ou l'extraordinaire entreprise canadienne du fléchois Jérôme Le Royer de la Dauversière*, La Flèche, 1947, p. 7.

27. (Adele-Josephine Grosjean, R.H.S.J.) *Notions abrégées sur Jérôme Le Royer de la Dauversière et Marie de la Ferre, leur mission et les interventions surnaturelles qui s'y rattachent*, Laval, France, 1887, p. 95; Leslie Roberts, *Montreal from mission colony to world city*, Toronto, 1969, p. 12. The wild oats story undoubtedly originated from the misinterpretation of the term "conversion" in "Copie fidelle de la lettre écrite au Reverand (sic) Père Chaumonot, Jésuite, au Collège de Kébec, sur la mort de Monsieur de la Dauversière, en l'année 1660," by Fr. Pierre Chevrier, Baron de Fancamp, in Marie Morin, *Histoire Simple et Véritable, Les annales de l'Hôtel-Dieu de Montréal, 1659-1725*, edited by Ghislaine Legendre, Montreal, 1979, p. 108.
What exactly did Fancamp mean by Le Royer's conversion? The great 17th-century spiritual writer, Louis Lalemant, S.J., quoted by Henry Pinard de la Boullaye, S.J., in "Secondes conversions" in *Dictionnaire de spiritualité ascétique et mystique, doctrine, et histoire*, Vol. 2, Paris, 1953, col. 2259, clearly defines the sort of conversion Jérôme Le Royer underwent: "Two conversions ordinarily take place in the lives of most of the saints and

religious who strive to attain perfection; one by which they give themselves up to the service of God; the other by which they give themselves up entirely to perfection." (Translation mine.) In Fancamp's letter, Le Royer's conversion relates to the second conversion referred to by Lalemant.

Chapter II

The Acacia Trees

IN THE LA DAUVERSIÈRE YARD, acacia trees thrived. The beauty of their white blossoms, and the pleasant shade their pinnate leaves threw upon the clipped lawn beneath, were popular in the gardens of pre-revolutionary France. As late as 1922, one of these trees was still standing.[1] When it was cut down, the trunk was a yard wide. So disappeared a silent witness of Jérôme Le Royer's childhood, youth, and manhood.

In 1617, at the age of twenty, Jérôme completed his studies at the Jesuit college.[2] As he prepared for his final examinations, he would gather together his philosophy notes and seek refuge within the walled garden of his home. There he could study without being disturbed.

Though never much a weaver of words,[3] he was as finely educated as any gentleman of his day. Quite probably better than our twentieth century bachelor of arts. A well rounded-out curriculum, roughly the equivalent to that provided by a rigorous secondary school today, was provided for the students in the Jesuit colleges of France— even ballet dancing and military engineering were taught to those who wished to take these electives.

Jérôme was well-mannered also. He knew as well as the aristocratic boarders at the Royal College better than "to pick his teeth with his knife... except, maybe, at breakfast," better than "to let his bottle of wine fall down," better than "to eat his neighbor's portion," better than "to blow on his broth..." Neither did he "eat with his knife, nor gnaw away at a bone while holding it with both hands." When his fingers were smeared with gravy, he never forgot "to whiten them, first with a cob of bread, without seeming to

13

Jérôme, in his capacity as a former student of the Jesuits, participated in the festivities. To begin with, for the gaining of the plenary indulgence granted by the Pope for the occasion, he and his wife, Jeanne, certainly fulfilled the necessary conditions, particularly the reception of the sacraments of Penance and of the Holy Eucharist.

On the afternoon of Sunday, July 22,[14] a procession in honor of St. Ignatius and St. Francis was organized, without doubt the most stirring in the history of the city. The streets were gay with bunting; the windows of the houses were swarming with people to the very gables; and, in the streets, had the policemen not been on active duty, it would have been impossible for anyone to get by. When the first of the marchers appeared, deep silence settled on the crowds and it was not disturbed, except for an occasional murmur, a sigh of admiration, wavelets running to the shore.

A city captain with a body of the military followed by six trumpets opened the march. Then came a Benedictine prior, enrolled for a course of theology lectures at the college, bearing the great standard of the entire student body. It was of blue taffeta, 12 feet by six, sprinkled with golden fleurs-de-lys, on both sides of which was emblazoned in gold the name of Jesus. Twenty little children from the ABC classes, sumptuously dressed as angels, their hands full of olive and orange branches, served as a guard of honor to the Holy Name.

In close succession, two by two, from the smallest to the tallest, walked the pupils. On one side of their banner fringed with blue silk was portrayed St. Ignatius to whom the Almighty revealed the mystery of the Trinity; on the other, was pictured St. Francis Xavier elevated in ecstasy as he distributed Holy Communion to the faithful.

In grand array, with waving pennants, banderoles, and guidons, next marched the students of the fine arts and rhetoricians, the philosophy and theology students,

16

everyone holding a lighted candle. Before each corps of students, musicians or choristers heralded the glory of the two saints.

In their wake, 400 participants represented the Sodality, with its crimson, blue and white flags, glittering with bullion, honoring the Blessed Virgin and the recently canonized Jesuit saints. The section dedicated to the Purification of Our Lady and reserved to the gentlemen of the city, had voted to contribute the sum needed to release a debtor from jail. Jérôme Le Royer, it may safely be assumed, was one of its members.

Two hundred and fifty boarders, "the flower of French nobility," made up one of the most colourful groups of the entire procession. The two oldest carried a banner, nine feet high by seven wide, on one side of which appeared life-sized portraits of Ignatius of Loyola and of Francis Xavier; on the other, the Name of Jesus raised in gold on a background of green damask. The young noblemen were garbed in new outfits of taffeta, satin, or scarlet silk, and adorned with strands of pearls, gems of all sorts, and plumes. Their coloured toque displayed the distinctive emblems of their respective families.

After the 2,000 and more men and boys, came the Capuchins and the Recollects, the Cistercians and the Carmelites, the male religious of Fontevrault, a mixed monastery governed by an abbess; the clergy of the thirteen parishes of La Flèche, headed by the priests from Jérôme's St. Thomas Church; and, in their white surplices and cowled amices, the Canons Regular of St. Augustine from the Abbeys of Melinais near La Flèche and of All Hallows at Angers.

The shrill cry of the fifes and the rat-a-tat-tat of drums then announced the giant float, 15 feet high by 12 wide, which it took 25 men to shoulder. The whole float was in pure Corinthian style, with gilded columns on which stood

17

four magnificent angels, all of which were fashioned out of wax. At each corner a different cardinal virtue was personified as an adult human being. In the center could be seen the animated figure of Christ blessing St. Ignatius and St. Francis Xavier prostrate at His feet. On the upper level of the float, God the Father smilingly approved of His Son's gesture, while the four angels like so many Greek stylites on the top of their pillars, extended a hand to crown the two saints. The 12 personages, exquisitely wrought, were clothed in rich silks gleaming with golden trimmings.

The procession would have been incomplete without Jesuits. There was a throng of them—80 in white surplices and black cassocks—divided into three bands, the first one bearing the dazzling reliquary of St. Placidus; the second, that of St. Messina; and the third consisting of the rest of the Fathers. In the footsteps of the community appeared the Rector carrying the great banner of the college with the assistance of the theology students. A host of little human angels beautifully attired went with them. Not only angels but also the mayor and the city magistrates with their liveried archers.

At this point of the unprecedented manifestations accompanied by 50 well-trained musicians alternately singing hymns and playing on their *cornetti curvi*, oboes, and violins, followed the Bishop of Le Mans, Emmanuel Philibert de Beaumanoir de Lavardin, in his resplendent pontifical vestments, his household, and not a few priests from his own cathedral and that of Angers. Besides the church dignitaries, the governor of the Province with a numerous escort of noblemen graced the celebration. Finally, the city authorities, the gentlemen of the presidial, the officers of the Election of La Flèche, and scores of others, each one with a lighted wax candle in hand, brought the procession to a close.

The first stop was as St. Columba's, a suburb of La

Flèche. Because of the length of the procession, it was obliged to go a roundabout way taking the highway through the countryside. After a visit at the local church for a prayer to the new saints by the Bishop, the worshippers moved through the main street of the city towards St. Thomas's, Jérôme's parish church, which had been emptied of its pews to accommodate as many of the participants as possible. A new organ pealed forth as they filed in. Another prayer to the two saints was offered by the Bishop and finally the procession turned to the Royal College.

Night had fallen when the Sodality members entered the portals of the college chapel. Jérôme Le Royer blinked in surprise. The sanctuary and the nave were illuminated with hundreds of lights, which brought out its magnificent ornamentation. The main altar, in particular, was ablaze with gold, silver, and burning candles. The Corinthian embellishment above the altar was 34 feet wide by 28 high. Behind the tabernacle, an arch 10 feet deep, resting on six huge pilaster, served as a frame for the eight-feet high and six feet wide painting of the saints. The frontal of the altar table, 12 feet long, a gift of the governor's wife, was of silver brocade. The lunette of the vault was illumined with the name of Jesus in gold, 35 feet in circumference, on a field of azure.

As soon as the Bishop made his appearance, the *Te Deum* was sung to the accompaniment of the organ and of an orchestra, and Vespers were chanted. As it was then nine o'clock, fireworks, a gift the gentlemen of La Flèche had prepared to top off the procession, were postponed until the following Tuesday. The congregation withdrew tired and happy to prepare for the next day.

At four o'clock on Monday morning, the chapel was packed tight. In those times, when concelebrations were not thought of, its six altars were not sufficient for all the priest who wanted to offer the Holy Sacrifice. Confessors kept busy during the entire morning and Holy Communion was distributed until noon.

Precisely at half past nine, the Bishop of Angers began the Pontifical Mass. The vicar-general of Angers served as deacon and that of Le Mans as subdeacon. After the celebration, 1,000 one-pound loaves of bread were distributed to the poor.

Despite the fatigue of the previous evening and the torrid heat heightened by the crowd, at two o'clock in the afternoon, Bishop de Beaumanoir delivered a panegyric on Ignatius of Loyola and on Francis Xavier. In the 17th century, a sermon little resembled the eight-minute homilies of the post-Vatican II era. The Bishop vividly depicted the lives and virtues of both saints, stressing their missionary activities for a full hour and a half. That it was a complete success is hard for us to believe. However, according to one of the Fathers present, "the congregation was so attentive that at the end it seemed the prelate had just ascended the pulpit!"

At the close of the festivities, which lasted for a full week, a report was sent to the King. He must have been pleased that his instructions had been so well carried out. The Fléchois who had taken part as well as the onlookers never forgot the homage rendered to the two Jesuit saints. Thoughts of the distant mission lands took seed in the hearts of many, and quite probably in that of young Jérôme Le Royer as he returned home to take up his everyday life.

The place he called home, built over a century before, was a three story dormer-window stone structure. From the front rooms, he could see the heavy coaches as they rumbled by, coming from the St. Germain Gate on their way to the heart of the city, on what in 1625 was named the Nuns' Hail Mary Street, la Rue des Religieuses de l'Ave, eventually shortened to Hail Mary Street.[15] At the rear of the house, two wings had been added on. One served as the office of the collector of taxes, the other with its paintings and carved woodwork as the family oratory. Beyond the noise and bustle of the outside world, from the main building and the two wings forming a Greek pi, stretched his garden as far as the city wall, behind which ran the murky waters of a moat. Outlined against the heavy masonry of the city fortifications, stood the familiar acacias.

As time went by, once again little children began to play beneath their leafy branches. Jérôme's firstborn was now four years old. At the birth of his second son on March 21, 1624,[16] what else could he have named him than Ignace, the French version of Ignatius? His first daughter, Jeanne,[17] was baptized in 1628.

Simplicity of life and a great love of God and of neighbor were the mainstays of the home with the acacia trees. It is not surprising then that four out of five of the Le Royer children, five out of six if we count adopted Renée Le Royer de la Roche, later consecrated themselves to God as priests or religious.

Chapter II

Notes

1. Camille Bertrand, *Monsieur de la Dauversière*, Legend of illustration following p. 32.

2. *Cenomanen*, p. 3.

3. *Les Véritables Motifs des messieurs et dames de la société de Notre-Dame de Montréal, Pour la conversion des sauvages de la Nouvelle France*, 1643, facsim, in Marie-Claire

Daveluy, *La Société de Notre-Dame de Montréal*, Part III, p. 37. Henceforth: *Les Véritables Motifs.*

4. Ferrier, Gustave Dupont, *Du collège de Clermont au Lycée Louis-le-Grand (1563-1920)*, Vol. 1; *Le Collège sous les Jésuites (1563-1762)*, Paris, 1921, p. 105.

5. Charles Mennetrier, Lettre à Soeur Mondoux, La Flèche, le 10 mai 1946, MS, ARHSJ, Montréal.

6. *VJLD*, Vol. 1, p. 12.

7. *Ibid.*, Vol. 2, p. 462.

8. *Ibid.*, Vol. 1, p. 13.

9. *Ibid.*

10. Alphonsus Marquet, *Cenomanen Beatificationis et Canonizationis Servorum Dei Hieronymi Le Royer de la Dauversière Necnon Sororis Mariae de la Ferre, Fundatorum Instituti Sororum a S. Joseph in Oppidum "La Flèche,"* La Flèche, 1934, p. 3. Text in French even if the title is in Latin. Henceforth *Cenomanen*; Camille Bertrand, *Monsieur de la Dauversière*, p. 12.

11. Franz Funck-Brentano, *La Société sous l'Ancien Régime*, (Paris) 1934, p. 3.

12. *RPA*, Vol. 2, p. 94.

13. François Lebrun, *Histoire des Pays de la Loire*, "Les XVIIe et XVIIIe Siècles, les Cadres Institutionnels et la Vie de l'Esprit," Toulouse, 1972, p. 283.

14. *RPA*, Vol. 2, pp. 83-93.

15. *VJLD*, Vol. 1, p. 13. Today Rue de la Dauversière.

16. *RPA*, Vol. 2, p. 94.

17. *Cenomanen*, p. 4.

Chapter III

An Order From Above

LIFE in the Le Royer household, then, was Christian to the core. Speaking of Marie Le Royer, Jérôme's second daughter, a Visitation nun who knew her well recalled that she came from a well-ordered family in which the exercises of true devotion were favored. The young lady formed excellent habits there, such as meditating daily in the morning and evening. The same religious did not hesitate to add that the beautiful home surroundings[1] to which Marie was accustomed interfered nowise with her practice of prayer nor with her piety, which kept her free in the midst of the social whirl even though she appeared in it to great advantage. When the collector of taxes' daughter entered the Visitation Order, she was richly dressed. No sooner had the doors of the cloister closed upon her than she divested herself of her finery and chose the poorest habit at her disposal.[2]

Jérôme Le Royer's active membership in the Gentlemen's Sodality and in the Third Order of St. Francis,[3] his work for the Recollects as their syndic[4] or temporal guardian, influenced his outlook as well as that of his family. He saw Christ in the numerous, needy orphans spawned by the wars and epidemics of his century. In the wordy legal style of his time, he would often draw up and sign documents in which he pledged himself to act as their tutor.[5] To be sure, Christ was present not only in these little ones, but also in the poor, the ill, and the aged. Jérôme knew this from his previous experience as a sodalist. His home was a haven for the afflicted, who were assured they could always find a remedy for their sufferings with him. And there was the La Flèche hospital beckoning to him with a bony finger, a finger of want, inviting him to come and serve the Master disguised in rags and tatters, in the solitude and death of its unhappy occupants.

A dilapidated building, so antiquated that it was ready to buckle, housed the indigent sick inadequately. It was comprised of a ward with a partition for female servants and above a room with two beds. In the garden there was a small bakehouse and, close by, a chapel dedicated to St. Marguerite, built to all appearances by pious Marguerite de Lorraine, Duchesse d'Alençon and Baronne de La Flèche.[6] Also, for the chaplain there was a small dwelling of three rooms, a cellar, and an attic. It was sometimes called the Almonry, for it was there that the priest occasionally distributed to the destitute alms donated by the kindhearted public.

As early as the middle of the 12th century, an association of laymen of limited means, the Confraternity of St. Gilles,[7] had dedicated itself to the upkeep of the seedy institution while a few well-intentioned volunteers without any legal or ecclesiastical ties took charge of it. At the beginning of the 17th century, the Confraternity no longer existed. On March 10, 1623, Mademoiselle Rachel Moreau,[8] a young cousin of Jérôme's, donated 50 livres tournois[9] to St. Marguerite's. She also promised to turn over to it whatever she might later inherit. Then taking the name of Gabrielle, she devoted herself to the care of the inmates. Unfortunately, Gabrielle's good intentions and hard work, coupled with those of a few other girls, did not provide sufficient help. Conditions were so bad that the next year Bishop Charles Miron of Angers agreed with the civil authorities of La Flèche that distaff Augustinians of Orleans should be invited to run the hospital. Feelers went out to the administrators of the Orleans Hôtel Dieu (or hospital) and to the Official[10] of the diocese, but the invitation was declined for want of vocations, a phenomenon not reserved to the late 20th century!

25

In the meantime, Fr. Philippe Boisricher, the almoner, had been enjoying the endowment settled long before on the hospital chapel by the House of Alençon, though the establishment had not succeeded in making ends meet since the beginning of the century. In 1604, the headstrong Marquise de la Varenne, displeased with the Cordelier Fathers, had had them ousted from their monastery and their revenue turned over to the Hôtel Dieu.[11] Legal complications arose, however, and no benefit resulted for the Hôtel Dieu, which was going from bad to worse.

In 1605, a poor woman, out of the kindness of her heart, left the hospital 110 sous, truly the widow's mite. Three years later, a bequest of 12 livres and 10 sous was recorded. Slowly, very slowly, its finances grew. The mayor and the city magistrates finally decided that a thorough investigation of its resources must be made. As a result it was deemed urgent to appoint several administrators, known as the "fathers of the poor." As the almoner was entrusted with the paupers' alms and, as the "fathers of the poor" were appointed to control the use of these funds, complications were possible, to say the least. They did occur a few years later.

In 1627, André Souchard, attorney at the presidial court of La Flèche, administrator of St. Marguerite's and "father of the poor," took the hospital to heart and left it there.[12] Although Le Royer's name appears in no legal document at this time, he was certainly interested in the busy lawyer's activities.

Worried by the sorry state of the Hôtel Dieu's accounts, Souchard sought energetically for ways and means to better it. He began by asking for an appraisal of the almonry benefice. Fr. Boisricher's book-keeping left him highly indignant. So on May 4, 1627,[13] he hied himself off to visit His Honor Benjamin Sol, mayor of the city and lieutenant-general of the presidial bench. In the interview that followed, he presented a written request that a summons be served upon Boisricher, who, incidentally, was not even residing at the almonry but at Savigné, where he was pastor.

A hearing was called for the afternoon of June 14, 1628. On the appointed date, Souchard stated that during Fr. Boisricher's fifteen or sixteen years of tenure and during the fifty previous years his uncle had been almoner, neither the one nor the other had ever attempted any repairs. On that, the "father of the poor" petitioned that the almonry be torn down and rebuilt at the defendant's expense.

The priest replied testily that the income of half a century would not suffice for the undertaking. Besides, he could not afford to give up the benefice without harm to himself. After much bickering, Fr. Boisricher declared he was ready to surrender the building and property of the almonry in perpetuity on condition that Attorney Souchard meet the cost of all future repairs. The City Council ratified the transaction on June 28th,[14] and a year later Bishop Claude de Rueil signed it without any restrictions.[15] The case was still not settled, for the sanction of the King and Parliament was needed, a tiresome, drawn out procedure.

What with Souchard's efforts in favour of the ailing poor and Rachel Moreau's devotedness to them, the attention of the collector of taxes was gradually focused on the Hôtel Dieu. But what was it that spurred him on to the point of involvement?

Fr. Louis Lalemant, S.J., former novice master of St. Isaac Jogues and St. Antoine Daniel, and one of the great spiritual directors of his day, wrote the following lines, which, of course, do not necessarily refer to the 20th century: "Of all the gifts of the Holy Spirit, that of piety seems to be the portion of the French. They possess it more strikingly than any other nation. Cardinal Bellarmine, on coming to France, was charmed with the devotion he observed everywhere; and he afterwards said that his compatriots seemed to him scarcely like Catholics when he compared them in piety to the French." [16]

Jérôme Le Royer was particularly blessed with this gift of the Holy Spirit, at one with his profound love for Our Lord in the Blessed Sacrament and His Blessed Mother. It was the foundation-stone of his spirituality, indeed, of his entire life.

In 1539, Pope Paul III had officially erected the Archconfraternity of the Blessed Sacrament. This pious association, it was made known at its inception, was to be established in parish churches throughout the world and would share in the indulgences of the Roman Archconfraternity. At St. Thomas's in La Flèche, the Archconfraternity was organized in 1614 or 1615, and Jérôme Le Royer became one of its members and eventually its treasurer.[17] Visitors to his home may see a niche in the wall, where in all likelihood there used to be a statue of the Blessed Virgin. On each of her principal feastdays, he gathered his family about him, placed a lighted taper in each one's hands, knelt, and for all of them renewed the consecration to the Queen of Heaven which he had been taught as a student.

His love for Mary had already made of him an ardent champion of her Immaculate Conception. It kept him faithful to his obligations as a member of the Gentlemen's Sodality of the Purification of Our Lady. This mystery always appealed to Jérôme, and the Blessed Virgin often rewarded him with special graces on this feast of hers.[18]

Fr. Etienne, the guardian of the local Recollect monastery, his confessor, summed up the distance his penitent travelled in his spiritual odyssey: "The spirit of God residing and operating in him taught him to combine marriage with continence, the world with religion, honours with humility, the most perilous duties and charges to salvation with

28

innocence of life, and, finally, wealth with poverty." [19] At the age of thirty-three, Jérôme Le Royer had approached closer to God than many of us at seventy. Still, a long, strange road was to unfold before him. His first perception of it took place at the Shrine of Our Lady of the Head of the Bridge.

In the following year, February 2, 1630, Feast of the Purification, after receiving Holy Communion, he consecrated himself anew, with his wife and children, to the Holy Family. As he made his thanksgiving, he felt his entire being afire with love and ravished in ecstasy. It seemed to him that His God requested him to work at establishing a hospital of St. Joseph at La Flèche.[20]

The first candidate for the future community was revealed to him and the initial chapter of its Constitutions dictated to him.

Now the effects of true ecstasy, according to St. Teresa of Avila, Doctor of the Church, are so evident one cannot doubt that the soul's vigour is increased. There consequently follows an expanding of the intelligence. For Jérôme, the resulting illumination enabled him to grasp fully what was being asked of him and, simultaneously, all his limitations, better than he had ever measured them before.

"Alas, dear Lord," he cried out in anguish, "who am I for so great a task?"

The divine answer seared his soul: "Obey! Obey! My grace shall be sufficient!"

His lengthy prayer ended, the collector of taxes wrapped himself in his cloak and returned home to write out the orders he had received from above and the first chapter of the Constitutions of the Congregation to be. He was determined to work at its foundation as soon as he could see his way to it.

Chapter III

Notes

1. Edmond Buron, former representative of the Public Archives of Canada in Paris, *Extrait des notes sur Monsieur de la Dauversière*, addressed to Sister Maria Mondoux of the Hôtel Dieu of Montreal, on December 22, 1939 wrote: "In the archives of Me Legrand of La Flèche, I found some interesting notes on La Dauversière. All the members of the family were of good position. The La Dauversières, at a sale of the personal property of René du Bois, Collector of Taxes for the salt storehouse, bought kettles, a chest, a pestle and mortar, small bench, a knife-box, sheets, a Turkish carpet, etc." MS, ARHSJ, Montreal. Translation by the Author.

2. *RPA*, Vol. 4, p. 372.

3. *Cenomanen*, p. 4; *NA*, p. 99.

4. Philippe Perrier, "Jérôme Le Royer de la Dauversière," in *Les Récollets et Montréal*. Huit manifestations commémorant le 250e anniversaire de l'établissement des Récollets à Ville-Montréal, 1692-1942, Montreal, 1955, p. 177.

5. *RPA*, Vol. 3, p. 175.

6. *Ibid.*, Vol. 1, p. 24.

7. *Ibid.*, pp. 9-10.

8. *Ibid.*, Vol. 2, p. 100. Rachel Moreau died in 1628: *NA*, p. 121.

9. The livre tournois (livre of Tours) was equivalent to 20 sous of 12 deniers each. The livre parisis (livre of Paris) was worth ¼ more. In 1667 the livre tournois was made the only legal one and when replaced by the franc in 1795, it was worth about 19.1 cents.

10. *RPA*, Vol. 2, p. 108. The Official is comparable to The Official (Principal) in the Church of England today, i.e., the presiding officer or judge in an archbishop's, bishop's or archdeacon's court," according to *The Shorter Oxford Dictionary*, Third Ed., Oxford, 1962, p. 1362.

11. *NA*, pp. 118-119.

12. *RPA*, Vol. 2, p. 108.

13. *Ibid.*, p. 109.

14. *Ibid.*, p. 114.

15. *Ibid.*, pp. 115-119. The Bishop of Angers, who would always favour Le Royer, was born in Paris, probably in 1575, son of the Superintendant of the Mint. He studied at the University of Angers and became Canon of Chârtres, Syndic of the Clergy, Almoner to Henry IV of Navarre and to Louis XIII, Grand Archdeacon of Tours, and in January 1622, Bishop of Bayonne. He was transferred to Angers and took possession of his See on July 6, 1626. See Moreri, *Le grand dictionnaire historique*, etc., Paris, 1795, Vol. 9, p. 427, Col. 2.

16. Louis Lalemant, S.J., *The spiritual doctrine of Father Louis Lalemant of the Society of Jesus*. Preceded by an account of his life by Father Pierre Campion, S.J. Edited by Alan G. McDougall, Westminster, Maryland, 1946, p. 155.

17. Adolphine Gaudin, R.H.S.J., *Inventaire et Extraits des Papiers de Famille de Monsieur Jérôme de la Dauversière*, La Flèche, ca. 1875, pp. 9-10, MS, ARHSJ, Montreal.

18. *RPA*, Vol. 2, pp. 135-136; *VJLD*, Vol. 1, p. 50: it became known as the Royal Devotion after 1638, when Louis XIII used the same formula to place himself, his family, and his kingdom under the protection of Mary, Queen of the Universe.

19. *RPA*, Vol. 6, p. 532.

20. (Joseph Jérôme Le Royer de la Motte) *Le Petit Mémoire ou Écrit Autographe*. De la Motte was Jérôme's grandson. A five-page copy of the *Petit Mémoire* was made at La Flèche, May 1938, by Sister Marie-Marthe Dupuis, R.H.S.J., the very year it disappeared; this transcription was published under the title of "Jérôme de la Dauversière. Mémoire de quelques particularités arrivées à l'établissement des filles de Saint-Joseph de La Flèche," in *La Semaine Religieuse, Semaine du Fidèle*, Diocèse du Mans, Le Mans, Vol. 85, No. 3 (15 Décembre 1946), pp. (27)-29; (Elisabeth Peret), *Histoire de l'Institution de la Congrégation des Religieuses Hospitalières de Saint Joseph*, Moulins, ca. 1740, pp. 3-4. MS (Photostat) ARHSJ, Montreal. Also known as *Les Annales de Moulins*, henceforth referred to as *AM*; *RPA*, Vol. 2, pp. 134-135; Marie-Claire Daveluy contends in *La Société de Notre-Dame de Montréal*, p. 96, note 1, that the date was 1633, implying this apparition could not have taken place before La Dauversière's "conversion." Beginning with St. Paul's great initial spiritual experience, too many examples in the lives of the Saints show that in these matters the Lord does not always follow the teachings of mystical theology; Rochemonteix, *Le collège Henri IV*, Vol. 4, p. 273.

Chapter IV

No More Daydreams

ALTHOUGH Jérôme Le Royer believed the voice he had heard was that of God, he knew that Satan sometimes, to confuse a soul, appears under the guise of an angel of light, and after winning its confidence, endeavours to lead it astray. Startling examples of the evil spirit's wiles are to be found in our own time in the life of Padre Pio (1887-1968) as well as in that of Blessed Anna Maria Taigi a century earlier (1769-1837). Now Jérôme had no intention whatsoever of tangling with a counterfeit angel of light and he promptly though reluctantly consulted Fr. Etienne, his spiritual guide.

The Franciscan superior who, until then, had never hesitated when called upon to assist Monsieur Le Royer in his spiritual life, could not deny the sincerity of his story, strange though it seemed. On the other hand, common sense told him to be careful, for here was a married man, father of three children, talking of founding a community of hospital Sisters! Sorely perplexed, the good priest told his penitent to consult one of the Fathers at the Royal College.[1]

With even greater reluctance, Jérôme found his way to his Alma Mater and asked for Fr. François Chauveau, Moderator of the Sodality and an old acquaintance.[2] Of the Jesuit's many consultations, this was the strangest. His caller was far from eloquent, but here again his profound sincerity dispelled in Fr. Chauveau's mind any thought of deception. Though Jérôme certainly did not wish to deceive, perhaps he was deceived. Was he not, perhaps, subject to a subtle diabolical illusion? This former student of the Royal College was a family man; his next obligation consisted in looking after His Majesty's Revenue. St. Ignatius, in the *Spiritual Exercises*[3] has a set of rules for discerning good and evil spirits. It was time to apply them.

Question followed question. Then Fr. Chauveau, in perfect agreement with Fr. Etienne, told Jérôme as kindly as possible to forget the pious day dreams and urged him to pray more and to do penance so that he should not fall a victim to the ruse of the devil. God had spoken through the Jesuit, and Jérôme, doubtless feeling asinine, returned home and obeyed the priest to the letter. A few days later, his fourth child was born and was named Marie in honor of the Queen of his home.[4] His first daughter, Jeanne, was barely two years old, Ignatius, his second son, six, and his eldest, Jérôme, ten.

Before the eventful month of February 1630 was over, the Letters Patent approving the settlement of the complicated Souchard-Boisricher case, begun in 1627, were issued by Louis XIII[5] and, in the middle of March they were approved by Parliament.[6] Fr. Boisricher was relieved of his position as chaplain of the hospital and, on the sixth of July, his nephew, Fr. Sébastien Cador, was presented as his successor by Souchard himself,[7] all of which no doubt interested Jérôme Le Royer, though he was not yet actively involved in the Hôtel Dieu.

Still Lawyer Souchard was not content. A perusal of the documents concerning the finances of the Hôtel Dieu convinced him that it was entitled to more income. The monies which the Cordelier Fathers had been supplied with for their works of mercy had been assigned to the hospital after their sudden expulsion from La Flèche by the Marquise de la Varenne in 1604, but they had never been collected by the administrators. At the cost of much troublesome litigation, Souchard went on to recuperate the interest of the Cordelier's holdings. The establishment was to profit by the noble lady's outrageous conduct and the tenacity of the "father of the poor" until the Revolution.

34

Since receiving the divine command to found a community of nurses for the Hôtel Dieu, the collector of taxes had become much more interested in Lawyer Souchard's activities. His brother, René, and his uncle, Florimond Le Royer de Chantepie, were already officially connected with the hospital.[8] Before the end of the year, Jérôme also took on the responsibilities of "father of the poor." [9]

Meanwhile, most of the inhabitants of La Flèche were living their lives as usual. Perhaps the graduates of the Royal College, who had had René Descartes as classmate discussed his recent discovery of the laws of refraction. About the same time, the general public was enjoying a veritable "opéra bouffe" (comic opera): "the war of frogs," which broke out between the Jesuits and the local aristocracy.[10] René Fouquet, second marquis de la Varenne, claimed fishing rights to the college moats. On the other hand, the Fathers intended to keep the fish for themselves. There followed a series of squabbles in and out of court, lasting until May 1634. To end them, the Rector of the college paid Fouquet 1,000 livres, a somewhat expensive price for small river fish such as bleak, roach, gudgeon, and perhaps an occasional larger fish. All along the marquis had been after the money and finally the Jesuits realized it.

To the general public, the truly important events lay hidden. After giving the idea plenty of thought, and probably not without Fr. Chauveau's consent, in the capacity of "father of the poor," Jérôme communicated his tentative project of an association of feminine nurses for the Hôtel Dieu to Lawyer Souchard, to his brother, René Le Royer de Boistaillé, and to his uncle, Florimond Le Royer de Chantepie, and perhaps to a few others.[11] They applauded his zeal, but not his project for a sisterhood.[12] He immediately responded by inviting them to pray that God make His will known to them.

With all his responsibilities as husband, father, tax-collector, syndic (temporal guardian) for the Recollects, active member of the Confraternity of the Blessed Sacrament, and "father of the poor," in the first weeks of 1632, Jérôme fell desperately ill.[13] The doctors who examined him were unable to diagnose his case. The rest he was obliged to take, gave him time to meditate, and then it was that he was favored with the "grace of conversion," the conversion of saints. It does not consist in withdrawing from serious sin to a life of fidelity to the Commandments, which must already have been achieved, but in the definitive detachment from created things and in the perfect submission on one's being to the Will of God. This illness and the ensuing "conversion" took six months.

Then in the early summer of 1632, Jérôme's mother died.[14] As his father's successor, it behooved him to take charge of the funeral arrangements and afterwards, with the help of his brother, René, wind up her affairs.

This death was followed by that of Lawyer Souchard's during July 1632.[15] In the capacity of administrator and "father of the poor," he left a record of competent and exceptional dedication to the patients of the ramshackle Hôtel Dieu and paved the way for Jérôme Le Royer, who was to supplement his efforts.

About this time, rapid spiritual progress followed for the tax collector, progress that later buoyed him up in the mysterious purifications that are the lot of mystics. He would especially profit from it during 18 months at a period of his life difficult to pinpoint, in which he would run the gauntlet of multiple anxieties, of interior abandonment like Christ's upon the Cross, and of multiple sorrows driving him to the very brink of despair.[16]

It was probably in 1633 that Jérôme began keeping a diary. Towards the end of his life, 27 years later, he had filled 200 of them with notes.[17] Three of these notebooks revealed that at the end of the year or at the beginning of

1633, Our Lord gratified him with extraordinary "caresses." During the three months covered by these diaries, not a day passed without his receiving special blessings from on high. Blessings that benefited not only Jérôme but many others also. For instance, the charism of guiding souls well advanced in the way of holiness: a few words would suffice to dispel their doubts and lead them on to wondrous undertakings for the glory of God. For six weeks, he was favored in the same manner as St. Catherine of Sienna three centuries before, by seeing the Sacred Humanity of Christ at his side, and by conversing familiarly with Him.[18]

After reading several of Monsieur Le Royer's diaries, Fr. Etienne asked a saintly religious of his acquaintances to examine them. The reply was not reassuring: perhaps the penitent's "divine favors" resulted from the interplay of nature and grace and not from grace alone. Jérôme complained about it to His Lord.

"Father is a man like any other man," the Saviour told him, "and without my enlightenment, he is nothing but darkness; in eight days he shall have completely changed his mind." [19]

And so it was, for the religious notified Jérôme's confessor that, after more prayer and reflection, he had come to the conclusion that the graces mentioned in the diaries were truly from God.

These heavenly illuminations, among other things, incited Jérôme to actively promote devotion to St. Joseph. In consecrating himself and his beloved ones to the Holy Family, and not only to Jesus and His Blessed Mother, had he not already favored the foster father of Jesus? And had he not also been called upon to found the Daughters of St. Joseph?[20]

Despite the well known writings of Jean Gerson, 15th century Chancellor of the University of Paris, and of St. Teresa of Avila, and the efforts of the Carmelites during the first half of the 17th century, St. Joseph was not very popular. In the provinces of Anjou and Maine, covered with chapels, churches, and monasteries, not one was dedicated to the great saint.[21] No boy was christened Joseph. To make up for this deficiency, Jérôme resolved to organize a Confraternity of the Holy Family, with the definite aim of spreading devotion to the great Saint.

In La Flèche, the drawing room of Madame Bidault de la Barre, a pious, well-to-do widow, attracted religiously inclined ladies and gentlemen, commoners of consideration, and no doubt, clergymen such as the pastors of the neighboring parishes, an occasional Recollect from his convent or a Jesuit from the Royal College.[22] Here much of the charitable work being done in the city took its origin. In this sympathetic environment, Jérôme Le Royer began to promote devotion to St. Joseph, perhaps as early as 1633. Here, also, it appears, he became acquainted with Mademoiselle Marie de la Ferre,[23] who was then forty or so. It had been revealed to him that she was destined to be of incalculable help to him in the years to come.

All her life, unknown to herself, Marie was being spiritually fashioned for the part she was to play. When she was about eight years old, her mother died.[24] Some four years later, her father remarried. Her stepmother, an ardent Calvinist, after dismissing her governess, a staunch Catholic, tried to win her over to her way of thinking. An aunt, Madame Françoise de Mondion, convinced the child's father that it would be preferable for the little one to live with another aunt, Madame Catherine de Goubitz at her domain of Grand-Ruigné,[25] a few miles to the south of La Flèche.

Aunt Catherine was a practising Catholic who never missed Mass on Sundays and holy days of obligation. Still, she found her niece a bit too devout for her taste. At first, she made life as pleasant as possible for the orphan. She rehired Marie's former governess, much to the child's satisfaction. She was also pleased when the teen-ager took a liking to Fr. Julien Le Royer, a cousin of Jérôme's who was pastor of the suburban St. Quentin parish.

Soon after Marie's fifteenth birthday, her aunt decided that she had completed her education and ordered her to make ready for her debutante ball. What better setting for this important event could be found than the manor of Grand-Ruigné, with its white facade standing out against a background of fir trees overlooking the Loire River? With its terraced gardens, its gushing fountains and the scenic view, which could be taken in from the curtained windows, beautiful Marie de la Ferre would appear as the radiant princess of a prosperous principality.

For the first time, however, the young niece refused to obey. Fr. Le Royer, who had become her spiritual guide, was inclined to agree with her. After giving considerable thought to the problem, he nontheless advised her to comply with the wishes of the autocratic aunt, who could pack her off to her stepmother. Choosing the lesser of two evils, Marie gave in.[26]

At first, Marie found the smart set into which her aunt had pushed her most agreeable. However, as time passed, the brilliant receptions and sumptuous meals began to pall. The elegant young ladies surrounding her noticed more and more often the melancholic droop of her lips and the far-away expression of her eyes during what should have been her happiest moments.

On Pentecost Monday, 1608, at Favernay in Burgundy, a strange occurence took place. It closely resembled the 8th century Eucharistic manifestations at Lanciano, Italy. In the 13th century church at Favernay, a fire consumed the chapel in which the Blessed Sacrament was exposed according to custom at that time of year. Some 10,000 people had flocked to the town for the day. To the astonishment of all, a ciborium containing two consecrated hosts arose out of the reach of the flames and remained motionless above the incandescent fragments of the altar, until a priest carried it off to safety.[27]

All France talked about this extraordinary happening. Marie was deeply shaken. The thought of the worldly life she was leading upset her. After much prayer and deliberation, on July 22, 1608, feast of St. Mary Magdalen, early in the morning, she made her way to St. Quentin and went to confession to Fr. Le Royer. She told him she intended to break with the world. And break with it she did, putting aside her jewelry, her fashionable clothes, and her light-headed friends of both sexes. From then on, the young lady, who was barely seventeen years old, gave up her comfortable well-furnished room to live in the garret. Her aunt and uncle, who feared she was thinking of the religious life, were properly indignant, but their indignation was no match for her.

Marie was indeed planning to become a nun. Fr. Le Royer advised her to pray, assuring her that God would enlighten her. Then because of the new way of life she was following, the opposition she met with, and the uncertainty concerning her vocation, she fell ill. On recovering, after a lengthy convalescence, she took up her austere life once again to the manifest displeasure of Madame de Goubitz. To her exacting daily schedule, she added the care of the sick and of the poor. The winter of 1608-1609 was so cold that the fine wines on the king's table froze. It snowed day upon day, seemingly without end. Her favorite occupation consisted in visiting the neighboring run-down quarters of St. Columba. She herself carried baskets of provisions to the indigent—no mean feat in those days for a lady of her circumstances.[28]

Life took on a rosier hue in 1612, when Marie's father died, leaving her well provided for. Instead of quitting Ruigné as she might have done, she asked and obtained permission to serve as her aunt's maid.[29] Two years later,

Monsieur de Goubitz also died. His widow found herself penniless, and Marie offered her little fortune to the unfortunate lady, who gratefully accepted it, interiorly thanking the Lord for not having been successful in marrying off her niece.

When Madame de Goubitz followed her husband in 1628, though Marie's Bidault cousins, to whom the manor belonged, insisted that she stay on with them, she bade farewell to them and moved to La Beuffrie, a suburb of La Flèche. There she cared for "a virtuous elderly lady," probably Fr. Le Royer's aged mother, until her death in the following year.[30] Marie de la Ferre now passed for a likable, efficient old maid.

About the same time, Monsieur Bidault succumbed to illness or old age. At his widow's repeated request, her unattached cousin took charge of the Ruigné manor and of her winter residence in La Flèche, where the family moved at the end of every summer. In this comfortable home, Marie, who was more interested than ever in helping the needy, now and then met Monsieur de la Dauversière, who was well acquainted with the Bidaults. Four times she had planned to join the Congregation of Notre Dame, which had recently opened a convent in La Flèche. Fr. Le Royer and Fr. P. Meslan, S.J., in whom she had confided, approved of her design, but a sudden illness always stopped her from realizing her hopes for a cloistered life.[31]

Although Marie was as yet unable to realize her dream of becoming a religious, she did her utmost to draw others to the love of her life—Christ Himself. A shining instance of her dexterity and grace in winning over even people of consequence will be sufficient. A worldly abbess in search of diversion was the talk of La Flèche.[32] In the company of several gentlemen, she peacocked about the streets of the little city, often crowded with the 2,000 students of the Jesuit college. The honest, hardworking population was of the opinion that she should have been behind the walls of her monastery praying for the upset world about them. They said as much quite openly, but not in her presence, for she was not only an abbess but also a lady of noble lineage.

After consulting several level-headed persons and after discussing the problem with Our Lord in her daily meditations, Marie de la Ferre decided to intervene. She did not dare ask for an appointment; instead she penned a carefully worded letter to the wayward nun. She extolled religious life in general and then went on to show her how she was degrading it as well as herself by not observing her vows. With perfect tact, Marie suggested that she quit La Flèche, where her reputation was not of the best, and affectionately urged her to put her trust in God and return to her abbey. Madam Abbess, who was simply lightheaded and not wicked, took to heart the good advice and was no longer seen in the city.

Doubtless Jérôme Le Royer thanked God for Marie de la Ferre with all her fine qualities. During 1633, he continued in prayer, begging the Almighty to enlighten him and to furnish him with all the means, including Fr. Chauveau's approval, of fulfilling His bidding. The sorry state of the poor, particularly of those who were ill, repeatedly threw him on his knees. His heart shuttled back and forth between their distress and what he deemed his inability to provide adequately for their needs. With the simplicity of a little child, he explained to His Maker his utter incapacity and lack of experience for the important task he had been entrusted with. And always there echoed within him the mysterious voice he had heard three years before on Candlemas (or the Feast of the Presentation), "Obey! Obey! My grace is sufficient!" [33]

For years visitors had been appalled by the sordid conditions of the hospital buildings. Jérôme now decided it was high time to rebuild them. He laid his plans accordingly, interested several wealthy friends in the project, and began soliciting aid. Among them was Pierre Chevrier, Baron de Fancamp,[34] who was to become his lifelong friend. He was born about the turn of the century, probably of Norman stock. Before Jérôme Le Royer launched his idea of a new Hôtel Dieu, the young nobleman had already come to live under his roof at the suggestion of Fr. Chauveau, the Baron's confessor as well as the collector of taxes' spiritual director extraordinaire.

Pierre de Fancamp was not, however, the first one to help Jérôme. An unknown woman and a little child approached the "father of the poor" with their offerings.[35] The little one gave him two deniers, roughly the equivalent of two pennies, and the mother, one. In them, he saw Jesus and Mary as his first contributors. At that he may not have been too far wrong.

Chapter IV

Notes

1. *Cenomanen,* p. 5.

2. *RPA, Vol. 2, pp. 136, 154, asserts that Fr. François Chauveau was Rector of the Henri IV College from 1630-1636;* so do other writers. This is not so: cf. Rochemonteix, *Le collège Henri IV,* Vol. 1, pp. 210-215.

3. Ignatius of Loyola, *The Spiritual Exercises,* translated by Thomas B. Moore, S. J., from the original Spanish in the "autograph," New York, 1948, pp. 163-164.

4. *RPA*, Vol. 2, p. 136.

5. *Ibid.*, pp. 128-130.

6. *Ibid.*, pp. 130-131.

7. *VJLD*, Vol. 1, p. 48.

8. *NA*, p. 121.

9. *VJLD*, Vol. 1, p. 23: An inventory at the La Flèche City Hall carries the following note: "Grosse d'un compte de reçettes et dépenses du bien des pauvres de l'Hôtel-Dieu de cette ville que MM. Florimond Le Royer et Hiérosme Le Royer auront rendu à MM. le maire et eschevins, depuis le 19 janvier 1632 jusqu'au dernier jour de décembre 1637."

10. Rochemonteix, Le *collège Henre IV*, Vol. 1, p. 169-175.

11. Daveluy, *La Société de Notre-Dame de Montréal*, p. 103, note 1, the author writes, "Dom Albert Jamet, O.S.B., dans sa *Marguerite Bourgeoys* Vol. 1, (Montréal, 1942, p. 385), ajoute au nom patronimique de Chevrier, celui de Keriallec... Malheureusement, le religieux bénédictin ne nous donne aucune référence sur cette nouvelle forme du nom de cet associé de Montréal." In a letter of July 19, 1954, Sr. Mondoux wrote to me:
"Je viens de découvrir—bien par hasard—la confirmation d'un nom que nous cherchions depuis longtemps. En tournant le premier feuillet d'un document de nos archives, j'aperçois sur la première ligne, comme premier mot: Keriallec! C'est le nom de Pierre Chevrier de Kériallec (orthographe un peu incertaine), baron ou seigneur de Fancamp. Je tenais ma référence, et du même coup celle de dom Jamet, car le savant bénédictin est venu consulter nos

archives au cours de la préparation de son ouvrage: *Marguerite Bourgeoys.*" The paper she referred to was "Document concernant l'établissement des hospitalières de Saint-Joseph à Montréal 3 mars 1656," MS, ARHSJ, Montreal. On further examination of this document, it definitely shows that what was taken to be Kériallec was Chevallier (Knight).

12. *AM,* p. 4. Though they are not named here, they could not have been any others than "the fathers of the poor" and Fancamp.

13. Morin, H*istoire Simple et Véritable*, p. 108.

14. Gaudin, *Inventaire et extraits des papiers de famille de Jérôme de la Dauversière*, p. 6.

15. *RPA*, Vol. 2, p. 134.

16. Morin, *Histoire Simple et Véritable*, p. 109; *Les véritables motifs*, p. 28.

17. Morin, *Histoire Simple et Véritable,* p. 108.

18. *Ibid.*, p. 109.

19. *Ibid.*

20. *Constitutions (primitives) des filles hospitalières de Saint-Joseph*, (Angers 1643), p. 1.

21. *NA*, pp. 125-126.

22. *Ibid.*, p. 128; RPA, Vol. 2, p. 142.

23. Mondoux, *L'Hôtel-Dieu, premier hôpital de Montréal*, p. 39.

24. Florence Moreau, *Présente à notre temps, Mère Marie de la Ferre, 1592-1652, Fondatrice de la Congrégation des Religieuses Hospitalières de Saint-Joseph*, Montreal, 1964, p. 19.

25. *NA*, p. 17.

26. E.-L. Couanier de Launay, *Histoire des religieuses hospitalières de Saint-Joseph*, Paris, 1887, Vol. 1, p. 37.

27. *NA*, pp. 43-44; "Le miracle de Faverney (1608)," in Jean Ladame and Richard Duvin, *Les prodiges eucharistiques*, Paris, 1981, pp. 120-126.

28. Couanier de Launay, pp. 41-42.

29. *Ibid.*, p. 44.

30. *RPA*, Vol. 2, pp. 138-139.

31. *Cenomanen*, p. 53.

32. *NA*, pp. 136-137.

33. *AM*, p. 6.

34. Daveluy, *La société de Notre-Dame de Montréal*, pp.103-108.

35. *RPA*, p. 151. Towards the end of his life, Lawyer André Souchard had begun gathering funds for this purpose: cf. *RPA*, Vol. 2, p. 143. Other donations were received, but they did not cover the expenses incurred:
   a) In 1633, Dame Jacqueline Chevalle, widow of Charles

de Maillé, Esquire and Seigneur de Brézé, bequeathed an annuity of 60 livres to the Hôtel Dieu. In 1643, her son, the Marquis de Maillé-Brézé, Marshall of France and of Anjou, redeemed it for 972 livres.

b) In 1634, Monsieur Peter Jouye, anticipating the carrying out of his testament and that of his wife Damoiselle Françoise de la Porte, willed to the Hôtel Dieu a ground-rent of 22 livres. In return, "every year on Holy Thursday (Jeudi absolu) the administrators of the hospital must prepare loaves of the finest flour of one sou each to be distributed to the poor of St. Joseph's after Holy Communion. One of these loaves must be sent each year to the benefactor and, following his demise, to his eldest son or to his inheritors..." For these and other offerings, see RPA, Vol. 2, pp. 151-152.

Chapter V

Permission Granted!

JÉRÔME DE LA DAUVERSIÈRE was not allowed to forget the words spoken to him in the chapel of Our Lady of the Head of the Bridge in 1630 and in 1631. To the initial order concerning the foundation of a congregation of hospital Sisters, another one of much greater consequence was added in 1634. It was unexpected, one for which he felt totally unprepared. He was entrusted with a mission in distant America. He was to found a settlement on the Island of Montreal far up the St. Lawrence River and establish there a hospital staffed by the still non-existent Daughters of St. Joseph, whose express aim would be the conversion of the native population.[1]

From a human point of view, a Hôtel Dieu one hundred and seventy-five miles west of Quebec, in a place that for decades could never possibly be bigger than a French hamlet, in the heart of territory constantly raided by the Iroquois, was preposterous. Then, too, there was the British threat. As recently as 1628, the Kirke brothers, with a commission from Charles I of England to oust the French from "Canida," had threatened Cap Diamant. Samuel de Champlain, founder of Quebec, putting on a bold front, managed to ward them off. "If they had pushed on," he mournfully wrote, "it would have been very hard for us to resist them, because of the wretched condition we were in; which shows that on such occasions it is a good thing to put on a bold countenance." [2] During the summer of 1629, the Kirkes dropped anchor once again in front of Quebec and on July 18, easily forced Champlain to surrender. Only in 1632 did he have the satisfaction of seeing the white and gold flag of France billowing once again over the heights of

Quebec. No one knew for how long.

Despite the slippery military and political situation in New France, the thought that a signal service was being required of him by God Himself provided Jérôme with the courage to confide anew in Father Chauveau. Besides a community of religiously oriented hospital nurses, he told the Jesuit what he had been ordered to do on the other side of the Atlantic. And he certainly pointed out that, since the previous year, the French were back in Canada as a result of the treaty of St. Germain-en-Laye between France and England.

More than ever before, Father Chauveau felt conscience bound not to allow Monsieur de la Dauversière to proceed. The old objection kept on haunting him: here was a married man with many children who talked of starting a community of nurses! Here was a man of ordinary means without title or influence, who proposed to make the desert flower in New France! Never before in the history of Christendom had anything like it been heard of!

What could the black-robed religious answer the quiet, earnest man seated before him other than, "Wait, wait, until God reveals His intentions definitely"? Although Jérôme was convinced the Lord had already clearly made known His intentions to him, in compliance with the priest's advice, he bided his time until Divine Providence intervened.

This forced inaction with regard to the future Sisters did not imply he was not to bend his efforts towards building a new hospital. After all, was he not a "father of the poor?" Nearly every day, he met with the simple, dedicated, but insufficient help at the Hôtel Dieu: Jeanne Cohergne, Catherine Le Bouc, and Julienne Allory,[3] along with Mathi Bertrand, janitor, and his wife,[4] who as early as 1627, had dedicated themselves with the little property they owned to the care of destitute patients. With the approval of his brother and uncle, also "fathers of the poor," Jérôme kept on these humble, devoted workers.

He then consulted many persons of known piety, who agreed to back him, if hospital Sisters were called in from Dieppe or Vannes to take charge of the Hôtel Dieu. They were of the opinion, and so was Father Chauveau, that to be adequately run, a hospital must be staffed by nuns. In direct opposition to the tax collector's orders from above, efforts were made to get a contingent of them, probably from Vannes. The attempt was as unsuccessful as a previous appeal to the Hospitalières of Orleans in the first quarter of the century.[5]

In the same year (1634), God once again drew back the veil of the unknown before Jérôme. In a series of visions, the Island of Montreal appeared to him in detail.[6] To Father Chauveau, "...he described it from end to end, not merely its shores and outline, but he also depicted it within with the same ease. He described the beauty and richness of the soil, the length and breadth of its different parts."[7] These celestial communications were so detailed they appeared to the Jesuit as a clear vision of reality. To imagine Jérôme de la Dauversière acting the part of one inspired with heavenly illuminations about Montreal, whereas, as it has been too frequently asserted, he may have borrowed them from Champlain's Third Voyage, 1611, possibly known to his acquaintances as well as to himself, is unmitigated nonsense. Purloining of this sort would have shown him up as a fraud.[8] Besides, it was completely out of character.

Jérôme also revealed to his spiritual mentor that he must set to work at realizing the divine commands. There was no time to be lost, he said, for the organization of a settlement in the heart of New France could not be effected in the twinkling of an eye. He pressed his point. Why hurry? "Because God as well as the Holy Family were to be honored there with special devotion, and because a Hôtel Dieu run by the nursing Sisters of the Congregation of St.

Joseph (which then existed only in the Divine Intelligence) would greatly contribute to His glory." [9] Furthermore, the Most High was incessantly soliciting him to set to work and he feared His wrath if he dallied longer.

The more Father Chauveau thought about the proposed undertaking the more grew his astonishment and admiration at the strange and enormous responsibilities vested upon his penitent. He was finally convinced of their heavenly origin. The precise description of a far-off spot in Canada had not alone solved the difficulty. What had helped most to solve it was the man's perfect obedience, his bedrock humility, and his sincerity. The priest could no longer withhold from Jérôme his consent to the hospitalières any more than to a Hôtel Dieu in Canada to be managed by them. "Have no doubts on the subject," he said, "work at it in earnest." [10]

Today, if a revenue officer in one of our cities received the command from on high to found a religious community in order to establish a hospital in the land of Ozymandias, finding a reputable counselor to approve of the project would be considered miraculous. In circumstances just as unheard of, Jérôme Le Royer de la Dauversière obtained the blessing of practical, clear-headed Father Chauveau.

Jérôme, understandably, was delighted. Permission was granted! His mission was important, and he saw it now. Father Chauveau had required a definite identification of its source, though it had taken nearly four years to get it! Then his spiritual director gave him some sensible advice. He must seek the assistance of devout people in La Flèche and elsewhere, able and willing to help him meet the heavy expenses this herculean venture would entail.

By 1634, the Jesuit had certainly heard about the new Society of the Blessed Sacrament, which a Parisian colleague had been instrumental in founding some years earlier. Men of influence from the nobility, the bourgeoisie, and from the humbler walks of life were flocking to its doors. So on advising the La Flèche collector of taxes to invite the mighty to cooperate with him, to whom could the priest's thoughts have turned more readily than to the Society of the Blessed Sacrament? And thus Jérôme learned about an organization that was to play a decisive role in his life. Father Chauveau thereupon concluded the consultation by insisting that his interlocutor look for the Will of God in all things and, on finding it, take the means of bringing it to a successful conclusion.

Another confirmation of Jérôme's extraordinary vocation strengthened his determination to follow it as soon as possible. It came from Mademoiselle Marie de la Ferre. In that same year, she "was transported in spirit to a very large room where she saw rows upon rows of beds. Not understanding the significance of the scene, she had recourse to God. Then she heard a voice saying, "This is to be your calling." [11] Upon recovering from this incident, Marie de la Ferre felt strongly inclined to reveal her experience to Monsieur Le Royer, and she did so the next time she met him. He manifested no surprise, for he already knew that she was to be the first Daughter of St. Joseph. His heart sang within him. "Mademoiselle," he said, "I believe God wants to make use of us to propagate the cult of St. Joseph and to honor the Holy Family; we must work at this undertaking." [12] Jérôme then divulged part of the orders he had received about the establishment of a new community of Religious Hospitaller Sisters dedicated to St. Joseph. He advised Marie de la Ferre to be discreet about the whole affair, allowing her, however, to disclose it to an intimate friend, Mademoiselle Anne Foureau.

This young lady's father, an alderman of the town of nearby Baugé and one of the most respected men of the region, was related to the Le Royers. For several years already, Anne, who was now twenty-five, had been attracted to Marie de la Ferre by her engaging personality and her unmistakable holiness. Everywhere that Marie went, Anne was sure to go. She accompanied her to the sick-rooms of the poor, assisted her in keeping fresh and clean the altars of St. Thomas's Church, and, like her companion, was a zealous promoter of devotion to St. Joseph.

When Marie de la Ferre informed her about the vision, Anne Foureau felt that she was treading on enchanted ground and asked her friend to arrange a meeting between Monsieur Le Royer and herself. Marie readily agreed, but not before urging her to pray for enlightenment.

Jérôme had not only one but also several other conversations with the two women. To test their mettle, he suggested that they work at the dilapidated Hôtel Dieu. It was not long before they were spending several hours each day taking care of the inmates of the hospital.[13]

One of the first tasks now awaiting the "father of the poor" was to procure more land for the future Hôtel Dieu. His plans demanded the acquisition of a good piece of adjoining property[14] and, also, of a quarter of a neighboring lot jointly held by five different people. On it stood a small building, a salt storehouse.

On the sixteenth of March, Jérôme Le Royer opened the doors of his comfortable home to several visitors: Françoise Préau, co-proprietress of this holding with her husband, Mathurin Souchard, son of the late "father of the poor," André Souchard. Françoise was accompanied by Royal Notary Jacob Lemercier, who in turn was followed by Mayor Pierre Bordeaux, and a few other officials, acting as witnesses. Jérôme's brother, René de Boistaillé, was also present as well as Baron Pierre Chevrier de Fancamp. The price agreed upon for the sale was 1,900 livres, a thousand of which Fancamp paid for in coins of the realm.[15] The rest of the sum seems to have come from funds collected by the late attorney Souchard. As soon as the papers, duly signed, were in Jérôme's hands, he gave orders to tear down all the buildings on the newly acquired property. A century and a half later, Dr. Charles Boucher, surgeon at the military Preparatory School in the dispossessed Jesuit college, wrote that the poverty and suffering of Monsieur Le Royer's fellow men had been up to this time the main cause of his worries, the object of his interest, and the passion of his life.[16] How much truer this would now be!

As the report of the sale and the talk of a new Hôtel Dieu made the rounds of the city, trouble flared up in different quarters. The Recollect Fathers, who had chosen Jérôme as their temporal administrator, were displeased with him, because the projected edifice, jutting forth beyond their church, would hamper traffic. For this reason and for a more serious one, the pastor of the St. Thomas parish voiced his dissatisfaction, and it must be admitted, he was not entirely to blame, for nearly 360 years later, following the reconstruction of the Hôtel Dieu, the main door of the church still cannot be used.

Without delay, Jérôme requested of City Hall the permission to demolish and rebuild the antiquated hospital. On the twenty-eighth of June, he got it but, to dissipate all opposition, was instructed to surrender to Fr. Hamelin a strip of ground fifteen feet wide by twenty long.[17]

The time was now ripe, Jérôme thought, to take a step ahead in promoting devotion to his beloved St. Joseph. He broached the idea of a Confraternity in honor of the foster-father of the Lord to his Bishop, Claude de Rueil of Angers,[18] who approved of it on July 2, 1634.[19] Six days later, the Bishop signed the authorization, requested by Jérôme and his brother, René, to tear down the chapel dedicated to St. Marguerite and to reconstruct it under the patronage of St. Joseph.[20] He was a devout man and a good canonist, so, in deference to St. Marguerite and in memory of the foundress, Marguerite of Lorraine, he commanded that a

54

side altar be erected within the confines of the new chapel in the saint's honor, in order that the customary devotion to her be maintained.

On July 14, the Lieutenant-General of La Flèche, René de Moré de Bresteau, Mayor Bordeaux, René de Boistaillé, and Florimond Le Royer met at the Hôtel Dieu. After consultation with architects and master masons, the Lieutenant-General granted them a warrant "to build and construct the said chapel and Hôtel Dieu." [21]

Now that all the legal difficulties were removed, Jérôme decided never to allow any modifications to the original plans, and this tenacity of purpose was to stand him in good stead. But if he then thought his troubles were at an end, he was mistaken. He found Fr. Hamelin in his way. The priest now wanted to institute proceedings against his brother, René, and his uncle, Florimond, "fathers of the poor."

When questioned, the pastor complained that the administrators intended to expropriate a strip of land 15 feet long by six or eight feet wide in front of the church, close by the presbytery and the former hospital chaplain's residence. He furthermore strongly objected to the new side door of the Hôtel Dieu, opening onto the grounds of the chaplain's residence. The ailing clients of the institution would greatly inconvenience Hamelin and his successors. In the 17th century the plague was no mere word.

To avoid legal action and out of a spirit of conciliation, Jérôme was willing to compromise. On August 4th, an agreement, seemingly satisfactory to the priest and to the hospital administrators, was signed by both parties. [22] The patients or their corpses, it was decided, would always pass through the main door, never through the offensive side door. As to the problem of the space in front of the church, the pastor was told that, with the ruling of June 28, he had obtained more than ever before. Despite these arrangements, knowing him for what he was, René de

Boistaillé and Florimond Le Royer politely reminded him that they had the right to build as they saw fit, since they were on hospital ground. For the time being peace reigned.[23] Regretfully however, trouble cropped up again and again in and out of court between the pettifogging Fr. Hamelin and the Hôtel Dieu of St. Joseph for all of twelve long years.[24]

During 1634, the "fathers of the poor" acquired other lots and buildings. Eleven contracts have been found,[25] and there are undoubtedly still more to be discovered. They were rarely made out in Jérôme's name, and even more rarely were they purported to have originated with him. His brother, his uncle or Pierre de Fancamp were his agents. Why did Jérôme Le Royer, "father of the poor," wrap himself up in mystery? A matter of prudence apparently.

Tax collectors are unpopular nowadays and so it was in the 17th century. Their position had to be bought and, once obtained a yearly charge for it had to be covered. All too often, it was siphoned out of the taxpayers' purse along with the legitimate taxes.

No one ever accused the La Flèche collector of taxes of exploiting the public, for his style of life was unpretentious. Still, he was careful to avoid charges of extravagant spending at the people's expense, which could drag him before the courts, ruin his reputation and undermine his efforts in favor of the Hôtel Dieu and later on of his foundation in New France. Jérôme was a business man faithful to the Master's advice, "Be cunning as serpents..." He was indeed cunning, without, however, forgetting the second part of Jesus' admonition, "...and yet as harmless as doves" (Matthew 10:16).

On October 7, with two clerks from the office of Philippe Hamel, Adjudicator-General of the important Salt Taxes of France, in La Flèche, René and Florimond signed a contract in which they obligated themselves to construct a salt storehouse fifty feet long by twenty wide, and to rent it to Hamel's men. It was to be built on the same spot as the old one, demolished by Jérôme's orders, after its purchase on March 16.[26] Naturally the contract could be annulled by any of the parties if the conditions agreed upon were not fulfilled.

The "fathers of the poor" did erect the storehouse, but not on its original site. To dispose of the empty plot, the joint owners must come to an understanding. Since acquiring a quarter-ownership of the property during March, the Hôtel Dieu was prepared to veto all suggestions contrary to its interests. The other owners soon realized that, under the circumstances, the land was no longer of much value to them, and, on November 21st, sold their rights to the hospital at the relatively low price of 1,050 livres.[27] Jérôme had planned the construction of the salt storehouse elsewhere so as to allow the administrators of the Hôtel Dieu to secure this land for the proposed chapel of the enlarged hospital-to-be. Fortunately, on December 22nd, the Adjudicator-General of the Salt Taxes made no bones about accepting the new storehouse in a different location than the one specified in the contract.[28]

The collector of taxes' interest in other good works did not lag either.[29] He devoted the little spare time he had left to several religious communities and associations for orphans and paupers, swept by the same giant wave of love of neighbour that was simultaneously carrying St. Vincent de Paul through the slums of Paris.

Sixteen hundred and thirty-four was a period of transition for Jérôme. After Father Chauveau had said, "Permission granted!" he had obtained the approval of the religious and civil authorities to carry out his plans. Old St. Marguerite's Chapel, as well as the hospital, which had been falling to pieces with age, had been razed. In the heart of the city, the "fathers of the poor" held a large tract of land on which the walls of the new Hôtel Dieu and its chapel were now rising under the skillful direction of Jean and Michel le Coiffe, architects and master masons, while the roof and the woodwork were being completed by Lucien Malteste, a competent architect and master carpenter. Better still, Marie de la Ferre and Anne Foureau were faithfully at work tending the sick, and Jérôme Le Royer alone really knew why they were there. There was only one inconvenience, a rather serious one, it must be admitted: for the first time in his life, he was in debt.

Chapter V

Notes

1. *Les véritables motifs*, p. 26, published in 1643 and, no doubt already partially written before the end of 1642, declare "Le dessein de Montréal a pris son origine par *un homme de vertu (Le Royer de la Dauversière) qu'il pleut à la divine Bonté inspirer, il y a sept ou huit ans, de travailler pour les sauvages de la nouvelle France, dont il n'avoit auparavant aucune particulière cognoissance...*" NA, p. 8.

2. Samuel de Champlain, *The Voyages of the Sieur de Champlain, Book Two*, in H. T. Biggar, *The Works of Samuel de Champlain*, translated by the late W. D. Le Sueur. The French text collated by J. Home Cameron, Toronto, The Champlain Society, 1933, Vol. 5, p. 286.

3. AM, p. 21.

4. RPA, Vol. 2, p. 134.

5. *Ibid.* Vol. 3, p. 176; Vol. 2, pp. 107-108.

6. *Les véritables motifs.* p. 26.

7. François Dollier de Casson, *A History of Montreal*, 1640-1672, from the French of Dollier de Casson, translated and edited, with a life of the author, by Ralph Flenley, Toronto, 1928, p. 63.

8. Olivier Maurault, "Question de mesure," in *Les Cahiers des Dix,* No. 11, Montreal 1946, pp. 15-17.

9. AM, pp. 8-9.

10. Dollier de Casson, *A History of Montreal*, 1640-1672, p. 63.

11. Mondoux, *L'Hôtel-Dieu, premier hôpital de Montréal*, p. 39 and especially "Quelques mises au point d'ordre chronologique," p. 313.

12. RPA, Vol. 2, p. 142.

13. AM, p. 11; Florence Moreau, *Présente à notre temps, Mère Marie de la Ferre*, p. 55.

14. RPA, Vol. 2, pp. 143-144: "A two-storied building, a bakery, a yard, a big garden, and a tannery."

15. *Ibid.*, p. 144.

16. VJLD, Vol. 1, p. 62.

17. RPA, Vol. 2, p. 145.

18. Son of the President of the Paris Mint and grandson by

his mother of Aymon Boucherat, Advocate General of Parliament (a high judicial court) in the capital, Claude de Rueil was orphaned at an early age and brought up by his maternal grand-uncle, William Ruze, Bishop of Angers. He entered the priesthood and in 1622 was consecrated Bishop of Bayonne; he was transferred to the See of Angers in 1628. During his episcopate of 27 years, this good prelate invited many religious communities to his diocese and reformed various others. A lover of peace, he sought to establish it wherever his authority held sway. He died in 1649 at the age of 74. For more details concerning Claude de Rueil, see Louis Moreri, Le grand dictionnaire historique, Vol. 9, p. 427, col. 2.

19. Mondoux, *L'Hôtel-Dieu, premier hôpital de Montréal*, p. 45.

20. RPA, Vol. 2, pp. 146-147.

21. *Ibid.*, pp. 147-149.

22. *Ibid*, pp. 149-150.

23. *Ibid.*, p. 76. During that same year, the pastor and his assistants joined forces with the "fathers of the poor" in opposing the presence of the Carmelite Fathers in La Fléche despite the city's authorization granted to them in 1629. The opposition maintained that the population had as many religious houses to support as it could afford.

24. In those days in "France," a good fight in the courts of the land was one of the preferred pastimes of the people. During a parish mission of three months in 1640, in the little city of Nantes, to the disgust of the local lawyers, 500 cases were settled out of court by a conciliation board set up by the missionaries: See Frédéric Monier, Vie de Jean-

Jacques Olier, curé de la paroisse et fondateur du séminaire de Saint-Sulpice, Paris, 1914, Vol. 1, p. 246. Before the bench, the litigants and the public found the thrills that the western or detective motion picture provides the teenager and the diversion-seeking adult of the late 20th century. In 1668, Racine satirized this national foible in his well-known comedy *Les Plaideures*. These lawsuits were not to Jérôme Le Royer's liking; he was forced into them.

25. VJLD, Vol. 1, p. 67.

26. (Contract between René Le Royer de Boistaillé and Florimond Le Royer, concerning a salt storehouse, October 7, 1634, at La Flèche), MS, ARHSJ, Montreal.

27. (Deed of sale of a property to the Hôtel Dieu Hospital in La Flèche, November 2, 1634), MS, ARHSJ, Montreal.

28. (Deed of acceptance of a salt storehouse by the Adjudicator-General of the Salt Taxes in La Flèche, December 22, 1634), MS, ARHSJ, Montreal.

29. RPA, Vol. 3, p. 175.

Chapter VI

Paris

NOW THAT Jérôme had launched his Hôtel Dieu, begged or borrowed the money needed for the building of the new chapel dedicated to St. Joseph, and begun the formation of the first two members of the future Daughters of St. Joseph, the time had come to work at ensuring these initial realizations and at executing the second and more important task he had been entrusted with. In 1635,[1] probably in the last months of the year,[2] he went to Paris.

Fr. Chauveau had a close friend, Fr. Claude Bernier, S.J., who was stationed from 1633 to 1637 at Meudon in the vicinity of the capital.[3] He admired him and defended him against his fellow Jesuits who did not understand his way of life, for his mystical experiences may well have surpassed those of the foremost saints of all times. Chauveau suggested that Jérôme call on him. The priest may have wanted to subject him to the keen scrutiny of a man granted special insights in matters spiritual. On the other hand, he may simply have wanted to entrust him with copies of letters in Bernier's defence addressed to the Most Reverend Mutius Vitelleschi, General of the Society of Jesus.

As to Jérôme, he planned to discuss several aspects of his future community of hospital nurses with competent people, and quite probably to meet the leaders of the Society of the Blessed Sacrament (not to be mistaken with the Confraternity of the Blessed Sacrament).

The originator of the Society, Henri de Lévy, Duc de Ventadour, Pair de France, Lieutenant of the King in Languedoc, and Viceroy of Canada,[4] was taken up as early as 1627 with the idea that an association of this sort would promote the glory of God by carrying out the reform of the

Church begun by the Council of Trent and pursued by Pope Pius V. A book written by a friend of his, Fr. Philippe d'Angoumois, O.F.M., Cap., *The Triumph of the Love of God in the Conversion of Hermogené*, strongly influenced him. "People living in the world," according to the friar, "are properly called upon to labor from without at all the works of piety, and to their piety are reserved the success and rewards of their charitable efforts." [5]

The Duke's idea of restoring Catholic life in France took on a more practical turn in March 1630.[6] Fr. Jean Suffren, S.J., confessor to the King, and the Most Reverend Charles de Condren, General of the French Oratorians, helped to start it. Authority was vested in a superior, more often than not a layman; its director, always a clergyman, had the obligation of seeing to the spiritual welfare of the associates and to the observance of the rules and regulations. A secretary and six counselors made up the executive. As in many modern fraternal organizations, the Society of the Blessed Sacrament enjoined secrecy upon its members. It never imposed on them what they should do, but encouraged them incessantly to do as much good as they possibly could, suggesting ways and means of facilitating their efforts, while leaving the responsibility to them.[7] The Society immediately won royal favour and Cardinal de Richelieu approved of it. In a letter to Cardinal de Gondi, Archbishop of Paris, Louis XIII requested that he encourage it, ". . . for I find only much advantage in it for my kingdom." [8]

For the "father of the poor," the shortest and most practical way to Paris was the paved Gallo-Roman road followed by Louis XIII in 1614: La Flèche, Le Mans, Chartres, and then on to the capital.[9] It is most probably the itinerary Jérôme followed for this, the first of many such journeys. It took the King fourteen days to reach his destination, but not much more than a week for Jérôme, even though he may have stopped beyond Le Mans at La Ferté-Bernard to pray at the Renaissance church of Our Lady of the Marshes, a paean in freestone to the Queen of Heaven, and at Chartres, where he would not have bypassed the cathedral of Our Lady, a masterpiece created by the combined love and intelligence of centuries of ardent faith at their best. Like so many pilgrims since the third century, he knelt before the Black Virgin, and also venerated what has been considered down the ages as Mary's veil. Heartened and renewed, he proceeded in a north-easterly direction until he reached the capital of the kingdom.

In Paris a man was awaiting the traveller, a stranger who, nevertheless, was to back him in his endeavors and become his lifelong friend, Fr. Jean Jacques Olier, future founder of the Sulpicians, and already on the threshold of the mystical life. The abbé was born on September 20, 1608, in his father's beautiful residence on the rue du Roi de Sicile in the French metropolis.[10] He was baptized Jean; later on, at his Confirmation, he added Jacques to his first Christian name. In 1617, he began his education in Lyons, at Trinity College, a Jesuit institution. According to the bizarre custom of the time, he was tonsured at the age of twelve, and a few years later, named Prior of Bazainville in the diocese of Chartres. The newly acquired dignity did not change the impulsive, impetuous, and undisciplined youngster, and it took St. Francis de Sales, a few days before his death on December 28, 1622, to reassure Jean's parents regarding him.[11]

In 1625, at the age of eighteen, and in the following two years, he received priorship after priorship, and was finally made Abbot of the Canons Regular of St. Augustine at Pibrac, Canon and honorary Comte de Saint-Julien de Brioude. The young Prior-Count-Abbot was no dullard. He went on to obtain his master of arts degree from the Collège d'Harcourt and then studied theology at the Sorbonne, the surest road to positions of distinction in the Church.

The life of theology students in those days was often quite worldly. Many of them, particularly if they were of the nobility, did not dwell together in seminaries as the Council of Trent had recommended. So Jean lived in high style with his valets, his two splendid coaches, and his gourmet dinners.

One afternoon during February 1629, with five other clerics, Olier was strolling through the arcades of the St. Germain fair grounds, a spot described by the poet Pierre de Ronsard as something less than a Cistercian monastery. Articles of luxury awaited the well garnished purse, and the allurement of pleasure baited whosoever was able to afford it. The young abbots and priors were conspicuous in their violet satin jerkins, their silk hose and cravats of the same vivid hue. Coming out of the arcades, they paused to chat in front of a wine-house owned by a widow of about thirty years of age, Marie de Gournay Rousseau. On seeing the young clerics she quickly crossed the street and addressed them in no uncertain terms, "Alas! gentlemen," she said. "What trouble you are giving me! I have long been praying for you. I hope that some day God shall heed my prayers." [12] In later years, Olier acknowledged that the origin of his conversion was due to this holy tavern-keeper.

The young man's total conversion took place, however, during 1629 in Italy, where he had planned to continue his studies. Shortly after the opening of the academic year, his eyesight failed him. The empirical remedies of the day proved of no avail and he resolved to seek a cure at the sanctuary of Our Lady of Loreto. Within the walls of the famous shrine, which, according to popular belief, contains the Santa Casa, his eyesight was restored and his soul definitively won over to Christ His Savior.

Before the year was over, his father's death brought Jean back to Paris. There he was ordained a priest, with the warm approval of Fr. Vincent de Paul, on the eve of the feast of the Holy Trinity, 1633. During the following year, his family name and his good reputation drew attention to him and he was pressed to accept the episcopate as successor to Bishop Sébastien Zamet of Langres.[13] Thoroughly persuaded that by the sanctification of the hierarchy, the Church of France would benefit immensely, Fr. Vincent de Paul urged him to respond favorably. On the other hand, Fr. Charles de Condren, whom the young priest also consulted, advised him to refuse. During 1635, he found himself betwixt and between. This was the man the tax collector from La Flèche was to meet during his stay in the capital of France. Of all the notables he would contact at the time, this was the one who was to stand by him through thick and thin.

Soon after his arrival, Jérôme made his way to the ancient Notre Dame Cathedral to pay his respects to the Mother of God. He attended Mass and received Communion. Afterwards, among the lights and shadows of the beautiful nave, at the Lady altar, he prolonged his thanksgiving, imploring the Blessed Virgin to help him with his work. Suddenly he fell into ecstasy and plainly saw Jesus, Mary and Joseph. As Jesus turned to his Mother, Jérôme heard Him ask, "Where shall I find a faithful servant, a faithful servant, a faithful servant?" [14] At this question with its triple insistence on fidelity, did not the collector of taxes' heart overflow with love, in a silent offering of himself to His Master? It was Mary who answered her Son's query, "Behold, Lord, this faithful servant," and taking Jérôme by the hand, she presented him to her Son, who greeted him with great kindness.

"Henceforth," He promised, "you shall be my faithful servant. I will clad you with strength and wisdom. Your guardian angel shall be your guide. Work hard at my affairs. My grace shall be sufficient for you and never lacking. Receive this ring and give one like it to all those who consecrate themselves in the Congregation that you are about to establish."

Then Christ Himself, after showing Jérôme the ring, inside of which were engraved His own sacred name and those of Mary and Joseph, placed it on the annulary or ring finger of His faithful servant.

All over the world, to this day, the Religious Hospitallers of St. Joseph wear a ring like the one miraculously offered to their founder by Jesus Himself. Jérôme Le Royer's ring was of the purest gold; theirs, regrettably, perhaps, are of silver, "this being deemed more in conformity with the prescriptions of holy poverty."

According to St. Ignatius of Loyola and St. Teresa of Avila, these ecstasies, if truly inspired by God, produce in the soul a profound and lasting peace and the desire of accomplishing the Will of the Most High in all things.[15] So it was with Jérôme, who was quite beside himself with joy and determined more than ever to carry out the orders he had received, as he left the great Gothic pile and stepped out into the noisy street.

The effects of the divine assistance began to make themselves quickly felt. Acting on Fr. Chauveau's suggestion, Jérôme got in touch with Fr. Claude Bernier at Meudon, a pleasant town built on a hillside overlooking the left bank of the Seine, some five miles west of Paris. Its Renaissance château was fine enough for the king and the court to occasionally grace with their presence. It was the residence of the Duchesse d'Elbeuf, whose confessor was none other than Fr. Bernier. As Fr. Chauveau's penitent waited for the Jesuit in a hall of the château, a secular priest, unpretentiously dressed, appeared: it was Fr. Olier, who had also come to pay a visit to Fr. Bernier.[16] On seeing each other, drawn by a strong fellow-feeling, they warmly embraced in true Gallic style. It seemed to both of them that their hearts were one, and being pious 17th century men, with verses from Holy Scripture, they manifested their joy.

No further mention is made of Fr. Bernier. The two new friends certainly saw him and afterwards proceeded to the ducal chapel, where Fr. Olier offered the Holy Sacrifice of the Mass during which Jérôme received Communion. After a devout thanksgiving, they made their way to the grounds[17] surrounding the château. For three hours, the priest and the "father of the poor" walked and talked of things spiritual as if they had known each other for years.[18] Jérôme revealed his mission concerning Montreal and the nursing Sisters he was founding for the conversion of the Indians of New France. At these words, Olier admitted that he, too, desired to spend himself for Christ and that he was moved by the same urge to work for the Christianization of the native people. "On finding myself bound," he later wrote, "as if miraculously, in fellowship with the one to whom Our Lord inspired this idea and commited the design and enterprise of Ville Marie, a town to be built in Canada on the Island of Montreal, I felt myself drawn to go and end my days in those parts, putting my heart and soul into dying there for my Master..." [19]

In 1635, Olier had no intimation that, as founder of the Sulpicians, without ever embarking for Canada, he would do far more for the first inhabitants of the New World than if he himself labored in their midst. This meeting with Jérôme Le Royer prepared him undoubtedly for the revelation made to him in the following year concerning his Canadian vocation.

As their conversation came to a close, the saintly priest assured the "father of the poor" from La Flèche that he would do his part in helping him accomplish his mission, and he was faithful to his word. Before bidding his new friend farewell, Olier gave him eighty gold pistoles,[20] "to begin the work of God."

What other visits did Jérôme make during his stay in Paris? One of them was surely to a close relative of Fr. Olier's, the recently appointed Lord High Chancellor of France, Pierre Séguier, Marquis de Châteauneuf, Keeper of the Seals, Governor and Lieutenant-General for His Majesty in Touraine.[21] As La Flèche belonged to the generality of Tours, it was normal for the collector of taxes to call on His Lordship at his opulent hotel on rue de Bouloi. A painting at the Louvre by his protégé Charles Le Brun does not minimize his questioning eyes and his eagle's nose, imparting to his features an expression of finesse and strength. In 1635, he was putting the finishing touches to the French Academy in collaboration with Richelieu; four years later, he would energetically if not ruthlessly quell a revolt of "the Shoeless" of Normandy against their over-burdening taxes. Beyond the report on the exercise of his duties, as far as we know, Jérôme had little enough to say and nothing to fear.

An indication of still others whom he may have seen in 1635 and in subsequent trips to the capital, is to be found in a petition addressed to the Marquis de la Varenne, Governor of La Flèche in 1673, by Mother Marie Grasset, Superior of the Hôtel Dieu Sisters, challenging Jansenist Bishop Henri Arnauld's intriguing to undermine the founder's life-work.[22] According to this well informed lady, the community was established only after Monsieur Le Royer had subjected his revelations to the spiritual discernment of the most experienced men of the kingdom, among them Fr. Claude de Lingendes, S.J., Fr. Charles de Condren, and St. Vincent de Paul, who all lived in Paris.

It is not unlikely that Fr. Bernier advised Jérôme to consult his confrère Lingendes, known as "the prince of sacred orators"[23] of his day and as one of the best spiritual masters of a period noted for them. St. Jeanne Frances de Chantal could think of no better priest to assist her on her deathbed.

It is not far-fetched either to conclude that Fr. Olier, with whom the founder of the Daughters of St. Joseph discussed the patterns within which they would operate, introduced him to his cherished spiritual directors, Fr. Charles de Condren and Fr. Vincent de Paul.

The future St. Vincent de Paul, founder of the Fathers of the Mission (the Vincentians), was also the originator of a distaff community, the Daughters of Charity. The Saint of the Poor succeeded, where Francis de Sales had failed, in liberating his Visitation Sisters from strict enclosure on account of the prevalent opposition springing up from a narrower conception of religious life with grill and cloister. "For your monasteries," Vincent de Paul told the young women who wanted to dedicate themselves to the care of the poverty-stricken, "you shall have the houses of the sick, for cell a hired room, for chapel your parish church, for cloister the city streets, for enclosure obedience, for convent grill the fear of God, and for veil holy modesty." [24]

When the Parisian saint informed his spiritual children that they were not members of a religious community, but Daughters of Charity, he was applying the principles contained in the above paragraph. Jérôme le Royer simply echoed his words when he repeated to his Sisters; "You are not members of a religious community with grill and cloister; you are Daughters of St. Joseph!" [25]

As to Condren, General of the French Oratory of Jesus, he was so esteemed that Pierre de Bérulle, the Founder and first General, who had received the red hat, used to kiss the threshold of his cell, whenever he visited the residence of the Oratorians (a habit cardinals do not seem to be given to nowadays, perhaps because there are not too many Condrens about). The new General maintained and perfected Bérulle's spirituality in his men, a spirituality aptly described by contemporary Catholic intellectual Jacques Bossuet. "His immense love for the Church," he

70

said, "inspired him with the design of forming a society to which he did not intend giving any other spirit than that of the Church, no other rules than its canons, no other superiors than its Bishops, no other bonds than its charity, no other solemn vows than those of Baptism and Holy Orders." [26] Much of this was in harmony with Jérôme's idea of a dedicated life for his Hospitallers.

Getting in touch with the leaders of the Society of the Blessed Sacrament seems to have been Jérôme le Royer's final concern. During the first few years of its existence, the associates would gather "in the King's apartment" at the Capuchin monastery in the St. Honoré suburb; by 1635, to preserve anonymity, they were holding their meetings in the homes of different members.[27] Still, with Fr. Chauveau's recommendation and, perhaps, with that of Fr. Jean Suffren, whom the tax collector may have seen while calling on Fr. de Lingendes at the Professed House of the Jesuits on rue St-Antoine, he would have been told at which door to knock. He was soon assured that among the good works the Society took to heart was aid to the underprivileged suffering from bad health. Would he not be willing to set up a branch in his city? It would seem so, for before the end of 1635,[28] the Society of the Blessed Sacrament had taken root in La Flèche. This was his first contact with a powerful group of men advantageously placed to help him realize his Montreal mission.

On his journey home, as he rode down the old Roman road, he wove his thoughts, multicolored strands illuminated by his Notre Dame vision and by his talks with men who walked with God, into a tapestry of epic dimensions, of heroic labors, and of far-reaching foundations in honor of Jesus, Mary, and Joseph.

Chapter VI

Notes

1. (Joseph-Jérôme Le Royer de la Motte) *Le Petit Mémoire...*, see Chap. 3, Note 20. RPA, Vol. 3, p. 155; Mondoux, *L'Hôtel-Dieu, Premier Hôpital de Montréal*, p. 319.

2. VJLD, Vol. 1, p. 98.

3. Monsieur Olphe-Galliard, art. "Bernier (Claude)," in *Dictionnaire de Spiritualité Ascétique et Mystique, Doctrine et Histoire*, Vol. 1, Paris, 1937, Cols. 1521-1522.

4. Daveluy, *La Société de Notre-Dame de Montréal*, pp. 268-276; E. R. Adair, "France and the beginnings of New France," in *The Canadian Historical Review*, Vol. 25, No. 3, (Toronto, September 1944), p. 258. Adair calls Lévis "a great *but* pious nobleman..." Italics mine.

5. Georges Goyau, *Une Épopée Mystique, Les Origines Religieuses du Canada*, Paris, 1925, p. 50. Adair in "France and the beginnings of New France," describes the friar as "a mystical fanatic." Fanatic and fanaticism are so often applied to the French in this article, that it is with considerable relief one finds Geneva simply qualified as "militant." René de Voyer d'Argenson, *Annales de la Compagnie du Saint-Sacrement*, Marseille, 1900, p. 12.

6. Eugène Lévesque, art. "Compagnie du Saint-Sacrement," in *Dictionnaire de Spiritualité*, Vol. 2, Paris, 1953, Part 2, Col. 1302.

7. Albert Bessières, *Deux Grands Inconnus, Précurseurs de l'Action Catholique et Sociale: Gaston de Renty et Henry*

Buch, Paris, 1931, p. 157. Because Adair was unaware of this guiding principle of the society of the Blessed Sacrament, he ascribes the foundation of Montreal to the Society of the Blessed Sacrament. See his article (referred to in note #4 on page 72), pp. 272-274.

8. Voyer d'Argenson, *Annales de la Compagnie du Saint-Sacrement,* p. 22; Albert Tessier, "La compagnie du Saint-Sacrement, 1627-1665," in *Les Cahiers des Dix*, Montreal, 1942, No. 7, p. 38.

9. Monsieur le comte Jean de Montgascon, maire de La Flèche, par son adjoint, Bruneau, *Lettre au lieutenant de Trétaigne* a l'institution nationale des Invalides, Paris, le 16 juillet 1953. The letter is now in my possession.

10. Etienne Faillon, *Vie de Monsieur Olier, Fondateur du Séminaire de Saint-Sulpice,* 4th edition, revised and completed by the author, Vol. 1, Paris, 1873, p. 2.

11. *Ibid.,* pp. 12-13.

12. Paul Renaudin, "Une voyante parisienne, Marie Rousseau," in *La Vie Spirituelle,* Vol. LIX, (Paris, April 1, 1939), pp. 45-46; Faillon, *Vie de Monsieur Olier,* Vol. 1, pp. 26-27.

13. Frédéric Monier, *Vie de Jean-Jacques Olier, Curé de la Paroisse et Fondateur du Séminaire de Saint-Sulpice*, Vol. 1, Paris, 1914, pp. 128-129.

14. *AM,* pp. 12-14. In a marginal note, Mother Péret gives her sources, "de vision de Monsieur Le Royer qui le confirme dans son dessin, assure par son propre récit à nos premières mères, recueilly par nos soeurs d'Obeilh, Baudet, etc." These Daughters of St. Joseph heard Jérôme Le Royer relate this vision during one of his talks to the community

at Moulins in 1652. *RPA,* Vol. 3, pp. 156-157.

15. Adolphe Tanqueray, *The Spiritual Life, a Treatise on Ascetical and Mystical Theology*, Second and revised edition, translated by Herman Branderis, Tournai, 1932, p. 706.

16. Louis Tronson, *L'Esprit de Monsieur Olier d'Après Les Notes de Monsieur De Bretonvilliers*, Vol. 2, document No. 106, pp. 369-370. MS, ASS, Paris. The following excerpt is self-explanatory: "Estants tous deux (Olier and Le Royer) il y a environ 18 ou 20 ans au Chasteau de Meudon pour visiter le Père Bernier. Et l'attendants (sic) dans une salle, par un mouvement intérieur, ils se jetterent au Col l'un de l'autre sans s'estre jamais cogneus, avec des tendresses et une cordialité si grande, qu'ils leur sembloient qu'ils n'estoient qu'un mesme Coeur, et avec certaine parole de l'Ecriture qui leur furent (sic) mise en la bouche. Ensuite Monsieur Olier dit la Ste. Messe ou il le communia. Après l'action de grâce ils allèrent dans le Parc..."

17. In *La Société de Notre-Dame de Montréal*, p. 21, Note 3, Marie-Claire Daveluy, writes,"... Le château de Meudon ne possédait alors ni galerie ni parc." Tronson or better still, his source, Bretonvilliers, did not use the word "galerie" but "salle," translated as a large room. In her effort to prove that there was no park at Meudon in 1635, Mademoiselle Daveluy states, "à la fin du siècle, le ministre Louvois le dotait d'un parc." Tronson asserts there was a park. That Louvois, who acquired the château in 1690, added a park, does not imply there was no park half a century earlier.

18. Tronson, *L'esprit de Monsieur Olier*, Vol. 2, p. 370: "...ils allèrent dans le Parc dans lequel ils furent trois heures entières ensemble à s'entretenir des choses de l'autre vie, que l'esprit de Dieu et leurs zèles leurs fournissoient."

19. Jean-Jacques Olier, *Mémoires Autographes*, Vol. 1, Paris, begun in 1642, p. 17. MS, ASS, Paris.

20. This farewell undoubtedly took place before Jérôme Le Royer returned to La Flèche at another meeting of the two friends. Marie Morin, *Histoire Simple et Véritable*, p. 36; Adolphine Gaudin, *RPA*, Vol. 3, p. 157. and Elisabeth Péret's *AM*, p. 14, all say "eighty louis d'or." But the louis d'or was first minted in 1640. In his *History of Montreal*, p. 65, Dollier de Casson uses both "louis" and "pistoles."

21. Le Royer must have seen Chancellor Séguier during his visit to Paris, though not at Meudon. See Joseph Jérôme Le Royer de la Motte, *Le Petit Mémoire*, Chap. 3, No. 20; *RPA*, Vol. 3, p. 157; *AM*, p. 14.

22. *VJLD*, Vol. 1, p. 100.

23. Elesban de Guilhermy, *Ménologe de la Compagnie de Jésus*, assistance de France, 1st part, Paris, 1892, p. 489.

24. Etienne Canitrot, *Le Plus Familier des Saints, Vincent de Paul,* Paris, 1947, p. 104.

25. *VJLD,* Vol. 1, p. 99.

26. André Georges, *L'Oratoire,* Paris, 1928, p. 104: quoting Arc. nat., MS 628, p. 112.

27. Albert Tessier, "La compagnie du Saint-Sacrement," *Les cahiers des Dix,* No. 7, Montreal, 1942, p. 38.

28. Pierre Dufay, "Réponses: La compagnie du Saint-Sacrement," *Intermédiaire des chercheurs et curieux*, (Paris, January 15, 1938), col. 14.

Chapter VII

An Important Birthday

IN 1635, THE ISLAND OF MONTREAL, the keystone of Jérôme Le Royer's project, was not for sale: The Company of New France had already disposed of it at the beginning of the year.

With the approval of Louis XIII, Cardinal de Richelieu had organized the Company in 1627 to colonize Canada and convert the Indian population to Christianity. He named Jean de Lauson, Councillor of State and President of the Grand Council,[1] its *intendant* or administrator of the board of twelve directors who administered its affairs, including the right to buy, sell, and distribute land grants or concessions.

To hasten the colonizing of New France, starting from Quebec, Lauson began to carve out vast tracts of land, which he granted to wealthy aristocrats and merchants on condition that they themselves promise to dwell in the new seigneuries and settle them. One of the first concessions he made was to his son, François, on January 15, 1635: all the land extending from the Richelieu River to the Châteauguay, beyond the Lachine Rapids.[2]

This was not enough for Jean de Lauson. True, the eleventh article of the edict of the establishment of the Company of the One Hundred Associates prohibited him or anyone else from acquiring more than 200 acres of land in New France without the written consent of the administrator and of 20 of the associates. But why let a few lines in a legal document deter an ambitious family-minded gentleman from achieving his ends, and even from doing so under the cover of respectability? The little intrigue that placed in the hands of a single individual a territory with which many European sovereigns would have been satisfied as a kingdom could well support a modern thinker's statement that it is essential not to have faith in human nature.[3]

Some time during the first two weeks of January 1636, Administrator de Lauson convened three puppets of his: Jacques Girard, Seigneur de la Chaussée and de la Callières, Simon le Maître, King's Councillor and Collector of Taxes for Normandy, and Jacques Castillon, a Parisian bourgeois. He explained to them a plan which he had carefully prepared. Would they collaborate with him? They would. At the hour set for the annual meeting on January 15, Lauson welcomed the directors and associates of the Company to his residence. After disposing of the usual business (a report on its financial state and the election of officers), applications were made for land grants in Canada. Simon Le Maître asked for and obtained a stretch of the Chaudière River six leagues long with three leagues of land on each side.[4] He was to enjoy the proud title of seigneur or lord for 15 days. On January 29, he admitted in a notarized act that he was holding it for Jean de Lauson, who could not acquire any property during his tenure of office.

The administrator, using Cheffaut de la Regnardière for dummy, also managed to appropriate part of the Beaupré seigneury and, with the help of Castillon, a fine slice of the Isle of Orleans.[5]

Jacques de la Chaussée then reminded the board of directors that during their previous annual meeting they had granted to Lauson's eldest son, François, sixty leagues on the south shore of the St. Lawrence, extending westward from the Richelieu River to the Châteauguay, and southward well into what is the present state of New York. The seigneury even comprised the islands within its limits, not excepting Montreal. Now La Chaussée requested and obtained that the Island of Montreal be withdrawn from young François de Lauson's concession and made over to himself. He played the same game as Castillon and Le Maître, for in 1638, he would relinquish it to the Councillor of State, after the latter's resignation as administrator.[6] And Lauson was an honorable man!

The administrator thus became the greatest landowner of the new colony, without the least protest official or otherwise. Here was a powerful man with whom Jérôme Le Royer would have to contend before many years went by.

Scarcely two weeks later, another event took place in the capital of France, which was to favor the Montreal venture. On February 2, Candlemas Day, Le Royer's new friend, Fr. Olier, knelt in silent prayer in the Parisian monastery of St. Germain des Prés. With regard to the coadjutorship of Langres, which Bishop Sébastien Zamet wanted him to accept, the young priest besought Our Lord to enlighten his two spiritual guides, Fr. Vincent de Paul and Fr. Charles de Condren. He would do whatever he was told.

Suddenly there came to him, with so great an intensity that it could not be denied, the conviction he must be "a light of revelation to the Gentiles." [7]

In 1636, when "Gentiles" were mentioned to a Frenchman, he immediately thought of the Indians of New France. Fr. Olier no longer saw a mitre and a crozier in store for himself but the far-off shores of Canada. Later Fr. de Condren got him to refuse the episcopate, which was being urged upon him, but also dissuaded him from sailing off to New France as a missionary. Quite a few years would elapse before the full meaning of the St. Germain communication became clear to him.

Unaware at the time of these distant Parisian doings, in La Flèche Jérôme was executing the orders he had received at Notre Dame as best he could.

His first step in this direction was to organize the

Confraternity of the Holy Family, a prelude to his community of nursing Sisters. Before his trip to the capital, at the home of Mme Bidault de la Barre, he had discussed and roughly planned it. He had even spoken to his Bishop about it two years earlier. He enthusiastically explained to whoever would listen to him the advantages which would result if each family modeled its conduct on that of the Holy Family of Nazareth.[8] After listening to him, a good many of the La Flèche people agreed to honor the most perfect family that ever lived.

Assured of the collaboration of the people of his city, M. Le Royer drew up a set of rules for the association. During the first weeks of February 1636, he and his brother, René, in their capacity of administrators of the Hôtel Dieu, asked Bishop de Rueil to examine the regulations of the Confraternity and to grant them a decree establishing its seat in the new hospital chapel. La Flèche desired it, the Bishop was informed, and the Confraternity, dedicated to St. Joseph, would be the living proof of the city's devotion to the Holy Family.

Claude de Rueil hastened to accede to the request of the two administrators in a four page rescript of February 17, 1636, which he signed and sealed with his coat of arms. The parchment, beautifully written in Latin, and carrying a short note in Le Royer's handwriting, contains an introduction by the Bishop, followed by the rules of the association.[9]

Even a cursory glance at the nineteen articles[10] clearly manifests the large dose of common sense with which Jérôme was blessed. The order of the day proposed to the new associates is indicative of that followed by the founder himself:

"On arising in the morning, they shall humbly adore God, and acknowledge His blessings; they shall offer themselves and all their deeds for the greater glory of God. Resolving to please Him throughout the day, they shall implore divine aid so as to accomplish works of piety and Christian justice and avoid all occasions of offending God. Throwing themselves upon their knees, they shall say three Our Fathers and Hail Marys to the glory of the Most Holy Trinity and of the humanity of Jesus. Each evening they shall examine their consciences, recalling to mind the faults of the day, and begging pardon of God with all their hearts; and after saying the Our Fathers and Hail Marys as in the morning, they shall place themselves in the keeping of Jesus, Mary, and Joseph."

The administration of the Holy Family Confraternity was both simple and practical. On a convenient day close to the Feast of St. Joseph, a prefect, two assessors, a treasurer, a secretary, and other officials were to be elected by the members. Their tenure of office was to last a year, but they were eligible for another term. These men were to give freely of their time and, at the end of the year, the treasurer had to render an account of the association's financial condition to the associates. This was the origin of the Holy Family Confraternity, which would be the first of a long line of many other associations even in far-off Canada.[11]

During these months, Marie de la Ferre and Anne Foureau were faithfully carrying on their prosaic labour at the hospital. The hope they entertained of consecrating themselves once and for all to the inmates of the institution convinced its head administrator that the time had come to fulfil it.

After their day of nursing at the Hôtel Dieu, the two devoted ladies and Jérôme Le Royer often discussed the ways and means of improving the treatment of the patients. Madame Bidault de la Barre, Marie de la Ferre's widowed cousin, with whom she lived, was unenthusiastic about the whole matter. Indeed, she feared she would soon be left alone to run her estate. Anne Foureau lived close by the hospital, while each day, Marie had a long walk home after many trying hours of caring for the sick. Would she not end up by taking quarters at the Hôtel Dieu? After one of Jérôme's visits, Madame de la Barre asked the younger woman if she were thinking of leaving her.

"Don't worry, dear cousin," Marie answered. "Nothing but death will ever separate us!"

Madame felt relieved, but she died shortly afterwards, some say at the beginning of 1636,[12] others during May of the same year.[13]

As Jérôme never acted hastily, he sought the advice of a few Jesuit friends, no doubt Frs François Chauveau,[14] Pierre Meslan,[15] and Claude Dubreuil[16] stationed at the Royal College. Following several consultations, these religious came to the conclusion that the vocations of Marie de la Ferre and of Anne Foureau were not to be taken lightly, and advised the "father of the poor" to foster them as much as it was in his power to do so.[17] He immediately decided to retain a room at the Hôtel Dieu for both of them.

Although Madame Bidault de la Barre was no longer there to cling to Marie, her other relatives as well as Anne Foureau's protested angrily on hearing of their decision to spend their lives in the wards of the hospital.[18] Knowing full well that "A man's enemies will be those of his own household" (Matthew 10:36), the two gentlewomen calmly awaited Jérôme's orders.

On May 18, 1636, Feast of the Most Blessed Trinity, the very day the spanking new hospital, now ready to welcome needy patients more adequately, was dedicated to St. Joseph, Jérôme had them enter the Hôtel Dieu on probation.[19] If Jérôme Le Royer had not destroyed most of his spiritual diaries before his death, we might know more about this historic Feast of the Blessed Trinity, which has always been considered as the birthday of the Daughters of St. Joseph.

Three kind-hearted volunteer workers at the hospital,

Jeanne Cohergne, Catherine Lebouc, and Julienne Allory[20] welcomed the two ladies. The lives of the five would soon be inextricably bound together for the service of the needy patients who knocked at the door of the new establishment.

Despite Jérôme's many occupations, he immediately began to look after the religious formation of Marie de la Ferre, who was already well advanced in the way of perfection, and of her friend, Anne Foureau. The "father of the poor" carefully prepared his talks to them on their new way of life. One after the other, he explained the future Constitutions, which he was then in the process of writing out in detail. The apparent incongruity of a layman in the role of a spiritual director did not surprise these probationers, for "his holy life was the perfect exemplar of all his teachings." [21]

Much stinting on their part notwithstanding, the yawning maw of the empty strong-box of the hospital reduced Marie de la Ferre and her companion to their personal resources and, finally, to begging. Along with scorn, mockery, and derision, they obtained dishes, table linen, clothes, furniture, and even dead twigs and small, dried branches, no doubt the best kindling they could find.[22] It is easy to imagine the dismay of their families. Although this situation was to last only a few years, it sufficed to envelop the apprentice nurses with an aura of holiness, which ungarnished the purses of many a wealthy nobleman or landowner in favor of the needy patients.

As for Jérôme Le Royer, he tried to improve the living conditions at the hospital for staff and patients alike. With this aim in view, at the end of 1636, on learning that a neighboring property was for sale, he set out to buy it. Acting as his go-between, Baron Pierre Chevrier furnished the necessary 1,500 livres and signed the contract.[23] An interesting stipulation, perhaps suggested by Jérôme himself, carried that the Baron would have the exclusive right to burial in St. Joseph's Chapel. It was a token from his friend considering the young nobleman's charity to the hospital; at the same time, it shielded the administration of the Hôtel Dieu from bothersome requests on the part of the Holy Family Confraternity members to be interred within the chapel precincts.

In the midst of his labours and difficulties, the New Year of 1637 brought joy to Jérôme and to his wife, Jeanne, on February 14, in the birth of his third son, the last of five children. Madame Anne Bodereau was chosen godmother, and the "high and mighty Pierre Chevrier, Baron de Fancamp," godfather.[24] The little one was baptized Joseph. Later on the son of his brother, René, and a cousin were also called Joseph, a name that soon became commonplace in and about La Flèche.

A week before the birth of Joseph, trouble had again begun to rear its ugly head. After keeping quiet for a few years, Fr. Hamelin, Jérôme's pastor, craved for more excitement. The pugnacious priest served a writ on him in his quality of "father of the poor" and alderman of the city, as well as on Mayor Fontaine and two other aldermen, enjoining them to answer questions he considered important.[25]

During their previous two years of tenure of office, Hamelin wanted to know, had they presented a petition to the Grand Council in Paris, requesting an intervention in the dispute between the presbytery and the Hôtel Dieu? And had Maître[26] Marsolier, President of the Presidial Court, been commissioned to draw it up and dispatch it to the capital?

As Jérôme thought the problem had been solved in 1634, the petition was never taken into account and Marsolier never called upon to do anything about it. He told the priest what he probably expected to hear and saw him retreat into sullen silence, a silence that was not to last very long.

For several years now, besides the busy hours devoted

to his duties as collector of taxes, Jérôme Le Royer also kept on with his active service as syndic or administrator of the Franciscan Recollects, treasurer of the Confraternity of the Blessed Sacrament, and legal tutor of poor orphans.[27] As if this were not enough, in 1637 and in the following years, he bent his efforts not only to strengthen his new Holy Family Association but also it would seem, to build up firmly and discreetly the Society of the Blessed Sacrament (not the Confraternity) launched during 1635 in La Flèche and the surrounding districts. Above all he was faithful to his responsibilities as "father of the poor" at the beautiful new hospital.

In the first half of 1637, the *Jesuit Relations* for 1636 reached Jérôme's office. On pages 18 and 19, Fr. Paul Le Jeune, S.J. thanked Cardinal de Richelieu's niece, Marie Madeleine de Combalet, future Duchesse d'Aiguillon, for providing funds for a Hôtel Dieu at Quebec, the first one in New France if not in North America. "Verily, there is nothing so powerful as this device," wrote the Jesuit Superior, "to win these poor Indians..."[28] Since this device was so powerful in Quebec, would it not be just as powerful if not more so on the Island of Montreal? Jérôme Le Royer was convinced it would.

In the following issue of the *Relations,* the story of Governor de Montmagny's trip up the St. Lawrence in September 1636 was described in detail. It corroborated Jérôme's visions of 1634. After a stop at Trois-Rivières, with his suite, the governor had sailed westward. The little party noticed that there were many islands in the immense watercourse, three of which were worthy of mention.

"This is the way these Islands are divided," wrote Le Jeune: "the great river Saint Lawrence bathes the lands of one of our Gentlemen on the South; passing to the North, it makes two Islands: one, perhaps a league and a half long, but very narrow, (Ile-Bizard); the other the great Island called Mont-Real. This island appears to be divided in the midst by a double mountain which seems to cross it. In the vicinity of these mountains is the Sault Saint Louys, in the Saint Lawrence river." [29] The Jesuit then goes on to say that Indians had lived there long ago, but finally abandoned it, as they were too often molested by their enemies—a harbinger of things to come, which must have given Jérôme food for thought. "We disembarked at these three islands and found them very fine and agreeable. I celebrated the first Sacrifice of the Mass which had ever been offered, as I was told, on the Island of Montmagny (Ile-Jésus)... After having viewed the beauties of the country, we set sail for Three Rivers."

Jérôme Le Royer was one of many to read these issues of the *Relations*. Most educated Catholics read this annual publication and it is probable that a copy fell into the hands of 27-year-old Count Baron Gaston de Renty. With Olier and Fancamp, he was to help the La Flèche collector of taxes more than anyone else. He was the scion of one of the most illustrious families of France. At the age of seventeen, he had been sent off to the Military Academy,[30] where he became an expert fencer, an excellent officer, and an exceptional mathematician. He is credited with several treatises on the art of fortification, geography, and cosmology.

One day, after reading the *Imitation of Christ*, which a kindly bookseller had urged upon him, he resolved to become a whole-hearted Christian. So whole-hearted indeed, that he ran away to become a Carthusian. The Rentys, were, to say the least, influential, and it was not long before the disgruntled would-be monk found himself home again.

To the relief of his parents, at the age of twenty-two, he had married Elisabeth de Balzac, who was to bear him five children. The young lord lived an exemplary life. In 1638, what he called his "conversion" took place; it was similar to Jérôme's in 1632. Among the works of mercy he then gave himself up to was the visiting of English Catholics forced into exile for their faith.

He would embrace them tenderly and discreetly slip a roll of coins into their hands. "Here are good Christians," he once remarked to a friend who was accompanying him, "they have abandoned everything for God. As for us, we have an abundance of earthly goods and are in need of nothing. They are satisfied with two crowns a month after having foregone an income of 15 to 20,000 pounds... Ah! Monsieur, Christianity does not consist in words but in deeds!" [31]

It did not take long for the Baron de Renty to join the Society of the Blessed Sacrament,[32] to which Jérôme had undoubtedly belonged since 1635. He was soon to take over the helm of the society and guide it masterfully for ten years. About the time of his election, he awoke one night and found tears streaming down his face. He had just been favored with a revelation informing him that he had an important role to play in the establishment of the Church on the Island of Montreal.[33] No wonder that he and Jérôme became intimate, lifelong friends.

Of less consequence but worthy of note was a trip Jérôme could have found pleasant and relaxing in the spring of 1638, had he not been wearing his penitential instruments. The Angevine countryside famed for its beauty was at its best when he left for Pouancé, a little town on the confines of Anjou and Brittany. On the first of May, he reached his destination, the Abbey of Claretz, where the Right Reverend François Etienne de Caulet, Abbot of Foix, and Fr. Ludovic Damourettes, confessor at the monastery, were awaiting him.[34]

Caulet was a friend of Fr. Olier's. He was one of the young, violet-clad clerics whom Marie Rousseau chided at the St. Germain Fair in 1629. On one of his visits to the

Abbey of Claretz, he had seen an important relic of St. Marguerite, which he certainly mentioned to Fr. Olier, who in turn must have informed Le Royer about it. At the new La Flèche Hôtel Dieu, an altar in the St. Joseph Chapel had been dedicated to its former titular, St. Marguerite, Virgin and Martyr. Perhaps "the humble Abbess of Claretz," as she signed her letters, could be induced to share part of it with Monsieur Le Royer de la Dauversière. Caulet's power of persuasion must have been excellent, for we find him with Fr. Damourettes and the La Flèche collector of taxes in the presence of the abbess, Mother Catherine Duprat, accompanied by a few nuns. Then a quill scratched loudly in the silence of the room. Jérôme gratefully accepted a piece of arm bone nearly an inch and a half long, "in consideration of the great devotion which the inhabitants of this city of La Flèche have for the Saint." [35]

Chapter VII

Notes

1. The Grand Council, which met in Paris, was established in 1498 by royal decree to take care of cases generally relating to the clergy.

2. J. Edmond Roy, *Histoire de la seigneurie de Lauson*, Vol. 1, Levis, 1897, p. 53.

3. Herbert Butterfield, *Christianity in History,* London, 1960, p. 47.

4. Roy, *Histoire de la seigneurie de Lauson*, Vol. 1, pp. 37-38.

5. *Ibid.,* p. 44.

6. *Ibid.,* Monier, *Vie de Jean-Jacques Olier*, Vol. 1, p. 213, Note 1.

7. Olier, *Mémoires autographes*, Vol. 1, p. 17. Furnished by Archivist Irénée Noyes of St. Sulpice, Paris.

8. *RPA,* Vol. 3, p. 167; *VJLD,* Vol. 1, p. 124.

9. *RPA,* Vol. 3, pp. 168-175. The decree is preserved in the Archives of the La Flèche Hôtel Dieu, A 1er, M. Bis.

10. *Ibid.,* pp. 172-173.

11. Adrien Pouliot, "La devotion à la Sainte Famille en Nouvelle-France au XVIIe siècle," Cahiers de Joséphologie, Vol. 29, (Montreal, 1981), pp. 1000-1033.

12. *RPA,* Vol. 3, p. 179.

13. *NA,* p. 148.

14. *RPA,* Vol. 2, p. 154: Fr. Chauveau was stationed at the Royal College of La Flèche from 1630-1636; appointed elsewhere from 1637-1638; he was again at La Flèche from 1639-1641.

15. *Ibid.:* Fr. Meslan taught theology at La Flèche from 1630 to 1641.

16. *Ibid.:* Fr. Dubreuil (or Du Breuil), who preached far and wide, was a member of the La Flèche college community from 1634 to 1641; from 1642 to 1665, he often returned to the Royal College for relatively long stays.

17. *AM,* p. 20.

18. Morin, *Histoire Simple et Véritable,* p. 27, Note 2.

19. *VJLD,* Vol. 1, p. 135.

20. Morin, *Histoire Simple et Véritable,* p. 27.

21. *AM,* p. 23.

22. *RPA,* Vol. 3, p. 196.

23. *Ibid.,* p. 182. The contract was signed on January 16, 1637. Fancamp, who later became a priest, was buried in parts unknown.

24. *Ibid.,* p. 183.

25. *VJLD,* Vol. 1, p. 136.

26. A title applied to advocates and councillors.

27. *RPA,* Vol. 3, p. 175.

28. *JR,* Vol. VIII, p. 23.

29. *Ibid.,* Vol. XII, pp. 130-135.

30. Bessières, *Deux grands inconnus, précurseurs de l'action catholique sociale: Gaston de Renty et Henry Buch*, p. 67.

31. Ch. Clair, "La compagnie du Saint-Sacrement, une page de l'histoire de la charité au dix-septième siècle," *Etudes religieuses, philosophiques, historiques et littéraires,* Vol. 45 (Paris, Dec. 1888), p. 564.

32. Bessières, *Deux grands inconnus, précurseurs de l'action catholique sociale: Gaston de Renty et Henry Buch*, p. 155.

33. Monier, *Vie de Jean-Jacques Olier*, p. 216, quoting J.-B. de Saint-Jure, La vie de Monsieur de Renty, Paris, 1651, p. 144.

34. *RPA*, Vol. 3, pp. 183-184.

35. *Ibid.*, p. 184. By the end of the 19th century, the relic given to the founder of the new Hôtel Dieu had been divided up. A fragment, placed in a gilded reliquary of wood, was exposed in the hospital chapel. A smaller piece was set in a miniature reliquary for lending to pregnant women. "Never," wrote Mother Gaudin, compiler of *RPA*, "has any misfortune befallen on any of those having recourse to the saint's intercession."

Chapter VIII

"I Was Sick and You Took Care of Me!"

BY JANUARY 1639, the Hôtel Dieu was in a much better condition than ever before. The completed construction was worthy of God's poor and the volunteer nurses under Marie de la Ferre cared for the sick in clean quarters. The competent directress devoted herself unsparingly, not only because Jérôme Le Royer had spoken to her about the extraordinary circumstances leading to her admission, but also because the sight of the large ward with its beds in neat rows, occupied by well tended patients, was exactly what she had seen in the vision that had determined her vocation several years before.[1]

For all that, Jérôme still had plenty of work laid out for him before his religiously oriented nurses would be recognized by the Church and the State. To begin with, the title of the almonry must be cleared. The benefice attached to it had no doubt been established to procure spiritual assistance for the patients of the Hôtel Dieu. Eleven years earlier, Fr. Philippe Boisricher, who was then enjoying it without complying with any of the obligations it entailed, had given up living at the almonry for an annuity of 40 livres.[2] In 1639, besides this annuity, the retired priest was still holding on to the other benefits of the office. The building of a new chapel and the changing of its patron from St. Marguerite to St. Joseph in no wise affected his rights. So the "father of the poor" planned to get Boisricher to relinquish them, but on account of the press of his many occupations was unable to achieve his aim until later in the year.

It was only on July 15th, at the home of Jacques Deniau, esquire and councillor, that Fr. Boisricher and Jérôme Le Royer came to terms. With Marin Pierre, royal notary, were present as witnesses the Baron de Fancamp and a certain Nicolas Lefranc. The almoner renounced his benefice and the corresponding rights in favor of Monsieur Le Royer, hospital administrator, and of all the succeeding administrators.[3] The Hôtel Dieu thus obtained the almoner's field with its hedges and ditches located near a plot of land belonging to the Jesuits. It also got a vineyard in the country and several ground rents.

In exchange for the loss of the benefice, Jérôme gave the priest 35 livres and promised to supply him with an annuity of 85 more. He also discharged him from all his obligations such as that of reading a Mass in the hospital chapel on the Feast of St. Marguerite.

The priest was satisfied. So was Le Royer, since he thought the arrangement important enough to sign it himself. It was one of the rare business transactions for which he did not have his brother or Fancamp do it for him. To be sure, the termination of the preferment obliged him to repeated outlays of money, but he knew it would not last very long, for Fr. Boisricher had acquired it 29 years before and, it seems, was quite aged. The Hôtel Dieu would profit fron this move until the French Revolution.

To be valid, the Boisricher agreement needed the approval of the Bishop of Angers and of the mayor and aldermen of La Flèche. The "father of the poor" hurried home to write up two petitions: one to the prelate, followed by another to the city authorities.[4] Why did he go to the trouble of drafting the second paper for Rueil even before sending the first one to the mayor? The answer may be found in a trip that was to keep him away from home for some time. On his way eastward, as he passed through Angers, he would leave the document with his Bishop. During July of the previous year, Fr. Olier had converted the nuns of the lax priory of la Régrippière, six miles or so from his own priory at Clisson. Before the first days of spring 1639, through Jérôme's influence, he had obtained that Fr. Chauveau, stationed since the beginning of the year at Nantes, should take charge of the now reformed leader of the laxists, Sr. Claude de Vauldray, as her confessor and spiritual guide.[5] Truly an act of charity, for the nun was "as vain as a rooster, the vainest human being not only of the monastery but also of the entire Province of Touraine." [6] This service rendered by Le Royer at the request of Olier indicated, to say the least, that the two men were on friendly terms.

About the same time the "father of the poor" was working on the almonry problem, he learned that Fr. Olier, who was preaching at Montdidier in Picardy, was on the point of accepting the coadjutorship of the diocese of Châlons-sur-Marne, one of the most honorable sees of the kingdom. Its aging Bishop, Henri Clausse de Marchaumont, had convinced Richelieu that here was the ideal man for the post. Since the appointment was signed by Louis XIII, it was difficult for the young priest to refuse. On July 30, he was in Paris and there wrote to His Eminence asking that he put off the official publication of his accession to the mitre and the crozier until he had discussed the matter with him.[7] During his audience with the cardinal minister, he definitively refused the episcopate.

What had happened? His spiritual director, Fr. de Condren, did not favor the acceptance of crozier and mitre, but he was not a man to order his penitent to turn his back on them. Before the end of July, when Olier wrote to the cardinal, Jérôme Le Royer had reached him, most probably at Montdidier, and with the familiarity of friendship told him, "The episcopate is not for you, God has other plans for you!" [8]

Jérôme was at least partially aware of the spiritual mission prepared by God for his friend. Besides, in informing Olier of the will of the Almighty with regard to his vocation,

93

he was also protecting the capital issue of his own mission. He felt that, without the assistance of Fr. Olier, the creation of Ville Marie would be impossible. His intuition was later corroborated. Fr. Olier relates that his calling was manifested to him several times under the symbol of a pillar on which two churches were joined, one of which was old, the other new; at the same time he grasped that he was to serve both these churches through his followers. "I saw myself," he wrote, "as the foundation stone on which the two archways or two churches rested and, as if I were receiving into my bosom a great number of persons who afterwards left it quite animated with the desire of serving God and of carrying His holy Name throughout the world." [9]

In the course of these conversations and perhaps in other unrecorded ones, Le Royer and Olier considered means of bringing about the settlement of the Island of Montreal in the near future. One of the first that came to their minds was the possibility of founding an association of well-fixed ladies and gentlemen sympathetic to their project. The more they thought about it, the more they liked it. Not unexpectedly, its first members were Fancamp, Olier and Le Royer,[10] though the latter could not have been called wealthy.

Whether or not they knew anything about Jean de Lauson's maneuvres, the matter of the ownership of the island surely came up. Jérôme would have to look into it.

On arriving home from his talks with Fr. Olier, Jérôme found himself confronted with a growing wall of hostility. His acquisition of the almonry rights from Fr. Boisricher was now common knowledge. Like little mice, rumors concerning the volunteer nurses were pitter-pattering through the streets of the city.

Fr. Etienne, his director, was hesitant, it has been asserted, about the timeliness of a new sisterhood, and along with a few grey-beards incapable of stomaching the idea of a mere layman founding a community of hospital nurses, he may have resurrected the twice-tried measure of staffing the hospital with Augustinian nuns.[11] More probably, the opposition originated in Fr. Hamelin's office at the presbytery (rectory).[12]

A rescript from Bishop Claude de Rueil gave teeth to the opposition. It was dated the sixteenth of August, and instructed the La Flèche Hôtel Dieu to make ready for the hospital nuns from Dieppe, who would take charge of it and eventually receive Mademoiselle de la Ferre and her associates into their ranks.[13] There is no evidence that the "father of the poor" was overly concerned. In Notre Dame at Paris, Christ Himself had assured him that His grace would be sufficient and never lacking. "Work hard at my affairs," he had added. Jérôme intended to keep on doing so.

The most immediate affair to which he had to attend was a proviso in the Boisricher contract of the middle of July obliging him to notify Fr. Michel Hamelin about the redeeming of the almonry title and, if possible to win his approval. In what he must have felt was a vain attempt, he knocked at the door of the nearby presbytery. What thoughts came to his mind on finding himself in the presence of his pastor? If public opinion was no longer favorable to what was known about his plans, if the threat of the Dieppe nuns' coming was hanging over him like a mushroom cloud, here in all likelihood was the man responsible for the mischief. The preceding skirmishes between the two had been desultory. Now the real fighting was on the verge of beginning. Hamelin and Le Royer both had razor-honed juridical minds. The priest had in him the stuff of an expert canonist and the "father of the poor" that of a high-priced 20th century corporation lawyer. One was no less spirited in attack than the other in riposte.

The details of the meeting are not recorded; however, they were certainly disheartening for Jérôme. As pastor,

Hamelin claimed the customary right of choosing the candidate to be proposed for the King's sanction. Since it had been ignored in 1610, he obstinately held that Boisricher's appointment was invalid and all the subsequent acts, too. This right he meant to have recognized, and not long after Jérôme Le Royer's visit, he took his case to the local authorities.

Jérôme was ready for him. He did not need to be very astute to see that his adversary's measure would void his contract with Fr. Boisricher and halt the establishment of the new community of nurses begun without official ratification. Having in hand, since the middle of July at least, the papers concerning the almonry, he had a copy of the retired almoner's appointment deposited at the office of the clerk of the court. The original drawn up on April 5, 1610, in Henri IV's name with the endorsement of Cardinal du Perron, Grand Almoner of France, carried the royal seal and signature.[14] Jérôme was of the opinion that the persons of His Majesty and of His Eminence were sufficiently vested with authority to assume responsibility in this matter. Besides, the late King's orders had been executed by the Seneschal of Beaumond and of La Flèche: ample proof that Henri IV had not infringed the rights of the duchy to which it belonged. He was convinced that, when the time came for the city council to settle the affair, this document would prove his point.

During the rest of the summer, autumn, and into the winter season, Jérôme did not sit at home idling away his time. He was on the road in search of settlers for his Montreal foundation, and in Paris for consultation with the Baron de Renty and others.[15] Most of the time, Fr. Olier was preaching missions close enough to the metropolis to be reached without too much difficulty. Then, during the last three months of the year, he was unexpectedly drawn into the vortex of a terrible spiritual ordeal, which left him incapacitated for months on end.[16]

Well before the winter season a bright ray of light dissipated the heavy fog hanging over the magnificent project of the "father of the poor." The Dieppe nuns cancelled their engagement to staff the La Flèche Hôtel Dieu.[17] This change of attitude on their part appears strange. It could not have been caused by the lack of proper quarters, for the nuns were aware that a new hospital was at their disposal. Neither was the sailing earlier in the year of three Dieppe Sisters to open a new house of their order in Quebec, Canada, a satisfying explanation, since their departure for New France had already been decided when the La Flèche foundation was accepted. Was it then, perhaps, a new administration of the Dieppe Augustinians that viewed the problem with a different eye? At Notre Dame in 1635, Our Lord had promised "His faithful servant" that He would never abandon him. Is there a better explanation?

Public opinion has always been a weathercock. When the Dieppe decision became known, Monsieur Le Royer's ideas emerged in a much better light, and the people of the little city began to favor the devoted women working at the hospital.[18]

Jérôme moved without hesitation. On December 23, 1639, he requested the city council to ratify his acquisition of the title and benefice of the almonry. As he expected, the royal seal and signature, and the presentation of Boisricher as almoner at La Flèche by the Grand Almoner of France impressed the Marquis de la Varenne, president of the council, the mayor, and all the other members. The contract was officially confirmed.[19]

On the same day, backed by his brother, René, Jérôme urged the city fathers to approve the outline of the charter that, after long months of prayer and consultation, he had prepared for Marie de la Ferre and her companions at the

Hôtel Dieu. This they did without a single opposing vote. It was the first formal recognition of the new body of "distinguished widows and girls,... desirous of taking charge... gratuitously,... under certain common rules in the form of statutes of a religious community, without, however, making profession of the religious state."[20] In those days, solemn vows and the strictly cloistered life were considered essential to the religious life.[21]

Every candidate was to enter of her own free will. For legitimate reasons—and this decision was certainly a Vincentian inspiration—any member was free to quit. The subject's dowry was to be handed over to the administrator, and he in turn was to supply the bursar with the funds needed for the upkeep of the community. Each month the bursar was to render an account of expenses to the administrator in the presence of the superior. The administrator was to be chosen among three candidates proposed by the hospital staff. It was also stipulated that for their maintenance, the hospitallers should not depend on the sums of money entrusted to the Hôtel Dieu for care of the sick.

For several years now, Mass was being offered regularly in the St. Joseph Chapel, though no Reservation of the Blessed Sacrament was permitted. Until then, Jérôme had not thought it expedient to ask his Bishop for the necessary authorization to keep it there. The chapel's proximity to the parish church seemed to banish any hope of obtaining it. However, after Fr. Hamelin had appealed to the courts for the annulment of Boisricher's appointment, there was no longer any need of trying to humour him. A petition was consequently submitted to Bishop Claude de Rueil, and in a rescript of May 28, 1640, he granted this much desired favor "to the chaplain, to the administrators of the hospital, and to the members of the Confraternity of St. Joseph," [22] on behalf of the future nursing Sisters and their patients.

On June 3, after receiving the episcopal document, Jérôme Le Royer presented the Hôtel Dieu with a register in which were to be inscribed the name of all who joined the Daughters of St. Joseph. The first to be accepted were Marie de la Ferre and Anne Foureau, whose names Jérôme himself wrote in.[23] On October 27, he added the name of forty-year-old Mademoiselle Anne de L'Espicier.[24] During a serious illness, her confessor had advised her, should she be cured, to consecrate her life to God in a fervent community. She did promise to do so, regained her health, and asked to be admitted alongside of Marie de la Ferre and Anne Foureau to care for the bedridden poverty-stricken.

More than nine years had passed since Jérôme Le Royer first began to plan and work for the hospital. The obstacles he met with seem to have accelerated rather than delayed success. His pastor's opposition hastened reconstruction of the Hôtel Dieu, the official admission of the first hospitallers to it, and offered the founder the opportunity of having approved a set of rules which gradually helped to transform the cluster of volunteer nurses into a religious institute. The Dieppe negotiations also favored the initiative it would normally have destroyed, for the agreement that Jérôme Le Royer and his brother, René de Boistaillé, signed with the mayor and aldermen, just about withdrew the Hôtel Dieu from city'jurisdiction. St. Joseph's Chapel became a place of worship for Marie de la Ferre and her three associates, or better still, for the incipient Daughters of St. Joseph. It was no longer a simple hospital chapel set aside for the Confraternity of the Holy Family.

On his knees before the Blessed Sacrament, Jérôme could now thank the Savior for not having abandoned him. And Jesus in the tabernacle could look down on him and answer lovingly, "I was sick and you visited me" (Matthew 25: 35-36). Indeed he was doing much better than simply visiting Him. He was also housing and caring for Him.

Chapter VIII

Notes

1. *NA,* p. 152.

2. *Supra,* pp. 14, 18.

3. *RPA,* Vol. 3, pp. 185-188.

4. *VJLD,* Vol. 1, p. 140; Bertrand, *Monsieur de la Dauversière,* between pp. 80-81, gives a reproduction of the letter to Bishop de Rueil, the original of which is preserved in the archives of the La Flèche Hôtel Dieu, A 1er Q.

5. Pierre Pourrat, *Jean-Jacques Olier, fondateur de Saint-Sulpice,* Paris, 1932, p. 68; Eugène Lévesque, Editor, *Lettres de Monsieur Olier, curé de la paroisse et fondateur du Séminaire de Saint-Sulpice,* Vol. 1, Paris, 1935: Letters 37, pp. 74-75; 38, p. 77; 39, p. 79; 40, p. 80. These letters also clearly indicate that Olier knew Le Royer before the spring of 1639.

6. Monier, *Vie de Jean-Jacques Olier,* Vol. 1, p. 187, Note 1, quoting Alexandre de Bretonvilliers, *Vie manuscrite de Monsieur Olier,* Vol. 1, p. 332.

7. *Ibid.,* p. 224.

8. More probably at Montdidier rather than at Paris, for Olier arrived in the capital on July 30, already resolved, it would seem from his letter to Sister de Vauldray, to refuse the episcopate. NA, p. 180; Faillon, *Vie de Monsieur Olier,* Vol. 1, p. 229, 257; (Joseph Le Royer de la Motte) *Le petit*

mémoire. See Chap. 3, Note 20.

9. Faillon, *Histoire de la Colonie Française en Canada*, Vol. 1, Ville-Marie, 1865, p. 386, note quoting Olier's *Mémoires*, Vol. 3, p. 266.

10. Monier, *Vie de Jean-Jacques Olier*, Vol. 1, p. 214; Daveluy, *La Société de Notre-Dame de Montréal*, p. (24).

11. *RPA*, Vol. 3, p. 189.

12. *VJLD*, Vol. 1, p. 144.

13. *RPA*, Vol. 3, p. 190. It has been asserted that Le Royer, in the capacity of "father of the poor," negotiated the coming of the Dieppe nuns to La Flèche. I have found no evidence for this assertion.

14. *VJLD*, Vol. 1, pp. 144-145.

15. *Ibid.*, pp. 149, 153.

16. Monier, *Vie de Jean-Jacques Olier*, Vol. 1, pp. 230-232; Jacques-E. Ménard, *Les dons du Saint-Esprit chez monsieur Olier*, Montreal, 1951, p. 38.

17. *RPA*, Vol. 3, 190; (Jérôme Joseph Le Royer de la Motte), *Le petit mémoire*, p. 2. See Chap. 3, Note 20.

18. Mondoux, *L'Hôtel-Dieu, premier hôpital de Montréal*, pp. 54-55.

19. *RPA*, Vol. 3, p. 191.

20. *Ibid.*, pp. 191-193.

21. Germain Lesage, *L'accession des congrégations à l'etat réligieux canonique*, Ottawa, 1952, pp. 150-154.

22. "Copie du MS de Mgr de Rueil, conservé aux archives R.H.S.J. de La Flèche, A. 1er S., traduit par Monsieur Jean-Baptiste Jupin, un de nos aumôniers," in *RPA*, Vol. 3, p. 194.

23. *Ibid.*, p. 195.

24. *NA*, pp. 224-225.

Chapter IX

"After Great Vigilance and Care"

THE LA FLÉCHE COLLECTOR OF TAXES did not lay aside his Montreal preoccupations as he bent his efforts towards consolidating the organization of the Hôtel Dieu.[1] In late 1639, he began to think of recruiting settlers for his foundation and immediately foresaw the necessity of having provisions ready for them on the day they disembarked at Quebec. With Pierre de Fancamp, he set to work accumulating the commodities, tools, and ammunition they would need.[2] By the last days of the spring of 1640,[3] he had crammed into large wooden barrels—the containers of the times—20 tonneaux (approximately 350 cubic feet) of supplies. He had reserved space for them on one of the ships sailing for the New World, and obtained two pinnaces, the *St. Joseph* and the *Notre Dame*,[4] to transport them from Quebec to the Island of Montreal. Not very far from the chapel of Our Lady of the Head of the Bridge at Port Luneau, today Promenade du Maréchal-Foch, the precious cargo was stowed away in the holds of several river-craft.

According to a local tradition, Marie de la Ferre and a few helpers added a feminine touch by putting in a few stones—not that there was a lack of them in Canada—into the well-filled barrels.[5] From old France, from La Flèche, these stones, chosen, perhaps from among those left over from the building of the St. Joseph Chapel at the hospital, were destined for New France, for the settlement thousands of miles across the ocean.

As was to be expected, the loading of the 20 tonneaux (i.e., barrels) provoked much chatter in La Flèche. Fortunately, the clacking of tongues was sympathetic to Jérôme. The size and importance of the shipment proved that he

103

had found the means to proceed with his plans; this substantial consignment for Canada would gain sympathy for the Montreal project and might enable him to find colonists for the distant foundation. And thus the barges sailed off for Nantes, where Fr. Chauveau supervised the transfer of all this material into ocean-going ships.[6] It was the first of many cargoes that Jérôme was to send to New France in the course of the next 14 years.

The twenty tonneaux were sent to Quebec in the care of Fr. Paul Le Jeune. In the Relation of 1640, the Jesuit wrote: "We learn through this year's fleet, that some brave and virtuous persons have resolved to send hither a number of men next year; having already sent over supplies for this purpose." [7]

One admires Jérôme Le Royer's optimism, or is shocked by it. It was all well and good to forward supplies and munitions to the Montreal of the future, but of what avail would they be if the pioneers were not allowed to set foot on the far-away island? Its proprietor, Jean de Lauson, then held the charge of Administrator of the Provinces of Provence and of Dauphiné. As it was imperative for Jérôme to become the owner of the Island of Montreal, which Providence had spread out before him in his vision, he resolved to leave for Dauphiné[8] as soon as he could.

Accompanied by the Baron de Fancamp, he rode out of La Flèche on horseback, in early May or June,[9] and headed for Tours, Lyons, and Vienne. About daybreak, before kissing his wife and children goodbye, he had slipped a hairshirt over his shoulders,[10] still sore from his daily penances, for he rejoiced to be able to share in the sufferings of Christ. The trip was a long and tiresome one, lasting more than two weeks.

Le Royer had never been to Vienne before. It is built on a hillside dominated by Mt. Solomon, Mt. St. Blandine, and Mt. St. Justus, and extends down into the plain to the banks of the Rhône River. This is a very old city, pre-

Roman in origin and full of monuments dating back to Emperor Augustus, but it is doubtful whether the two visitors paid much attention to them, preoccupied as they were with their coming visit to the Administrator. It is not out of order to imagine that Jérôme and his companion stopped to pray at one of the churches, perhaps at Saint-André-le-Bas, the first Gothic edifice built in Dauphiné.

To the Hôtel de Maugiron,[11] where Administrator de Lauson was in residence, went Le Royer and Fancamp. The collector of taxes from La Flèche must have given much thought to the preparation of this interview. He was a man of business, and he understood that one does not simply stalk into the presence of a high and mighty lord, and request that he dispossess himself of acres, thousands of them, even though they are situated beyond the seas! He would speak to the Administrator of the glory of God and of the salvation of the Indians. Should Lauson be receptive, he would explain his plans to him in detail for sending forty pioneers to Montreal in the immediate future.

As soon as Jean de Lauson learned the whys and wherefores of the visit, his manner became brusque, and he dismissed the two callers with a curt refusal.[12] On the Administrator's refusal to part with the Island of Montreal, many would have read into it a manifestation of the Divine Will and would have abandoned the project. Not so with Jérôme Le Royer. Both he and the Baron saddled their horses and took the road to Paris. In the capital, they would knock at doors and ask for help. Nothing definite is known about this trip. At Lyons, if the two travellers had time, they certainly paid homage to Our Lady of Fourvière in her hilltop shrine,[13] quite popular since the plague of 1628, because of the many cures obtained there.

In Paris, Jérôme made the rounds of the relatively few friends and acquaintances he had. Olier was not among them. During the last three months of 1639, the priest had been unexpectedly drawn into the vortex of a terrible spiritual ordeal, which left him incapacitated for months on end. He describes this tribulation in his Memoirs: "It seemed that our good Lord wanted me to be affected simultaneously with all sorts of interior trouble: the pains of reprobation and divine scorn, a continual impression of pride, the loss of the power of elevating my heart to God, the dark night of the spirit, confusion, encompassment by the devil, the disdain of important people, the abandonment of my spiritual director, the universal contempt of all—relatives, friends, servants, the great and the small—the conviction that I had become a Judas..." [14]

At the Royal College of Clermont, Le Royer and Fancamp sought out the procurator-general of the Canadian Missions, Parisian-born Fr. Charles Lalemant, the future St. Gabriel Lalemant's uncle.[15] Since the missionary's return from New France in 1638, everyone interested in the Canadian Missions made it a point to call upon him. Besides, Jérôme had at least a nodding acquaintance with him, since Fr. Lalemant was completing his philosophy course at the Royal College of La Flèche when he began his studies, and reading theology when he graduated.

When Monsieur Le Royer and the Baron de Fancamp told him how they had been received by Lauson, the Jesuit, who was acquainted with the Administrator, offered to accompany the collector of taxes on a second visit to Vienne. Fancamp, it was decided, should return to La Flèche, where he could work at recruiting settlers for Montreal.[16] The Baron set out for Anjou and arrived at La Flèche in the second week of July and on the twelfth he had notaries Pierre de la Fousse and Jacques Guillier draw up a deed granting power of attorney to Jérôme Le Royer in order to negotiate, not only in his own name, but also in that of his friend, the transfer of the Island of Montreal.[17] The procuration was then sent to Jérôme by post.

Lauson received Fr. Lalemant and his friend from La Flèche cordially. He held the Jesuit in high esteem. Perhaps he also realized that he had too closely followed St. Paul's advice to proprietors, holding the island as though he possessed it not. Indeed, he had done nothing to settle it, as his contract with the Company of the One Hundred Associates obligated him to do. Fr. Lalemant may have very tactfully hinted that a refusal on the Administrator's part to make over the land would force to take up the matter with the members of the Company. Lauson, who was not unintelligent, signed over the Island of Montreal to Jérôme Le Royer and Pierre Chevrier de Fancamp. At what price? A document published in 1643 mentions "certain conditions quite reasonable and favourable."[18] No one really knows what the outlay was, if any.

At the Hôtel de Maugiron in Vienne, on August 7, 1640, Notary Gounon[19] drew up two deeds. In the first one Jean de Lauson "ceded, gave and transferred purely and simply the Island of Montreal,... situated in the St. Lawrence River above Lake St. Pierre, just as it had been given by the Gentlemen of the Company of New France to Monsieur de la Chaussée... under the same terms and conditions.."[20] In the second one, Jean de Lauson, in the capacity of administrator for his son, François, granted sailing rights to Jérôme Le Royer on the entire length of the St. Lawrence River as well as permission to fish within a two-league limit of the Island.[21] In exchange for this privilege, according to the feudal system then in force, as "a token of simple acknowledgement" ten pounds of fish were to be supplied to Lauson every year.

Gratified by the turn of events, it appears that Jérôme invited Jean de Lauson to become a member of the Company of Montreal and that the invitation was accepted. The same invitation, it is said, was subsequently proffered to Jacques Girard de la Chaussée, the Administrator's straw man, who also joined the little group of devoted planners.[22]

Father Lalemant and Monsieur Le Royer knew, or if they did not know then, they found out upon arriving in Paris that their contract with Administrator de Lauson had to have the official sanction of the Company of New France. To begin with, it flatly refused to recognize as valid the transfer of Montreal to Le Royer. Because Jean de Lauson had never sent a single settler to the New World, he had lost his rights to his Canadian seigneury and was unqualified to dispose of it. How many visits to the Company's headquarters did Jérôme make, how many discussions with the administrators did he have? Fr. Lalemant certainly put in a good word for him. His plans to establish a new settlement in Canada and his chances of success were carefully estimated. The situation of the Island of Montreal was examined and a map of it, sent from Canada by Governor de Montmagny, was scrutinized, signed by the directors of the Company and by Jérôme Le Royer,[23] with the intention of adding it for future reference to the grant once it was drawn up and approved. Finally, assured that all would be well, the collector of taxes from La Flèche quit the capital.[24]

He arrived home worn out. During the previous two years, the worries, the travels, and the obstacles that had been his lot, in addition to his daily corporal penances, had considerably weakened his resistance. He was happy to be back with his wife and children. It would be so easy to be with them constantly.[25] Temptations of discouragement flitted through his mind and, as the days went by, beset him more and more. Why keep on with the Montreal enterprise? There was plenty of good to be done in Anjou and in France. He had no experience in this kind of venture, no resources, and he probably would never have any. What did he intend to do about his wife, five children, and Renée Le Royer de la Roche, the niece whom he had adopted? Who would take care of them if he suddenly died? More insidious were the doubts concerning his revelations, in particular the order from above to found Montreal and the assurances God had given him that He would bless his efforts and always be with him. He was sick to the inner core of his being with the bitterness of it, and with the darkness into which he was plunged. His entire existence was tied up in a knot, and then all at once unravelled. God strengthened him interiorly and he placed all his trust in the divine assistance.

Since the autumn of 1639, his friend Fr. Olier had also found himself buffeted by the high seas of illness and desolation and unable to be of any use to him. On December 13, 1640, Henri de Marchaumont, Bishop of Châlons died, and his young coadjutor, Félix de Herse, succeeded him much sooner than had been expected. "If Father Olier," people crowed, "had accepted the coadjutorship that had been offered to him, he would now be Bishop of Châlons!" The man who could have become a powerful prelate became the laughing-stock of Paris. "The King," he wrote in his *Mémoirs*, "Cardinal de Richelieu, my Lords the Bishops, and the Chancellor, especially the Chancellor Pierre Séguier, and all my relatives, began to make much fun of me."[26] All this scorn and derision delayed the unhappy priest's cure until several months of the following year had passed.

Other backers would come to Jérôme's assistance. Sixteen hundred and forty one walked in joyfully, their arms overflowing with blessings for the Hôtel Dieu, assuredly a harbinger of good things to be. These blessings took the form of young ladies, some of them very young, inspired by the example of Mademoiselle de la Ferre and her two companions to seek admission among them.[27] The first one to knock at the door of the little hospital was Anne Le Tendre on January 7, 1641; she was followed by Renée Busson on the 25th day of the same month. The candidate who filled Jérôme with the most joy, a joy tinged with an understandable sadness, was that of his little daughter Jeanne, who was barely thirteen years old. She had long been aware of her father's dedication to the poor and the ill, she had seen the new hospital and its chapel rise from their foundations, and at last had solemnly requested the permission to dedicate herself to God's forsaken ones at the new establishment.

On February 1, eve of the Feast of the Purification of the Blessed Virgin Mary, the eleventh anniversary of the manifestation Jérôme had received from above, he accompanied his child to the nearby hospital, where he entrusted her to the maternal loving-kindness of Mother de la Ferre. On the same day, two other youngsters, Marie and Thérèse Havard de la Tremblaye also joined her. Others were soon to come, among them Anne Baillif, who requested admission as a lay Sister, on May 7.[28] On October 8, Marie, daughter of Charles Gyrot, "master of penmanship" at the Royal College, and of Roberta Le Queüe, was welcomed as a novice; her brother, Father Jean furthermore dedicated himself for life as chaplain at the Hôtel-Dieu.

In early 1641, Jérôme Le Royer was informed that on December 17, 1640, the administrators of the One Hundred Associates had signed the Island of Montreal transfer in his favour and in that of Baron de Fancamp.[29] This document created what was to become the metropolis of Canada. Though closely resembling Lauson's deed of transfer to Le Royer, it contained significant differences.

The new seigneury did not take in the entire island, for the Company restricted the concession made to La Chaussée and passed on to Lauson by retaining to its own advantage the western end, enclosed within a line drawn from the Rivière des Prairies to Lake St. Louis, about four leagues from Mount Royal. There it intended erecting a trading post. On the mountain top, the Company furthermore preempted five acres or so, which were to be used when it saw fit for the construction of a fort. In compensation, to the east of the Island of Montreal, the One Hundred Associates granted a small fief, later to be known as St. Sulpice's, to the two gentlemen from La Flèche.

The deed of concession clearly deliniated the political and military position of the future settlement. Le Royer, Fancamp, and their successors were to manifest their faith and homage by the customary manifestations of feudal tenure, not excluding the *aveux* and *dénombrement*[30] according to the custom of Paris, a system that was to endure for years in Canada.

In regard to justice, whenever an appeal was to be made, the local judges appointed by the new seigneurs must look to the Sovereign Court, which would be set up in Quebec or elsewhere in New France.

The deed contained several other restrictions. The fur trade with the aborigines and for that matter with anyone else was only allowed insomuch as the need of individual people was involved. Furthermore, the erection of any fortifications other than those required for the protection of the inhabitants was strictly forbidden. Finally, no land grants were to be allotted to colonists previously come to the New World, but only to future immigrants.

It was finally stated in the deed that orders were to be sent to the Governor-General of Canada, so as to facilitate the establishment of the settlement.

Truly, December 17, 1640 had been a red-letter day for Jérôme Le Royer, and for Canada also. He now owned the Island of Montreal, some 250,000 broad acres of it, admirably situated in the heart of New France, and he intended to use it for the greater glory of God. After ten years, he had won a round in the fight for souls, but, as Dollier de Casson wrote in the last quarter of the 17th century, only "after great vigilance and care." [31]

Chapter IX

Notes

1. *VJLD*, Vol. 1, p. 155.

2. Dollier de Casson, *A History of Montreal*, p. 69.

3. *RPA*, Vol. 3, p. 193; Bertrand, *Monsieur de la Dauversière*, p. 97.

4. Bertrand, *Monsieur de la Dauversière*, p. 103, Note 2.

5. *NA*, p. 98; Mondoux, *L'Hôtel-Dieu, premier hôpital de Montréal*, pp. 71-72.

6. *NA*, p. 221. According to Sr. Grosjean, Fr. Chauveau was living at Nantes. If so, he was in temporary residence only: See above, Chap. 4, Note 4.

7. *JR*, Vol. XVIII, p. 245.

8. Edmond Esmonin, in his paper, "Les Intendants du Dauphiné des origines à la Révolution," Allier, 1923, pp. 46-47, taken from *Les Annales de la Faculté des Lettres de l'Université de Grenoble*, quoted by R. Azevou, Chief Archivist of the Departmental Archives of Isère and of the former Province of Dauphiné, in a letter to Lieutenant de Trétaigne at the Invalides in Paris, June 14, 1954, refers to "a commission of June 23, 1638, naming him (Lauson) to establish the Board of Excise at Vienne..." In this document he is called "administrator or intendant of justice, police, and finances of our Province of Provence at Vienne..." Had he not been administrator of both Provinces, he would not

have received this commission. Esmonin's article is now reprinted in his *Etudes sur la France des XVIIe et XVIIIe siècles*, Paris, 1964, pp. 71-112.

9. I have followed *VJLD's* (Vol. 1, pp. 159-161) chronology for Le Royer's trip to Dauphiné and to Paris. It is more complete than any other and does not differ substantially from *RPA's* version.

10. Baron de Fancamp, "Copie fidelle de la lettre écrite au Reverand Père Chaumonot, Jésuite, au College de Kebec, sur la mort de Monsieur de La Dauversière, en l'année 1660," in Marie Morin, *Histoire Simple et Véritable*, p. 109.

11. Not Montgiron, as Faillon wrote in *Histoire de la Colonie Française en Canada*, Vol. 1, pp. 394-395, but Maugiron. See "Donation et transport de la concession de l'Ile de Montréal," par M. Jean de Lauson aux Sieurs Chevrier de Fouancant (sic) et Le Royer de la Dauversière (sic), in Dollier de Casson, *Histoire du Montréal*, (Mémoire de la Société Historique de Montréal, 4), Montreal, 1968, Appendice, pp. 246-248.

12. *RPA*, Vol. 3, p. 199.

13. A sanctuary had been erected in the 10th century on the ruins of Trajan's Forum, *Forum vetus*, but was destroyed by the Huguenots in 1562. Another chapel was constructed in 1586. This was the shrine at which Le Royer may have prayed. It was rebuilt in 1751 on a larger scale, and a last time in the 19th century (1872-1894).

14. Lévesque, *Lettres de Monsieur Olier*, pp. 144-145, and note referring to Olier's *Mémoires*.

15. Leon Pouliot, art. "Lalemant, Charles," in DCB, Vol. 1, pp. 423-424.

16. *NA*, p. 204; Daveluy in *La société de Notre-Dame de Montréal*, p. 106, gives another reason: "M. de Fancamp est empêché d'y aller (to Vienne), car il surveille le premier envoi de vivres et d'outils dirigé, de la Flèche, vers la Nouvelle France. Il signe une procuration autorisant Monsieur de la Dauversière à transiger en son nom."

17. Etienne-Michel Faillon, *Vie de Mlle Mance, et histoire de l'Hôtel-Dieu de Villemarie dans l'Ile de Montréal*, Vol 1, Villemarie, 1854, Introduction, p. xxxiv, referring to "Actes de Pierre de La Fousse, notaire à La Flèche, 12 juillet 1640: "Archives de la Marine, Canada, t. 1." Henceforth: Faillon, *Vie de Mlle Mance*.

18. Les Véritables Motifs, p. 27. Bertrand in *Monsieur de la Dauversière*, p. 91, "On a pretendu que l'Ile de Montréal avait été achetée et payée 100,000 ou 150,000 livres... Il n'y a rien la qui ressemble à une vente..." Desrosiers, *Paul de Chomedey, sieur de Maisonneuve*, p. 25, "...Par donation pure et simple, Lauson remet l'Ile de Montréal à Jérôme Le Royer et au Baron de Fancamp." On the other hand, without furnishing any proof, Robert Lahaise asserts in "L'Hôtel-Dieu du Vieux-Montréal," *L'Hôtel-Dieu de Montréal 1642-1973*, p. 13, "Elle (the Company of Montreal) obtint l'Ile du Montréal,... au prix de 150,000 livres." Gustave Lanctot, *Montréal sous Maisonneuve, 1642-1665*, Montreal, 1966, pp. 150-151.

19. Not Courdon as Faillon wrote in *Histoire de la Colonie Française en Canada* Vol. 1, p. 394; as *RPA*, Vol. 6, p. 491, and Mondoux, *L'Hôtel-Dieu, premier hôpital de Montréal*, p. 336, spell the name. Their error comes from a copy of "Donation et transport de la concession de l'Ile de Montréal

par Monsieur Jean de Lauson aux Sieurs Chevrier de Fancamp et Le Royer de la Dauversière," (7 aout 1640) made on March 10, 1664, by Frs. Le Ragois and Queylus. However, R. Azévou, in his letter quoted above in Note 8, writes, "J'ai le regret de vous faire connaître que je ne trouve aucune trace, ni à Vienne, ni à Grenoble, ni dans le departement actuel de l'Isère, d'un CAUDRON, COURDON, GAUDRON ou GOURDON. Le nom le plus approchant est celui de GOUNON, notaire à Vienne, dont les minutes sont conservées seulement depuis 1648."

20. "Donation et transport de la concession de L'Ile de Montréal par M. Jean de Lauson aux Sieurs chevrier de Fouançant (sic) et Le Royer de La Dauversière (sic)." See note 11 on page 113.

21. Faillon, *Histoire de la Colonie Française en Canada*, Vol. 1, p. 394-395. The author gives as reference "Archives du Séminaire de Montréal." The document disappeared a long time ago.

22. Etienne de Montgolfier, *La vie de la vénérable Marguerite Bourgeois dite du Saint-Sacrement...*, a Ville-Marie, 1818, p. 19.

23. "Concession d'une grande partie de L'Ile de Montréal par la Compagnie de la Nouvelle-France a MM. La Dauversière et Fancamp," in *Edits, ordonnances royaux, déclarations et arrêts du conseil d'Etat du roi concernant le Canada*, Vol. 1, Quebec, 1854, p. 21. The correction is mine; the Editor writes: a MM. du Séminaire de Saint-Sulpice."

24. *VJLD*, Vol. 1, p.162.

25. *Véritables Motifs*, pp. 27-28.

26. P. Pourrat, *Jean-Jacques Olier, fondateur de Saint-Sulpice*, Paris, 1932, p. 87.

27. *RPA*, Vol. 3, pp. 214-215. Anne, daughter of René Busson, Sieur de la Galoisière, also a La Flèche lawyer, and of Renée LeBarbier, a relative of Jérôme Le Royer; Jeanne, her youngest sister later became a Daughter of St. Joseph; Mary, aged 14, and her sister Theresa, aged 10, were daughters of Anthony Havard, Sieur de la Tremblaye, judge of the presidial court of La Flèche, and Hibon de la Hibonnière.

28. *Ibid.*, p. 216; Anne Baillif, aged 25, daughter of a La Flèche mason. During the month of August, Jérôme accepted Renée Hurst, aged 75, widow of lawyer Papin of nearby Durtal, as an 'associate.' She died in October of the same year (1641), leaving 1,100 livres to the poor of the Hôtel Dieu.

29. "Concession d'une grand partie de L'Ile de Montréal par la Compagnie de la Nouvelle-France a MM. La Dauversière et Fancamp," in *Edits, ordonnances royaux*, Vol. 1, pp. 20-23.

30. An avowal of the grants of the seigneury from the Crown and the census of the seigneury with the names of the concessionnaires, the amount of lands granted them and under cultivation, together with the number of heads of cattle, etc., as defined by William Henry Atherton in *Montreal Under the French Regime*, p. 63, note 3.

31. Dollier de Casson, *A History of Montreal*, p. 67.

Chapter X

Ladies and Gentlemen and Others

FROM SEPTEMBER 1640 well into 1641, Jérôme was on the lookout for more men and supplies for his distant foundation. With his brother, René de Boistaillé, his friend, Pierre Chevrier de Fancamp, and an unknown party at Dieppe, he laboured untiringly with the slender means at his disposal to send an important contingent of pioneers across the ocean in 1641.[1] He wanted young men—farmers, craftsmen, and soldiers—all unmarried.

It is not difficult to imagine the collector of taxes with a copy of Fr. Le Jeune's *Jesuit Relations* of 1634-35 in which Frenchmen were urged to come and open up the land and build cities and towns in Canada, and with a copy of the 1636-37 issue, in which there is a description of the Island of Montreal. He knocked at one door and then at another of the candidates he had already screened in an attempt to persuade them to go into exile to the other side of the world for the greater glory of God. To hamlets, towns, and cities he travelled, unmindful of fatigue, persistent even when dogged with unsuccess. Although he was not silver-tongued, he discussed with pent-up fire the pros and cons of Fr. Le Jeune's invitation and applied it to the fantastic adventure to which he was now inviting these compatriots of his.

A great deal was demanded of the future immigrants. the prospect of extraordinary monetary benefits was not dangled before their eyes, nor was that of broad acres of landed property; besides, constant military service was compulsory and religious worship was communal.[2] In other words, theirs were to be lives subject to strict discipline: religious, social, economic, and family discipline, exacting nothing less than outstanding generosity on the

117

part of each one. All this, to settle the Island of Montreal with fervent Christians whose good example would attract the Indians and lead them to Christ,[3] much as the Benedictines had done in Europe after the fall of the Roman Empire.

Once they had committed themselves, he had their contracts drawn up by notaries at La Flèche, Nantes, La Rochelle, and Dieppe. The newcomers took service for three, four or five years with the promise of an annual salary and subsistance during the entire length of their engagement.[4] Jérôme was responsible for their transportation to Canada and for their return home at the end of their employment. This method of recruiting was advantageous to all concerned. Enough land would be cleared and sufficient houses would be built to ensure the viability of the nascent establishment. By that time, the soldiers, farmers, and craftsmen would have acquired adequate experience of life in the Canadian wilds, earned their upkeep, and could, as they wished, either remain in this new land or return to France. In both cases, the little colony would have profited from their coming and the men would have been compensated for their contribution to it.

Stouthearted soldiers were of course necessary to stem the incursions of the Iroquois, but there was even greater need of a suitable commander to lead them. Not only a skilled warrior but also a man of ideals and of tact, capable of assuring the success of the Montreal undertaking. This leader for whom Jérôme, his brother, and Pierre de Fancamp had been praying, unknown to them, was twenty-nine-year-old Paul de Chomedey, a gentleman of Champagne.[5] He was all they hoped for and much more.

The documents Paul de Chomedey later drafted and signed with his elegant hand bear proof that as a child he benefited from the lessons of excellent teachers. At the age of thirteen, it appears that, in the wake of the young nobility of his time, he began his military career during the Thirty Years' War against Austria, serving his country in the Netherlands, and even rose to the rank of colonel. His favourite pastime was the lute—the guitar of his day— which he enjoyed playing in his tent on foggy evenings. It would help him while away long winter hours in Canada.

His sister, Mother Louise de Chomedey de Ste. Marie, a religious of the Congregation of Notre Dame at Troyes, a city on the Seine, in northeastern France, describes her brother's martial appearance, with bangs falling over his forehead and giving him the appearance of a crusader. An avid reader of the *Jesuit Relations*, Mother Louise was fascinated by the Canadian missions and she yearned to cross the ocean to evangelize the Indians. This was not to be, but she did much better by calling Paul's attention to the peoples of the world who, through no fault of theirs, knew nothing about the Saviour and His Cross.

With these thoughts in mind, during one of his leaves of absence, in early 1641 he went to Paris, where he was welcomed by his friends the Trumenys. During his stay in Paris, in his hosts' study he found a copy of the *Jesuit Relations*, which he read attentively. He fell upon the name of Fr. Charles Lalemant, the same man who had accompanied Jérôme Le Royer to Vienne, and learning that he was in the city, made his way to Clermont College. There he knocked at the door of the Jesuit's little cell and having introduced himself, confided his developing interest in Canada to him.[6] With an annual income of 2,000 livres, he would be willing to dedicate his life to God as a layman. He was above all a soldier and used to giving orders. Where could he best use the talents God had given him? After a long conversation, the Jesuit was convinced that he had before him a man of extraordinary disinterestedness, with a heart devoid of all fear except that of God. With the promise he would hear from him in the near future, Fr. Lalemant wished him well.

On his next visit to Paris, Jérôme Le Royer also knocked at Fr. Lalemant's door. The religious had been of great help to him at Vienne; perhaps he would be of assistance again. A good leader was needed for the lot of men he was sending to New France. Did the priest have anyone in mind? He did, and smilingly answered, "I know a gallant gentleman of Champagne, named Monsieur de Maisonneuve who has such qualities and who might suit you very well." [7]

After hearing Fr. Lalemant's description of Paul de Chomedey de Maisonneuve, Jérôme was eager to meet him. Upon hearing the name of the inn where he was staying, on the Jesuit's advice, he was determined to get immediately acquainted with him. This he achieved quite skillfully, taking care at first not to make himself known. After taking a room at the inn as any ordinary traveller would, during the following meal he began to speak of the New World to his table companions, of the immense good that could be done in that remote land, and finally of his plans for the Island of Montreal. Jérôme, who had recognized the gentleman from Champagne from Fr. Lalemant's description, drew him along with the others into a spirited conversation. After walnuts and wine, or more precisely pears and cheese, or parsley and ox tails, Chomedey arose and invited Monsieur Le Royer to his room, for the idea of a new colony on the Island of Montreal appealed to him. When the men were alone, the young soldier, who felt strangely attracted to this (at first glance) nondescript collector of taxes from La Flèche, got down to business.

In response to Jérôme's questions, he candidly expressed himself on his own qualities. He would be very glad, he added, "to escape from his idle life, and... if he could help in his enterprise, he would offer his service willingly... Besides, having no preoccupations, and sufficient wealth for his limited aims in life..., he would use his life and his purse in this enterprise without other ambition than the honour of serving God and the King, his master, in the calling and profession of arms which he had always followed."

Before allowing Monsieur de Chomedey to commit himself once for all, Jérôme told him about his two trips to Vienne, one of them with Fr. Lalemant, and about Jean de Lauson, Administrator of the Province of Dauphiné, and, perhaps, about the latter's friend Jacques Girard, Lord of la Chausseé and de la Callières. Three other men already deeply interested in the project were also the subject of conversation: Fr. Jean Olier, a relative of Chancellor Séguier; Baron Gaston de Renty; and, finally, Baron Pierre Chevrier de Fancamp. With the La Flèche collector of taxes, this was the nucleus of the group that was to be known in history as the Company of Montreal. For assets, it had only 25,000 crowns to cover the expenses of the first shipment.[8] Was Paul de Chomedey ready to join it? He was. There was no hesitation to his answer. Was he willing to be at the seaport of La Rochelle by the end of April to take command of the Montreal-bound pioneers? He was. This unexpected volunteer, thought Jérôme, was a heaven-sent gift. He was never to change his mind about him.

Later on, when the young officer's father, a man of letters eulogized by Ronsard, heard of his decision, he energetically opposed it. Paul was his only living son, the hope of the family, a family of old and noble lineage. A sinister affair, this Montreal venture was, and detrimental to his son's best interest! To win over his father, Paul explained that, in taking charge of the settlers he would gain a fine reputation and that before very long he would be very, very wealthy. He did not reveal, however, that he was referring to Our Lord's promise, "And everyone who has left houses, brothers, sisters, father, mother, children or land for the sake of my name will be repaid a hundred times over, and also inherit eternal life" (Matthew 19:29).

Understanding that the wealth alluded to was of this world, the old gentleman consented to his son's involvement with Le Royer.

By the time Paul de Chomedey succeeded in convincing his father, Jérôme, his business finished, had left Paris. The cobblestones echoed the beat of his horse's hooves. "Thank the Lord for Paul de Chomedey! Thank the Lord for Paul de Chomedey!" their resonance seemed to say. And he thought of the work in store for him. Besides his regular occupation as collector of taxes, which had to be seen to, the search for more men willing to cross the ocean had to be accelerated. Fortunately he could now count on an experienced soldier as well as on his brother and Fancamp. Then he had to be at La Rochelle on the distant Bay of Biscay on the Atlantic coast some 290 miles southwest of the capital, in early May at the latest, for the first sailing of the year.

As he rode along the chilly countryside, he certainly felt gratified at the thought of a visit he had made while he was in the capital. Of all persons, to a taverner he apparently had met during a previous stay, perhaps after his return from Vienne with Fr. Lalemant, or even earlier. The taverner was a woman, Marie Rousseau,[9] the same one who had upbraided Olier and his companions for their worldliness in 1629.

Marie de Gournay had married David Rousseau in 1612, when she was about sixteen years of age. Her husband was listed among the twenty-five purveyors of wine by special appointment to the Court, which he followed in its changes of residence. He was also a wholesale liquor dealer and a licensed tavern keeper with an establishment at Bussy Arch. Following the unfortunate example of Henri IV, all the classes of society rubbed shoulders in the taverns, the gambling dens, and the brothels of Paris. During 18 years, Marie Rousseau waited on this motley crowd of clients, often made up of the residents of the vicious St. Germain quarter of the city.

This woman, who was a good businesswoman and an excellent wife, to the extent that she was careful not to stay too long in church so as to avoid getting her husband's dander up, bore him four sons and one daughter. She brought them up as a good Christian mother should and, after David Rousseau's death, while her daughter became a nun, she established her sons in a trade of their own.

Now why should Jérôme Le Royer have anything to do with her? This unassuming widow was favoured by God with mystical graces, and had received the mission of converting the tough St. Germain underworld, of helping Fr. Olier found the Seminary of St. Sulpice, and of being the spiritual guide of many eminent members of the clergy and laity alike. People of both sexes, advanced in the ways of holiness, consulted her. Pious noblewomen—they did exist—such as the Princesse de Condé and the Duchesses d'Aiguillon and d'Elbeuf commended themselves to her prayers. St. Jean Eudes, Monsieur du Coudray, organizer of the Near Eastern Missions, Chancellor Séguier and other notables sought her advice.

Thanks to Olier, we know that Jérôme Le Royer profited by his talks with Marie Rousseau. "It is she also," he wrote, "who is serving as a guide for this man, whom God has chosen for the establishment of the Church in Canada... Although this great servant of God is quite enlightened about everything concerning his mission, he considers it a signal favour to converse with her and to receive her advice on the most important affairs of this country." [10]

Marie Rousseau does not seem to have spoken to Jérôme about a distinguished lady who had paid a visit to her during the previous winter, Mademoiselle Jeanne Mance. With Chomedey she was to be the mainspring of Montreal. She came from far-off Langres in one of the distant marches of southeastern Champagne. Apparently, she had first gone to Olier, still seriously ill, who sent her to Marie, the taverner. She was then thirty-three years old, poor in health, and determined to sail to Canada.[11] She was the second of a family of twelve, which belonged to the legal profession. Her father, a judge, saw to it that she and her sister, Marguerite, received a thoroughly Catholic education, very likely with the Ursulines. At the early age of seven, she had consecrated herself to God by a vow of chastity. When she was nineteen or twenty years of age, she lost her mother and in 1635, her father, whom she tenderly loved. These deaths as well as the war—the Thirty Years' War, then in its seventeenth year, trailing in its wake the other three horsemen of the Apocalypse—gave rise to serious thinking about life and death and their significance.

It was in mid-April 1640 that Jeanne Mance first felt drawn to the Canadian missions.[12] A cousin of hers, Fr. Nicolas Dolebeau, chaplain of the famed Holy Chapel in Paris and future Canon of Langres, spoke to her enthusiastically about New France and the good that was being done there by men and women alike. Never before, in the history of the Church, had women quit their native land to work in the foreign missions. He mentioned his brother Jean, a Jesuit, who that very spring of 1640, was leaving for Canada. Then the priest explained how a person of distinction, Madame de la Peltrie, had led a group of Ursulines to Quebec; how Madame la Duchesse d'Aiguillon, one of St. Vincent de Paul's penitents, had furnished the Augustinian nuns of Dieppe with the means to found a Hôtel Dieu or hospital in the little capital of the French colony. This conversation with her cousin resulted in Jeanne Mance's foreign vocation.

In the following days, the inclination, which she had so strongly felt and which had produced such joy in her, disappeared. Objections sprouted up in her mind, in particular her poor health. For hours and days, she seesawed from yes to no, and the more she drew back, the more she was pursued with the thought that she was resisting God's will. She finally consulted her spiritual director, a Jesuit. At first, he opposed her going to Canada, but to no avail. As Pentecost was approaching, he invited her to pray to the Holy Spirit for guidance. When she again sought his advice, after breathing a prayer to the Holy Spirit, he answered without hesitation: "You may leave for Paris on Wednesday after Pentecost; there, you will be able to speak to Fr. Charles Lalemant, who is in charge of Canadian affairs. For your spiritual guide, take the rector of the Jesuit house nearest to your lodging." [13]

So on May 30, she left her hill city of Langres to visit her Dolebeau cousins in Paris, there to be seen and admired, thought her friends.[14] The trip took her from three weeks to a month and was exceedingly tiresome. Down the chalky roads of Upper Champagne, through Lower Champagne, her coach rolled along. Part of the time, she travelled on horseback. She doubtless stopped at Troyes, and at the royal city of Rheims with its towers and white walls. Before the end of June, the majestic silhouette of Notre Dame cathedral appeared in the distance. Finally, her coach halted at the strand an open space on the banks of the Seine in the heart of Paris, swarming with lords and ladies in their silks and velvets, magistrates in their caps and gowns, and merchants and tradesmen in their working clothes.

Jeanne Mance soon discovered that the home of Madame de Bellevue, née Antoinette Dolebeau, a first cousin of hers where she was welcomed, was close to the Church of St. Sulpice and in the neighbourhood of the Jesuit novitiate. Making a mental note that she must soon call upon its superior, she bypassed it and made her way to the Royal College of Clermont. Fr. Lalemant welcomed her and on her following visit, strengthened her in her resolve to go to Canada.

Shortly afterwards, she asked for Fr. Jean Baptiste de Saint-Jure at the Jesuit novitiate on the rue du Pot-de-fer. Father Rector was one of the most eminent Jesuits of his time and the author of the well known ascetical work, *Of the Knowledge and of the Love of the Son of God, Our Lord Jesus Christ*. From all the corners of France and even from beyond the frontiers, people came to consult him. Baron Gaston de Renty was one of his penitents.

Mademoiselle Mance related the story of what she thought was her vocation to the noted priest, so well versed in the psychology of extraordinary souls. He listened attentively without any sign of approval or of disapproval. For the next three months she was unable to get an appointment with the busy Jesuit.

During this time, she became the friend of an elderly Parisian lady, one of the former spiritual children of St. Francis de Sales, now one of St. Vincent de Paul's. This great lady, Madame de Villesavin, on learning that her young friend wanted to meet Fr. de Saint-Jure once again, told her to be at the parlour of the Jesuit novitiate the next day.

At the appointed hour, Jeanne Mance was at the rendezvous with her elderly friend. Fr. de Saint-Jure was called and he chatted with the two women until Madame de Villesavin begged to be excused. The Jesuit then told Mademoiselle Mance that he had never seen God's will manifested so clearly with regard to a vocation as to hers. And he suggested that she make it known to her friends and acquaintances.[15]

Quickly her intention to work in Canada became public knowledge. In the 17th century, as the departure of a woman for the foreign missions was a novelty, it caused quite a stir. She was in great demand in the drawing rooms of the fine ladies of the land. Even the cold and apathetic queen, Anne of Austria, received her in her private apartments. To their numerous questions, she answered, "that she well knew that God wanted her to be in Canada, though why, she did not know; and that she surrendered herself implicitly to His commands for her there."

She learned during the last months of 1640 that the Very Reverend Charles Rapine de Boisvert, Provincial of the Recollects of St. Denis,[16] was in Paris. As she knew him, she told him how matters stood. The kind Franciscan congratulated her on surrendering to God's will and promised that friends would concern themselves with the matter. A few days later, she received a word from Fr. Rapine telling her, as soon as she received an invitation, to wait upon Madame Angélique Faure de Berlise, Duchesse de Bullion, at her residence on Platrière Street.[17] Her husband, the late Claude de Bullion, Marquis de Gallardon, had been the Superintendant of Finances in France, Minister of State and an intimate friend of Richelieu. According to his solicitor, Le Cannes, he could count on a yearly revenue of 700,000 livres, to which on each New Year's Day, His Eminence added a bonus of 100,000 more. The portly widow, whom her husband used to call "ma grosse amie" (my fat friend), was well provided for.

When the time came, Jeanne Mance was introduced into the presence of the great lady, seated on a high-backed chair carrying the coat of arms of the Bullions. Fr. Rapine was standing beside the Duchess, and Jeanne immediately felt at ease. Her eyes took in the dark dress, low-necked and point-laced, the velvet hassock, a crimson splotch at her feet. After the friar took his leave, the two women continued their conversation. Madame de Bullion was aware of the foundation of the Hospitallers of St. Joseph in La Flèche, for Mother Marie de la Ferre was one of her correspondents.[18] She may well have known they were founded for the New World. Perhaps on the occasion of that first visit, the illustrious hostess decided that her visitor had been sent to her by God to help establish the Hôtel Dieu on the Island of Montreal. At all events, Mademoiselle Mance had made a lifelong friend.

Some time after returning to La Flèche, Jérôme received a letter from Mademoiselle Mance. Though he was unknown to her, she revealed to him her ardent desire to work as a lay missionary in the New World.[19] What else did she say? She needed at least to know if it would be possible to sail on one of the same ships as his men, for some priests were bound to accompany them, and she planned, if it were possible, to attend daily Mass on the long passage across the Atlantic. He promptly replied, urging her to hasten to La Rochelle, where he would meet her. There they could discuss her plans for the future.

Chapter X

Notes

1. Dollier de Casson, *A History of Montreal*, p. 69.

2. *VJLD*, Vol. 1, p. 167.

3. Léon Gérin, *Aux Sources de Notre Histoire*, Montréal, 1946, p. 170.

4. Bertrand, *Monsieur de la Dauversière*, pp. 106-109.

5. Léo-Paul Desrosiers, *Paul de Chomedey, sieur de Maisonneuve*, Montreal, 1967, p. 32; p. 37.

6. *Société de Notre-Dame de Montréal*, p. 121.

7. Dollier de Casson, *A History of Montreal*, p. 69.

8. *Ibid.*, p. 73. But Mother Jeanne-Françoise Juchereau de la Ferté de Saint-Ignace in *Les annales de l'Hôtel-Dieu de Québec, 1636-1716*, Albert Jamet, ed., Quebec, 1939, p. 39, says 50,000 crowns, p. 37.

9. Paul Renaudin, "Une voyante parisienne Marie Rousseau," in *La Vie Spirituelle*, Vol. LVIII, No. 234 (Paris, March 1, 1939), p. 268.

10. Faillon, *Olier*, Vol. 1, p. 341.

11. William Henry Atherton, *The Saintly Life of Jeanne Mance, First Lay Nurse in North America*, St. Louis, MO., 1945, p. 7.

12. Dollier de Casson, *A History of Montreal*, p. 75.

13. *Ibid.*, p. 77.

14. Morin, *Histoire Simple et Véritable*, p. 40.

15. Dollier de Casson, *History of Montreal*, p. 79.

16. Damase Laberge, "Le père Charles Rapine, récollet," in *Les Récollets et Montréal*, pp. 143-145.

17. Today 3, rue Jean-Jacques Rousseau.

18. *NA*, pp. 226-229.

19. Morin, *Histoire Simple et Véritable*, p. 46; AM, p. 29.

Chapter XI

Down to the Sea in Ships

JÉRÔME'S HOME, on Ave Maria or "Hail Mary" Street in La Flèche, must have seemed good, so very good to him after his weeks of traveling from one corner of France to the other. Jeanne de Baugé, his understanding wife, joyfully welcomed him back. During his absence, she, too, had been working in the interests of Montreal. The collector of taxes had taken the habit, before leaving for one of his trips, of granting his wife power of attorney so that she could borrow in his name 14, 18, and even 30,000 livres.[1] His brother, René de Boistaillé, or friends like Olivier de la Guittière, offered themselves as surety for both of them, confident the loans would be reimbursed as promised.

In the earlier weeks of April, Paul de Chomedey went to bid farewell to his two sisters at Troyes, Madame de Chevilly and Sr. Louise de Sainte-Marie. With three other nuns, the latter offered to accompany her brother to Canada, but the time was not ripe for a teaching Order on the Island of Montreal. So she gave him a holy picture on the back of which she wrote her hopes of some day joining him across the sea.[2]

After a hasty farewell, with the recruits Jérôme had garnered in the capital and perhaps a few of his own, Paul de Chomedey set out for the coast, no doubt by way of La Flèche.[3] He must have reached the little city on the Loire early in May. The founder of Montreal and the Baron de Fancamp, with recruits from Maine, Anjou, Perche, and Normandie, were awaiting him.[4] The two groups may have then gone on together by barge as far as Nantes, and from that city to La Rochelle. Most likely Jérôme hurried on before them to prepare for their coming. The Jesuits or perhaps some of the members of the Company of the Blessed Sacrament gave him the address of a Catholic merchant, Jacques Mousnier, who gladly lodged him.[5]

In 1641, La Rochelle was emerging from hard times. Its people had been Calvinists for nearly a century; only thirteen years before, its inhabitants had sided with England against France and, in retaliation, at the end of 1627, Louis XIII and the Cardinal Prime Minister had marched against the place. After his Majesty's return to Paris, Richelieu decided to isolate the city. He established a line of field works consisting in ramparts, entrenchments, 13 forts, and plenty of artillery, the whole line of circumvallation extending to no less than nine miles. In the spring of 1628, the blockade had become a veritable siege. To cut off all possible assistance from English allies, Richelieu did not hesitate to erect an immense dike, some 747 yards long, to seal up the port. Finally, on October 30, 1628, La Rochelle capitulated after 12,000 of its population had perished.[6] The scars of war were still apparent.

During the days that remained before sailing, as the colonists walked down the rue du Palais with its porched houses harking back to the Middle Ages, they passed the Hôtel de Ville with its storied battlements and examined the three towers guarding the port, which had been spared by the Cardinal. It was easy for them to imagine the horrendous year of the great siege. The thought of all these deaths and desolation clutched at their hearts like an icy hand. Perhaps more than one wondered if, in the not too distant future, they too might be assailed, not by the King's men but by fearsome Indians. The presence of their leader, whom they knew to be an experienced soldier, helped to allay their misgivings.

In distant Paris, the Gazette de France had quickly brought to its readers' attention the preparations under way for the Montreal expedition with its batch of settlers-to-be, adding, "There is also a Demoiselle Mance, a native of the city of Langres, who leads a very exemplary life and lives only on bread and water, and to whom they say God grants many graces." [7] The "only" was pure exaggeration, to which the press was already prone in the 17th century.

If we are to believe the Véritables Motifs published in 1643, before departing, Jeanne Mance foretold in detail to Frs. Rapine and Saint-Jure what would happen to her at La Rochelle and in New France during the following year; to mystic Marie Rousseau she gave a written account of these events as she bade her goodbye. [8]

After a tiresome trip, Jeanne Mance reached the seaport. Her first visit was to the Jesuit college, where Fr. Jacques de la Place, whom she had met in Paris, was staying. He was pleased she had persisted in her determination to go to Canada and remarked he had feared she would not arrive on time before the ships put out to sea.

"Did you see that gentleman," he inquired, "who left me in order that I might be free to see you? This year he has given 20,000 livres for an enterprise in that country. He is called the Baron de Fancamp and is joined with several persons of quality who are incurring great expense on behalf of an establishment that they wish to set up on the Island of Montreal in Canada." [9]

During the conversation that followed, Jeanne told the Jesuit how well she had been received at every stop on her way from Paris. Innkeepers refused to take her money and went out of their way to be gracious to her. As she was about to go, Fr. de la Place asked her where she roomed and she answered that a good Huguenot lady had a room for her. At his suggestion, she decided instead to put up with one of his acquaintances, who lived close to the Jesuits, until the ships weighed anchor.

The next day as Jeanne was about to enter the recently

constructed Jesuit college church, Monsieur Le Royer
came out. They had never seen each other before, but
recognition was immediate.[10] By a special illumination,
Jérôme was granted a knowledge of the interior workings
of Jeanne Mance's soul and of her plans for the glory of God;
a similar knowledge was imparted to her concerning the
founder of Montreal.

There on the doorsteps of the college church, they
talked of the coming foundation, of the group of men
dedicated to its realization, and of their aim in this enterprise—the conversion of the native inhabitants. During
this first meeting, Jeanne Mance may have spoken to the
collector of taxes from La Flèche about a great lady who
wished to remain unknown and who was interested in the
Canadian missions.

Shortly afterwards when they again discussed the
future of the island colony, Jeanne revealed to its initiator
how time and time again she had returned to call on the
"Unknown Benefactress," as this open-handed personage
was soon to be known. She was weighed down by the rolls
of gold coins the benefactress had donated for her work in
New France. Now Jeanne used to go to her residence in a
sedan. One day, her chairmen became inquisitive. "Why is
it, Mademoiselle," they asked, "that when you come here
you are less heavy than when you leave? Surely this lady
is fond of you and gives you presents!" This remark
frightened her. Perhaps these men would steal the money
she was carrying and kill her. So in the following visits, she
always took a different sedan with different chairmen and
made her appointments for different hours.

On her fourth visit to the noblewoman, Jeanne Mance
had been asked to take charge of a hospital in the wilds of
America. The "Unknown Benefactress" was planning to
endow a hospital for the sick and the wounded. She
intended to organize one like the Quebec Hôtel Dieu, the

result of the generosity of Richelieu's niece, the Duchesse d'Aiguillon. Would it be possible for her guest to inquire among her acquaintances about the terms agreed upon by the pious Duchess for the Quebec institution? The only objection Jeanne had been able to muster against this design was the poor health she had been suffering for over seventeen years. Still, she had promised to examine the proposal under the direction of her spiritual Father. Before leaving the princely residence, her aristocratic hostess solemnly charged her to never, for any reason whatsoever, reveal her name without her express permission.[11]

Jeanne Mance had then called upon Fr. de Saint-Jure, Rector of the Jesuit novitiate on the street of the Iron Pot,[12] who suggested that she make a retreat. As she was about to begin it, she had begged prayers of her friends, among them Marie Rousseau. After her meditation on the Two Standards during the Spiritual Exercises, she made her election and submitted it to her director. On approving it, Fr. de Saint-Jure had declared that God wanted her to cross the ocean; she must accept the offer of the "Unknown Benefactress;" furthermore, she was not to take into consideration her frail health.

As Jeanne informed Jérôme Le Royer, when the ten day retreat was over, she had hurried to her patroness and told her it was God's Will she should sail for New France. She had also been able to apprise her that the Duchesse d'Aiguillon and her uncle the Cardinal Minister had begun by providing the Quebec Hôtel Dieu with 22,000 livres tournois, and that during the previous year they had increased it to 40,500 livres.[13] Jeanne Mance's wealthy friend had done even better for the hospital she wanted to build, with the promise of a contribution of 42,000 livres.[14] It was also understood that during her entire life, Jeanne Mance would receive an annual income of 1,000 livres; on the other hand, she was to be responsible for the temporal administration of the Hôtel Dieu.

On saying goodbye to the "Unknown Benefactress," she had received "religious jewelry" of considerable value—two gold crosses, one in white enamel set with nine rubies, the other of wood decorated with mother-of-pearl, and a silver clock "which could ring," a casket set with agates of a superior quality containing a miniature portrait of the donor in a gold frame enriched with fine pearls—and to cap it all, a burse of 1,200 livres for her upkeep during the year, with this encouraging promise, "Take this as an earnest of our good will, until we complete the matter, which we will do when you have written us from the place where you are going, and have reported the state of affairs." [15]

To Jérôme, no mean judge of character, the thought came that a woman of this caliber, furthermore a woman who had the backing of a wealthy aristocrat, would be a rare prize for Montreal. He explained to her his motives in establishing a settlement on the distant Canadian island and in founding a Hôtel Dieu in La Flèche, which would eventually be of great help to Ville Marie as the Montreal foundation was soon to be called. He informed her that he already had a leader for the colonists, a soldier and a gentleman, M. Paul de Chomedey, but that someone like her was needed to ensure the success of the affair. Wouldn't she cast her lot with the Montrealers and not simply travel with them across the sea? She would assuredly be of much service to them. She could even build the hospital of the "Unknown Benefactress" in their midst, once they had settled down. There would be the sick and probably the wounded to take care of. Meanwhile she could act as the supervisor of the stores and directress of the household. This invitation to join the Montreal group dovetailed so well with Jeanne's plan that she gladly accepted it.

The La Flèche tax collector also spoke to her of the small circle of friends interested in promoting the future settlement. M. De Chomedey belonged to it. Why should she not, too? At first, she was apprehensive about committing herself, for she was poor and most of the associates were wealthy. With her modest thousand livres' annuity and her poor health, she would be a hindrance rather than a help. As Jérôme kept on urging her to become a member of the Company of Montreal, she finally disclosed why she was so hesitant, "If I do so, I shall be dependent on human aid and so can count less on aid from on high." [16]

"You will no less be a daughter of Providence," he answered her, "for this year we have expended 75,000 livres, and I do not know where we shall find the first penny for next year. True, I am confident that this is the work of God and that He will carry it on, but in what way, I have no idea."

On this, Jeanne agreed to join the Company of Montreal, provided Fr. de Saint-Jure, her spiritual director, approved her decision.

"Do not lose a moment," advised Jérôme. "Write by this post to the Reverend Father."

Jeanne immediately took his advice, communicating not only with the Parisian Jesuit but also to several friends, and, as Jérôme expected, her spiritual guide counseled her wholeheartedly to join the new association. The founder of Ville Marie was of course pleased with the turn of events and introduced Mademoiselle Mance to the Baron de Fancamp and to Paul de Chomedey. In the name of the seven other associates, the three received her into the Company of Montreal.

A few days before the ships set sail, at Jeanne's suggestion, Jérôme put down in writing his design for Montreal, had several copies made and handed them over to the new member of the Company. To each one, she added a letter of her own and addressed them to the great ladies who had received her so well in Paris, among them, the Princesse de

Condé, Madame Séguier, wife of the Chancellor, her dear friend Madame de Villesavin, and above all, Madame de Bullion from whom she hoped most.[17] Before the year was out, the founder was to use these letters to great advantage for the island colony.

Each day now, more and more often, the thirty-seven Montreal recruits wandered down to the wharves. These inlanders had become used to the tang of the salt air. Sometimes, early in the morning, they watched the men in the Chain Tower haul in the heavy iron chain extending to the St. Nicolas Tower across the entrance to the inner port, thus opening the channel, which was shut nightly. This was one of the four chains, according to satirist and humorist Rabelais, that Gargantua had forged to keep his son, Pantagruel, bound hand and foot in his cradle.

As the future Montrealers sauntered and loitered about the streets of the port city, did they comment on the absence of a carpenter among them, an indispensable workman for a land where practically everything had to be built from scratch? Le Royer, Fancamp and Chomedey had sought far and wide for one and had offered the most tantalizing salary, but to no avail. What were they to do?

As they worried over this problem, someone came running with the message that the barrel maker who had signed up for Montreal had been offered a better salary and had embarked on a ship that was already underway.[18] At a word from Jérôme, two of his agents jumped into a shallop and rowed furiously to catch up with the fugitive. Despite all their efforts, they would never have boarded the vessel had a sudden calm not halted it in the roadstead. As soon as they got their fugitive and were on their way back to the shore, the wind rose and the ship sailed on. But not for long. Scarcely had it gone a few leagues out to sea when a terrible storm raged and broke the mainmast. The captain was obliged to return to La Rochelle and dismiss

137

his crew. Among these sailors was a skilled carpenter, who hastened to offer his services to Jérôme Le Royer. He was engaged on the spot.

May 9, 1641 was the date set for departure.[19] Jeanne Mance was generally bright and cheerful, but that morning, at the thought of being the only woman for nearly two years among half a hundred men, she felt downcast. While the captains of the two ships waited for the wind and tide, a dispatch arrived for Jérôme Le Royer from his agents in Dieppe, who had charge of preparing the exodus of ten recruits from that part of the country. It said that two of the hands hired for Montreal had refused to sail without their wives, who had finally accompanied them. A young lady of good repute had also forced her way on deck and, despite all the efforts to dissuade her, had gone off to New France, where she intended to serve God as best she could.[20]

When Jeanne Mance heard the good news, her spirits soared and, with joy and alacrity, she made her way to the wharves. With the two Jesuits, Fr. de la Place and Bro. Ambrose Brouet,[21] and twelve Montrealers, she climbed on board the first ship, while Monsieur Le Royer and the Baron de Fancamp accompanied Fr. Antoine Fauls, bound for the Quebec Ursulines, and 25 more settlers on the other one.[22] Paul de Chomedey joined them a little later.

Each priest had his band of men kneel and recite with him the acts of faith, hope, charity, resignation to the Will of God, and of contrition, followed by the litanies of the Saints and of the Queen of Saints.[23] In those days, crossing the ocean was a serious matter, and it was customary to commend the voyage to the Master of the wind and waves. Then Jérôme Le Royer wished them all God-speed, and with Fancamp, he slowly descended to the shore. Half an hour later, the ships, with their sails billowing in the wind, passed under the archway joining the St. Nicolas and Chain Towers and disappeared in the direction of the

Island of Ré and the New World.

After the noise and bustle of the immediate preparation for sailing, and after the long years of expectation and organization, now that the task he had been given to do was on the crest of realization, relief must have flooded Jérôme's being, a great relief culminating in an outpouring of thanks to God. For the settlers who had left their native land for Canada, he also prayed with all his heart. And well he might, since three weeks or so later, he received the bad tidings that after eight days of good sailing, a squall had separated the two ships.[24] Chomedey's had sprung a leak and had been forced back to port. When the time came to cast the hawsers off once more, three or four of the recruits did not answer the roll call. Twice again, the ship put back to port for repairs before it headed out to sea again and this time into stormy weather. Then for months on end, no message of any kind reached Jérôme. More than once, as he worked at his books as collector of taxes, his mind wandered westward. Had the ship carrying the Dieppe contingent, had those carrying Mademoiselle Mance, Paul de Chomedey and the other recruits, successfully berthed at Quebec or had they foundered with all aboard?

Chapter XI

Notes

1. NA., pp. 246-247; Gaudin, *Inventaire et extraits des papiers de famille de monsieur Jérôme Le Royer de la Dauversière;* See, for instance, loans during 1643, pp. 11-12.

2. Desrosiers, *Paul de Chomedey, sieur de Maisonneuve,*

pp. 39-40. In 1653, Saint Margaret Bourgeoys discovered the picture, foxed and dusty, pinned up on the wall of the Hôtel Dieu chapel in Montreal.

3. VJLD, p. 172.

4. Compagnie des associés amis de Montréal, *La Flèche et Montréal ou l'extraordinaire entreprise canadienne du fléchois Jérôme Le Royer de la Dauversière,* La Flèche, (1947), p. 15.

5. G(abriel) Debien, "Engagés pour le Canada au XVIIe siècle, vus de La Rochelle," *Revue d'Histoire de l'Amérique Française,* Vol. IV, No. 4, (Montreal, March 1951), p. 479.

6. Hilaire Belloc, *Richelieu, A Study,* Philadelphia, 1929, p. 266.

7. William Henry Atherton, *The Saintly Life of Jeanne Mance, First Lay Nurse in North America,* p. 18, quoting *La Gazette de France,* No. 96, p. 291, 1641.

8. *Véritables Motifs,* p. 31; where she is qualified as "une personne de grande piété." Daveluy, *Jeanne Mance,* 51, where Marie Rousseau is quoted, calling her "une des plus grandes âmes qui vivent."

9. Dollier de Casson, *A History of Montreal,* p. 83.

10. *Véritables Motifs,* p. 30. One reads, "s'etans tous deux saluez sans s'estre jamais veus," and adds, "n'y ouy parler l'un de l'autre." Despite the letter or letters exchanged between the two, they could have known practically nothing about one another.

11. Morin, *Histoire Simple et Véritable,* p. 42.

12. The street of the Iron Pot is now rue Bonaparte.

13. Daveluy, *Jeanne Mance,* p. 46, Note 16.

14. Morin, *Histoire Simple et Véritable,* p. 42, Note 3.

15. Dollier de Casson, *A History of Montreal,* p. 81.

16. *Ibid.,* p. 85.

17. *Ibid.,* p. 87.

18. *Véritables Motifs,* pp. 32-34.

19. Daveluy, *La société de Notre-Dame de Montréal,* p. 50.

20. *Véritables Motifs,* p. 31.

21. *JR,* Vol. XXI, p. 107.

22. Atherton, *The Saintly Life of Jeanne Mance, First Lay Nurse in North America,* pp. 18-19.

23. *AM,* p. 30.

24. Dollier de Casson, *A History of Montreal,* pp. 87-89.

PART TWO

Hard at work

Chapter XII

"A Foolish Enterprise"

THE FIRST NEWS about his colonists reached Jérôme Le Royer in the last two months of 1641. In August, with his men, Paul de Chomedey had sailed into Tadoussac Bay, where, between two mountains, the dark waters of the Saguenay River rush into the St. Lawrence. To his delight, he found ships flying the colors of France, and his delight was heightened when he discovered *L'Espérance,* the flagship of the One Hundred Associates, under the command of Admiral de Courpon, an old friend of his.[1]

After embracing in true continental fashion, the two had much to say. The commander of the Montrealers related the incidents of his stormy passage and inquired about the other two ships and the rest of the recruits. The Admiral reassured him: they were safe in Quebec. Mademoiselle Mance had disembarked on August 8[2] and had entrusted him with letters for his friends in France, in particular for Monsieur Le Royer. She was anxious, he added, because of Monsieur de Chomedey's delay in arriving.

In the course of the conversation, Paul de Chomedey told his friend that he was worried on account of the death of the group's surgeon during the crossing. Courpon instantly offered his own practitioner[3] to the commander of the Montreal settlers on condition that the man consent. There were no objections and the surgeon's trunk was loaded into the shallop that was being made ready. Seeing

142

that it sometimes took several weeks to sail upstream as far as Quebec when the winds and tides were unfavorable, Chomedey had decided to row on ahead with a few of his settlers. He thanked Admiral de Courpon, bade him farewell, and speedily departed, perhaps reaching Quebec on August 20th, certainly before September 20th.[4]

From the ramparts of Fort St. Louis, his boat, flying the white and gold colors of France, was detected. As the St. Lawrence is but two-thirds of a mile wide at Quebec, nearly all the settlement of the 150 inhabitants were soon aware that men from the long expected vessel were about to land. Mademoiselle Mance hastened down to the shore to welcome Monsieur de Chomedey. How happy she was! In response to her questions, he related all the details of his perilous crossing. There was no longer any reason for concern regarding Fr. Fauls and the rest of the settlers, whose ship would be casting anchor any day at the foot of Cap Diamant.

Jeanne Mance then told the commander the story of her voyage across the Atlantic. After a gust of wind had torn the ships apart, the sea had been very calm, even in the Gulf of St. Lawrence and on the great river itself. And then she was at Quebec. In France her health had been poor, but after setting foot in New France, the fulsome air of the country and the expectation of great things to come had wrought wonders for her.

Not long after landing, she had found the ten Dieppe recruits working on a storehouse on the north bank of the St. Lawrence at a spot chosen for them by Governor Charles de Montmagny, Knight of Malta, according to orders received from the One Hundred Associates. Not only a storehouse, but a haven also in case the Iroquois obstructed the foundation of a settlement on the Island of Montreal.[5]

Turning to the twelve men of her own ship, she had asked them to join the Dieppe contingent in their work.

143

Paul de Chomedey was quick to grasp that her virtue, intelligence, and common sense had already won the esteem of the settlers, who honored her, despite her relatively young age, as if she were their mother and carried out her slightest wish with alacrity.[6]

Even before its leader's appearance at Quebec, attempts were being made to nip the Montreal foundation in the bud. It has been asserted without proof that the Company of New France were the instigators,[7] piqued by the powers granted to Monsieur de Chomedey as a result of the engagement signed by Le Royer on December 17 of the previous year. Nothing more than the apparent harebrainedness of the venture was needed to stir up the people against it. The most articulate among them did their utmost to win Jeanne Mance over to their way of thinking.[8] Since she was an associate of the Company of Montreal and exercised considerable influence on the recruits, had they succeeded, willy-nilly Commander de Chomedey would have been forced to abandon his efforts to settle his men on the Island of Montreal. But no objections of human prudence could alter Jeanne Mance's outlook after her conversation with Jérôme Le Royer in La Rochelle and the numerous approbations she had received in Paris concerning her vocation.

This initial failure of the probably well-meaning troublemakers did not deter them. They would have been delighted had the Society of Jesus sided with them. According to Sulpician Dollier de Casson, the Jesuits had been instrumental in giving body to the enterprise.[9] The Fathers, who knew the country and its dangers as well as anyone, would have been powerful allies. They had, however, foreseen the practical utility of Montreal as a permanent center for religious activities and this implied a strong garrison on the island to withstand the Iroquois inroads.[10] The Jesuit's position, summed up in the Relation

144

of 1641, did not favor the opponents: "We took satisfaction in seeing the men of the Gentlemen of Montreal, because their design is wholly for the glory of our Lord, should it succeed." [11] Charles Huault de Montmagny was the growing opposition's last hope.[12] The 53-year-old governor, renamed Ononti-O, "Big-as-a-mountain," by the Iroquois, was a man of imposing stature and profound religious convictions, along with an ample supply of the common sense so useful to a good administrator. He had been sent to Canada in 1636 and was acutely aware of the Ho-de-no-sau-nee or Five (Iroquois) Indian Nation menace. When the foundation of the little known La Flèche collector of taxes, Jérôme Le Royer, was being discussed, he knew the criticism surrounding it was not unwarranted. As recently as the previous February, two colonists, Thomas Godefroy and François Marguerie, had been captured at Trois-Rivières. The Iroquois later freed them, for they hoped to conclude a treaty of peace with the French so as to obtain firearms from them. They went as far as to promise that they would be French and Iroquois at the same time, "Not only shall our customs be your customs," they pretended, "but we shall be so closely united that our chins shall be reclothed with hair, and with beards like yours." [13]

There was a fly in the beards; a big fly. The treaty would take effect contingent on the exclusion of the Laurentian Coalition, France's allies composed of the fur-purveying Huron, Algonquin, and Montagnais. From a shallop at Trois-Rivières on June 10, Montmagny had presided over the negotiations, which proved unsuccessful. Meanwhile, a detachment of Iroquois blocking the St. Lawrence at Lac St. Pierre (a broadening of the river), fell upon a flotilla of Huron and French canoes laden with pelts, capturing and killing most of the men. Fr. de Brébeuf and a few Frenchmen managed to escape. The situation had become so precarious that in conference with the Jesuit Superior, the

Governor delegated Fr. Paul Le Jeune, author of the Relation of 1641, to Richelieu for help.[14] He would return to France on the ship that had carried Chomedey across the sea.

And now, this leader of the Montrealers, a stranger to the country, intended colonizing an exposed section of New France. Unthinkable! He must listen to Governor de Montmagny.

Soon after his arrival, Paul de Chomedey paid his respects to the King's representative. After the usual greetings, he was told: "You know that war has broken out again with the Iroquois, and that they declared it on Lake St. Peter last month, where they broke the peace in a way which shows they are more active than ever. You will hardly consider establishing yourselves in so remote a spot. You must change your plans; if you like, you can have the Isle of Orleans. In any case the season is too far advanced for you to reach the Island of Montreal this year even if you thought of so doing." [15]

Paul de Chomedey's answer was worthy of the great leader that he was, proof also of his utter confidence in Jérôme Le Royer, true founder of Montreal: "Sir," he said, "what you tell me would be excellent if I had been sent to look about and select a place. But as it has been decided by the company who sent me that I should go to Montreal, my honor obliges me to go there and found a colony, were every tree on this island changed into an Iroquois, and you will, I am sure, approve my decision. In view of the advanced state of the season, you will agree that I should limit myself before the winter to reconnoitring the place with the most active of my men, so that I may see where I can plant all my people next spring."

Other visits followed to the Jesuits in their temporary quarters in which the Governor of New France had housed them after the fire of 1640; to Mother Marie of the Incarnation, superior of the Ursulines, in their narrow quarters

146

in the lower town, which they called their Louvre; and to the Hospital Sisters of St. Augustine in their new stone Hôtel Dieu at Sillery, in the outskirts of Quebec. As Chomedey walked through St. Louis, St. Anne, Mt. Carmel, and St. Geneviève streets, carefully laid out by Montmagny, visiting the persons who could be of some use to him in the future, he gathered a well-rounded picture of what public opinion thought of the Montreal venture, summed up in the terse designation: a foolish enterprise!

The above details, in great part, Jérôme Le Royer learned from letters sent to him by Jeanne Mance and by the head of his pioneers, Paul de Chomedey. During February 1642, Jérôme also met Fr. Le Jeune in Paris and from this interesting and sympathetic eyewitness got his impressions of the Montreal pioneers, their chief, and Mademoiselle Mance. The founder's recruits were then in Quebec and the man to whom he had entrusted them was faithful to his directives. Why worry? Conditions, true enough, were bad,[16] but his "Foolish Enterprise" was "in the sight of God and within the hands of the Almighty accompanied by a more lofty wisdom than the human mind could ever attain to." [17]

On his way to the capital in the interest of his colonists, Le Royer's itinerary generally led him through Chartres. On one of these trips, he probably learned of Fr. Olier's partial cure. Although his friend was not yet entirely free from the noxious effects of his illness, he preached retreats to the clergy and to the laity. Olier and his companions occasionally went on pilgrimage to the subterranean dark Virgin, Notre-Dame-Sous-Terre, of the cathedral. On one of these visits to our Lady, he perceived "the first ray which began to scatter the shades of night"—the long night of his strange illness. The complete cure came gradually. Light. Then joy. On the Octave of Corpus Christi, 1641, the bells of the cathedral had awakened him, and he found himself in complete good health.[18]

By the beginning of 1642, Le Royer knew that his friend had taken up residence with the Abbot of Foix and Father du Ferrier in a suburb of Paris. The priest's interest in the Montreal settlement was keener than ever before, and he was ready to second his friend in any way he could.

Fr. Olier had received special lights from above. Marie Rousseau, the saintly widow whom Jeanne Mance had consulted before leaving for Canada, revealed to him that his efforts would result in much glory for God in the New World.[19] Another messenger from heaven to Olier was the celebrated Claude LeGlay, a married man despite the popular appelation of "Brother" given to him by the pious Parisians of his time. Although he is practically unknown nowadays, his prayers were of no little help in establishing what for a long time was to be Catholic French Canada. Olier does not hesitate to compare his zeal to that of the prophet Elijah. One morning as the Abbé was offering the Holy Sacrifice for the success of the Montreal venture, "during the entire Mass," he later wrote, "LeGlay did nothing but request on my behalf what our Lord, on the Feast of the Purification, 1636, had indicated that he wanted to give me; and, furthermore, he petitioned God that I become the general of his captains, who could later train a good many soldiers. These prayers that he said were inspired by a pure movement of the Holy Spirit, for he knew nothing of my vocation for the clergy, and I know no one who could have ever spoken to him about it." [20]

This encouragement coming from two so remarkable servants of God, added to the communications received from on high, led Olier, founder of the Company of Montreal, with Jérôme Le Royer, into renewed activity. For his part, Jérôme, thanks to the letters to which Jeanne Mance had appended a note of her own before sailing for New France, had struck a common chord for the great ladies to whom they were addressed. Magic resulted from the combined efforts of the two men. By February 1642, for a small body of pioneers wintering in Quebec with the unknown staring bleakly at them, Le Royer and Olier had found a good number of new associates, among them "magistrates, counts, dukes, ladies of the highest degree..." [21]

On February 27, the last Thursday of the month, a few minutes before ten o'clock in the morning, by foot, horse, sedan or coach, approximately thirty-five distinguished worshippers gathered at Notre Dame. All were fasting. Among them were nine saintly priests such as Jean Jacques Olier and Pierre Le Gouvello de Kériolet, "the penitent baron." [22] Passersby must have wondered what ceremony was attracting notables as important as Henri de Lévy, Duc de Ventadour, Prince de Maubuisson, Pair de France, former Viceroy of New France, founder of the Company of the Blessed Sacrament, and recently ordained subdeacon;[23] Baron Gaston de Renty; Marquis Roger du Plessis, who, a year later was to be created Duc de Roche-Guyon and Pair de France; Jean Antoine de Mesmes, Seigneur d'Irval and Cramayel and Comte de Vandeuil; and Jean de Garibal, Baron de St. Sul-pice. Unknown to the general public, seventeen of them were also members of the Company of the Blessed Sacrament.

Seven or eight ladies, most of them titled, passed through the portals of the great cathedral on that far-off forenoon, not the least of whom were Charlotte de Montmorency, Princesse de Condé; Jeanne de Schomberg, Marquise de Liancourt and future Duchesse de la Roche-Guyon; and Marie de Gournay Rousseau, so well known to Jeanne Mance and to Jérôme Le Royer.

Fr. Olier offered the Holy Sacrifice at the Lady altar close by the rood-loft at the entrance of the chancel. The lay members of the assembly received communion from his hands; the other priests offered the Holy Sacrifice at nearby altars. The Island of Montreal was consecrated to the Holy Family, under the special protection of Our Lady,[24] at the very spot where Jesus, Mary, and Joseph had appeared to Jérôme in 1635. Was it at this moment that he proposed the future settlement be called Ville Marie, the name by which it would officially be known until 1705?[25] Then this exceptional band of people dedicated itself to the Montreal Enterprise, "uniting in this good work with so much concert and union that they treated one another only as brothers and sisters." [26]

After Mass, the friends of the Montreal venture assembled at the hotel of Jean de Lauson, who had become somewhat more sympathetic to the project. To translate their good intentions into deeds, the members contributed 40,000 livres for the further recruiting of men and for the purchasing of provisions for the next shipment to Montreal. Was it at this reunion or at one of the three subsequent ones held during 1642 that Lauson was named administrator and director of the Company of Montreal?[27] Jérôme assumed the more modest but vital position of procurator, and Renty that of secretary.

The following lines written in 1643 admirably evaluate the founder of Montreal and his efforts at this period of his life: "If we ponder carefully the case in point, it is out of the ordinary for a man, sole author of so high and so new a design; a stranger, unknown in Paris, without means, support, or the magic of fine words, to be received and welcomed in so short a time by so many persons of different standing, mentality, virtue, experience, and influence, and sufficiently particular about not letting themselves be easily deceived; and to persuade them to join in a holy company, which does not have any aim, obligation nor interest other than pure charity, unless they were moved, inspired and called by God..." [28]

Chapter XII

Notes

1. Dollier de Casson, *A History of Montreal,* p. 89.

2. Louis-Bertrand de la Tour, *Mémoires sur la vie de Monsieur de Laval,* Cologne (Montauban) 1761, pp. 129-130.

3. Probably Jean Pouppée: see Mondoux, *L'Hôtel-Dieu, premier hôpital de Montréal,* p. 94, Note 6.

4. Dollier de Casson, *A History of Montreal,* p. 89. Earlier than Sept. 20, despite Marie-Claire Daveluy's assertion to the contrary in "Paul de Chomedey de Maisonneuve," in *DCB,* Vol. 1, 1967, p. 219. See *infra,* Appendix 1.

5. Marie de l'Incarnation, ursuline (1599-1672), *Correspondance, Lettere IX,* Dom Guy Oury, Ed., Solesmes, 1971, p. 144, Note 15. William Henry Atherton, *Montreal, 1535-1914,* Vol. 1: Under the French Regime, 1535-1760, Montreal, 1914, p. 65, states the Great Company also gave the Company of Montreal a site at Trois-Rivières to house its provisions safely. Henceforth, Atherton, *Montreal,* Vol. 1.

6. Faillon, *Histoire de la Colonie Française en Canada,* Vol. 1, p. 430.

7. Dollier de Casson, *A History of Montreal,* p. 89.

8. *Ibid.*

9. *Ibid.,* p. 87.

10. Atherton, *Montreal,* Vol. 1, pp. 69-70.

11. *JR,* 1641, Vol. XXI, p. 107.

12. Dollier de Casson, *A History of Montreal,* p. 91.

13. *JR,* 1641, Vol. XXI, p. 45, 47.

14. Leo-Paul Desrosiers, *Iroquoisie* (1534-1646), Montreal, 1947, p. 235.

15. Dollier de Casson, *A History of Montreal,* p. 91.

16. As a matter of fact, conditions were worse than Jérôme Le Royer thought, worse even than the governor of New France, the Jesuits, and the settlers thought. See in Desrosiers's *Iroquoisie,* pp. 224-229, a keen analysis of the Franco-Iroquois situation at the time.

17. Dollier de Casson, *A History of Montreal,* p. 91.

18. Pourrat, *Jean-Jacques Olier, fondateur de Saint-Sulpice,* pp. 105-106.

19. Faillon, *Histoire de la Colonie Française en Canada,* Vol. 1, p. 387.

20. *Ibid.*

21. Faillon, *Vie de Mademoiselle Mance,* Vol. 1, p. 34.

22. Daveluy, *La société Notre-Dame de Montréal,* pp. 34-35, where she lists 31 of the associates present at Notre Dame on February 27, 1642.

23. Though Marie-Claire Daveluy qualifies Henry de Lévy as a priest as early as 1642, on p. 35 of *La société Notre-Dame de Montréal,* but on p. 272, she writes, "le duc de Ventadour dut recevoir la prêtrise vers 1643."

24. *JR,* Vol. XXII, p. 209. According to Faillon in *Vie de Monsieur Olier, fondateur du séminaire de Saint-Sulpice,* Vol. 3, p. 403, it was Olier who convened the associates at Notre Dame and was responsible for the dedication of the Island of Montreal to the Holy Family under the special protection of Our Lady. See also his *Histoire de la Colonie Française en Canada,* Vol. 1, p. 436.

25. Mondoux, *L'Hôtel-Dieu, premier hôpital de Montréal,* pp. 95-96. In official religious documents, the old name, Ville-Marie (Marianopolis) is still used.

26. Chrestien LeClercq, *The first establishment of faith in New France.* Now translated, with notes by John Gilmary Shea, Vol. 2, New York, 1881, p. 41.

27. Montgolfier, *La vie de la vénérable soeur Marguerite Bourgeois,* p. 21.

28. *Véritables Motifs,* pp. 37-38.

Chapter XIII

A Grain of Mustard Seed

GOVERNOR DE MONTMAGNY, seeing that the private meeting he had had with Paul de Chomeday had been of no avail, called an assembly of the notables of Quebec, which may have numbered a baker's dozen or more. Once again the Montreal leader listened attentively to Montmagny's propositions. They were, it must be admitted, excellent. The governor publicly reiterated his offer of the Island of Orleans to the Society of Montreal. There were many advantages in settling there rather than a hundred and eighty miles farther inland. Jérôme Le Royer's colonists would be much safer from the Iroquois, and Quebec would profit from the proximity of the new establishment. Otherwise the distance between the two groups, with scarcely five hundred people in all,[1] would weaken the French position in America.

Chomedey expressed surprise that a meeting had been summoned to discuss his affairs without his consent. He insisted that he had no intention whatsoever of founding a colony on the Island of Orleans. He had been sent to found a habitation on the Island of Montreal and not at any other place. If this project were even more perilous than the Governor and his men asserted, he would set to work at the risk of his life. All apparent opposition melted, and Charles Huault de Montmagny, with deep misgivings, approved of the "Foolish Enterprise."

Indeed, the Governor, Fr. Barthélemy Vimont, S.J., and several persons who knew the St. Lawrence well, accompanied Paul de Chomedey, or perhaps one of his most trusted followers,[2] up the river in order to select a site for the settlement. The island with its long sloping hill loomed up before them on October 15, 1641,[3] and they made ready to land. Although Governor de Montmagny and his men meant well, the spot that was decided upon for the establishment was unfortunate. None worse of the island could have been chosen, for part of it was marshy, often flooded, and difficult of access,[4] but according to the Governor, easy to defend. This strip of land, named Place Royale in 1611 by Samuel de Champlain,[5] was later called Pointe-à-Callière.

By the end of the month, Paul de Chomedey was worrying more than ever about the pioneers. Winter, he had been told, could be very grim in this wild land, and adequate quarters were lacking. However, his fears were soon to be allayed. The unexpected happened when he visited St. Foy, near the outlet of the Cap Rouge River, and met Pierre de Puiseaux, master of Mont-Renault.[6] This gentleman of 75 years of age had made a fortune in Mexico. After coming to Quebec he acquired two holdings, one at St. Foy, a day's journey from Quebec,[7] and the other at St. Michel, about a mile lower than Sillery. The two pieces of land were said to have been worth 100,000 livres.[8]

The old seigneur was probably lonely and he may have been approaching the borderline of dotage; at any rate, his heart was as big as the New World. When he learned of the Montreal venture, of its La Flèche Founder, and of the apostolic ideals of the Society of Montreal, that is, its aim to convert the Indians by means of a stable French colony, he was moved to enthusiasm. In the previous year, Puiseaux had lent his home to the Augustinian Hôtel Dieu nuns. Now he placed it along with all his possessions, even his livestock, at the disposal of the Montreal commander. He then proposed that the pioneers spend the winter at St. Foy. The many oaks that grew on his land could be cut down for the building of boats to transport the humble possessions of the party up the river, and his joiner's shop at St. Michel could be used advantageously too.

The Montreal leader was elated. Not only would his followers be lodged for the winter, they would also be able to prepare for their departure in early spring. He accepted Pierre de Puiseaux's offer provisionally, promising to submit his name as a candidate for membership among the Montreal Associates. Of this arrangement the generous benefactor heartily approved and immediately turned over St. Foy to Paul de Chomedey. The latter, leaving his surgeon in charge of several men, went with Pierre de Puiseaux to the St. Michel fief. There the owner put the leader of the Montreal expedition in possession of the property, keeping nothing for himself, not even a room to welcome his friends. To his guest, Madame Marie-Madeleine de Chauvigny de la Peltrie, who had moved to St. Michel's in order to be close to the Indians, he ventured the following idea: "Madame, it is no longer I who provide your lodging, for I no longer own anything here, it is to Monsieur de Chomedey that you are now under an obligation, for he is the master of everything."

Madame de la Peltrie, the lay foundress of the Ursuline monastery at Quebec, had first become interested in the Canadian mission after the Relation of 1635 came off the press.[9] If she were cured from a serious illness, she had promised to devote her life to the care of Indian children. As she obtained her cure, with the approval of Vincent de Paul and of other saintly priests, on May 9, 1639, she set sail for Quebec, where she arrived on August 1, in the company of three Ursulines, among them Marie de l'Incarnation, and several other religious.

Almost immediately, living with the nuns in a small uncomfortable house, she busied herself with the housekeeping. She saw to the laying of the cornerstone of the monastery on July 9, 1640, in what was to be the Upper Town site of the present monastery. During the following

156

year, the new building was blessed and made ready for use. A few weeks later, charming and saintly Jeanne Mance walked into Madame de la Peltrie's life. The high motives animating her, Paul de Chomedey and Jérôme Le Royer in France as well as the other Montreal associates, touched her as much as elderly Pierre de Puiseaux's offer. Madame de la Peltrie had been disappointed because the One Hundred Associates had been amiss, despite their formal promise, in settling Indians near Quebec. Convinced that the Montreal pioneers, at the cost of fantastic sacrifices, intended to found a settlement for this very purpose, it is easy to understand why she was drawn to them.

So it was, during the winter of 1641-1642, that Madame de la Peltrie, Mademoiselle Mance, Monsieur de Chomedey, and the soldiers and laborers of the Montreal enterprise were housed in their new property, known as "the jewel of the colony." In reality the jewel was not of the first water, for it contained only three small, low-ceilinged rooms.[10] The weather was extremely cold; still, under the snow-capped house and sheds, the carpenters and joiners worked steadily. The commander and the two ladies helped them as best they could. Jeanne Mance had charge of the food and clothing; she also had the responsibility of distributing the munitions. Once, having given each man the materials he needed, there resulted a squabble, which though unfortunate, relieved the monotony of daily life.

On January 25, 1642, Paul de Chomedey was thirty years old. For some time, Jeanne Mance had been wondering how to celebrate the event in this land of snow and ice. She finally decided that a military display would please the leader of the Montreal venture. Therefore, on the eve of the Conversion of St. Paul, she gave the soldiers plenty of shot. On Paul de Chomedey's birthday, an hour and a half before daybreak, they fired their muskets, three or four perriers, and a little cannon called *espoir*. To show his appreciation,

157

the commander granted his men a holiday and regaled them for the first time with excellent French wine. In the evening, an hour before twilight, they renewed the same exploit in his and Jeanne Mance's presence. Thus, they thought, happily ended the day.[11]

In the quiet of the night, however, the detonation re-echoed as far as Quebec. Governor de Montmagny was highly offended. He was convinced that the salvos should not have been ordered without his express permission. Obviously this was an exaggeration on his part, for Chomedey and his men had the authorization to carry firearms. Of what use was this privilege if each time they wanted to use them, they must obtain permission from the Governor? Furthermore, as ship's captain, Monsieur de Chomedey had this right and it was enhanced by the fact that the order had been given in the St. Michel fief, which then belonged to the Society of Montreal. It was the first difficulty in the colony concerning rights of precedence, about which the nobility was so touchy; unfortunately it was not the last.

The Governor of New France had Jean Gorry, the soldier responsible for the firing of the cannon and the perriers, chained and jailed. A native of Ponthaven in Lower Brittany, the cannoneer, then about thirty years of age, had come to New France in 1639. With Isabeau Panie, whom he had married in Quebec shortly after his arrival, he joined the Montrealers with four years of experience of the New World behind him. His desertion of the Quebec group coupled with the commander's refusal of the previous October to settle on the Island of Orleans displeased Charles Huault de Montmagny.

In these difficult circumstances, the man chosen by Jérôme Le Royer as chief of his pioneers showed great discretion and moderation. He did not challenge Gorry's imprisonment and was determined not to do so no matter how long his subordinate spent in jail. Not that he did not pity the prisoner—his heart went out to him—but he knew that the Governor had acted "ultra vires" (without authority). Indeed, had not Louis XIII given a commission to Governor de Chomedey for his men to bear arms? What the Montreal leader expected happened: the Governor being unable to justify his action soon released the prisoner.

Still, the incident was not closed. The commander could easily have lost face along with his soldiers' esteem. So being informed of Gorry's release and return, he made a point of welcoming him at the door of his residence, an unbending not often seen in the noblemen of his day, embraced him, and had a fine repast served in his honor.

A week elapsed and on Saturday, February 1, once again he granted his men a holiday, not only because it was the octave of his feast day but also through consideration for Gorry, whom he wanted to compensate publicly for the harsh treatment he had undergone. At his command, a banquet was served with wine for all. On this occasion no firearms were discharged, not even a musket, either before or after, out of respect for Monsieur de Montmagny. Monsieur de Chomedey joined the diners at the festal board and to put fresh heart into them, he openly manifested his affection for them, something officers rarely did. On drinking to their health, he carefully refrained from making any statements that would hurt the Governor's feelings.

To Gorry, he was particularly kind. Having embraced him once again, he had him take a place of honor at table and said to him in the presence of all: "Jean Gorry, you have been in chains for the love of me; you suffered the punishment and I received the slight; because of this I love you all the more, and that is why I am raising your salary by ten crowns." [12]

To the others he said: "Children, although Jean Gorry has been ill-used, do not lose courage because of that; drink now to the health of the Master of the Chain!" Turning to Gorry, he asked him, "Why aren't we in Montreal? There we would be the masters! When we shall be settled there, no one will stop us from firing our artillery!"

Governor de Montmagny was soon informed of the commander's kindly treatment of the solders and of the warm welcome he had extended to Jean Gorry. He decided to investigate the conduct of the Montreal leader during the two previous weeks. Thanks to the gubernatorial tiff, several names of settlers that might otherwise have remained unknown, have come down to us, for Montmagny had them appear before him: François Robelin of Paris; Augustin Hébert of Caen; Antoine d'Amiens, a native of Saens-Ville, in the vicinity of Rouen; Jean Caillot of Lyons; Pierre Laimery of Hâvre-de-Grace, and of course, Jean Gorry.[13] All were obliged under oath to reveal everything that had been said and done on the two holidays that had been granted to them by Monsieur de Chomedey.

The information Monsieur de Montmagny got must have given him some insight into the sagacity, the disinterestedness, and the moderation of the man who had perhaps been reported as a dangerous rival striving to supplant him as governor of New France.

Now that a better understanding had been established between Montmagny and Chomedey, life was much more pleasant at St. Michel and at St. Foy. For diversion and for firsthand knowledge of the country, the ladies and gentlemen frequently visited the Hospital Sisters and the Jesuit Fathers.

During the winter of 1642, three Jesuits were stationed at their residence of St. Joseph at Sillery: Frs. Jean de Quen, Joseph Imbert Duperron, and Jean de Brébeuf.[14] The man we know today as a saint had remained at Quebec for the year in the interests of the Huron missions. It was a good occasion, he thought, for preparing the conversion of a few transient Hurons, who were invited to stay with the Jesuits during the cold months. Only two of them benefited by this offer and were converted: Atondo, about thirty-six years of age, and Okhukwandoron, some eleven years younger.[15]

As Paul de Chomedey and Jeanne Mance were interested in these neophytes, Fr. de Brébeuf chose them as sponsors. These Hurons were solemnly baptized; the godfather gave the name of Paul to Atondo, the godmother, Jean-Baptiste to Okhukwandoron. The two converts went to Confession and received Holy Communion for the first time on Easter Sunday. Through Jean de Brébeuf we know that the Governor had them go to Communion alongside of him. Mademoiselle Mance was present and so was Monsieur de Chomedey. On the part of Montmagny, it was an elegant and public acknowledgement that the misunderstanding between himself and the head of the Montreal group was cleared up. Here Governor de Montmagny appears in true perspective—a good and sincere man, though somewhat quick to take offense.

Slowly the winter of 1641-1642 rolled by. The first warm days of April freed the St. Lawrence from its icy yoke. Foodstuffs and other materials arrived daily from St. Foy. It was decided that as soon as the weather permitted, the settlers would set sail for their final destination, and on May 8, Paul de Chomedey and Jeanne Mance prepared to set out. With approximately 40[16] people comprising the women and children, they boarded the small flotilla, composed of a fine pinnace or small three-masted craft, a gabbard or flat-bottomed barge with sails, and two shallops. With them, at the request of Jérôme Le Royer,[17] went black-robed Fr. Barthélemy Vimont, Superior of the Jesuit Missions of New France. Despite his advanced age, Pierre de Puiseaux joined the pioneers, as did Madame de la Peltrie and Charlotte Barré, her maid. Governor de Montmagny, in one of the shallops, led the expedition as it left the cliffed shoreline.

In those days, the voyage from Quebec to the Island of Montreal generally took ten days. The weather must have been favorable, for they reached their goal a day sooner than expected, on May 17, 1642.[18] In later years, Jeanne Mance often recalled how, for a half a league before their landing, the shores of the river were bright with wild flowers.[19]

At the first sight of the Island of Montreal, covered with trees, the settlers broke into hymns of joy. An hour or so later, with the current making the going up stream more difficult, they came to a small island at the mouth of the little St. Pierre river, into which they sailed. Almost immediately, they were forced to drop anchor. This was their destination, a triangular piece of land, bounded by the St. Lawrence, the St. Pierre stream, and swampy ground. Thirty-one years before, Champlain had it cleared and called it Place Royale.

On landing, the commander threw himself upon his knees to adore God, and all present followed his example. Governor de Montmagny officially entrusted to him the government of the Island. Mademoiselle Mance and Madame de la Peltrie prepared what was needed for Mass. As it was to be the first Eucharistic Celebration on the Island, they worked at it with great love and care. With the other women, they decorated it with their modest jewelry,[20] and its humble beauty was not unworthy of the day.

Before offering the Holy Sacrifice, Fr. Vimont intoned the grand old hymn, *Come, Holy Ghost,* and the entire party joined in.[21] A few minutes later, he approached the makeshift altar, covered with gleaming linen, and uttered the beautiful opening psalm of the old Tridentine Mass, "I shall go unto the altar of God, to God who gives joy to my youth."

Save for his voice, the silence was broken only by the woodnotes of numerous birds, the sighing of the wind in the trees, the purl of the little St. Pierre contrasting with the onrush of the mighty St. Lawrence.

After reading the Gospel of the day, in his capacity as superior of the Canadian Missions, Fr. Vimont made these far-sighted remarks:

"Look, gentlemen," he said, "what you see is but a grain of mustard seed, but it is sown by hands so pious and so moved by the spirit of faith and piety that Heaven must doubtless have vast designs since it uses such workmen, and I have no doubt that this seed will grow into a great tree, one day to achieve wonders, to be multiplied and to spread to all parts." [22]

The Blessed Sacrament was then exposed for the day, which passed in devotions, thanksgivings, and hymns of praise to God. For want of oil, lamps were not lit for the Eucharistic King, but, according to Dollier de Casson, "there were some fire-flies which shone very pleasantly day and night, hung by threads in a beautiful and marvelous manner..." [23]

Besides Jeanne Mance, Madame de la Peltrie and her maid, who were the women present? The most noteworthy was Françoise Gadois, wife of Nicolas Godé and sister of Pierre Gadois, first future grantee of Montreal, whom Dollier de Casson for this reason regards as the first inhabitant of the metropolis of Canada. Godé, then about fifty-nine years of age, was an excellent joiner. With them were their four children, François, Françoise, Nicolas, and Mathurine, the youngest aged five, the first Montreal family. The other female emigrants were Isabeau Panie, Gorry's wife, and Marie Joly, probably the girl who had forced her way onto the ship that sailed from Dieppe in 1641 and married Antoine Damien at Quebec on October 6, 1641. [24]

As leader of the new settlement, Paul de Chomedey cut down the first oak or pine, [25] and the men, following his example, set to work felling trees to build a 320-foot stockade surrounded by a moat.[26] For the time being, they all lived under canvas, and the young leader must have recalled the many times he had slept in a tent during his military campaigns as a soldier in the armies of the King.

When Governor de Montmagny was satisfied that the colonists were secure behind their paling, with his suite he sailed down the river to Quebec. Fr. Vimont accompanied him with some of the Montreal party, who were to finish the storehouse that they had begun during the previous year. The remaining colonists worked hard at constructing a fort behind the palissade, which, it was hoped, would be ready for occupation by the first cold days of autumn.

In July, on Fr. Vimont's order, Fr. Joseph Antoine Poncet de la Rivière[27] took charge of the spiritual needs of the little community, where he was to stay for a year. On July 28, a small party of friendly Algonquins discovered the French on the Island of Montreal, and tarried with them for several days.[28] Atcheast, their chief, presented his four-year-old son to be baptized.[29] Fr. Poncet christened the little boy and, at the request of Paul de Chomedey and of Jeanne Mance, named him Joseph. Sententiously, the Jesuit later wrote: "This is the first fruit that this Island has borne for Paradise; it will not be the last." [30]

In early August, the first French ships for the year dropped anchor at Quebec. Admiral Pierre Legardeur de Repentigny hastened to Montreal,[31] where he was welcomed by the jubilant cheers of the settlers. Jubilant, too, was the friendly Admiral, for he came with all sorts of provisions, munitions, and funds. Better still, he brought twelve new men to the settlement, not the least valuable of whom was Gilbert Barbier, nicknamed "Le Minime" or "The Tiny One," a clever carpenter and, despite his diminutive size, a valiant fighter when the time came to fight.

"Monsieur (le Royer) de la Dauversière, who knew him

well," wrote Dollier de Casson, "in order to win and please him gave him the charge of several cannon which he brought to this place." [32]

Shortly afterwards, in the main room of the new fort, Commander de Chomedey, Fr. Poncet and perhaps Fr. Vimont, if he accompanied Repentigny, Mademoiselle Mance, Madame de la Peltrie and Monsieur de Puiseaux gathered. The Admiral then gratified them with an account of the doings of the Company of Montreal concerning the island habitation.

Paul de Chomedey and Jeanne Mance were particularly pleased on reading their letters from France. The membership of the Company of Montreal had increased to 35 ladies and gentlemen,[33] through the publicity spread by copies of the report distributed as agreed upon by Jeanne Mance and Jérôme Le Royer in the past year at La Rochelle.

The Algonquins and other compatriots who had joined them were still present on August 15, when the white men celebrated the Feast of the Assumption of the Blessed Virgin. A fine tabernacle, the gift of the La Flèche founder and of his associates, was placed upon the altar of the humble bark chapel. All these good people went to Holy Communion. Their names and those of their companions in Quebec had been placed next to the paten and chalice. The *Te Deum* was sung in thanksgiving to God for granting the colonists the favor of partaking in "the first great Festival of Our Lady of Montreal." [34] After Mass, the thunder of cannon re-echoed through the island, without incurring anyone's displeasure. Fr. Poncet then catechized the Indians, explaining the significance of the day. After the chanting of Vespers, a procession was organized, following the recent custom, which was becoming popular in France since Louis XIII had consecrated his kingdom to the Blessed Virgin in 1638.

After the liturgical ceremonies were over, the French and the Algonquins entered the forest and made their way to the top of Mount Royal. From this vantage point, stretching out their hands to the ancient hills that lie to the East and South, the Indians said that their forefathers had lived there before they were driven away by their enemies.

Before these well-disposed visitors departed, Atcheast promised he would return in the spring with his family. His companions, also, were willing to come back, but, out of fear of the Iroquois, would not give their word that they would settle down next to the French. Paul de Chomedey understood their fear, and Fr. Vimont stressed it in the Relation of 1642 by admitting he had difficulty in believing there would ever be a very large number of congenial Indians living on the Island of Montreal until the Iroquois were subjugated or had agreed to peace.[35] In the same manuscript he gave the pith of what was needed for the ultimate success of the Montreal project: "...no one is brought to Jesus Christ except through the Cross;... the plans that are formed for his glory in this country are conceived in expense and in trouble, are carried out amid difficulties, are completed by patience, and are crowned in glory." [36]

Perhaps on the same ship that carried Legardeur de Repentigny to France, went a letter from Fr. Vimont, Superior of the Canadian mission, to Fr. Cellot, Rector of the College of La Flèche, asking for hospital Sisters for the distant establishment. Seventeen years were to elapse before Jérôme Le Royer would be able to comply with his request.

Chapter XIII

Notes

1. Marcel Trudel, *Histoire de la Nouvelle-France,* III, La Seigneurie des Cent-Associés, 1627-1663, Vol. 1, Les événements, Montreal, 1979, p. 154, Note 35.

2. Marie-Claire Daveluy, art. "Chomedey de Maisonneuve," in *DCB,* Vol 1, p. 215. It seems that Chomedey did not go to Montreal during the autumn of 1641. Besides Daveluy, see Léo-Desrosiers, *Paul de Chomedey, sieur de Maisonneuve, p. 47.*

3. *JR,* Vol. XXII, p. 211.

4. Aristide Beaugrand-Champagne, "Les origines de Montréal," in *Les Cahiers des Dix,* Montreal, 1948, No. 13, p. 51.

5. Samuel de Champlain, "Les voyages de Samuel de Champlain," *La découverte du Canada,* Vol. 2, Montreal, 1969, p. 113.

6. Daveluy, *La Société de Notre-Dame de Montréal,* p. 171, and by the same author, *Jeanne Mance,* p. 76, Note 9.

7. Atherton, *Montreal 1535-1914,* Vol. 1: Under the French Regime 1535-1760, p. 71, Note 8. St. Michel subsequently became the residence of the Lieutenant Governors of Quebec, first under the name of Spencer Wood, then under that of Bois de Coulonge.

8. Dollier de Casson, *A History of Montreal,* p. 95.

9. Guy-Marie Oury, *Madame de la Peltrie et ses fondations canadiennes,* Solesmens, 1974, pp. 34-40; Marie Emmanuel Chabot, art. "Chauvigny de la Peltrie, Marie Madeleine de," in *DCB,* Vol. 1, pp. 207-208.

10. Jeanne-Françoise Juchereau de Saint-Ignace et Marie-Andrée Duplessis de Sainte-Hélène, *Les annales de l'Hôtel-Dieu de Québec, 1636-1716,* p. 29.

11. Faillon, *Histoire de la Colonie Française en Canada,* Vol. 1, p. 430.

12. *Ibid.,* p. 433.

13. *Ibid.,* p. 434.

14. *JR,* Vol. XXII, p. 41.

15. *Ibid.,* p. 139.

16. Marcel Trudel, *Montréal, la formation d'une société, 1642-1663,* p. 13.

17. Mondoux, *L'Hôtel-Dieu, premier hôpital de Montréal,* p. 99.

18. Léon Pouliot, *Etude sur les relations des Jésuites de la Nouvelle-France (1632-1672),* Montreal, 1940, pp. 133-134; and by the same author, in *Premières pages du Journal des Jésuites de Québec,* 1632-1645. *Rapport des Archives du Québec,* Vol. 41, Quebec, 1963, p. 90.

19. Morin, *Histoire Simple et Véritable,* p. 52.

20. *Ibid.;* Dollier de Casson, *A History of Montreal,* p. 97.

21. *JR*, Vol. XXII, p. 211.

22. Dollier de Casson, *A History of Montreal,* p. 99. Marie-Claire Daveluy is of the opinion that the first Mass was offered on May 17, and the first High Mass with Fr. Vimont's homily on Sunday, May 18. See her *Jeanne Mance,* p. 88.

23. Dollier de Casson, *A History of Montreal,* p. 99. That the fireflies shone day and night is a moot question; that they survived although they were strung together is indeed hard to take. This passage seems to be a development of Sr. Morin's account of what happened after a chapel was built, in *Histoire Simple et Véritable,* p. 54: "... Comme nos Israelistes n'avois (sic) point d'huille pour faire brusler une lampe jour et nuit devant l'hostel, ils s'avisèrent de mettre dans une phiolle de verre fin plusiers mouches qu'on appelles à feu,... qui fesois (sic) parestre cette phiolle aussi claire et réluisante pendant la nuit que s'y il y avoit eu plusieurs petites bougies alumée dedans..."

24. Daveluy, *Jeanne Mance,* pp. 90-91.

25. Morin, *Histoire Simple et Véritable,* pp. 90-91.

26. Desrosiers, *Paul de Chomedey, sieur de Maisonneuve,* p. 53.

27. Lucien Campeau, art. "Poncet de la Rivière, Joseph-Antoine," in *DCB,* Vol. 1, p. 551.

28. *JR*, Vol. XXII, p. 211.

29. *Ibid.,* pp. 211, 213.

30. *Ibid.,* p. 213.

31. Dollier de Casson, *A History of Montreal,* p. 101.

32. *Ibid.,* p. 103.

33. Daveluy, *Jeanne Mance,* p. 96, Note 4.

34. *JR,* Vol. XXII, p. 213.

35. *Ibid.,* p. 217.

36. *Ibid.,* p. 211.

37. Rochemonteix, *Le Collège Henri IV,* Vol. 4, p. 277.

Chapter XIV

Thrust and Parry

IN THE MOTHERLAND, during 1642 and 1643, Jérôme Le Royer would bend his efforts to building up his Canadian settlement as well as the La Flèche hospital with its nursing sisters.

In the first months of 1642, at the Hôtel Dieu, dedicated women and girls were serving Christ in the poverty-stricken patients. Beyond the circle of these selfless people, Fr. Hamelin was still on the warpath. The man enjoyed nothing as much as a good row. The contemporary court records show him continually at variance, not only with the "fathers of the poor," but also with practically all the civil and religious bodies whose trail he crossed.

At the beginning of 1642, Jérôme had addressed a petition to the Bishop concerning the canonical approval of the La Flèche Sisters.[1] In this document he recalled that the administrators had completely rebuilt the Hôtel Dieu with the chapel, and that every means had been taken to provide the little city with Dieppe Hospitaller Sisters, but to no avail. On the other hand, zealous and capable women had been found who were willing to devote themselves to the poor at the hospital out of pure love of God, under a written rule accredited by City Hall, a copy of which was enclosed with the petition.

To it Jérôme added another document[2] signed by the hospital administrators, which, he hoped, would still pugnacious Fr. Hamelin once and for all. Until Fr. Boisricher's acquisition of the title deed of the almonry of St. Marguerite on July 15, 1639, as its last almoner, he had been the rightful owner. Jérôme Le Royer decided to abolish the benefice, since the deed was now his and because, after Fr.

Gyrot's arrival, there was no longer any need of an almoner. Would the Bishop confirm the December 1639 contract between the Hospital Administration and the City? Thus Fr. Hamelin would no longer have any grounds on which to prop up his pretentions affecting the precious "pastoral rights" with regard to the Hôtel Dieu.

Bishop de Rueil had no choice. The second petition implied the suppression of a benefice—the old St. Marguerite almonry with all its responsibilities and, also, with its pecuniary advantages. There was furthermore the risk of other rights being encroached upon. On the twenty-eighth of March, the prelate wrote a brief ordinance enjoining that Fr. Hamelin be notified.[3] The pastor must be free to lay his case before the Church.

During the summer, nothing changed at the presbytery. As administrators of the Hôtel Dieu, did Jérôme and his brother, René, whom Louis XIII had recently named Chancellor, seek an amicable settlement with Fr. Hamelin? One gets the impression they did. In vain.

So, at their request, a meeting was called at City Hall for August 23, 1642.[4] His Honor Mayor le Barbier and the aldermen, having examined, article by article, the proposed statutes of the hospital Sisters, unreservedly endorsed them and requested that the "fathers of the poor" put the following requests before the Bishop: the formal establishment of the Daughters of St. Joseph at the Hôtel Dieu, the approbation of their statutes, and their position regarding the almonry.

True, the almoner had been replaced by Fr. Gyrot as acting chaplain. The City now wished the latter to enjoy the same advantages as the past almoners in matters concerning his appointment and his ministry. Despite the so-called rights of the pastor, the Council trusted Bishop de Rueil would maintain intact, without any concessions to Fr. Hamelin, those of the city of La Flèche, of the chaplain, and of the hospital nurses. In case of opposition, without intending any disrespect to the Bishop, the administrators were empowered to protect their rights even in the courts of the land.

The City Fathers also directed the administrators to include the minutes of the meeting and copies of Fr. Simon Benoit's and Fr. Jean Coign's appointments with other papers for the Bishop's inspection. The next two days, Jérôme transcribed them, had them certified by two notaries, and then delivered them to the prelate, who withheld his decision, for he had not yet heard from Fr. Hamelin.

It was towards the end of 1642, that our clerical Rip Van Winkle finally showed some sign of life in a counterclaim to the Bishop.[5] He wanted his prerogatives maintained to the point that in the chapel no sacraments were to be administered, no Masses offered, and no public ceremonies held, unless he himself officiated or expressly allowed another priest to do so. Moreover, the stubborn abbé was resolved to expel the Hospitaller Sisters, who were increasing alarmingly in number and influence. Since the pastors of La Flèche, he argued, had always enjoyed the title and rights of the almonry, why shouldn't he? Obviously, "the honors, profits, and emoluments" of the function belonged to him!

Bishop de Rueil was not impressed and simply turned Hamelin's protest over to Jérôme Le Royer for examination. The "father of the poor" read it attentively, annotated it, and filed it among his papers. Although the Bishop favored Jérôme, he did not force the pastor of St. Thomas' to desist. The reason seems to have been that he had agreed to the City Council's suggestion of a decision by the highest authorities in the land— His Majesty and Parliament.

While Jérôme and Fr. Hamelin thrust and parried, an immense scarlet letter quit Tarascon on the Ariège and

173

followed the Rhône River to distant Paris. His Eminence Armand Jean du Plessis Duc de Richelieu was going to his rendezvous with death. On December 4, 1642, he died at the French capital, one of France's greatest statesmen France has had, and a far-seeing friend and benefactor of Canada. Would his passing complicate matters for the island colony of Montreal?

About the same time, Jérôme received Paul Chomedey's report on conditions in the island colony. With eagerness tinged with anxiety, he broke the seal. The colonists were hard at work settling down and were grateful to him for the twelve new recruits he had sent. Among other things there was mention of the fortifications that were being put up. Now the 1640 grant had stipulated that no fort was to be erected by the Company of Montreal; but, it had also specified that the settlers might fortify themselves so their lives would not be in jeopardy. At Ville Marie, on August 15, 1642, Chomedey had repeated the consecration already made in Paris of the little colony to the Holy Family.[6] Then there was the joy of learning that the first child, to be baptized in the settlement, an Indian, was named Joseph. And, too, that the feast of the Assumption had been celebrated by the pioneers before a band of friendly Algonquins.

During the spring of 1643, Jérôme's comings and goings suggest that he stopped at the bishopric of Angers and, in order to obtain the legalization of his Daughters of St. Joseph, submitted a petition requesting the Bishop's approval of the Letters Patent, without which they were useless. Claude de Rueil signed them on June 29, 1643.[7]

The prelate's signature allowed the Letters Patent to go to Parliament. Once registered, they would allow Jérôme to establish his Hospitallers legally at the La Flèche Hôtel Dieu. On August 22, in Paris, Parliament did register the Letters Patent and on September 4, the Seneschalsy and the

Presidial Court of La Flèche added their paraphs and seals. After 15 years Fr. Hamelin's bark had finally lost its bite.

Month after month, as the La Flèche tax collector expended himself for the Hôtel Dieu of his town, he was far from neglecting his Montreal colony. In February 1642, we find him in Paris seeking help for Paul de Chomedey and his men. Olier, of course, was consulted. He was then busy with the founding of his Major Seminary in an abandoned dovecote at Vaugirard, in the vicinity of Issy, close by the French capital.

At the time of the priest's stay at Chartres, a colorful and zealous priest named Fr. Adrien Bourdoise, the initiator and superior of a group of clerics of the diocese, had instilled the idea of starting a seminary in his Parisian colleague's receptive mind. An institution of this sort, he believed, must be intimately associated with pastoral work. In this, Bourdoise had Vincent de Paul's approval, though he did not always support the future saint in his dealings with his subordinates, even to the point of calling him a "wet hen." [8]

Fr. Olier proved successful with his seminarians. Quite unknowingly he was making ready for his community of Sulpicians, who were to labor so effectively in Ville Marie, the very reason Jérôme had deterred him from accepting the episcopate. Richelieu, before dying, had offered his château at Ruel to the Messieurs (Misters) as the Abbé and his companions were already called.[9] They preferred poverty and solitude. During the summer of 1642,[10] Fr. Olier's felicitous pastoral activity would result in his appointment as Pastor of St. Sulpice in Paris, a wild run-down parish, haunted by troublesome Calvinists. There he also transplanted his seminary with its teachers and candidates to the priesthood, despite his mother's thin-lipped anger. Her Jean Jacques, a mere curé, when he could have been the Bishop of one of the great sees of France!

Later on in the year, the Company of Montreal convened three times in Paris. Fr. Olier noted in his memoirs that "the persons who were preparing to leave for Canada met with those who are interested in the affairs of religion in the country."[11] Le Royer must have attended at least one of these gatherings in 1642, most probably the first one. Its date is unknown; the second took place on the second of July, feast of the Visitation, at the chapel of the Visitation on St. Jacques (or St. James) Street; the third, on the sixteenth of July, feast of Our Lady of Mt. Carmel, in the Carmelite church of Notre Dame des Champs (Our Lady of the Fields), today demolished. Fr. Olier celebrated Mass and afterwards wrote that Fr. Thomas Le Gauffre, Nicolas Quatorze, mystic Marie de Gournay Rousseau, "Brother" Claude LeGlay and Jean Blandeau de la Croix were among the assistants.

To provide the next batch of men to be sent to New France and the wherewithal to feed and defend them, Jérôme knocked at many doors and managed to borrow large sums totalling 72,000 livres, 60,000 of which he got in January 1643 alone.[12] He jointly obtained these loans in his own name and in that of his wife, while his brother, René, and other relatives and friends such as Denyon de Pasty and Olivier de la Guittière stood surety for him, expecting nothing in return. It was understood that the Company of Montreal would cover these advances. On the twenty-fourth of January as he was on the verge of setting out for Paris, he gave power of attorney to his wife, enabling her to borrow as much as 15,000 livres for his distant settlers.

On his way to meet the members of the Company of Montreal, Jérôme assuredly encountered prospective candidates for the island colony. When at last he rode into the capital, he found plenty to do. He wanted to have Chomedey's predicament with regard to the construction of a fort on the Island of Montreal brought to the attention of Louis XIII. To ensure the safety of the settlement aborning, Baron de Renty, Fr. Olier or even Chancellor Séguier at the suggestion of his wife, Madeleine Fabri de Champauzé, an associate of the Company of Montreal, were in a position to apply gentle pressure on the king.

Someone was successful, for a letter from His Majesty to Governor de Montmagny declared he had been informed in detail by the Company of Montreal of its intention to labor at the conversion of the aboriginals of New France.[13] He willingly granted Commander de Chomedey the authorization to finish the little fort already begun. He also enjoined the Governor-General to assist Ville Marie with all the means at his disposal. No subject of his was to trouble in any way the island habitation. One restriction alone was maintained: the buying and selling of pelts remained the monopoly of the Company of New France.

On February 21, 1643, the same day on which Louis XIII advised Governor de Montmagny he had granted the Montrealers the right to build a fort, the Company of Montreal addressed a petition to Pope Urban VIII.[14] On the previous Feast of the Purification, the idea had come to Fr. Olier as he handed out to his seminarians the candles he had blessed. His thoughts reverted to the words he had heard during his vision of Candlemas 1636, "You must become," he had been told, "a light that will give revelation to the Gentiles." A distraction, which might be called holy, ensued: Why not appeal to the Holy Father for the authorization to send his priests to New France? The Archbishop of Rouen then claimed jurisdiction over Canada. The founder of the Sulpicians felt that the Island of Montreal should be officially designated as a foreign mission directly responsible to the Pope.

The answer from Rome readily granted the papal blessing, certain indulgences, and the right to two privileged altars, all of which had been requested, but no mention was made of the faculties for the future Montreal missionaries, Jean Jacques Olier's Sulpicians. The time was not yet ripe.

During March, probably at the beginning, Louis XIII again manifested his interest in Le Royer's project. Despite the war with Spain—and wars are always costly—he gave the Company of Montreal a ship of 250 tonneaux, fitted out at his own expense. It was promptly named the *Notre Dame de Montréal*.[15] He topped his gift with several pieces of artillery to help ensure the defense of the island. Jérôme and his collaborators fully appreciated the royal bounty: no longer would they be forced to count on the cooperation of the Company of the One Hundred Associates to transport each year the men, munitions, and other provisions needed to sustain the lives of the pioneers!

Then a meeting of the Company of Montreal was called for the morning of the thirteenth of March at Notre Dame. In the group, it is safe to assume that young Louis d'Ailleboust, master of Coulonge and of Argentenay, his wife, Marie Barbe de Boullongne, and his sister-in-law, Philippine de Boullongne, attracted considerable attention.[16] These three new members of the Company were bent on going to join Paul de Chomedey and Jeanne Mance in their missionary efforts. Jérôme had probably met them and, impressed by the young nobleman, may have already thought of entrusting him with his third batch of recruits and with the precious cargo of provisions eagerly expected by his settlers.

As Fr. Olier was about to vest for the Holy Sacrifice, Our Lord and His Blessed Mother inspired him to yield to another priest, Fr. Thomas La Gauffre, the honor of celebrating Mass at the Lady altar. "Our Lord told me," he wrote in his Memoirs, written by order of his confessor, "that as his representative in this charitable undertaking

178

[Ville Marie], it was necessary for me to act as the heart of the Company of Montreal. In the human body, the heart does its work by means of the members of the body, which are quite visible; however, its life remains hidden, though all the members are alive and active in subjection to it... 'You must be like the heart of my good works, you must give life and movement to all of them,' said Our Lord, 'and do my work secretly...' " [17]

The minutes of the meeting that followed the Mass have not been preserved. However, most of the points brought up for deliberation are obvious.[18] First of all, a letter of thanks to the King must have been voted for his authorization to construct a fort at Ville Marie and for his gift of the *Notre Dame* and of artillery pieces to the Montreal pioneers. The different aspects of the growing opposition, launched by political and religious interests to stifle the Company of Montreal by alienating influential members, on pretext, of all things, that sacred theology could not countenance its efforts, demanded a careful examination. And, surprisingly enough, at this early date, resulted in the idea of petitioning the Sovereign Pontiff to appoint a Bishop for Montreal!

During that month of March in Paris, as the "father of the poor" from La Flèche saw to the affairs of his island foundation, he was also hard at work trying to settle the difficult Hamelin problem. He may even have had an audience with Louis XIII. Before the month was out, His Majesty had signed the Letters Patent abolishing the almonry on condition that a priest reside at the Hôtel Dieu to minister to the needs of the patients—in other words a chaplain.[19] It was one of the last documents signed by the king before his death, and it still may be seen at La Flèche. Its tale of the efforts for the betterment of the hospital since Fr. Boisricher's removal in 1628 is so detailed that none other than Jérôme Le Royer could have drawn it up.

About this time, Louis XIII signed the following order, quite unthinkable before his late Prime Minister's demise. His mother, Marie de Médicis, had died the year before in distant Cologne[20] and her remains were to be brought back to Paris. In 1624, while young Bishop de Richelieu was serving as her Almoner, she had succeeded in having her son accept him as Prime Minister of the country. Almost immediately, he vigorously went to work at establishing order in a kingdom long upset by the wars of religion. The Queen Mother soon found herself at loggerheads with her protégé. Then hoist with her own petard, the outraged Queen Mother suddenly found herself stripped of all her possessions and condemned to perpetual exile.

Now after a lifetime of little joy and of much unhappiness, she was laid to rest at St. Denis's with the kings and queens of France since the time of 7th century Dagobert. Her heart, in accordance with her wishes, was to go to the chapel of the Royal College at La Flèche, where Henri IV's had been placed in 1610, when Jérôme was still a boy. The two hearts rarely beating in unison during life would rest together in death.

Fr. Louis Le Mairat, Jesuit superior of the Professed House of St. Louis in Paris, was chosen to transport the royal relic to its destination.[21] On April 12, the cortège reached the Angevine city on the little Loire River. The members of the Presidial Court and the gentlemen of the City Council received it with the deference due to the memory of the late king, signal benefactor of La Flèche. Jérôme was not at home on April 3, for his wife was still borrowing money in his name;[22] as royal tax collector, city alderman, administrator of the Hôtel Dieu, and graduate of the Jesuit College, he was assuredly there nine days later.

On April 5, 1643, Louis XIII had died and solemn Masses were offered in La Flèche for the repose of his soul as soon as the news reached the little city. Jérôme once again found his way to the college chapel and there is little doubt that he poured out his heart before God for the monarch, who had lent him a helping hand.

Though it hung fire for a while, a refutation of the arguments marshalled against the Montreal Associates was finally published to offset the adverse propaganda against them which was beginning to take effect. It was a book of 127 pages in quarto with an impressive title: *The True Motives of the Ladies and Gentlemen of the Company of Montreal for the Conversion of the Indians of New France.*[23] It came off the press in the last half of 1643. To this day, the author of this hastily-written, albeit well thought-out work, remains unknown. Should there ever come to light a copy of Jérôme Le Royer's "Plan for Montreal," jotted down at La Rochelle at Mademoiselle Mance's suggestion before she sailed for the New World, it might help to solve this problem. Fr. Olier, the Baron Gaston de Renty, Magistrate Laisné de la Marguerie, and Jérôme himself have, each in turn, been suggested as the author.[24] Its origin was also ascribed to Fr. Paul Le Jeune, S.J., the Canadian missionary, who had returned to France in 1641.[25] In all probability, however, it was put together in collaboration.

Only a few history buffs are now more than passingly acquainted with *The True Motives*. It masterfully treats of practical charity with regard to foreign missions, in this case the Montreal establishment dedicated to Our Lady; it also clearly spells out the hopes of the members of the Company of Montreal to have Urban VIII name a Bishop for Ville Marie.

What was the impact of *The True Motives*? Unsatisfactory. Could it have been otherwise? Many of the well-meaning aristocrats who were at first interested in Ville Marie practised a rather desultory charity. Their aim consisted not so much in a specific good work as in good works in general. One was as good as the other. Any pretext sufficed to draw their attention elsewhere and to open their purses to other worthy causes.[26] Not too many had the singleness of purpose that Jérôme Le Royer and his intimate circle of friends were blessed with.

Chapter XIV

Notes

1. *RPA*, Vol.3, pp. 218-219.

2. *VJLD*, Vol. 1, p. 225.

3. *RPA*, Vol. 3, p. 219.

4. *RPA*, Vol. 3, pp. 222-224.

5. *Ibid.* pp. 221-222.

6. *JR*, Vol. XXII, pp. 209, 211.

7. *VJLD*, Vol. 1, p. 248.

8. Pourrat, *Jean-Jacques Olier, fondateur de Saint-Sulpice*, p. 99.

9. Faillon, *Vie de Monsieur Olier*, Vol. 1, pp. 377-378.

10. Irénée Noye and Michel Dupuy, art. "Olier (Jean-Jacques)," in *Dictionnaire de spiritualité*, Vol. 2, Paris, 1982, Col. 738.

11. Quoted by Daveluy in *La Société de Notre-Dame de Montréal*, p. 28.

12. *RPA*, Vol. 3, p. 244; VJLD, Vol. 1, p. 241 says 87,000 livres.

13. *La Société de Notre-Dame de Montréal*, p. 37. The latter is given in *extenso* from a notarized copy of April 20, 1643, at the Archives of the Séminaire de Montréal.

14. "Lettre des Associés de Montréal au Souverain Pontife, Urbain VIII" (February 21, 1643), in Daveluy, *La Société de Notre-Dame de Montréal*, pp. 35-37.

15. *RPA*, Vol. 3, p. 245.

16. *Les Véritables Motifs*, p. 34.

17. Daveluy, quoting Olier in *La Société de Notre-Dame de Montréal*, pp. 226-227.

18. If the finances of the Company of Montreal were discussed, was provision made for Ville Marie? Probably. If so, not enough hard cash was set aside to cover Jérôme Le Royer's borrowing.

19. *RPA*, Vol. 3, p. 251.

20. Michel Carmona, *Marie de Médicis*, Paris, 1981, p. 565.

21. *RPA*, p. 249.

22. *VJLD*, Vol. 1. p. 259.

23. Fortunately, *La Société de Notre-Dame de Montréal*

contains a photocopy of a very rare copy of the original 1643 edition, preserved at the Huntington Library in San Marino, California. Another copy may be consulted at the Library of the City of Montreal. See Appendix II.

24. Albert Jamet, "Jérôme Le Royer de la Dauversière et les commencements de Montréal," in *Revue de l'Université d'Ottawa* (Oct.-Dec., 1936), Vol. 6, No. 4, p. 404.

25. Bertrand, *Monsieur de la Dauversière*, p. 143.

26. Léon Gérin, *Aux sources de notre histoire, les conditions économiques et sociales de la colonisation en Nouvelle-France*, Montreal, 1946, p. 181.

Chapter XV

The First Year

MORE AND MORE OFTEN Jérôme's thoughts now turned to New France and to the Island of Montreal a thousand miles inland from the sea. Until the return of the ships during the autumn of 1643, no news, either good or bad, would be forthcoming.

The founder of Montreal had ended up by entrusting that year's lot of settlers to Monsieur Louis d'Ailleboust. He could not have chosen better. The young aristocrat, who soon proved his worth to Ville Marie, was later to do as much for all of New France.

Louis d'Ailleboust was born in 1612 at Ancy-le-Franc, a little town of the Province of Champagne.[1] He belonged to the recent nobility, since Henri IV had ennobled his grandfather, Jean d'Ailleboust, royal physician, perhaps because of his effective bedside manner.

In September 1638, Louis, at the age of 26, had married Marie Barbe de Boullongne, who was six years younger than he. She came from Ravière, some nine miles from his home town. Their nuptials were celebrated in Paris with the express condition that he would always respect the vow of virginity which Marie Barbe had taken as a child.

Three years later, in 1641, the young couple wrestled with a serious difficulty. The husband's heart was filled with the desire of becoming a lay missionary in the New World. His wife, who was plagued with ill health, was homelier in taste. As time went by, Louis d'Ailleboust, not without the assent of Fr. Manart, his spiritual father, persisted in his hopes of sailing for Canada. But the more he felt like going, the less Marie Barbe wanted to go. Heaven seemed to set its stamp of approval upon her attitude, for her health rapidly deteriorated. The doctors who were consulted gave up all hope of recovery.

When it was thought the young woman had not long to live, she promised to accompany her husband to Canada if her health improved sufficiently. In Notre Dame Cathedral, where Jérôme Le Royer had been inspired to found Montreal, she suddenly found herself completely cured.[2] After some hesitation, Mme. d'Ailleboust informed her husband and Fr. Manart that she was ready to keep her promise. The Jesuit thereupon introduced them both to Jérôme's friend, Fr. Charles Lalemant, the very man who had helped him to win over Paul de Chomedey to his cause. Fr. Lalemant suggested that they join the Company of Montreal, and this, they immediately agreed to. As soon as their decision became known, Mme. d'Ailleboust's sister, Mademoiselle Philippine Gertrude de Boullongne, asked to accompany them to Ville Marie, where she intended to devote herself "to the service of God and the conversion of the Indians." Her request was granted.

In April or early May, Ailleboust, his wife and his sister-in-law went to hilly La Rochelle, with its narrow and crooked streets. Along the way, they were joined in all likelihood by some of Jérôme's recruits and rendezvoused with the rest of them at the seaport. With the purest of motives, these men were "ready to sacrifice their lives for the Montreal enterprise —the glory of God and the conversion of souls." [3]

The news of their coming spread from the quays of the lower town to the higher section with its cobbled streets. For anyone to cross the ocean with the intention of living in Canada qualified him as courageous; but to do so with the purpose of establishing himself at Ville Marie labelled him as heroic and somewhat foolhardy. Several wealthy Calvinists were impressed by the sight of these new Crusaders and embraced the old faith of their fathers. Some workmen of the same persuasion did likewise and even swelled the ranks of the Montreal emigrants.

Among the departing Montrealers were farmers and laborers. Only the name of one of them is recorded, that of Jean St-Père, "a man of fine piety, quick intelligence, and altogether, according to report, as sound in judgment as anyone..." [4] How many of them composed the third recruitment for Montreal is not known.[5] Other passengers were Fr. Noel Chabanel, who died a martyr, Fr. Gabriel Druillettes, the beloved apostle of the Maine Abenaki, and Fr. Léonard Garreau, who baptized Francis Xavier Tonsahoten, founder of the Mission of St. Francis Xavier, where Blessed Kateri Tekakwitha achieved union with God.

Jérôme Le Royer does not seem to have been present to bid farewell to Monsieur and Madame d'Ailleboust, her sister, and to this third party of colonists for Ville Marie as their ship, one of three, cast off. Only the most serious reasons could have kept him away from La Rochelle.

The passage proved rough and long, and two of the ships dropped anchor at Quebec as late as August 15, just as Fr. Vimont was about to begin high Mass.[6] All the passengers disembarked, priests, nuns, and laymen, and under the protection of the "Empress of the Universe," dedicated themselves to God and to the salvation of the native people.

News from Montreal was both good and bad. Approximately 55 pioneers from different parts of France, of divers ages and conditions, lived there harmoniously.[7] None had been ill during the winter and the only ones to make use of the tiny hospital were a few Indians. The inhabitants had their goods in common. They had very little money. Barter and interchange of commodities, of work and of service linked them with the early Christians. Fortified by the thought that they were toiling for the glory of God, there was a complete absence of crime. All frequented the sacraments. The resulting peace among the French edified the Indians who visited them and spoke well of it.

The newcomers were also informed of the Iroquois depredations in the colony. On their way to Montreal, they halted at Trois-Rivières and heard more about them. A month and a half before, on June 12, two of the Hurons who had been taken captive on the second of August of the previous year had managed to escape to the little French fort at Trois-Rivières, where they met Fr. Jean de Brébeuf. They told him of their capture and gave him news about Fr. Isaac Jogues and Guillaume Cousture,[8] who had become slaves of the Mohawks.

M. d'Ailleboust and the other emigrants learned still more about these fearsome enemies when they finally arrived at their destination. The lesson began quite concretely then and there. Although the settlers within the stockade saw their pinnace, for fear of an ambush, no one dared go out to meet the new arrivals, who for the same reason did not dare to disembark. Without any sign of rank, clad in the same grey serge as his men, it took courageous Paul de Chomedey to hurry to the riverside to welcome the new immigrants. From the palisaded fortifications, all watched with baited breath, "so true was it that over the threshold of the door no one was safe." [9]

After Monsieur and Madame d'Ailleboust, Mademoiselle de Boullongne, and the men reached the safety of the little fort and rested somewhat, they were plied with questions. Among other things, Louis d'Ailleboust confirmed the good tidings the inhabitants had already learned during the first days of July from Governor de Montmagny: The late King's donation to the Company of Montreal, a 250 tonner, the *Notre Dame*, had carried them safely to Canada. His Majesty had also added to his bounty several pieces of artillery with munitions, which Monsieur d'Ailleboust transported to Quebec on the new ship. Best of all, he had approved the building of the fort and ordered that the Governor of Montreal be helped as much as possible and that no obstacle be set up in his way. ...Paul de Chomedey then told the story of Ville Marie's first year. The location of the fort had been the cause of the first major difficulty. Hemmed in by the St. Lawrence River and its affluent, the St. Pierre, (today an underground stream in the vicinity of the Custom House), its very existence was threatened when their waters rose and spilt over into the nearby fields. The settlers had recourse to prayer. The commander himself was inspired to set a cross up on the bank of the smaller current close to the fortified building. God would listen to his plea. He would retain the waters in its bed. If not, He would doubtless make known which part of the island He wished them to build upon.

To the colony's spiritual guides, Jesuit Fathers Joseph Antoine Poncet de la Rivière and Joseph Imbert Duperrou, Paul de Chomedey submitted a project of his. They thought highly of it. As a proof of his sincerity, he wrote it down and read it out publicly.[10] The cross was planted on the riverside, blessed, and the written document attached to its base. Chomedey then pledged, should his request be heard, that he would carry a cross on his shoulders to the summit of Mount Royal.

Despite the pledge and the prayers, the waters continued to rise—a test of the pioneers's trust in Divine Providence. In large waves, they overflowed into the moat surrounding the fort and crept up to the door. It was Christmas night, a bleak Christmas night. It seemed to this band of strangers from afar that the next morning there would be no roof over their heads. Whatever the outcome, their faith in the Father in heaven never wavered. The waters lapped at the very threshold, hesitated and little by little began to recede. The place was safe and Paul de Chomedey had to accomplish his pledge.

Without delay, the co-founder of Montreal ordered his men to hew out a path to the top of the mountain. On January 6, 1643, feast of the Epiphany, he was made "the first soldier of the Cross, with all the ceremonies of the Church," [11] and a heavy wooden cross was blessed. He then loaded it on his shoulders and, accompanied by most if not all the inhabitants, carried it three miles to the highest point of the mountain. When it stood out stark against the winter sky, Fr. Joseph Duperron offered the Holy Sacrifice. Madame de la Peltrie was the first one to receive Holy Communion. After the final Deo Gratias, the worshippers venerated the Cross and the relics set in it. From that day on, the Cross triumphant stretched its arms protectingly over the hardy and deeply religious men and women Jérôme Le Royer had handpicked to found Ville Marie.

Thus the first-rate workmen under their commander's orders continued working with such alacrity that on the nineteenth of March, feast of St Joseph, within the fort, at least the framework of the main building was completed.[12] It comprised the chapel of Our Lady, the temporary hospital, stores, and rooms for some 70 people.[13] The occasion was celebrated with a joyful cannonade in honor of the great patron saint of Canada. Peace lay upon the land. But not for long.

In the first days of April, the French caught sight of Indians, soon recognized as Algonquins, on the south shore of the St Lawrence. They crossed it on the floating ice, fleeing at top speed to the security of the white man's fort.[14] In hot pursuit a band of Iroquois followed them to the river's edge: the Algonquins had killed and scalped one of their braves. Thus did the existence of Ville Marie become known among the Five Nations.

Many other Indians had begun to look upon the little settlement as a haven. During the previous October, an Indian girl was baptized, and in November and December, two other native children were received into the Church.[15] Towards the end of February 1643, a warparty of 25 had left their women and children under Commander de Chomedey's protection as they set out on the warpath against the Iroquois.[16]

Two or three days later, another band had come to hunt on the Island, for the game there was plentiful. Its leader, Oumasasikweie, soon learned that the purpose of the new settlement was none other than the salvation of the souls of the Indians. He was deeply touched and asked to become a Christian and live with the French. Rightly convinced of his sincerity, Paul de Chomedey promised him a field and two men to grub it for him during an entire year. After receiving the necessary instructions, Oumasasikweie and his wife, Mitigoukwe, were baptized about the seventh or eighth of March. As the first Indian male adult to become a Christian at the settlement, he was given the name of Joseph, which must have been very much to Jérôme Le Royer's liking when he learned about it. Mitigoukwe was named Jeanne after Mademoiselle Mance. On the same day, she and Joseph were married according to the rites of the Church, the first couple to receive the Sacrament of Matrimony at Ville Marie. As a baptismal and wedding gift, Joseph's godmother, Madame de la Peltrie, presented him with an arquebus. .... Joseph's uncle, Tesswehas, the "terror of the Iroquois," Algonquin chief of the Kichespirini, called by the French "Le Borgne de l'Isle" (Isle of Matches in the Ottawa River), attended the ceremonies with his wife and daughter. The most celebrated and famous of all Algonquins had joined his nephew on March 1. Until then, though strongly opposed to Christianity for himself, he had allowed his children to be baptized and had been the occasion for many others to embrace "Prayer." On the other hand, his example had retarded a considerable number of his people from doing so. On first meeting the commander, he said, "The single purpose which brings me here is prayer. It is here that I desire to pray, to be instructed and baptized; but if you do not agree to it, I will go away to the Hurons, where the Blackrobes who are there with the Algonquins will teach me..." [17]

As the conversion of Tesswehas would greatly benefit the Kichespirini, the leader of the French resolved to do everything in his power to facilitate it. He asked the Fathers to tell him that if he truly wanted to take instructions and settle down, this was the place for him. Furthermore he insisted that he would love him as a brother and assist him to the best of his ability.

The chief was grateful for these offers and made the most of them. He faithfully attended the common prayers, the instructions and the baptisms of several of his tribesmen. For hours on end, he listened to the Jesuits' lessons and sought help on all sides, even to reciting the Lord's Prayer with old women and children. "My daughter," he complained, "has no sense, not to be willing to teach me what she knows!"

On March 8, despite what he had previously said, he confided to Frs. Duperron and Poncet, "I never promised to be baptized, but to be instructed; but now I promise it to you." The following night, he informed his people of his decision and spent several hours urging them to imitate him. On the morning of the ninth of March, he went to the Blackrobes and urgently asked to be baptized and sacramentally married. "Come," he said to Fr. Duperron, "make haste; for there will be some, even till night--so many persons you will have to baptize. You will have plenty to do, as well as the Fathers; because the entire day cannot satisfy my people, who all wish to be baptized."

According to Chomedey's wishes, the baptism and the marriage following it were celebrated as solemnly as possible. Together with Mademoiselle Mance, he named the new convert Paul; Madame de la Peltrie and Monsieur de Puiseaux had chosen Madeleine for the wife's Christian name. Fr. Poncet preached on the Lord's goodness to the neophytes, and we are told that the good priest was nearly overcome by emotion. At any rate, tears streamed down the cheeks of the hardy settlers attending the ceremony. Commander de Chomedey afterwards gave Paul a splendid arquebus and had the couple dine with him and the other notables, while a hearty meal was served at the same time to the other Indians and French. This was a sample of what Jérôme Le Royer had founded Ville Marie for, but only a sample, a bright ray of light in what was quickly changed into a somber sky.

In a letter from Huronia, one of the missionaries wrote, "...if the place had more security, they [the Algonquins who had sought a haven among the Hurons] would forever leave this country here, in order to form a village at Mount Royal, and gather there those of the Island [the Kichespirini] and the other scattered nations, who see themselves to be the prey of the enemy here, and on the river where they have their haunts. They ask nothing better than to have a secure place of refuge, where they can live and rally together." [18]

But more security Ville Marie was not to offer for many years. Had a superman, either French or Indian, been able to analyse the situation correctly and quickly organize the migration of French settlers and aborigines to the Island of Montreal, so as to present the Iroquois with a united front, the following decades would not have been drenched with blood. But the superman did not exist. To make matters worse, none of the authorities in Quebec thought of arming the Hurons and their friends with arquebuses as the Dutch had done for the Iroquois.

On June 9, 60 unarmed Hurons in 13 canoes laden with pelts, on their way from Huronia to Quebec, were attacked by a band of 40 Iroquois, each one with a Dutch arquebus in hand. They took 23 prisoners, laid hands on their canoes, furs, letters, and the Relation written by the missionaries. The rest of the Hurons fled, naked, to Ville Marie.[19]

The amended version of the Relation, published in 1645, related that the enemy had hastily build a temporary fort about a mile and a half higher than the French Habitation and had invited the Hurons to spend the night with them. The invitation was accepted, but many never awoke, having been massacred in their sleep by their new friends.[20]

The victors decided to push their advantage to the utmost. Ten of their men were left to guard the surviving Hurons, 20 others simulated an attack on the French fortifications, with an arquebusade of more than 100 shots. The diversion was successful for the remaining ten surrounded five Frenchmen working at some carpentry about 200 paces from the Habitation. They took two captives and killed and scalped Guillaume Boissier, Bernard Berté, and Pierre Lafond, called Laforest, the first to shed their blood for the success of Jérôme Le Royer's enterprise. They had all received Holy Communion, some a few days before, the others on the very day of their capture.

After a nighttime of rejoicing and of deliberations in their makeshift retreat, the Iroquois began the day by beating 13 of the Hurons to death, not wanting to encumber themselves with too many captives on the way home. They embarked with as many of the beaver pelts as they could load into their elm bark canoes, and crossed the St. Lawrence in full view of the French, who dared not pursue them. On the south shore, they staved, or broke holes in the bottom of the canoes to make them unusable and set out for the Richelieu River near what was to become the town of Chambly. After two days, they untied the leather thongs which bound the white men. Eight days later, one of them escaped, found his way to the abandoned canoes, stuffed the better ones with grass, filled them with some of the beaver skins strewn about the shore, and rowed them back across the river. Thus the captive, who had been given up as dead, was welcomed safe and sound at Ville Marie.

One of the particularly disastrous effects of this raid and of several others during the rest of 1643 explains why the Algonquins no longer believed the protection offered by the French within their fortifications was adequate. Neither Le Borgne de l'Isle nor his nephew Joseph ever farmed the land they had been given. They soon permanently quit Ville Marie with their tribesmen. Never would the other Algonquins—the Mataouachkariniens, the Onontchateronons, the Kinoncheperiniks, the Weweskariniens, the Nepissiriniens, the Archirigouans, and the Archouguets— settle down in the shadow of Jérôme Le Royer's Habitation. Ville Marie had become a military outpost for Quebec.

However, Jérôme Le Royer, founder of Ville Marie, would be able to derive comfort at the thought of the 70 or 80 Indians baptized in the wake of Le Borgne de l'Isle.[21] The candidates had been severely screened and quite a few whose motives were judged too selfish, were rejected. To be sure the presence of these men and women had left the settlers in a predicament. The peas and maize planted by them had been shared with the friendly Indians; much of the food sent by Jérôme had also been distributed among the native visitors. Very little remained for Ville Marie itself. But Paul de Chomedey did not regret his open-handedness. "It is not easy to tell of the care that he took of the poor unfortunates, the kindnesses he did them, and how much all this cost the company in this first year when everything was so dear; in short, his goodness stopped at nothing." [22]

All the while, Louis d'Ailleboust had listened attentively to what his host, Jeanne Mance, and the first-year emigrants had to say. He strongly advised them to plant good French wheat, for the peas and the Indian corn were not sufficient.[23] As he was an engineer, a good military engineer, he felt he must help ensure the safety of the little colony. Already his active mind began planning four bastions for the little fort and a sturdy wall to surround it in lieu of the paling of 1642.[24] All this Louis d'Ailleboust achieved after communications with France were severed for the year.

One of the ships homeward bound in October or perhaps an earlier one, carried a letter from Jeanne Mance to Madame de Bullion.[25] Her talks with Fr. Jean de Brébeuf at Sillery during the winter of 1641-1642 and, no doubt with Madame de la Peltrie, who was becoming more and more interested in the missions of Huronia, had inspired it. She expressed the hope that the fund reserved for the hospital—which as yet had not a single French patient— be applied to the Huron missions so badly in need of assistance.

Chapter XV

Notes

1. Jeanne-Françoise Juchereau de la Ferté de Saint-Ignace, *Les annales de L'Hôtel-Dieu de Québec*, p. 70, Note 6.

2. *Véritables Motifs*, p. 34.

3. Ernest Gagnon, *Louis d'Ailleboust de Coulonge et d'Argentenay*, 2nd Ed., Montreal, 1931, p. 24.

4. Dollier de Casson, *A History of Montreal*, p. 221.

5. Marcel Trudel, *Montréal, la fondation d'une société, 1642-1663*, p. 17.

6. *JR*, Vol. XXIII, p. 287.

7. *Ibid.*, Vol. XXIV, p. 223. The 55 pioneers comprise the initial batch of 1641 plus the 11 brought over in 1642 by Le Gardeur de Repentigny.

8. *Ibid.*, p. 281.

9. Dollier de Casson, *A History of Montreal*, p. 113.

10. *JR*, Vol. XXIV, p. 225.

11. Léon Pouliot, "Premières pages du `Journal des Jésuites' de Québec, 1632-1645," in *Archives du Québec, Rapport 1963*, Vol. 41, p. 96.

12. Dollier de Casson, *A History of Montreal*, p. 107.

13. *Véritables Motifs*, p. 35.

14. *JR*, Vol. XXIV, p. 263; Dollier de Casson, *A History of Montreal*, p. 107.

15. *JR*, Vol. XXIV, p. 265. Faillon, *Histoire de la Colonie Française en Canada*, Vol. I, pp. 455-456.

16. *JR*, Vol. XXIV, pp. 231-235.

17. *Ibid.*, p. 239.

18. *Ibid.*, p. 267.

19. *Ibid.*, pp. 275-279.

20. *JR*, XXVI, p. 21.

21. *Premier registre de l'église Notre-Dame de Montréal*, Montreal, 1961, Facsimile, pp. 43-60.

22. Dollier de Casson, *A History of Montreal*, p. 115.

23. *Ibid.*, p. 123.

24. *Ibid.*, p. 117.

25. *Ibid.*, p. 125.

Chapter XVI

The Poorest of the Three

WHILE VILLE MARIE was holding its own in Canada, in France, Jérôme Le Royer's Hôtel Dieu was attracting new subjects to its doors. From distant Paris, on September 23, 1643, came little Marie Houzé,[1] the ten-year-old child of a man of independent means, perhaps a member of the Society of the Blessed Sacrament to which Jérôme belonged. The same day, the coach from the inland port of Nantes on the Loire, to the southwest, trundled into La Flèche and came to a halt. Mademoiselle Catherine Macé stepped down. The daughter of a merchant,[2] some say of a wealthy ship owner,[3] at any rate a business acquaintance of Jérôme's, she was then in her mid-twenties.

The story of Catherine's vocation was typically that of countless religious from devout families. Even as a little one, she felt the closeness of God. As she grew older she prayed to Him daily in her private oratory. At the age of nineteen, she began asking Divine Providence to guide her in the choice of a state of life. She persevered in her devotions for two years, leaving her comfortable home only for Mass and the divine office, which she often attended in the 15th-century cathedral of St. Pierre with its admirable nave over 100 feet high. It was through the Society of Jesus that she learned of the nascent community of the St. Joseph Hospitallers of La Flèche. She requested the Jesuits to arrange for her admission. Impressed by their recommendation, Marie de la Ferre agreed to accept her as an aspirant.

M. Macé, on learning of his daughter's decision, put his foot down. Catherine being a 17th-century Frenchwoman, had recourse to tears and, when these abated somewhat, revealed to her father how reluctant she was about quitting him. Nonetheless, seeing that God wanted her to become a Daughter of St. Joseph, to La Flèche she must go!

Her brother, Fr. René Macé,[4] pastor of the parish church of Our Lady of Montfaucon, later to become one of Fr. Olier's Sulpicians, opposed her vocation to the nursing Sisters. There were plenty of nuns in her own city; why couldn't Catherine enter one of the monasteries there? Otherwise her father would surely die of grief. He was fortunately made of sterner stuff than his son, the Curé.

With all her tears, Catherine had an iron will. She finally convinced René that the Hôtel Dieu of St. Joseph was the only place for her, and he in turn persuaded Monsieur Macé to consent to his daughter's departure. Catherine packed her bags, kissed her father and brother goodbye and was off to La Flèche, where Mademoiselle de la Ferre received her with open arms.

"We have been expecting you for some time," Monsieur Le Royer welcomed her, "for you are one of God's chosen ones!"

From the first day Catherine Macé lived up to the two founders' expectations, and Marie de la Ferre soon confided to Jérôme her excellent opinion of the newcomer.

"She will be a model," he said, "by her life unknown to all and hidden in God, of the sublime virtues Our Lord loved and practised most on earth."

In prayer, Jérôme was granted an extraordinary perception of Catherine Macé's future. God had picked her out to labor in Ville Marie. The next time the founder spoke to her, he inquired if she would object to being sent across the sea to Canada. No, she would not, she even desired to spend her life there despite her unworthiness, which made her fit only to hide away from the world. Beneath this answer, perhaps re-edited for posterity, pulsed sincere love and true missionary zeal.

Catherine Macé had arrived at La Flèche in the nick of time to share in the joy caused by a series of letters and decrees emanating from the pen of Bishop de Rueil. On the nineteenth of October, from Evantard, which he was then visiting, came the decree of establishment admitting to the Hôtel Dieu the Hospitallers of St. Joseph.[5] The prelate recalled that, because of the Royal College which drew from many corners of France and even from beyond its boundaries young noblemen and gentry trailing their suites of tutors and valets, the population of the city had increased. Hence the need for a bigger and better staff at the hospital. By the devoted women comprising the personnel, a common rule of life was to be followed as embodied in the Constitutions, a development of the Statutes already mentioned. Since human nature is generally prone to laxity, the Bishop ordered that a copy be always exposed in a prominent place in the community refectory and that another be kept in the Sisters' archives, where it could be easily accessible for reference.

Six days later, on October 25, 1643, at Angers, in a lengthy letter, which reproduced the Constitutions textually, the Bishop formally approved the 24 chapters drawn up by Jérôme Le Royer.[6] Running far ahead of his time, parallel to St. Francis de Sales, founder of the Order of the Visitation, and to St. Vincent de Paul, founder of the Sisters of Charity, the La Flèche tax collector was instrumental in adapting feminine convent life to the needs of the era.

On the eventful Candlemas of 1630—it must have seemed centuries ago to Jérôme—in the little bridge-chapel on the Loire, God had dictated to him the first chapter of the Constitutions. The spirit of the future institute had there been made clear to him. This layman, fortunately blessed with the gift of prudence and helped by Marie de la Ferre, had slowly prepared page after page of

201

the Constitutions and shaped them on the anvil of day to day experience. He had also been able to consult specialists in the field of religious life. Ever ready to study his problems and help him solve them, besides Fr. Vincent de Paul, Fr. de Condren, and Fr. de Lingendes, S.J., in Paris, he could count on Abbé Eveillon, a saintly priest called by his contemporaries, "the light of our Anjou," a less known Fr. Vallier, S.J.,[7] and also Fr. Dubreuil, S.J.,[8] who had helped him revise the entire document.

None better than a good chaplain could guide the Daughters of St Joseph in the observance of their brand-new rules. Three days later, on October 28, Bishop de Rueil appointed Fr. Jean Gyrot to this post.[9] The brief episcopal text of the appointment goes out of its way to specify that the nominee was duly authorized to administer the sacraments to the needy sick and to the "Servants of God" (in the feminine) even on Easter Sunday. In other words, to the touchy Frs. Hamelin present and future, "Hands off!" Jérôme was making good use of his time.

On October 30, Royal Notary Robert Couallier drew up the contract for Fr. Gyrot and his sister, Marie, binding them legally to the Congregation, the first as chaplain and the other as hospitaller.[10] Included in the settlement of all of the notarial red tape of the period was the important matter of the "portion" or dowry each candidate would be requested to furnish. Jérôme had decided upon 3,000 livres, the income of which would provide for the needs of each new subject. At the death of a Sister, the sum she had brought with her on entering would accrue to the community. In turn its members would hand over 300 livres to the Hôtel Dieu in reparation for the deceased hospitaller's shortcomings, particularly those even inadvertently committed against the penniless patients who had been under her care.

Sr. Marie de la Ferre, the co-foundress, was affected by

this ruling. As the administrators of the hospital were not ramrods, an exception was made in her favor.[11] For ten years, without a sou of salary, and while seeing to her own needs, Mademoiselle de la Ferre had served the destitute sick. So the 1,300 livres she had already given to the Hôtel Dieu and the little furniture she had brought with her, valued at 100 livres, were accepted in place of the regular dowry. At her request, 200 livres were diverted to the dowry of her niece, Sr. Marie Maillard, at the nearby convent of the Daughters of Notre Dame, an order founded by Montaigne's niece, Blessed Jeanne de Lestonnac.

That same day, Couallier notarized other contracts, for instance those of Mademoiselle de L'Espicier for 3,794 livres, and of Jérôme's daughter for a simple promissory note of 3,000 livres to be redeemed two years later.[12] Meanwhile, with his wife, Jeanne, he would pay the annual interest to avoid any loss on the part of the Hospitallers. The La Flèche tax-collector was already feeling the pinch of his many charities to Ville Marie.

All this ink, legal paper, and red wax finally came to life on November 23, 1643. That morning Jérôme and his brother, René represented the mayor and aldermen at the Hôtel Dieu. Several gentlemen interested in the welfare of the destitute of the city had gathered together with them as witnesses.[13] As they waited near the doorkeeper's lodge, a peal of the house bell shattered the silence of the hospital and almost immediately Fr. Gyrot's cassock darkened the door of the reception room. Seconds later Marie de la Ferre, Anne Foureau, Anne de L'Espicier de Ribère, Marie Gyrot, Anne Le Tendre, Jeanne Le Royer, and Renée Busson joined him. The hour had come to entrust legally Fr. Gyrot and the above-mentioned Sisters-to-be with the care of the Hôtel Dieu. The two "fathers of the poor" tendered a missal solemnly to the chaplain, who, on receiving it, promised to discharge his duties faithfully. To Mademoiselle de la

Ferre and her little group, they gave the heavy keys of the hospital. These devoted ladies assured the administrators they would conscientiously attend to God's ailing poor.

After all had signed the minutes written out by Jérôme himself, it is pleasant to imagine they were served an excellent glass of wine, despite Gresset's caustic remark a century later about the La Flèche vintages, un petit vin assez potable, a humble glass of wine sufficiently drinkable. It was the least they could do to celebrate the official conclusion of fifteen years' strife in the civil and ecclesiastical courts of the Kingdom of France.

The City Council had approved of the Constitutions in December 1639, and since 1641, several aspirants had folded away each today into the yesterdays illumined by this tentatively approved rule. They had stormed heaven to be allowed to pronounce their vows in the not too distant future. However, would Bishop de Rueil, who did not approve of their way of life until 1643, be satisfied with their uncanonical novitiate, carried out before his official stamp of approval was received?

In the first days of 1644, Jérôme Le Royer and René de Boistaillé decided to find out. The prelate received them favorably and set the date of the vesture, the vows, and the election of the first superior for January 22,[14] then celebrated in the diocese of Angers as the feast of the Espousals of Mary and Joseph, and one of the community Communion days according to the rule book.

On January 19, Bishop de Rueil commissioned Fr. Pierre Syette, one of Jérôme's friends, to preside over the ceremony. The La Flèche tax collector had known him as a young curate at Bazouges in the close neighbourhood of La Flèche. Now the list of Syette's attributions stretched out nearly as long as his bishop's train. He had a licentiate in church law and was Canon and head cantor of the 12th-century St. Maurice cathedral in Angers. Besides chanting the Divine Office daily, he was the Assistant Director of the officiality and Vicar-General of the diocese. The bishop, in his declining years, had taken the habit of sending his faithful Syette to represent him at those functions he would have taken part in had his health permitted. As for Jérôme, he could always count upon the Vicar-General to back him up in all his requests to Bishop de Rueil. Never once did Fr. Syette fail Monsieur Le Royer, not even in the turbid years ahead, after Claude de Rueil's death.

As soon as the date of the vow day was known, the "novices" began cutting out and sewing their black habits. They had previously dressed as their friends outside the hospital walls. A small headpiece, a dark skirt and a jumper had comprised the distinctive features of their apparel, without, however, any of the gewgaws or bright scarlet aprons so dear to the heart of La Flèche womanhood. The new linen wimple was square-cut, protecting only the front of the throat. Vaguely wattle-shaped on each side, it fell upon a large white kerchief and was topped by a white bandeau, all of the same material. A close-fitting bonnet and a piece of black taffeta for veil completed the attire.[15]

Little other manual labor was allowed them. With some friends, Jérôme took care of the material preparations for the long-anticipated day. He also took a good part in the readying of the Sisters spiritually, for during the month he gave a series of 30 lectures to the Hospitallers.[16] What a sight it must have been to see this collector of taxes, whom the American historian Francis Parkman depicts as "a squat, uncourtly figure, and not proficient in the graces either of manners or of speech," [17] moving his listeners to tears!

This extraordinary lay instructor then had the little band of women follow a retreat under the direction of one of his Jesuit friends, very likely Fr. Dubreuil.[18] Obviously the "praise, honor, and serve God" of the Ignatian Principle and Foundation were taken seriously by these virtuous women, when on January 22, 1644, dawned the great day of the full approval of the new group of nurses by the Church. Reaching La Flèche on the twenty-first and taking Fr. Sébastien Cador, a local Notary Apostolic as his secretary, with M. Le Royer, Vicar-General Syette made a first visit to the Hôtel Dieu.[19] The future Daughters of St. Joseph welcomed him and presented him with the original copy of the Constitutions. In a detailed report he afterwards dictated, he left the names of these valiant ladies for us to honor. The first ones were those of Marie de la Ferre and her followers, who had been legally commissioned during November of the previous year by Jérôme and his brother, René, to take charge of the Hôtel Dieu. To them must be added those of the "domestic" or lay Sisters —faithful Jeanne Cohergne, Catherine Lebouc, Julienne Allory, Anne Baillif, Louise Bidault. Finally, not to be forgotten, were the postulants: Marie Havard, Thérèse Madeleine Havard, Catherine Macé and little Marie Houzé, whose hearts went pit-a-pat beneath the somber workaday clothes that they were to exchange for the newly made habits 24 hours later.

The next morning at seven o'clock, before a brilliant congregation including representatives of the diocesan and regular clergies, the Marquis de la Varenne, Governor of La Flèche, the other notables of the region, Jérôme and his brother, René, Marie de la Ferre and her "novices," Fr. Syette formally presented his credentials in the new St. Joseph Chapel and read in a sonorous voice Bishop Claude De Rueil's decree of the previous October, establishing the Daughters of St. Joseph canonically, and promulgated their Constitutions. Probably at Marie de la Ferre's suggestion, the patients who were well enough to leave their wards and drag themselves to the chapel were present[20] and they, along with the nobility in their velvets and fine serges, served as witnesses.

After blessing the habits of the candidates, the Vicar-

General invited them to come for the new apparel and, as he vested in red for the Mass of the Holy Spirit, they filed decorously out of the chapel. Ten minutes later, they returned dressed in their habits and took their places at the altar railing as the congregation craned their necks to get a better view of them. The bishop's delegate then admonished Marie de la Ferre and her 11 companions to proceed in all sincerity and to consider attentively the significance of the vows they were about to pronounce.

Fr. Syette thereupon received the oath of the three scrutineers to accomplish faithfully their duty during the forthcoming elections. The oldest of them handed him the packets of ballots, some of which he in turn gave to one of the scrutineers for distribution to those designated by the Constitutions to cast lots.

During the Holy Sacrifice, the twelve women received Holy Communion from the celebrant's hand. After the Deo Gratias, they gathered round a table placed at the foot of the altar and, alternating with him and the rest of the clergy, chanted the *Veni Creator*. Following another prayer, the Daughters of St. Joseph took the simple vows of poverty, chastity, and obedience for one year. The fifth one to consecrate herself to Christ in His poor was Jeanne Le Royer, Jérôme Le Royer's and Jeanne de Baugé's flesh and blood—so different yet so beautiful in her unfamiliar dress. Not unexpectedly, the official report makes no mention of her parents' impressions on this day of days, but they can easily be imagined.

After Sr. Louise Bidault had read the last words of her vow-formula and the laity had withdrawn, the prelate requested the lay Sisters to leave also, because they were not empowered to vote. To one side he ordered the three scrutineers and to the other, the chaplain, Fr. Jean Gyrot, and Frs. Louis Lecerf and Etienne Gusson, his assistants for the elections. Each Sister wrote down her choice and when the votes were counted, Sr. Marie de la Ferre was designated as the first superior of the Daughters of St. Joseph for the next three years... one dissident vote was recorded—her own.

As the bells of the hospital chapel rang out and as the clergy and the Sisters sang their *Te Deum*, did Jérôme's thoughts revert to the first alms received for the new Hôtel Dieu from a poor woman and her child recognized by him as Jesus and Mary? Joseph, the poorest of the three, had given nothing at that moment, however the spiritual and material foundations of the hospital were entrusted to him. Hadn't the Holy Family been entrusted to his care?

Chapter XVI

Notes

1.*RPA*, Vol. 4, p. 272.

2. Morin, *Histoire Simple et Véritable*, p. 185.

3. *NA*, p. 292.

4. *RPA*, Vol. 4, p. 273. Our Lady of Montfaucon is in the diocese of Nantes. Morin, *Histoire Simple et Véritable*, p. 186, writes he was then "a young clergyman."

5. *Ibid.*, Vol. 3. pp. 252-257.

6. *VJLD*, Vol. 1, pp. 269-273.

7. *Ibid.*, Vol. 2, pp. 278-279.

8. *AM*, p. 35: Couanier de Launay, *Histoire des Religieuses Hospitalières de Saint-Joseph*, Vol. 1, p. 123.

9. *RPA*, Vol. 3, pp. 257-258.

10. *Ibid.*, p. 262.

11. *Ibid.*, pp. 258-259.

12. *Ibid.*, pp. 260-261.

13. Nicolas de Sol de la Brunelière, François Bertereau des Preaux, René Ollivier de la Guittière, and François Syette, practitioner.

14. *AM*, p. 37.

15. *Ibid.*, p. 36.

16. *RPA*, Vol. 4, p. 268.

17. Francis Parkman, *The Jesuits in North America in the Seventeenth Century, Vol. 2, France and England in North America,* (Boston, 1897, p. 13.) On p. [3], he gives a more favourable description of La Dauversière, "His look is that of a grave burgher, of good renown and sage deportment." Sage deportment must include some proficiency of manner. See above, p. 8.

18. *NA*, p. 312.

19. *RPA*, Vol. 4, pp. 268-272.

20. Eight women and nine men: Julien Goguelet, Urbain Biais, Michel Douesnard, Jacques Langlois, François

Mersanne, Mathurin Testu, Louis Chevalier, François Gaulin, and Jean Goueslard; Michèle Touret, Perrine Robin, Nicole Vaslin, Urbaine Coherne, Urbaine Bournault, Marguerite Porcher, Catherine Beaumont, and Martha Amelot.

Chapter XVII

Anne Baillif's Return

A FEW DAYS LATER, Bishop de Rueil complimented the new Institute for its choice of a superior, causing "great satisfaction on all sides." [1] On the following February 2, 1644, the elections of Mother de la Ferre's Council resulted in the appointment of Srs. Anne de L'Espicier as assistant, Renée Busson as mistress of novices, Anne Le Tendre as chief hospitaller, and Anne Foureau as bursar. [2]

In his decree instituting the Congregation, the Bishop had collectively declared it a member of the Holy Family Confraternity established at the Hôtel Dieu. [3] In those days, each hospitaller, taking Jesus, Mary, and Joseph as her models, served the sick poor with an ardor so communicative that it attracted the charity of "ladies of quality" and, eventually, many of the ladies themselves. The Sisters were faithful to their rules, in particular to that of interior silence, without which no deepening of divine love in the soul is possible. [4]

With the summer months, the first cross since the formal approbation of the Hôtel Dieu Sisters was thrown upon the shoulders of Jérôme Le Royer and of Marie de la Ferre: one of their lay Sisters, Anne Baillif, died. [5] She was only twenty-eight years old. The priests, her guides in the world before and after her entrance into religious life, urged the Daughters of St. Joseph to write up the virtues of this saintly woman in order to edify the generations of hospitallers to come. [6] Because of the burden of work at the time, no one was named to prepare the biographical notes. God, in His own way saw to it.

About ten o'clock on Wednesday evening, December 14, Mother de la Ferre, who had been deterred from retiring at the regular hour, made her way soft-slippered out of her cell down the corridor to one of the archways overlooking the chapel.[7] After a busy day, it was high time to ask the good Lord for a "quiet night and a perfect end." As she opened the shutters, she noticed a bright light. Her first impression was that it came from the wards below, next to the chapel. She had forgotten that all the doors were closed. After a moment of prayer, as she turned back towards her little room, she was halted in her footsteps by someone moaning. A second time, quite distinctly, the sound came up to her, drawing her down.

As she visited the wards on the lower floor a few minutes later, the heavy breathing of the patients told her all was normal. Since she was so close to Our Lord in the Blessed Sacrament, she opened the chapel door for a moment of adoration. Before her startled eyes, at the center of the altar steps, facing the tabernacle, loomed a white-covered form.*

Fear jumped at her and she quickly shut the door. With a quick-beating pulse, she ran to awaken Sr. Catherine

---

* Apparitions like Sr. Baillif's are not unusual in the history of the Church. Six days after her death in 1680, Blessed Kateri Tekakwitha appeared to Fr. Claude Chauchetière for two hours; she appeared again to him on September 1, 1681 and on April 21, 1682. (Beatificationis et canonizationis servae Dei Catharinae Tekakwitha virginis indianae (+1680), Positio super introductione causae et super virtutibus ex officio compilata, Typis polyglottis Vaticanae, 1938, pp. 218-220.) Another example, closer to us, was the apparition of Luigi Comollo shortly after his death, to his friend, St. John Bosco. In 1839, both were seminarians at the Major Seminary of Turin. The first apparition took place in their dormitory and was witnessed by some twenty seminarians on the night of April 2, 1839, as well as on the second, the following night. "Bosco, Bosco," cried out Comollo, "I am saved!" (Memorie Biografiche di Don Giovanni Bosco, recolta dal sac. Salesiano Giovanni Battista Lemoyne. Vol. 1, San Benigno, Canavese, Italy, 1898, pp. 469; 472-473.)

Lebouc, sleeping in the women's ward. Once more, Mother de la Ferre opened the door of the chapel, this time with the Sister beside her. There it was again, the very same form. Slowly it moved and advanced towards them.

Sr. Lebouc was intrigued. She didn't know who or what it was and decided to find out, "Who goes there?" she questioned.

All in a dither as you or I would be, her Superior ordered her to keep quiet and to shut the door promptly. Perhaps it was a soul from Purgatory. Suddenly in Sr. Lebouc's mind the thought flashed that it could be the late Sr. Baillif, a lay Sister like herself. For several minutes Mother de la Ferre and her companion tried hard to pray, but who shall blame them if a few distractions crept into their Hail Marys? At last they screwed up their courage and flung open the wooden door again. Except for the soft gleam of the sanctuary lamp, all was dark in the chapel. Nervously they climbed to the community cells on the upper story, but from the archway where Mother de la Ferre had first seen the white light, nothing unusual caught the eye. The visitor was gone.

Sleep did not favor the Superior during the ensuing night and, the next morning, she sent a note to M. Le Royer soliciting his advice. He hurried over and listened to her astonishing tale. What should she do if the spectre appeared once more? As Jérôme had had no experience with ghosts, and as he was convinced of the Mother's sincerity, he decided to consult Fr. Dubreuil at the Royal College. The apparition did not see fit to wait for the Jesuit's say before manifesting itself anew.

Towards the end of the afternoon, accompanied by lay Sr. Julienne, who knew nothing of the events of the previous night, Mother de la Ferre made the rounds of the community garden to see if all were in order. As they looked about they saw a strange being under the vine

213

arbor. It began walking unhurriedly towards them. Overcome by fright, the Superior would have slumped to the ground had not Sr. Julienne upheld her. "Reverend Mother," she urged, "let's go meet her; it's Sister Anne!"

Since Mother de la Ferre would have none of it, the little Sister helped her back to the security of the hospital. But not without several backward glances in the direction of the apparition, until it could no longer be seen. Neither of them turned into a block of salt, and much to the Superior's relief, M. Le Royer met them with Fr. Dubreuil's instructions. Now she would know how to welcome a visitor from the other world. Within the Hôtel Dieu, not a soul except Mother de la Ferre and the two lay Sisters had the slightest idea of the goings-on. They were determined to keep the secret to themselves.

During examination of conscience at half past eight in the evening, the Reverend Mother heard Sr. Baillif sighing. In a trice, she was at Sr. Lebouc's room and informed her of the latest development. With commendable self-mastery, she then returned to her cell and tried to sleep. Nobody will blame her for having placed a lighted lamp next to her cot. . . .

In the dark, cold building, once again all was quiet. The clock in the chapel rang out nine, then ten o'clock. The last stroke had scarcely echoed through the corridors when the bursar, Sr. Anne Foureau, heard someone knocking at her door. Then twice again she heard it. Thinking her superior was ill and in need of assistance, she arose and went to her door. The corridor was empty. Afraid, she knew not of what, she rushed to Mother de la Ferre's room. The door was shut tight, and her apprehension grew. She dared not return to her little cell, and not wishing to disturb the good Mother, hesitated as to what she had better do. Finally, her anxiety drove her to rap on the closed door, and a second later she was within the room.

Although she knew not a thing about the visitations, her fear changed into a visceral fright on learning that Mother de la Ferre had not knocked at her door. In a panic she threw herself on the foot of the superior's small bed. At that moment, robed in white, stood before them a figure of the same build as Sr. Baillif.

With trembling hand and quavering voice, Mother de la Ferre made the Sign of the Cross and, as well as she could, spoke as she had been directed by Jérôme Le Royer and Fr. Dubreuil, "If you come from God, speak!"

Without giving her a chance to continue, the ethereal visitor bowed slightly and spoke:

"I have come from God to tell you that you are too indulgent in having the Rules observed exactly. Many imperfections are being committed against them and before God you shall be held responsible for them. Love your Rules! Love your Rules! Love your Rules! They are from God. They were inspired by the Holy Spirit. See to it that the First, the Ninth, the Fifteenth Chapters[8] and the Chapter on union (among yourselves) be observed. Your charity is not perfect. It is made up of several elements, two of which are necessary for your Community: the first one does not see (the faults of others), the other sees (their qualities very well). Silence is not kept. Your recreations are quite imperfect and those on the Vigils of Communion Days greatly displease God, for lack of preparation. Be careful about lengthy conversations with outsiders: they are displeasing to God. There are little unfounded acts of envy; beware of them! You are all wanting in humility. I have suffered much, at death, having been faulty with regard to my vow of poverty concerning what you found in my chest and for a paper that was there. Also for my futile recreations and regarding obedience, for a lack of submission."

The little lamp flickered momentarily beside the bed and the voice paused briefly before continuing:

"Have compassion on the Lay Sisters: they are the weaker group. You do not support one another enough. Some commit serious faults. I'll not name them. Jesus Christ didn't name Judas. You are lacking in devotion to St. Joseph and are not getting others to honor him in this house, although he is your powerful protector with a throng of his intimates."

Then came the final admonition:

"O Love, O Love, O Love divine! May it prepare eternal crowns for you, provided that you keep your Rules well. Let nothing of all this disturb you. Be in peace and let your downfalls help you rise before God. Tell this to all the Sisters and write it down for perpetual memory and never allow it to be taken out of the house! Let not this apparition worry you. It was necessary for me to appear to several of you in order that none would have any doubts. Farewell, farewell, farewell! You will see me again only in heaven."[9]

As Sr. Anne Baillif disappeared, Mother Marie de la Ferre and Sr. Anne Foureau were plunged into bliss. The Superior's first thought was to send for Sr. Catherine Lebouc, who had witnessed the first apparition. She, too, shared in the happiness of the other two.

The next day, December 16, 1644, in compliance with Sr. Bailiff's instructions and at the suggestion of "persons of great piety, knowledge, and experience," namely, Jérôme Le Royer, Fr. Dubreuil, and Canon Syette, Mother de la Ferre wrote out on parchment a detailed account of the apparitions. Before the entire community met again, both she and Sr. Foureau signed it, and the two lay Sisters, who did not know how to write, added their crosses below. This document was countersigned by Canon Syette.[10]

What did Jérôme, the founder of the Daughters of St. Joseph, think about it all? He was aware of the deep flow of the Sisters' spiritual life. He knew that more than one highly experienced priest admired their interior and exte-

216

rior fidelity to the Constitutions. He was acquainted with Mother de la Ferre's perfect adhesion to the Will of God and must have quietly smiled when, in the report on the different visions, she depicted herself as frightened and the lay Sisters as courageous during the various manifestations. For years he had known, since Fr. Chauveau's approval of his plans, that the Rules were heaven-sent. He had unequivocally been commanded from above to prepare them. Now these sensitive visions, perceived by several religious, ratified the entire Constitutions in their eyes and in those of most of the Daughters of St. Joseph.

The reference to the "wanting in humility" and to the "little unfounded acts of envy" apparently applied to the Sisters who were still unconvinced deep down that the Constitutions were God-given, and were secretly desirous that their simple vows would some day be replaced by the solemn vows of the older monastic Orders.[11] Sr. Baillif unflatteringly qualified these religious as Judases. Jesus Himself had spoken even worse of St. Peter when He called him Satan. Furthermore, sins of pride and envy were conceivable among these Sisters, for the just man sins several times daily!

The message, it must be stressed, rests upon the topic sentence; otherwise the entire communication is thrown out of perspective. "You are too indulgent," the Superior had been informed, "in having the Rules exactly observed; many imperfections are being committed..." The Daughters of St. Joseph were called to high perfection and correspondingly, the graces they received were greater than the average. By rebound, their failings in the eyes of God took on a deeper malignancy, somewhat as in the eyes of St. Teresa of Avila a voluntary venial sin seemed serious.

This view is borne out by Anne Baillif's accusation that St. Joseph was not honored enough, of all places, in the Hôtel Dieu consecrated to him. Yet Jérôme Le Royer and

217

Marie de la Ferre were the first to promote devotion to him at La Flèche. They had established the Confraternity of the Holy Family, built the first shrine to St. Joseph in their province, and written into the Constitutions that each day after the noon recreation, during the visit to the Blessed Sacrament, the Sisters were to recite a prayer to their common patron for the patients and the hospital benefactors.[12] The same prayer was to be said in the wards, both in the morning and evening. On Saturday, abstinence was observed in honor of the Holy Family. On many other occasions, the Daughters of St. Joseph were directed to invoke the aid of their patron. Was the devotion of the Sisters to the foster father of Christ merely superficial? Of all of them, most of the time? Hardly.

At first glance, one is surprised on reading the list of Sr. Baillif's transgressions, coupled with her statement that, because of them, she had suffered much at death. One is even more surprised at Sr. Adèle Joséphine Grosjean, writing in 1887, that on account of venial sins, covered by a multitude of good works," [13] the soul of the young lay Sister had been detained for more than seven months in purgatory. As bad as Pandora's box, a chest in her room furnished the evidence of her guilt. She had deposited in it eighteen deniers (less than one cent), which had been given to her in the capacity of house seamstress to buy some needles, a leather discipline which she should have used but didn't. Sister simply kept it because she liked it as well as the poster. The poster advertised a play by the students at the Jesuit college! So much for her faults against religious poverty! [14]

During recreation she cracked a few innocent jokes. For this, one would think, her stay in purgatory should have been shortened. Perhaps, however, at the bottom of it all, there was a hidden seeking of self or an excess of purely natural fun, which may have resulted during evening silence in distracting the Sisters from the peaceful indwelling of the Blessed Trinity within their hearts. Bossuet in his sermon on the Assumption of Our Lady to the Court of France in 1663, draws attention to the divine jealousy of the Creator, brooking no competition in the souls of his intimates. If Sr. Baillif did suffer in purgatory, should it not be ascribed to occasional lapses of obedience, the corner-stone of religious life?

Be that as it may, Jérôme Le Royer and Fr. Dubreuil took steps to remedy the Daughters of St. Joseph's failing. The Jesuit, who had promised to give one instruction a week to the Sisters during Advent, decided to give two until the renewal of vows in the following January.[15]

With all the guarantees of the authenticity of the apparitions, a few members of the community pooh-poohed them. Infinitely gracious, God granted them a series of special manifestations. On January 15, 1645, in the community work-room, while the Sisters were busy together, a loud bang was heard.[16] Simultaneously the minutes of the apparitions appeared before all. The community was properly frightened. Some time later, after Mother de la Ferre had placed the document in her coffer, it was laid by unseen hands on the altar before the Blessed Sacrament. One of the sceptics obtained permission to hide it away under lock and key. It was then discovered beneath the cot of another Sister who had no faith in the story and was sorely tempted to leave the religious life. Only after it had been decided to read it each month to the community, did the document settle down. So well, in fact, that ever since, it has stayed put.

Chapter XVII

Notes

1. *AM*, p. 44.

2. *NA*, p. 316.

3. *Ibid.*, p. 317.

4. *RPA*, Vol. 4, pp. 279-280.

5. *Ibid.*, p. 274.

6. *Ibid.*

7. *Ibid.*, pp. 275-279.

8. The first chapter deals with the aim of the Institute and the means to attain it; the 11th, with the conduct of the Sisters with regard to outsiders; and the 15th, with the daily schedule.

9. When one compares the praises heaped upon the Daughters of St. Joseph at that period by the priests who knew them with Sr. Baillif's admonitions, one wonders what to think about the apparitions. Mother Adolphine Gaudin, writing two centuries and a quarter later comments, "It is clear that there were apparitions, but we don't know whether they were of divine or diabolical origin." (*RPA*, Vol. 4, p. 279) If one takes into account the Ignatian "discernment of spirits," however, they seem to have been heaven-sent.

10. *La Flèche Hôtel-Dieu Archives, Number f.C., 2nd Dossier, 1644*; *Apparition de ma soeur Anne Le Baillif*, according to *RPA*, Vol. 4, p. 279.

11. *NA*, p. 327.

12. *Constitions- [primitives] des Filles Hospitalières de Sainct Ioseph*, Ch. XV, art. 6; Ch. XVI, art. 2; Ch. XIV, art. 3; Ch. XIX, art. 6; Ch. XXIII, art. 8.

13. *NA*, p. 352.

14. *AM*, p. 54.

15. *NA*, p. 355.

16. *RPA*, Vol. 4, p. 280.

Chapter XVIII

The Duchess Was Adamant

DURING THESE IMPORTANT YEARS, Jérôme Le Royer had more to do than to give advice about an ethereal apparition, sympathetic though it may have been. On the afternoon of January 12, 1644, he left his room in Paris at the Fleur de Lys Inn on the still existing street of the Marmousets in the parish of St. Pierre aux Boeufs, and made his way to the study of Notary Chaussière within the stern walls of the Royal Châtelet.[1] He was joined by Bertrand Drouart, gentleman ordinary to the Duc d'Orléans and secretary of the Montreal group. Both were welcomed by Chaussière and his partner Pourcel.

Jeanne Mance's letter addressed to the "Unknown Benefactress," Madame de Bullion, and suggesting that the funds promised to the Montreal hospital be given to the Huronian missions had reached the great lady towards the end of 1643. Having decided to stand by Le Royer and his project, according to the God-given orders he had received, the duchess was adamant and rejected the transfer.[2]

Jérôme informed the notaries that the wealthy contributor had the intention of founding and building a hospital on the Island of Montreal in Canada "to treat, doctor, feed, and dress the wounds of the destitute sick of the said country, and have them instructed in the things necessary for salvation."[3] In honor of St. Joseph, she was donating 42,000 livres tournois to the undertaking. Of this sum, 4,000 livres were to be used for the food, upkeep, and salaries of the ten workmen gone to Montreal in June 1643 to erect the Hôtel Dieu, and, also, for food to be dispensed to the friendly Indians and other visitors who knocked at the door of the hospital. In the papers containing Madame de Bullion's "foundation for the sick of the Island of Montreal," it was stipulated that the remaining 38,000 livres were to be invested and the revenue applied as Jérôme Le Royer and Bertrand Drouart guaranteed, to the maintenance of the future Hôtel Dieu.

Backed by the generous duchess, Jérôme promptly set the new capital to work. A Parisian gentleman, Jacques Labbé de Bellegarde, owned quite a few estates in Normandy. Was it with the aid of the Baron de Renty, a native of this province, that Jérôme was introduced to Labbé? At any rate, not long afterwards through Drouart, who served as his agent, the founder of Ville Marie agreed to several transactions with him, all in the interest of the Montreal Hôtel Dieu.[4]

After the death of Louis XIII, Jérôme and his friends had counted on the Queen Regent, Anne of Austria, to further their efforts in New France. Rightly so. Some of the courtiers, Montreal Associates or their friends, drew her attention to conditions on the island. She graciously deigned to favor Ville Marie. On February 13, 1644, she signed the Letters Patent under the five-year-old King's name, taking the Island of Montreal under his protection.[5] She did this along with a pride of peers of the kingdom, among them His Majesty's uncle, the Duc d'Orléans, and Henri de Condé, sometime viceroy of New France.

The royal document's effects far surpassed those of Louis XIII's letter to Governor de Montmagny. The deceased king's letter had not, after all, given to the Montreal group a permanent, incontestable right to organize an island center in the St. Lawrence for the welfare of Indians desiring to become Christian.

Had Jérôme Le Royer been Peter Pan's identical twin he would have danced with glee because of the privileges granted to Ville Marie. The Crown, in effect, ratified the contracts providing M. Le Royer and the Baron de Fancamp with the title to the distant island, and allowed the former to name its own governor, who was to continue the construction of fortifications and homes for Christian Indians as well as for the French. The authorization was also given to further the whites and the aborigines with the necessities of life, even arms and ammunition, if necessary. The settlement was to be organized on a civic basis and the St. Lawrence River was unrestrictedly opened to the inhabitants of Ville Marie. Finally, Le Royer and Fancamp were empowered to give and receive legacies and endowments for the care of poor Indians and for "that of the clergy both regular and secular, living there at the time or who would live there in the future."

A month later, on the afternoon of March 25, with his friend, Pierre de Fancamp, Jérôme acknowledged this in an official document stating that the Island of Montreal—made over to them by Intendant de Lauson at Vienne in 1640 and then confirmed by the Company of New France in Paris—was destined to the Montreal Associates for the conversion of the Indians of New France, and not to themselves personally.[6]

The next day, in accordance with the Letters Patent of the previous month, on behalf of the Company of Montreal, Paul de Chomedey was commissioned governor of Ville Marie,[7] a nomination that proclaimed its autonomy to the world at large. By one of the early ships, probably the *Notre Dame*, sailing for New France that spring, Jérôme notified his friend he had been appointed governor of the island colony.

Unaware of his promotion, Chomedey was living up to Le Royer's fondest expectations. He watched over the little settlement bravely and prudently. Since the loss of five men in June 1643, he had issued orders to safeguard each and all of them. The sound of the bell gathered them together, whenever, well armed, they left for work outside the bastions. At noon, it called them back to the protection of the fort.[8] Meanwhile, the Iroquois lay hidden in the neighboring forest, ready to pounce on every solitary straggler.

The most restless of the pioneers were for an out and out attack against the lurking foe. Much to their disgust, the governor restrained them. Luckily their little pack of watch-dogs, with Pilotte at their head, were past masters at scenting out the assailants. If the Iroquois approached the Habitation, they howled and snarled in their direction, thereby saving the lives of many settlers. On these occasions, the more impetuous of Paul de Chomedey's men grumbled because of what seemed to them sheer lack of courage on their leader's part.

"If we chase them as you desire," he said, "since we are but a handful and little skilled in wood fighting, we shall all at once be caught in an ambush where there will be twenty Iroquois to one Frenchman. Only have patience until God gives us enough men, then we will risk these actions, but at the moment, if would be rash to risk losing everything at one blow; it would be to discharge very badly the trust committed to me." [9]

On March 30, as the dogs with Pilotte at their head were reconnoitring around the fort, they began to bark in the direction of the concealed enemy. Some of the hot-headed Frenchmen were then completely convinced that the governor was a coward since he always avoided engagements. When these comments reached his ears, "he decided that it would be better to risk everything rashly on one good throw than to let them believe what might continue to grow and even wreck his whole enterprise." [10]

As the dogs kept on howling, his men rushed to him. "Sir," they said, "the enemy is in the wood, in such a direction; are we never to go after them?"

Paul de Chomedey retorted, "Yes, you will see them; make ready to set out very soon; I trust you will be as brave as you say you are. I will lead you."

The snow was deep and there were only a few pair of snowshoes for all of them. Still they hurriedly prepared for the attack. After leaving the habitation in Louis d'Ailleboust's care, the commander marched out with thirty of his men. On entering among the shadows of the leafless trees, a volley of about 200 shots met them.

Seeing his men in danger, Chomedey ordered them to take refuge behind the trees in Indian fashion. Then followed a brisk exchange of musketry until the ammunition was exhausted. After several Frenchmen were killed or wounded, he gave the signal for retreat. This was no easy matter as the French and Iroquois were closely engaged, and the latter well equipped with native rackets (snowshoes) and skillful in their use. Accordingly the settlers, as Dollier de Casson noted, "were hardly as mobile as infantry compared with cavalry."

Still they obeyed their commander, at first without haste, making all the while for a track used to haul wood for construction purposes, because it was hard, and easy to walk on without rackets. On setting foot on the sleigh road, in a panic they dashed to the fort, leaving their leader, who had waited for the wounded to be evacuated, exposed to capture.

With a pistol in each hand, Paul de Chomedey now faced the Iroquois alone. They recognized him as the white chief and tried to take him alive with the purpose of torturing him at leisure. Then they made a serious mistake. They delayed somewhat, preferring to reserve the actual capture to their own chief. But the would-be captor fared badly. Chomedey, bothered by this Indian, who was, as it were, constantly on top of him, he turned about to shoot him. The chieftain ducked to avoid the shot, but as Chomedey's pistol missed fire, he leapt at him in fury. The weapon in the commander's other hand went off and killed the assailant outright. As he was much closer to him than his companions, his death allowed Paul de Chomedey the opportunity of outdistancing them, before they reached the slain warrior. Instead of continuing in hot pursuit of their fleeing enemy, they halted, lifted their dead leader from the blood-stained snow to their shoulders and carried him off, lest he fall into the hands of the white soldiers.

Their respect for their chief saved Chomedey, who had time enough to find security within the walls of the Habitation. There he learned that his men had nearly been blown to pieces. One of the pioneers inside the little fort, at the sight of his friends retreating helter skelter, set a match to the cannon without aiming it. Happily, the priming was so bad it did not go off. "Had it done so," commented Dollier de Casson, already quoted, "it was laid so truly along the little road by which they approached, that it would have killed them all."

What were the casualties on both sides? The enemy had mortally wounded Guillaume Lebeau, who was buried on the same day; killed Jean Mattemale and Pierre Bigot, whose funeral took place on the following morning, and made two captives, who would slowly be burnt to death during four days.[11] How many had the Iroquois lost? Nobody knows, for they took with them not only the body of their chief, but also the other dead, if there were some, along with the wounded. All in all, the sortie was beneficial to Ville Marie. The colonists were now convinced their leader was of the stuff heroes are made of and thereafter none blamed him for his prudent conduct.

In May or early June, the Habitation closed its door on three of the fold: Madame de la Peltrie with her maid, Charlotte Barré, and Monsieur de Puiseaux, who boarded the pinnace about to sail downstream to Quebec.[12] The idea of being close to the Indians had prompted the noblewoman to accompany Mademoiselle Mance to Montreal. There she had remained despite the efforts of Governor de Montmagny and the Jesuit Fathers to have her return to

227

the Ursuline monastery, where she could be useful to (Blessed) Marie de l'Incarnation. Since the Algonquins were avoiding the danger zone that the Island of Montreal had become, Madame de la Peltrie made up her mind to work with the missionaries at Fort St. Marie in Huronia. It had taken one of them to dissuade her. On the other hand there was no longer any point to her staying at Ville Marie, so, after a tearful good-bye to Mademoiselle Mance, Madame d'Ailleboust and Mademoiselle de Boullongne, she returned to Quebec where she would be in contact with at least a small band of Indian children and be able to devote herself to them.

A different reason explains Monsieur de Puiseaux's departure. Following an attack of paralysis, his mind had been affected, and he made it clear that he wanted to recover his donation to Ville Marie in order to return to Europe for treatment. This was no small request, for he had been extremely generous to Ville Marie.

"Sir," answered Paul de Chomedey, "we have done nothing for gain, everything is still yours, be easy on that point. I will give you what you need here, and I will recommend you to the gentlemen of the company in France, who will abundantly acknowledge the good that you have done."[13]

Puiseaux was well taken care of in Quebec until he sailed for France in the autumn of the year, and in the motherland until his death in 1647, at the age of 77 or 78, by Jérôme Le Royer and his friends.

The rest of the year, the Iroquois kept the population on the alert. From springtime on, divided into ten squads, they threw terror into the hearts not only of the white men but also of the Hurons and Algonquins. Five bands of warriors roved the St. Lawrence from Montreal to Trois-Rivières, the others higher up on the river and beyond, as far inland as Huronia.[14] As very few friendly Indians dared approach the settlement, no baptisms were then recorded.

Help finally arrived from France during the summer. The Queen Regent contributed a force of 60 men and 100,000 livres to train and equip them.[15] These soldiers were distributed among the Canadian posts, and several of them stationed at Ville Marie. With them came another party of at least 20 farmers and laborers hired by Jérôme Le Royer.[16] Two small cannons at La Rochelle, noticed by him during his frequent visits, of no use whatsoever to the busy port, were forwarded to Ville Marie, obviously at his suggestion.[17]

Of the new arrivals, two engaged by Jérôme or by his assistants proved unsatisfactory. Michel Chauvin, alias Sainte-Suzanne, settled in Ville Marie and three years later, in Quebec, married Anne Archambault. In March 1650, he had a child by her, but in October of the same year, it was discovered that he already had a wife in France.[18] There was no place for a bigamist in New France and he vanished from sight to lead a better life, it is hoped, wherever he was.

The leader of the 1644 recruits, Captain de la Barre, was the other unfortunate choice. His given name is unknown to us; The dramatist Molière would have called him the hypocritical Tartuffe. "At La Rochelle, he wore at his belt a large rosary with a big crucifix which he had almost continually before his eyes, so that he entered this country as a man of apostolic piety to whom had been entrusted the command. ...This person looking like Virtue itself, stayed in Montreal all the following year, but he was finally discovered through the frequent walks that he took in the woods with an Indian woman, whom he made pregnant, thereby making clear the falsity of his fine pretences..." [19]

These two men were exceptions, who did little enough to harm the settlement as a whole, since the island was rid of them almost as soon as their true colors were revealed.

On the same ship that had brought the two miscreants to Canada, came the news of the "Unknown Benefactress' " contract of the previous January. It left no doubt about her intentions regarding the hospital. Indeed, convinced it was already completed, the great lady forwarded Mademoiselle Mance "2,000 livres, three pieces of church plate and some household goods, sending her all as if she were living in the hospital." [20] Nevertheless, a year would escape before it opened its doors.

For the winter months ahead, the Montrealers were privileged to have as their spiritual guides two Jesuits of note: Fr. Isaac Jogues and Fr. Jacques Buteux.[21] In 1652, the latter was killed by the Iroquois on his way to Hudson Bay and his body thrown into a nearby river; Fr. Jogues, whose devotion to the Iroquois was to earn him martyrdom in 1646, had already suffered at their hands. Each morning as he offered the Holy Sacrifice, the colonists saw him lifting up the consecrated host with hands bereft of their two forefingers and his left thumb, which he had lost in 1642 during the tortures inflicted upon him at Ossernenon, today Auriesville, New York. The sight of this gentle priest, a man of culture, possessed of a heart patterned on that of Christ, gently serving the settlers as the days shortened and the nights grew longer, renewed their courage, their strength, and their faith in the "foolish venture."

Across the sea 1645 started with a significant change in the management of the Company of New France. The Quebec and Trois-Rivières settlers submitted to the Crown that New France would never prosper as long as the One Hundred Associates monopolized the Canadian pelt traffic. Because of this monopoly, the acquisition of a decent competency was impossible. New settlers were thus discouraged from emigrating to Canada. His Majesty was urged to suppress the Company of New France's exclusive control of the fur trade.[22] The fat was in the fire! In Paris, the administrators debated the issue at its annual meeting on December 6, 1644, and at a subsequent one on January

230

7, 1645.[23] Finally, on the fourteenth of the month, they drew up and signed a treaty with the French inhabitants in the New World whereby the latter were conceded all rights to the pelt trade in Canada, with the exception, however, of Acadia, Miscou, and Cape Breton.[24] Six months later, on July 13, the Crown ratified the arrangements.[25] The Colony gained very little from the treaty, "a beautiful scheme on paper." [26]

On January 20, only six days after the signature of the treaty, Jérôme concluded an accommodation regarding Montreal with Legardeur de Repentigny, the head of the pioneers' deputation. A warehouse was to be opened on the island for the exchange of pelts and of merchandise; a garrison was to be maintained there with part of the income derived from the fur trade; and the percentage of profits accruing to the inhabitants was clearly stipulated. The Montreal Associates, furthermore, were to be notified of the arrival of the furs on French soil. In the person of their delegate, they were empowered to supervise the sale of the pelts and other goods in the homeland.[27] Neither Le Royer nor Repentigny foresaw that the hapless barter would soon be doomed for many years.

Although none of the colonists were allotted land before 1648, precisely because they had not yet consented, according to the terms of their contracts, to reside for good in Ville Marie, a sagacious initiative by Paul de Chomedey succeeded in creating a municipal corporation out of Ville Marie. An officer called a syndic, was chosen to watch over the interests of the people. He was to look after the general welfare of the island, see to the taxes needed for the upkeep of the garrison and bring to justice the evildoers who stole their neighbors' property. The position, however, was unremunerated, and could not be held for more than three consecutive years. The election generally took place in the depot of the Company of Montreal, to which the pioneers

231

resorted for all necessary food, clothing, and tools. This step in popular representation was the first in New France.[28]

During 1645, nobody in Jérôme Le Royer's little colony suffered from the Iroquois. His settlers, however, killed several of the attacking enemy. One of the latter, though he escaped unhurt, got the scare of his life. As the bell called the white men back to dinner, he advanced towards the fort and "climbed into a very thick and wide branching tree, most suitable to conceal him, and good for spying out when anyone returned.[29] After dinner, when the bell rang again, the Frenchmen returned to work in the woods. To his dismay they set a guard under the very tree on which he was perched, unknown to them. Dollier de Casson tells us this Indian ran a high fever all the time the tree was under guard, and well he might!

Before the last ship had sailed for France in 1644, Jeanne Mance had written to the charitable Duchesse de Bullion, acknowledging that she had been wise in refusing to change her endowment into one for the Huron missions as she had begged her, since the hospital was so much needed. She then added, "As soon as the house in which I now am was finished, it was at once filled... Therefore, if you could make a further gift, whereby I and one servant might be provided for, the 2,000 livres income could be given entirely to the poor, who would then be better provided for. Will you consider this? I scarcely dare propose it because I can hardly ask you for more." [30]

During the following summer of 1645, the gracious benefactress replied, "I am more anxious to give you what you need than you are to ask for it. To this end, I have placed 20,000 livres in the hands of the Company of Montreal, in order to invest for you; thus you may care for the poor without its being an expense to them; in addition I send you 20,000 livres this year." [31]

In the capacity of agent for the Company of Montreal,

Jérôme had sent Jeanne material aplenty, "to begin with, chapel furnishings, a chalice, a ciborium and a silver monstrance, candlesticks, a cross, a lamp, three altar adornments with all the linen, a Bergama tapestry, two covers or carpets, and other objects meant for church services; likewise the necessary furniture for the Hôtel Dieu, such as mattresses, bedclothes and linen, pewter and copper tableware, kettles and all the other household utensils; medicines for the ill, surgical instruments. Last of all was forwarded to her a menagerie composed of ten oxen, three cows and twenty sheep." [32] With the successful wheat crop Louis d'Ailleboust had persuaded the men to sow,[33] there would be enough for the sick and the wounded to enjoy a little variety in their menus, the best way to avoid scurvy!

For the newly arrived stock a stable was built, 30 feet in length by 12 in width and the four-acre pasture set aside for it was surrounded by a wall of thick logs.[34] This was no problem for Governor de Chomedey; the problem of the Hôtel Dieu, on the other hand left him in a quandary.

Fr. Jérôme Lalemant, S.J., en eye-witness, writing in October 1645, tells us the story: "When I arrived..., they had prepared a timber dwelling for our Fathers, and it seemed that there was nothing more to be done than to raise it; but, when they were on the point of doing so, the vessels arrived, bringing word and orders... to those who commanded at Montreal, to employ all the workmen for other things—namely, in erecting a hospital, for which large funds had been received in the preceding years; and yet no beginning had been made."

Governor de Chomedey found it hard to inform the Fathers of the news, and Fr. Lalemant took it upon himself to do so, and to persuade them to regard the matter favorably. "Afterward," he noted, "they flung the cat at my legs, as if I were the one who had hindered the work." [35]

What with the Jesuit and his cat, the Hôtel Dieu went up and was finally completed. The Christmas flood of 1641 was still fresh in the minds of all and the hospital was built on a knoll eight acres from the walls of the fort and farther away from the river than the other buildings. More precisely, it was located at the corner of the present St. Paul and St. Sulpice Streets, on land conceded to Jeanne Mance by Paul de Chomedey acting for the Company of Montreal, four hundred acres in all. Later on, Mademoiselle Mance, unable to farm them because of the Iroquois incursions, retained only seven or eight acres.[36] The hospital made of stone, soon known as "Mademoiselle Mance's house," was 30 feet long by 25 wide and had four rooms—a kitchen, a partition for Mademoiselle, another for the maids, and still another for the patients, "for whom she was a nurse and a mother." [37] With time she added a larger room which was used as a presbytery by the Reverend Gentlemen of St. Sulpice.[38] A little stone chapel, nine feet by ten, arched and properly made, was also added. The Blessed Sacrament was kept there for the comfort of the sick, as well as in the chapel within the fort wall, which served as the parish church until 1658.[39]

Besides the tidings of the treaty concerning the Company of New France and the colonists, Admiral de Repentigny brought a letter for Governor de Chomedey notifying him of his father's death.[40] Shortly afterwards, in September, at Trois-Rivières, peace was concluded with the Iroquois by Governor de Montmagny. The governor of Montreal made the most of the situation and, on October 24, 1645, he sailed from Quebec to France on the *Notre Dame*.[41] Returning with him was the unwanted La Barre. Before his departure, the Governor had entrusted the government of Ville Marie to the capable hands of Louis d'Ailleboust.[42]

At Jérôme Le Royer's request, Fr. Paul Le Jeune, S.J. along with Fr. Isaac Jogues, who was already there, had been assigned to winter in Montreal.[43] As the September peace rapidly attracted many former enemies to the island fort, the two Fathers promptly struck up an acquaintance with them as well as with the sympathetic Algonquins. In the early colonial documents preserved at the presbytery of Notre Dame in Montreal, one may see a burial record, dated October 10, 1645, of one Mathurin Parisien, a child of two or three years, signed by Isaac Jogues, and another of an Indian named Elie, with Fr. Le Jeune's signature.[44]

Mme. D'Ailleboust, already acquainted with the Algonquin language, soon became popular with the aborigines. In fact, a convert asked her one day, during the absence of the two blackrobes, "Since you understand us so well, couldn't you replace the priest and marry us publicly in church?" The acting governor's wife burst into laughter and blushing somewhat, told him he must wait for the missionary or go to Quebec where it would be easy to find a priest to marry the couple.[45]

So the uncertain peace of 1645-1646 allowed the two priests and the laymen to inaugurate a missionary effort which, at the cost of heroic efforts, was to grow over the years and result, in the latter part of the century, in the crowning glory of the Indian race—saintly Kateri Tekakwitha and five Iroquois martyrs.[46] Another of Jérôme de la Dauversière's principal aims was by way of becoming a reality—the conversion of the Indians!

Chapter XVIII

Notes

1. Now the site of the century-old Châtelet theatre.

2. Dollier de Casson, *A History of Montreal*, p. 125.

3. "Fondation pour les Malades dans L'Isle de Montréal" (January 12, 1644), in Mondoux, *L'Hôtel-Dieu, Premier Hôpital de Montréal*, p. 324.

4. "Vente Jacques Labbé, aux Pauvres de l'Isle de Montréal," (January 16; 28; March 25, 1644), *Ibid.*, pp. 326-335.

5. *Edits, Ordonnances Royaux...*, Vol. 1, pp. 24-25.

6. "Déclaration à la Compagnie de Montréal" (March 25, 1644), in Mondoux, *L'Hôtel-Dieu, Premier Hôpital de Montréal*, pp. 336-337.

7. Desrosiers, *Paul de Chomedey, Sieur de Maisonneuve*, p. 91. Note 10.

8. Dollier de Casson, *A History of Montreal*, p. 127.

9. *Ibid.*, p. 117.

10. *Ibid.*

11. *Premier Registre de L'Église Notre-Dame de Montréal*, p. 366; Desrosiers, *Iroquoisie*, p. 282.

12. Dollier de Casson, *A History of Montreal*, p. 115.

13. *Ibid.*

14. *JR*, Vol. XXV, p. 193.

15. Dollier de Casson, *A History of Montreal*, p. 123; Faillon, *Histoire de la Colonie Française en Canada*, Vol. 2, p. 29.

16. Mondoux, *L'Hôtel-Dieu, Premier Hôpital de Montréal*, p. 115, referring to Teuléron's minutes at the La Rochelle Archives; Gabriel Debien, "Liste des engagés pour le Canada au 18e siècle (1634-1715)," *RHAF*, Vol. VI. (Dec., 1952), pp. 376-377.

17. Faillon, *Histoire de la Colonie Française en Canada*, Vol. 2, p. 29, Note (4) *Archives du Ministère des Affaires Etrangères, Volume intitulé: Amérique, de 1592 à 1660*, fol. 154.

18. Trudel, *Montréal, La Formation d'une Société*, pp. 97-98.

19. Dollier de Casson, *A History of Montreal*, p. 123, 125.

20. *Ibid.*, p. 125.

21. Mondoux, *L'Hôtel-Dieu, Premier Hôpital de Montréal*, p. 143.

22. Atherton, *Montreal*, Vol. 1, pp. 91-92.

23. Faillon, *Histoire de la Colonie Française en Canada*, Vol. 1, p. 141.

24. *Edits, Ordonnances Royaux*, Vol. 1, p. 28.

25. *Ibid.*, p. 29.

26. Atherton, *Montreal*, Vol. 1, p. 92.

27. Bertrand, *Monsieur de la Dauversière*, pp. 162-163.

28. Atherton, *Montreal*, Vol. 1, p. 88.

29. Dollier de Casson, *A History of Montreal*, p. 127.

30. *Ibid.*, p. 125.

31. *Ibid.*, p. 129.

32. Faillon, *Vie de Mademoiselle Mance*, Vol. 1, pp. 41-42.

33. Dollier de Casson, *A History of Montreal*, p. 123.

34. Robert Lahaise, "L'Hôtel-Dieu du Vieux-Montréal," in *L'Hôtel-Dieu de Montréal, 1642-1973*, p. 18.

35. *Journal des Jésuites*, Editions François-Xavier, Montreal, 1973, p. 11; *JR*, Vol. XXVII, pp. 93, 95.

36. Mondoux, *L'Hôtel-Dieu, Premier Hôpital de Montréal*, facsimile of the document signed by Jeanne Mance on February 6, 1666, in which she explains why she did not keep all the island in 1644, p. 108.

37. Morin, *Histoire Simple et Véritable*, p. 55.

38. Lahaise, "L'Hôtel-Dieu du Vieux-Montréal," in *L'Hôtel-Dieu de Montréal*, p. 18, Note 21.

39. Morin, *Histoire Simple et Véritable*, p. 54; Mondoux, *L'Hôtel-Dieu, Premier Hôpital de Montréal*, p. 112.

40. Dollier de Casson, *A History of Montreal*, p. 127. Louis de Maisonneuve had died sometime between April 24, 1645 and June 1 of the same year: See Daveluy, *La Société de Notre-Dame de Montréal*, p.123.

41. *Journal des Jésuites*, p. 8.

42. Dollier de Casson, *A History of Montreal*, p. 129.

43. *Journal des Jésuites*, p. 4.

44. *Premier Registre de l'Église Notre-Dame de Montréal*, p. 366.

45. Ernest Gagnon, *Louis d'Ailleboust*, 2d ed. Montreal, 1931, p. 49.

46. Henri Béchard, S.J., *The Original Caughnawaga Indians*, Montreal, 1976, pp. 203-227.

Chapter XIX

A Friendly Governor-General

IN FRANCE, Jérôme Le Royer was hard at work stocking supplies for the next shipment, something he was to do each year until the end of his life. He met when he could with the Montreal Associates, notably with Fr. Olier. For the previous three years, Jérôme's good friend, the Abbé, had been laboring tirelessly in the St. Germain quarter of Paris. The Queen Regent and the Court esteemed this enterprising pastor and upheld his reform of the clergy and of the parishes. In his own presbytery, he had taken upon himself the rehabilitation of the twelve listless curates who never troubled much about their motley flock. Fr. Olier began to sweep away vice from the dirty streets and alleys in which St. Sulpice was enmeshed.

Opposition was bound to come. It came whence it hurt most, from the former pastor, Fr. Julien de Fiesque.[1] This worthy decided he should be reinstated as pastor, and after intrigue and intimidation failed, did not scruple at assault and battery. On June 8, 1645, a disorderly crowd of sympathizers broke into the presbytery, seized Fr. Olier and dragged him through the streets, railing at him and raining down blows upon his shoulders. It took no less than St. Vincent de Paul, at the risk of his life, to extricate his brother priest from the frenzied rabble. Olier finally found refuge at the Luxembourg palace, where he enjoyed a little respite for eight days. Profiting from his absence, the rioters tore things to shreds in his presbytery and only on the tenth of July was the law able to throw them out. No sooner was the pastor home again than a mob milled round the house and threatened to burn it. The Queen's guardsmen were called in to quiet the disturbance and a number of

240

them posted there for the pastor's safety.

On June 12, while the boy King and the Queen Regent made ready to attend the celebration of a French victory over Spain at Notre Dame cathedral, the high officials of the kingdom prepared to join them. A throng of lusty-throated females crowded into the Parliament building, one of the major courts of justice of the land, as the magistrates entered. Not content with shrieking their dislike of Fr. Olier, they jeered at them, hoping thus to intimidate the Court.[2] It was a mistake. A decree was quickly issued ordering the denunciation of the instigator and forbidding large gatherings under pain of death. Law and order were to be maintained at any cost. A certain quiet followed, but even after a second contract signed by Fr. de Fiesque confirming the suppression of his rights to the pastorate of St. Sulpice on behalf of Fr. Olier, the latter was harassed for months on end by the criminal element of his parish.

Conditions gradually cleared up, however, and his seminary, destined to prepare priests not only for France but also for Ville Marie,[3] would soon be functioning more efficiently than ever. Once before, but to no avail, Jérôme Le Royer and Fr. Olier had tried to pave the way to sending secular priests to the island foundation by requesting the Holy See to take it under its wing. Now the two friends and doubtless other Associates of the Company of Montreal discussed a new solution. Why could Canada not have its own Bishop? Perhaps one of the Associates would be a suitable candidate. It would bear looking into.

Sometime in December, Governor Paul de Chomedey was certainly back in France again. Monsieur le Royer sympathized with him in his bereavement over the loss of his father; at the same time, he made the most of the opportunity to obtain firsthand information about his beloved Ville Marie. The Governor may have accompanied him to Paris or at least met him there before December 12, when the Company of Montreal, or rather Jérôme himself, gave the Montreal settlement two pinnaces, the *St. Joseph* and the *Notre Dame,* for transporting men and provisions from Quebec to Ville Marie.[4] Admiral Legardeur de Repentigny agreed to take them to Quebec. All this may well have been at the suggestion of Paul de Chomedey.

Many questions faced the founder and the Governor, a prime instance being that of a Canadian bishopric. Monsieur de Puiseaux's case, too. Although the Company of Montreal was no longer bound to him by any legal ties, how were they to treat him? And Madame de la Peltrie wanted to dispose of her property in France: what could the Associates do about it? There were others, but little enough time was given the two friends to find answers to all of them, for before January 9, 1646, Paul de Chomedey was back at Neuville-sur-Vanne, his native town.[5] On that day, kneeling bareheaded, without sword or spurs, before his liege lord, the Baron de Villemort, he promised fealty and service, sealing his vow by kissing the bolt of the main door of the baronial château. He thus became the "sieur" or master of Maisonneuve. Then devolved upon him the responsibility of validating and registering his father's last will and testament. Even nowadays probate work is often long and difficult; so it was in those times. Perhaps Paul de Chomedey de Maisonneuve was able to shorten it somewhat even though it unquestionably took many weeks, perhaps several months.

In Paris, Jérôme Le Royer, in concert with the other Montreal Associates, was now actively involved in promoting the idea of a Bishop for Canada. The most likely candidate appeared to be Fr. Thomas Le Gauffre.[6] This clergyman, a former master of accounts in the capital, converted to the interior life by saintly Father Claude Bernard, called "the poor priest" a friend of Fr. Olier's. "His

242

love for the glory of God, his devotion to the Blessed Virgin, his friendship with Fr. de Condren, founder of the Oratorians, were the source of his close union with Fr. Olier. But especially what seemed to have insprired them with the same sentiments was their tender and ardent love for the poor." Fr. Bernard died at Paris on March 23, 1641 at the age of 53 years. (Faillon, *Vie de M. Olier*, Vol.1, pp. 249-250.) On the latter's death, Le Gauffre took over his work at the Parisian Almshouse, at the Conciergerie with its prisoners and its criminals condemned to death.

Fr. Le Gauffre was as generous as he was wealthy, and on learning about the project of a bishop and a diocesan clergy for the French colony, he donated 30,000 livres for this purpose. Cardinal Mazarin, Richelieu's successor as Prime Minister, also countenanced an episcopal see in New France, and Fr. Le Gauffre, whose zeal he was aware of, seemed to him the ideal candidate for Bishop. His Eminence then suggested that the Society of Jesus be consulted since its missionaries alone were at that time in charge of Canadian missions. Fr. Georges Delahaye, S.J., then responsible for the Jesuits of New France, was approached and after debating the problem with other men of his Order, who were well acquainted with Canada, was enthusiastic about the proposal. On the King's behalf and in accordance with the Gallican privilege, the Cardinal Minister named Fr. Thomas Le Gauffre to take charge of the future diocese.

The good priest was aghast. He felt he was suited for something else, for work in the Parisian jungle among the paupers, the outcasts, the unruly crowd of misfits. His fellow priests insisted that, since he had had nothing to do with his nomination, it was obviously the will of God. Even so, before accepting his new role, he felt he should consult with his spiritual director. Fr. Hayneuve, S.J., to whom he put his case, and who advised him to make a retreat. Then, indeed, he received an answer from above. On the third day of the retreat that was to be decisive, during March 1646, he unexpectedly died.

In his testament, this man of God bequeathed all his fortune to worthy causes. To the 30,000 livres already promised for the bishopric, he had added 10,000 more for the propagation of the Faith in the New World.

Jérôme Le Royer and his supporters did not abandon the idea of a Bishop for Canada. In his memoirs, Fr. Olier wrote that the Church in New France would be the handiwork of Jesus, Mary, and Joseph, and that, despite unworthiness, the Father in heaven wished him to take the place of His Son.[7] In other words, Jean Jacques Olier's mission with regard to Ville Marie was, above all, to give Christ to the distant island through the priests he would send there, precisely what Jérôme expected of him.

The presence of a Bishop in that country, they were now more and more convinced, would facilitate that of diocesan priests there. So the General Assembly of the Clergy was petitioned to study this design. On May 25, 1646, Bishop Godeau of Grasse brought up the question before his assembled colleagues.[8] He stressed the need of a bishop in far-off Canada, which without one was "half a Christian Church." The colonists needed a bishop to confirm their children, and the converted Indians likewise, to become strong in faith. He then concluded by asking the prelates to submit the matter to the Queen.

The matter was apparently not settled when Jérôme wished Paul de Maisonneuve a happy voyage to Canada.[9] A little later when Anne of Austria was sounded about a bishopric for Montreal, she proved sympathetic to the idea and Cardinal Mazarin endorsed it at the Assembly of Wednesday, July 11, 1646.[10] He even offered a pension of 1,200 crowns of his own money towards the erection of the future See. Once again the Jesuits were consulted. This time, however, they apparently demurred.[11] Conditions in the New World now seemed too uncertain to them. Any day, they felt, the cold war between the Iroquois and the French might blaze out into a red hot one! The project was accordingly abandoned. Still, it must be noted, Le Royer's and Olier's efforts were not totally vain: they opened the way to the eventual erection of a See in Quebec.

While these negotiations were going on, Jérôme Le Royer came to a decision that we find surprising three centuries later. The founder of Ville Marie wrote to its Governor inviting him to return to France. The letter was forwarded to him by a ship sailing shortly after his own. Perhaps it had been meant to reach him before he embarked at La Rochelle.

Why was he recalled? It has been suggested that because of his engrossing family problems, Maisonneuve had not had sufficient time for a serious discussion of conditions in Ville Marie with his friend, Jérôme. This explanation does not hold water, for neither the one nor the other would have missed the opportunity to carefully review the difficulties concerning their mutual undertaking, before the Atlantic Ocean separated them. Elsewhere it is alleged that Paul de Maisonneuve's mother was on the verge of contracting a disastrous second marriage. Perhaps. If so, would he not have had some inkling of it before his departure?

At any rate, Jérôme was eagerly awaiting him. On October 31, the Governor of Montreal found the grounds for returning good enough to sail for France,[12] where he arrived in December. On his trip from the coast, there is reason to believe that he stopped at La Flèche to spend some time with the man responsible for the existence of Ville Marie. The two partners examined the events, whatever they may have been, that brought them together. The Governor also reported on his activities during the six weeks he had spent in the little capital of New

France. He had not thought it expedient to go to Ville Marie, but he had expended care in its behalf.

On October 12, for 23,000 crowns, in the Baron de Fancamp's name, he had acquired Madame de la Peltrie's property in the motherland.[13]

Elderly Pierre de Puiseaux's property had also demanded attention. On October 19, 1646, Paul de Maisonneuve ratified the retrocession already made to the elderly benefactor of the fiefs of St. Michel and of St. Foy as well as of the goods and chattels he had transferred to the Montrealers in 1641.[14] Governor de Montmagny, perhaps at Maisonneuve's suggestion, then decided that the funds contributed by the Company of Montreal for the grubbing of St. Foy had to be reimbursed. Thus Jérôme Le Royer, through his *alter ego*, his second self as Cicero would have expressed it, protected the interests of his little colony.

The Governor of Ville Marie also related to Jérôme his dealing with the "Inhabitants of New France." When the Company of New France relinquished its fur rights to the colonists, a board of administrators was formed with headquarters at Quebec. During October 1646, Monsieur de Maisonneuve spent some time attending the meetings of this new body. Instead of stamping out the former abuses, the members of the board thought of allocating themselves an exhorbitant salary. Maisonneuve, who would have profited by the proposed ruling, refused his consent.[15] His healthy obstinacy forced the others to desist.

After his conversations with Jérôme, did the Governor then go to Neuville-sur-Vanne to meet his new stepfather or did he ride to Paris with Le Royer? Whatever he may have done, when he did reach the French capital, he favorably impressed the Montreal Associates and the other notables he met. In Ville Marie, he dressed simply as the other settlers. Now with his powdered wig, his broad-brimmed felt hat and his dress sword, he was quite the

246

gentleman. His manners, his discourse, and his reputation as leader for the past five years of the settlement of Ville Marie, constantly threatened by the Iroquois, marked him out as a man to be taken seriously. He was taken seriously.

He had made the crossing in the company of Robert Giffard and Guillaume Tronquet,[16] Governor de Montmagny's secretary, who hoped to settle certain problems which had cropped up during the past year. Together the three men presented the Royal Council with a list of complaints about the administration of the recently formed Habitants' Company. Not without Jérôme Le Royer's knowledge and perhaps at his suggestion, three devoted Montreal Associates, Fr. Elie Laisne de la Marguerie, Jean Antoine Mesmes d'Irval, and Antoine Barillon de Morangis, were called upon to use their influence to obtain from the boy King and the Royal Council the establishment of a council at Quebec. A royal decree issued on March 27, 1647,[17] ruled that the government of Canada, in matters of police, commerce, and war, should be in the hands of the Governor-General, the Superior of the Jesuits, and the Governor of Montreal or if the latter was absent, the acting governor. Problems demanding an immediate solution were to be resolved in Quebec by a plurality vote of the three men. Consequently, Ville Marie was to have its say in the matter!

The royal decree went so far as to allot the Governor of Montreal a salary of 10,000 livres a year and 30 tons of freight, free of charge, but he was also saddled with the upkeep of 30 garrison soldiers. The Jesuits got 5,000 livres for their missions, and the Governor-General, 25,000 with other privileges.

As Paul de Maisonneuve wove his way among the high dignitaries, the first impression he had made was confirmed. Now talk of recalling Governor de Montmagny, who had served for eleven years, was in the air. To the surprise of the Governor of Montreal and no doubt to the dismay of its founder, he was offered the governorship of New France. Le Royer need not have worried. "With a wisdom, which will be better recognized in the next world than in this," later noted Dollier de Casson, "he (Maisonneuve) had refused the office."[18] What a relief it must have been for the La Flèche tax-collector to have his friend stick by him!

Who then should replace Montmagny? Paul de Maisonneuve could think of no worthier candidate than Louis d'Ailleboust, whom he had left in charge of Ville Marie. This suggestion was taken under consideration, and later in the year on returning to Canada, Maisonneuve would also be able to inform Ailleboust that he was to be appointed Governor of New France and that he had to return to France to receive his commission.

Before the Governor of Ville Marie's departure, Jérôme examined with him the ways and means of encouraging more men to emigrate to the Montreal island and those who were already there to stay on. From the very beginning, the founder had clearly specified the conditions to which they must subscribe: four or five years of salaried service and free subsistence followed on their part by the decision to remain at Ville Marie or to return to France. Until then only a few had built homes outside the fort. To the others, according to Jérôme's initial plans, it was decided between him and the Governor, were to be quickly made grants of land in conformity with the easy terms of feudal tenure. In the face of the Iroquois aggression and the uncertainty concerning the future, it was the best manner to lessen the departure of settlers from Ville Marie.

In the late spring or early summer of 1647, Jérôme wished Paul de Maisonneuve "bon voyage." Towards the end of the year, he was happy to embrace an emigrant he had sent to Montreal in 1643 with his wife and sister: Louis d'Ailleboust, the Governor-General to-be, who had boarded

248

ship at Quebec on the twenty-first of October[19] after seeing Paul de Maisonneuve off to Ville Marie. News from New France was not good. The sham peace between the French and the Iroquois had degenerated into open war.[20] Ville Marie had suffered, for two settlers and three Hurons had been captured by the much feared enemy earlier in the year.

Accompanying the young nobleman were a few colonists delegated by the Canadian population to voice their complaints against the administration and request several amendments to the decree of the previous spring. Since the dealings of the delegation might effect life in Montreal, Jérôme kept his eyes and ears open.

At the end of February, the grievances presented by Louis d'Ailleboust and his companions were examined by the Royal Council in the presence of the Queen Regent. The decisions of this august body were embodied in the decree of March 5, 1648.[21]

The governor-general's term of office would no longer last more than three years, though a second term was permissible. The colonial council was to comprise five members instead of three as in the initial decree. The governors of Montreal and of Trois-Rivières would also have the right to sit in at its meetings whenever they were in Quebec.

The salary of the governor-general was reduced to 10,000 livres and he was entitled only to 12 tons of freight annually and to a garrison of a dozen soldiers. The local governors of Montreal and Trois-Rivières had theirs slashed down to 3,000 livres and were allotted but six tons of freight each year, and half a dozen guardsmen each.

The 19,000 livres thus saved were to be diverted to the foundation of a flying party of forty militiamen, ready to go at a minute's notice, wherever they were needed; the surplus, if any, was to be used to buy arms and ammunitions and was to be used for the protection of all, friendly Indians as well as Frenchmen.

These changes would have a bearing on the next governor-general's administration, and, as Jérôme Le Royer was well aware, he would be Louis d'Ailleboust, whom he considered a trump for Ville Marie. Outgoing Governor de Montmagny had done little enough to protect the Island of Montreal; indeed, he had checked many would-be settlers, convinced there was no likelihood the habitation would last, from going there.[22] On the second of March, Ailleboust's commission as governor-general was signed and ten days later he was sworn in before the nine-and-half-year-old King and Anne of Austria.

In Paris Jérôme Le Royer and Louis d'Ailleboust roomed at the same inn. Despite all the fuss preceding and accompanying the swearing in, neither neglected Ville Marie. Together they discussed the financial state of the island settlement across the sea. The largess of the "Unknown Benefactress" was gratefully considered but judged inadequate. To be sure, she had put up 42,000 livres for the Montreal hospital, 6,000 of which had already been spent, while 36,000 rested with the Company of Montreal. For reasons unknown to us, the sum entrusted to Monsieur de Bellegarde in 1644 had been returned to Jérôme Le Royer and to Bertrand Drouart, secretary and procurator of the Company. The income resulting from these funds and other donations had been used for the administration of the Ville Marie Hôtel Dieu, for the acquisition of furniture, and for food needed by the settlers.

Fr. Rapine was always available and feelers were thrown out to the "Unknown Benefactress," who promptly responded by adding 24,000 more livres to her past bounties, bringing them up to 60,000 livres.

This donation became legal in a deed of gift prepared in Paris by Notary Chaussière and signed on March 17, 1648 by Jérôme Le Royer, Pierre de Fancamp, Louis d'Ailleboust, and Louis Séguier.[23]

250

Several articles of the act betray Jérôme's fine touch. Mme. de Bullion insisted on seeing to Mademoiselle Mance's upkeep and on retaining her as administratrix of the hospital until her death. On the other hand, both Jérôme Le Royer and Madame de Bullion agreed to the condition that neither capital nor income should ever be used for anything else than Hôtel Dieu, and finally that the endowment must never be transferred outside the island of Montreal.[24]

At the same time, at the Benefactress's request another contract was signed committing the investment of 44,000 livres to the Baron and Baronne de Renty and the rest, 16,000, to the Baron de Fancamp.

On April 15, before Governor-General d'Ailleboust shipped again for Canada, he approved a brief instruction for administrative purposes in Montreal[25] with Jérôme and several other associates. Every year, second-hand furniture and clothing were forwarded to Ville Marie. Jérôme or his agent would henceforth include in each shipment two invoices indicating the value of each article. The administration of the Hôtel Dieu, that is, Mademoiselle Mance, was enjoined to keep a copy and return the other with her signature to France. She was also to furnish a yearly report of her accounting to the Governor of Montreal, to the priest in charge, and to the syndics, who were to return a copy duly signed to the headquarters of the Company of Montreal in Paris. This regulation was not intended to disparage Jeanne Mance's capable management; it was for Jérôme Le Royer simply a means of accrediting his own transactions in behalf of the Hôtel Dieu.

When Louis d'Ailleboust disembarked at Quebec on August 20,[26] he had the satisfaction of embracing his wife, Barbe, and his sister-in-law, Philippine de Boullongne, who had quit Jeanne Mance and the settlers of Montreal to come to welcome him. During his first three-year term and later during his second term (1657-1658), Ailleboust did not betray Jérôme Le Royer's expectations, and showed himself the staunch friend of Governor de Maisonneuve and of Ville Marie.

In the spring of 1649, following his arrival at Quebec, the Governor-General ordered 40 men off to Montreal, under the command of his nephew Charles d'Ailleboust des Muceaux.[27] They were to ensure its protection. Lack of experience in Indian warfare prevented Muceaux from rendering all the help that was expected of him. The noise of the oars of his shallops on the tholepins warned the enemy, who disappeared into the underbrush and thickets.

During that same spring, the Governor-General also sailed up to Ville Marie for his first official visit with his friend Governor de Maisonneuve and his pioneers, who were delighted to see one of the Montreal Associates as governor of New France.[28] He informed Paul de Maisonneuve that the Company of New France, pleased with his leadership, had increased his funds by 1,000 livres and his garrison by six men. He also gave him the regulations concerning the Hôtel Dieu: the surgeon must now treat the sick and wounded free of charge, whether they were French or Indian; in addition, the administration's accounts must be addressed to the capital every year.

On the third of May, before leaving Ville Marie, Governor-General d'Ailleboust formally handed over to the Jesuits the Seigneury of the Magdeleine, which was to become the Mission of St. Francis Xavier.[29] This was a strip of land, two leagues in width by four in depth on the south shore of the St. Lawrence river, extending from the point opposite St. Helen's Island almost to Sault St. Louis (Lachine Rapids). Twenty-eight years later, this mission was to become the home of Kateri Tekakwitha.

The official document was signed and notarized within the walls of the fort. Only in 1667, however, was the Jesuit seigneury opened to the French and the Christian Indians who wished to settle there. Though few of the Montrealers could have foreseen it, this was another big step in the Christianizing of the native people.[30]

In France, Jérôme, who had already faced great troubles, would have been jubilant had he been able to foresee the Indian saints and martyrs who were to live at the Mission of St. Francis Xavier under the protection of Ville Marie; he would also have rejoiced had he anticipated the destiny reserved to the baby girl for whom Governor d'Ailleboust stood sponsor on March 19, 1649. The child's name was Marie Morin and she was to be the first Canadian-born Hospitaller of St. Joseph and the first annalist of Jérôme Le Royer's Hôtel-Dieu in Montreal.[31]

Chapter XIX

Notes

1. Faillon, *Vie de Monsieur Olier*, Vol. 2, pp. 149-152.

2. *Ibid*. pp. 172-173.

3. *Ibid*., Vol. 3, pp. 400-401.

4. Desrosiers, *Paul de Chomedey*, p. 97.

5. Daveluy, *La Société de Notre-Dame de Montréal*, p. 123.

6. *Ibid*., pp. 224-232.

7. Faillon, *Vie de Monsieur Olier*, Vol. 3, p. 423.

8. *Ibid.*, p. 407.

9. Maisonneuve arrived at Quebec on September 20, see *Journal des Jésuites* 24, p. 65.

10. Faillon, *Histoire de la Colonie Française en Canada*, Vol. 2, pp. 50-52.

11. *Ibid.*, p. 52.

12. *Journal des Jésuites*, p. 68.

13. G. Oury, O.S.B., *Madame de la Peltrie et Ses Fondations Canadiennes*, p. 101.

14. Faillon, *Histoire de la Colonie Française en Canada*, Vol. 2, p. 57.

15. *Journal des Jésuites*, p. 68.

16. *Ibid.*

17. Daveluy, "Le Conseil de Québec," *La Société Notre-Dame de Montréal,* p. 60; Atherton, *Montreal Under the French Regime*, Vol. 1, p. 95.

18. Dollier de Casson, *A History of Montreal*, p. 137.

19. *Journal des Jésuites*, p. 95.

20. Marie de L'Incarnation, "Lettre CX," *Correspondance*, p. 323. The first overt mark of hostility was the martyrdom of Saints Isaac Jogues and Jean de la Lande, who shed their blood at Ossernenon on October 18, 1646 (perhaps October 19 for Jean de la Lande).

21. Faillon, *Histoire de la Colonie Française en Canada*, Vol. 2, pp. 92-93.

22. Dollier de Casson, *A History of Montreal*, pp. 139-140.

23. "Conventions, Pierre Chevrier et Louis d'Ailleboust" (March 11, 1648), in Mondoux, *L'Hôtel-Dieu, Premier Hôpital de Montréal*, pp. 338-342.

24. In the long run, the investments proved to be anything but gilt-edged. The importance of the "Conventions" lies in the fact that, despite the contrary efforts of Blessed François de Laval, first Bishop of Quebec, despite those of a few well-meaning Jesuits and of the apostolically aggressive Fr. de Queylus, the Hôtel Dieu of Montreal still stands as a monument to Jérôme de la Dauversière and to the Duchesse de Bullion, the enduring proof of their wisdom and foresight.

25. "Endos-Règlement," (April 14, 1648), in Mondoux, *L'Hôtel-Dieu, Premier Hôpital de Montréal*, p. 120.

26. *Journal des Jésuites*, p. 115. Philippine entered the Ursuline novitiate on December 2, 1648.

27. Dollier de Casson, *A History of Montreal*, p. 147.

28. Faillon, *Histoire de la Colonie Française en Canada*, Vol. 2, pp. 96-97.

29. Yvon Lacroix, *Les Origines de Laprairie* (1667-1697), Montreal, 1981, p. 46.

30. Henri Béchard, S.J., *The Original Caughnawaga Indians*, *in extenso*.

31. Esther Lefebvre, *Marie Morin, Premier Historien Canadien de Ville-Marie*, Montreal, 1959, pp. 37-38.

Chapter XX

"As a Fruitful Olive Tree"

WHILE VILLE MARIE struggled to hold its own, how had the Sisters of St. Joseph of La Flèche fared under the leadership of Mother de la Ferre, counselled by Jérôme Le Royer? Since the first vows of January 1644, as a whole they had profited spiritually, especially after Sr. Baillif's apparitions. Jérôme continued training them and guiding those who turned to him for help.[1] It was probably after the deceased Sister's message, "Love your rules" and her mention of Judas that the founder revealed to the community the mystical origin of its foundation.[2]

His talks were so appreciated that, in the style of the period, one of the listeners wrote about all the Sisters coming out suffused with tears and about the good odor of their virtues drawing public esteem and veneration upon them without having wished it.[3] Faithful to his resolve, Fr. Dubreuil explained the different articles of the Constitutions to them from the beginning of Advent 1644 to the third week of January 1645. In the spirit of Sr. Baillif's remarks, he stressed the importance of the simple vows.[4]

On January 22, eleven of the twelve Sisters who had pronounced their initial vows renewed them, this time for two years.[5] The absent twelfth was, of course, Anne Baillif.

Life and death kept knocking at the community door. In the summer of 1644, young Anne Vedie of La Flèche had been welcomed as a lay postulant.[6] This admission may have been of some consolation to Mother de la Ferre, but again and again death struck: Sr. Louis Bidault expired on March 19, 1645,[7] followed by another veteran, Sr. Anne Foureau, a cousin of Jérôme's and Mother de la Ferre's friend of pre-Hôtel Dieu days. Sr. Anne died at the relatively early age of forty on April 19,[8] four months to the day of Sr. Baillif's final apparition when she had said, "I shall see you only in heaven." At the moment of her death, before standing in the presence of her Judge, Sr. Anne did not retract a word of the evidence she had given concerning the extraordinary manifestations she had witnessed.

Another blow to the superior and to Jérôme Le Royer was the death of Sr. Jeanne Cohergne a year later, on February fourteenth.[9] She had worked at Hôtel Dieu as early as 1635 when it was still known as St. Marguerite's. These deaths were soon offset by the flow of candidates, however.

Until then, most of them were from La Flèche and had been spontaneously attracted to the life of the Hôtel Dieu Sisters. Sr. Catherine Macé, it will be recalled, though, had been introduced to the Hospitallers by a Jesuit. After their official establishment, most of the Fathers at the Royal College constituted themselves ardent propagators of this change brought to religious life, and their students imitated them.

The first one to respond to their influence was Renée Le Jumeau des Perrières de la Naudière,[10] daughter of Jean Le Jumeau, Seigneur of Blou, a village close to Baugé. As the family was large, her father, at the request of his sister, Madame de Milon, entrusted his daughter's upbringing to her care. She had only two sons and was delighted to have Renée with her. This kind aunt brought her up as if she were her own child. Under the wing of Mme. de Milon, at Le Mans, capital of the Province of Maine, her niece, on becoming of age, enjoyed the mundane life. Then the unexpected happened.

As the tale is told, it was at Midnight Mass on Christmas in the Cathedral of St. Julien that Renée fell into convulsions.[11] It was the first of many attacks and dashed all her worldly hopes to the ground. Instead of resorting to bitterness and recrimination, she resolved to retire to some convent, where she could spend the rest of her life in work, prayer, and penance. A Jesuit, to whom she mentioned her plans, suggested the nursing Sisters of St. Joseph, recently founded in La Flèche.

At first Madame de Milon thought favorably of the idea; then, after consultation with Renée's parents, opposed it. How could a sick girl, raised in the lap of luxury, survive as a Hospitaller Sister? But she was a kindly soul and a good Christian and finally gave in to her niece's pleas. Indeed, if she were to give Renée to God, she would do it in grand style. Towards the end of December 1644, Madame de Milon and Renée Le Jumeau des Perrières were off to La Flèche with a veritable caravan of servants, lackeys, litters and coaches.

Letters had assuredly been exchanged between the girl's aunt and Mother de la Ferre. So Renée was cordially received as a postulant. Time would tell if she were fit to take her vows. One of the oldest manuscripts at the La Flèche Hôtel Dieu relates that the superior advised Renée to ask Our Lady to cure her. She did so before a statue of the Blessed Virgin in the dormitory and, after hearing Jérôme Le Royer speak of the Canadian missions, promised, if she regained her health, to devote her life to the care of the ailing and wounded in the Hôtel Dieu of Ville Marie. She was delivered of the falling sickness. Mother de la Ferre quite prudently did not allow her to take the habit and begin the novitiate until three years had elapsed, three years completely free of the slightest trace of epilepsy. Much later Sr. Le Jumeau went to Montreal where she died in 1709 at the ripe old age of ninety-two after a remarkable life of service to the sick.[12]

On January 2, 1645, a forty-year-old spinster, Mlle. Anne de France, daughter of a rich merchant of Angers, applied for admission. Her mother, Nicole Le Peintre, was a native of La Flèche, certainly known to Le Royer. Anne brought some property with her—a small garden in the neighborhood of the Hôtel Dieu, an annuity of 90 livres, and a life pension of 30 livres.[13] This dowry and the others that followed would soon make the community financially independent. More than once, Jérôme must have wished that the Ville Marie enterprise were as well off as its counterpart in La Flèche.

Twenty-four-year-old Mlle. Anne Aubert de Cléraunay of Le Mans donned the habit of the Daughters of St. Joseph on August 5, 1645. As a child of ten, she had lost her parents. As they were well-to-do, her tutor saw to it that she lacked nothing, not even dancing lessons and plenty of new shoes, which she wore out prodigeously. Her personal maid, her monthly allowance, her silk dresses, gloves and dainty slippers of perfectly matching hues, her green petticoats, her biscuit and flesh-colored stoles, her ribbons and hongrelines,[14] would be the delight of the cinema starlets of today.

At the La Flèche Hôtel Dieu on New Year's Day 1646, Jérôme Le Royer, representing the Daughters of St. Joseph, and René Arnoul de la Corbinière, Anne de Cléraunay's brother-in-law, acting for the family council, verified the trusteeship accounts. The papers were in good order and Anne was legally declared of age—women of the Province of Maine, to which she belonged, attained their majority at twenty-five years.[15] She had inherited 22,874 livres. When the dowry contract was signed in the La Flèche study of Notary Robert Couallier, the Hospitallers also acquired a small farm in the vicinity of Laval and other advantages.

Four months later, Jérôme was informed by Mother de la Ferre that a young lady, highly recommended by a Jesuit Father,[16] was seeking admittance among the Daughters of St. Joseph. Not a penny did she have to offer for her dowry. Judith Moreau de Brésoles's story is pure melodrama, which simply serves to stress her goodness. In a letter to Madame d'Ailleboust, sometime between 1660 and 1665, the Jesuit who had sent her to Mother de la Ferre wrote, "So you are staying with the nursing Sisters of Montreal. I think you are fortunate. I know one of them called Judith Moreau de Brésoles, since childhood; I always served as her spiritual guide until a few years before she quit France for Canada, and I consider her one of the most faithful to follow the voice of the divine Spouse."[17]

Judith began to follow this voice when she was still very young. As she was the baby of the family, her noble parents, François Moreau and Françoise Gallard, cherished her particularly. When she was still a little tot, she would distribute food to the needy children of the nearby towns. As she grew older, she taught them their prayers and their catechism. She learned how to care for the ill, even to the point of leeching them after the manner of the contemporary barbers and surgeons, and to compound remedies for them. The day came when she admitted to her family that she intended to become a hospitaller in a hospital not far from her home town of Blois. The answer was negative; not until the death of her father and mother would she be allowed to enter the convent!

From time to time, Judith would urge her Jesuit confessor to help her with her vocation, but he prudently kept putting her off. Not until she was twenty-six years old did he finally advise her to apply to the Hospitallers of St. Joseph at La Flèche for admission. There in distant Anjou, she could remain unknown and would have nothing to fear from her people. He then gave letters of recommendation for Mother de la Ferre, for one of the Fathers of the La Flèche college, and for the Abbess of Fontevrault, Jeanne-Baptiste de Bourbon, legitimized daughter of Henri IV.[18]

A trustworthy acquaintance agreed to help the young lady escape. The night before her departure, she managed to appropriate the keys of the house, prepare a small bundle of linen, and gather her clothes together. The next morning before the cock crowed, she put on her dresses, one on top of the other, while her helper went to the stable, saddled her horse and led it quietly into the street. She then let herself out, walked away in the opposite direction and, at one of the city gates was joined by her escort, who helped her to mount. The trip had been well planned. Each evening she reached the town that had been decided upon beforehand. Along the way, the Abbess of Fontevrault, thanks to the letter from Judith's confessor, welcomed her most graciously and put her up for the night.

Mother de la Ferre received the courageous young lady warmly. On November 10, 1646, Judith Moreau de Brésoles declared in writing that, since her parents were opposed to her vocation, she had nothing to offer for her dowry.[19] The postulant was assigned to the hospital pharmacy and within six months she was more competent at her work than the expert pharmacist who taught her. It is not difficult to imagine Jérôme's satisfaction. The newcomer was a lady not only of distinction but also of decision. Some day, perhaps, he would make use of her in Ville Marie.

On January 10, 1646, two months after Judith de Brésole's arrival, Françoise Pilon, a relative of Jérôme's wife, Jeanne,[20] was admitted as a postulant. In the footsteps of Françoise came a niece of his wife, Marie Lamé of Le Mans. Jérôme's and Jeanne's connections were generally from moderately wealthy families of deep faith.

Of the numerous candidates who, during that decade, flocked to join the Daughters of St. Joseph, there is one more to whom I here wish to draw attention: Marie Maillet[21] of the Angevine town of Beaufort. At the time of her entry on April 5, 1646, she was thirty-six years old. Marie had enough income to live comfortably and she could have continued thus to the end of her days. Her love of God led her to the complete gift of self in the service of the ailing poor. She chose as her spiritual director none other than

261

Jérôme Le Royer himself, and he guided her perfection along the paths of obedience, humility, poverty, and fidelity to the rules of the Hospitallers.

Although her health was middling, she was one of the first chosen by Jérôme to go to Ville Marie. There the Indians loved her and called her their mother. In distant Canada, she was to reach the heights of mystical prayer. Several times after their deaths Jérôme Le Royer and Fr. Olier appeared to her,[22] for she feared that, from lack of funds, the Hôtel Dieu in this last outpost of civilization would be abandoned. Reassuringly these two servants of God told her that their work was His and that it would last despite the opposition of men acting blindly and ignorant of His intentions; the good Lord would derive glory from all these mishaps and the Hôtel Dieu would benefit thereby, since it had been founded and sustained by the Cross.

As a result of the many postulants and novices, the Sisters' quarters in the La Flèche hospital were bursting at the seams. Already in April 1646, Mother de la Ferre, not without consulting Jérôme, rented a house on Port Luneau belonging to a merchant of Nantes. The high rent she paid—53 livres tournois—shows how pressing the need was. This building was insufficient, however, and in September, for 7,700 livres, the Daughters of St. Joseph acquired a domicile next to the premises in which they were then established. For an annuity of 61 livres, a neighboring garden and shed were added to it.[23]

At the beginning of 1647, Mother de la Ferre's term of office expired.[24] The founder's good friend, Canon Syette, Vicar-General of the diocese, presided over the elections for a successor to the first superior. On January 22, Mother de la Ferre was at the helm again with one dissident vote— her own, as three years before. Her reinstatement had to be ratified by Bishop de Rueil and after drawing up the minutes of the procedure, Jérôme penned a request for ratification on the fold of the document. Three days later it was back in his hands with a commission authorizing Father Gyrot, the chaplain, to receive the vows of the Sisters who were to renew them in February. Among these was Jérôme's daughter, Sr. Jeanne Le Royer.

With Mother de la Ferre reelected for three more years, Jérôme Le Royer felt he could forge ahead with his plans for the Daughters of St. Joseph. A problem even more important than the housing of the community must be dealt with. Better attuned to conditions after several years' experience, Jérôme grasped that his conception of the Hospitaller Sister had been wrongly pivoted, and this, unexpectedly, because of his love for the poor. He had not discerned at first that not only did his group of nurses have responsibilities with regard to their patients but also that the community lives of these nurses, bound together by vows, implied other equally important obligations.

Now the original Constitutions had not drawn a fine enough distinction between the revenue of the Hôtel Dieu and that of the Daughters of St. Joseph.[25] All the income, whether it came from the Daughters or from bequests to the destitute patients, was to be turned over to the administrators, and any capital in excess of what was necessary for the care of the ill and for the upkeep of the Daughters was to constitute a reserve fund, which could not be tampered with for any other but the above necessities. As Jérôme and his brother, René de Boistaillé, were the two administrators, they would have made no bones whatsoever about settling the allotment of the funds to the satisfaction of the Daughters of St. Joseph.

It must be noted, however, that they held their mandate from the mayor and the aldermen. As a matter of fact, the latter hoped the sick of the Hôtel Dieu would profit from the dowries and inheritances of the Daughters of St. Joseph. On the other hand, as the two brothers pointed out, the articles of the Constitutions on which the city pressed its claim could equally apply to the Daughters. Should they ever need land on which to build a convent, the Hospitallers would have the right to turn to the reserve funds, made up not only of their own contributions but also of the gifts and donations to the Hôtel Dieu itself. The reserve fund, then, was the root of the difficulty.

The notables of La Flèche, including Mayor Gabriel Le Gaigneur de Poislé, crowded into notary Pierre La Fousse's study on the afternoon of September 20, 1647 to weigh Jérôme Le Royer's solution. Mother de la Ferre was present, too, accompanied by Srs. Anne de L'Espicier, Anne Le Tendre, Marie Gyrot, Renée Busson, Jeanne Le Royer, Marie and Thérèse Havard, and Catherine Macé. In return for complete financial autonomy, the Daughters of St. Joseph were now ready to offer the city 300 livres, that is one tenth of each one's dowry three months after the death of a Sister, with the exception of the first four to die and of the lay Daughters, who were generally admitted without any monetary consideration. They also agreed to see to the upkeep of the chaplain who would administer the sacraments not only to themselves but also to the needy patients.[26] This answer to the problem was too elegant to be turned down, and the mayor and the aldermen gladly signed the papers of the transaction, which Mother de la Ferre and her Council countersigned.

On the Feast of the Assumption 1647, twenty-three-year-old Jeanne Le Tendre joined her sister, already a Hospitaller, and on September 7, eve of the Nativity of the Blessed Virgin, Marie Bidault de la Ferre, age twenty-four, a relative of the superior, was accepted as a postulant.[27]

Since the community was flourishing, the practical founder judged the time was ripe to obtain Letters Patent for his institution, which would grant it the authorization to hold property in Mortmain[28] and guarantee for it, as

264

nothing else could, the independence and stability enjoyed by religious orders.

Jérôme did not waste a minute. On his way to Paris, it is likely that in Angers he obtained Bishop de Rueil's approval, dated December 30, of the settlement reached by the city of La Flèche and the Hospitallers of St. Joseph.[29] Perhaps it was on this occasion that he left for the Bishop's sanction the manuscript of the custom book prepared by Mother de la Ferre with his aid, and revised by the Jesuits, for the use of the Daughters in their different obediences. The sympathetic prelate may have even informed Jérôme that he had in mind a canonical visit to the Hôtel Dieu and the Daughters of St. Joseph. It was expedient that in accord with church law the latter benefit from a thorough comparison between their ideal as vested in the Constitutions and the reality of their everyday life.

To get the King's and the Parliament's consent to the modification of existing laws or privileges, in 17th-century France, the question of time was irrelevant. Months and years could go by in the process. But Jérôme Le Royer's Letters Patent were signed by ten-year-old King Louis, who was also Baron of La Flèche, in the first days of February 1648, registered by the Chancellery of France on the ninth of the same month, by the audit office on April 6, and by Parliament six days later.[30] This expedition may be explained by Fr. Olier's influence with the Queen Regent, who had not hesitated to send her guardsmen to protect him when he was in danger. Before the end of April, Jérôme was home again.[31] On June 5, the Letters Patent were finally registered at La Flèche and henceforth had force of law. Mother de la Ferre and her successors could freely govern the Daughters of St. Joseph and later build other hospitals as they saw fit, without submitting to outside pressure of any kind. And the community property was truly that of the Hospitallers. Jérôme had seen to that.

In the second week of July, he was called upon to draw up an inventory of the papers of his first cousin Jacques Le Royer de la Roche, who had died from a stroke during the previous April. He left three children, two daughters, one of whom was a nun, and a son. In Jérôme's absence, the family council had named him curator for Renée, then eighteen years old. This cousin made her home with him and his wife, Jeanne de Baugé, until she entered the Visitation Sisters in La Flèche.[32]

On July 28, during one of Jérôme's absences, took place the first canonical visit to the Hôtel Dieu and to the Sisters of St. Joseph.[33] The Bishop's delegate was the founder's good friend, the Vicar-General, Canon Syette, who had countersigned the report on Sr. Anne Baillif's apparitions in 1644. In the parlor of the Hôtel Dieu, he informed Mother de la Ferre of his commission to conduct the visit. She assembled the community at once and notified them about the Vicar-General's arrival, inviting them to pass the next few days in prayer and silence. On August 1, he offered the Holy Sacrifice in honor of the Holy Spirit in the chapel dedicated to St. Joseph and immediately began his tour of inspection.

With Fr. Gyrot, the chaplain, and with Fr. Etienne Busson, attached to the parish church, according to the prescription of Canon Law, the Bishop's delegate examined the altar, the tabernacle, the sacristy with its liturgical vestments, the chalices and missals: everything was in perfect order.

How could one see better what Jérôme Le Royer's plans had come to regarding the Hôtel Dieu and the Hospitallers than by accompanying Canon Syette, his assistants, Mother de la Ferre, and a few of her Sisters as they made the rounds of the place?

In the wards he spoke to each and everyone of the bedridden patients. All were clean and well taken care of.

"Things couldn't be better," he reported. The indigent sick were loud in their praise of the Daughters of St. Joseph concerning their bodily and spiritual well-being.

From the hospital proper, the little group went on to the rooms of the Sisters, to refectory, kitchen, infirmary, pharmacy, credenza, laundry, grounds, and exits: all things were in as good a shape as could be expected in the little space allotted to them.

At one o'clock in the afternoon, in a brief talk, the good Canon explained to the community the advantages of the canonical visit, promised to do what he could to make it a success, and guaranteed that everyone could count on his complete discretion. Then, beginning with the superior, he received each Sister privately, a task taking two or three of the warm summer days.

What were Canon Syette's conclusions at the end of the visit? There was much to praise, but from a spiritual viewpoint, there were faults against the Constitutions, due in part to the lack of a custom book. To remedy the situation, he would leave the Daughters of St. Joseph a detailed memorial of his visit to which they must refer on occasion; he would also give them back completed and amended the manuscript of the custom book the founder had submitted to Bishop de Rueil many months before.

He had not taken into account the financial situation, since Jérôme Le Royer, "their Father Bursar and director of temporal affairs" was absent. The agreement with City Hall was not yet effective and, as a result, the bookkeeping of the community was still done by the two administrators. But the Daughters themselves would attend to it after Jérôme's return.

All in all, the founder's plans were thriving as "a fruitful olive tree." There was, it is true, some dissatisfaction. Canon Syette pointed it out in alluding to Sr. Baillif's admonition, "Love your rules: they are from God!" A nucleus of stubborn Sisters were not content with their simple vows. They wanted to change the Daughters of St. Joseph into a cloistered community with solemn vows. To them may be applied these verses of Gresset, unfairly written for women in general:

Désir de fille est un feu qui dévore,
Désir de nonne est cent fois pis encore. [34]

The desire of a girl is a devouring fire.
The desire of a nun is a hundred times worse.

Chapter XX

Notes

1. Morin, *Histoire Simple et Véritable*, p. 57; *AM*, pp. 23, 56-57.

2. *AM*, p. 56.

3. Morin, *Histoire Simple et Véritable*, p. 57.

4. *AM*, p. 56.

5. *NA*, pp. 360-361.

6. *Ibid.*, p. 322.

7. *RPA*, Vol. 4, p. 285, Note 1.

8. *Ibid. AM*, p. 57, and *NA*, p. 362 give April 15.

9. *NA*, p. 389.

10. *RPA*, Vol. 4, p. 281.

11. *NA*, p. 323.

12. Morin, *Annales de l'Hôtel-Dieu de Montréal*, Ed. by A.E.Fauteux, E.-Z. Massicotte and C. Bertrand (Mémoires de la Société Historique de Montréal, No 12), Montreal, 1921, pp.168-169, Note C. Sister Le Jumeau set foot in Montreal in 1669, was fourth superior of the Hôtel Dieu, where she died on May 25, 1709 at the ripe old age of 92.

13. *RPA*, Vol. 4, p. 285.

14. *Ibid.*, p. 287. The *hongrelines*, an undergarment of Hungarian origin, are still worn (or were until Vatican II), Larousse tells us, by the Sisters of Charity.

15. *Ibid.*, p. 288.

16. Referred to as Fr. Diet by Morin in *Histoire Simple et Véritable*, pp. 162, 165. However, Fr. Edmond Lamalle, S.J., archivist of the Society of Jesus in Rome, in a letter dated April 14, 1963, writes: "Nous avons deux catalogues de cette année de la Province de France (catalogue triennal de 1645 et catalogue annuel de 1645 exeunte). Dans aucun des deux, je ne trouve de nom qui se rapproche de celui-ci, non seulement dans le personnel du collège de Blois, mais dans tout le catalogue..."

17. Morin, *Histoire Simple et Véritable*, pp. 162-163.

18. *NA*, pp. 374-375.

19. *RPA*, Vol. 4, p. 290.

20. *Ibid.*

21. *Ibid.*, p. 291.

22. Morin, *Histoire Simple et Véritable*, p. 198.

23. *VJLD*, Vol. 2, p. 333.

24. *RPA*, Vol. 4, pp. 293-294.

25. *Constitutions [primitives] des Filles Hospitalières de Sainct Ioseph.* Chap. VIII, art. 2 and 7.

26. *RPA*, Vol. 4, pp. 300-305.

27. *Ibid.*, p. 305.

28. The condition of property left in perpetuity, especially for religious, charitable or public purposes.

29. *RPA*, Vol. 4, p. 305.

30. *Ibid.*, p. 312.

31. *Ibid.*, p. 314: a notarized act drawn up and signed on April 26, 1648, testifies to his presence in La Flèche and that he was proprietor or lessee of three small farms in the vicinity of Tours.

32. *Ibid.*, pp. 313-314: Renée had taken the private vow of chastity at the age of twelve. As Sr. Renée Pacifique, she became one of the truly great superiors of the La Flèche Visitation monastery during her 66 years of religious life.

33. *Ibid.*, pp. 320-321.

34. Gresset, [Jean-Baptiste-Louis] "Vert-Vert," *Poésies choisies de Gresset*. Avec une notice bibliographique, par L. Derome, Paris, 1883, p. 1.

Chapter XXI

Mostly Laval and Moulins

WHILE THE HOSPITALLERS of St. Joseph at La Flèche were increasing daily, and while Jérôme Le Royer was traveling back and forth from La Flèche to Angers, from Angers to Paris, from Paris to La Rochelle, in the interest of Montreal, another possible development drew his attention. Requests began coming in for other Hôtels Dieu in different parts of the kingdom.

Already during September 1647, in the act providing financial discretion to both the hospital and to the Hospitallers, mention is made of "some other Hôtel Dieu" to which the Sisters could be sent.[1] This, of course, referred to the future Montreal Hôtel Dieu, but not exclusively. The hospitals to-be of France, under the care of the Daughters of St. Joseph, would be financed by benefactors of the cities and towns in which they would be erected. But Ville Marie's Hôtel Dieu would remain Jérôme Le Royer's responsibility. As he furnished the income for the little colony without drawing a sou of revenue from it, common sense dictated that he delay sending his Daughters of St. Joseph across the Atlantic until later. Moreover, in the important March 1648 contract, drawn up at the request of the "Unknown Benefactress," it was stipulated that the Hospitallers would be established at the Montreal Hôtel Dieu following Jeanne Mance's death.[2]

As far as we know, the city of Laval, astride the picturesque Mayenne River, was the first to call for nursing Sisters of St. Joseph.[3] Since 1644, Jérôme Le Royer was linked with it through his founding there of a branch of the Society of the Blessed Sacrament.[4] Acquaintances and probably friends were consequently not lacking in that city. On May 22, 1648 at Laval, he discussed the eventual erection within its limits of a Hôtel Dieu modelled on that of La Flèche. A few weeks later, once again he rode north into the hilly district of Lower Maine, lush with its green fields checkered by quickset hedges, fruit trees, oaks and beeches, perhaps the ancestor of all the fairy woodlands conjured up in our modern minds by Walt Disney's magic! But Jérôme's thoughts were foreign to magic of any kind. In his pouch he carried papers drawn up June 16 in his home town by Notary de la Fousse and signed by the Superior of the Daughters of St. Joseph and by her assistants, conferring upon the bearer the power of attorney to negotiate an agreement between the authorities of Laval and the Hospitallers of St. Joseph.[5]

In Laval, during the forenoon of June 20, Jérôme Le Royer was admitted into the presence of Louis de Cossé, Seigneur de Vauthorte and President of the Brittany Parliament, as well as of several other notables.[6] At the previous May meeting, with his wife, Dame Renée Picard, he had promised to cooperate with Jérôme. Although nothing was then specifically noted in writing, with regard to this promise, doubtless it was a respectable sum for the construction of the new establishment. Others now contributed to it in land or money, particularly Jean Bérault des Essarts, President of the King's Bench and of the Exempt[7] of Laval. The arrangement then signed guaranteed that six Daughters of St. Joseph would take over the future Hôtel Dieu. It definitely favored the city of Laval.

Jérôme Le Royer and Marie de la Ferre had intended it should be so. The people of Laval donated the land, the hospital, and the adjoining buildings; they also agreed to provide the new institution with a chapel or a small church.[8] The lay administrators would provide monthly whatever was needed for the impecunious sick by way of food and clothing or the equivalent in hard cash.

On the other hand, the Hospitallers committed themselves to supply their own furniture, to retain nothing of the alms destined to the patients and to find the sufficient income to cover the cost of their own food and upkeep—concretely a revenue of at least 100 livres. On the death of each Daughter of St. Joseph stationed at Laval, as for those at La Flèche, the community would contribute out of the deceased's dowry 300 livres for the benefit of the poor.

Since this understanding between Laval and the Daughters of St. Joseph was practically the same as that which was to exist wherever Hôtels Dieu were founded, it is worth while noting a few provisos which Jérôme tacked on. He had the lay administrators pledge they would never force the Sisters to accept any candidate of theirs into the community, not an unnecessary clause in those troubled days. All too often the younger children of the nobility were flooded with preferments: this had been the case for his friend Olier. He had them promise no chaplain would be assigned to the Daughters of St. Joseph unless he were acceptable to them and approved by the Ordinary. Finally he had them pledge no contagious patients would be admitted to the Hôtel Dieu and that all the sick, before being assigned to a ward, would be examined by a competent physician or surgeon.[9]

The Laval authorities promptly carried out their part of the agreement and had work begin on the hospital and the Sisters' residence, which was completed by mid-September 1650. With the blessing of Bishop Emmanuel de Beauvoir of Le Mans, the first batch of Daughters of St. Joseph moved into the new Hôtel Dieu on the fifth of December of the same year.[10]

Laval was not the only iron in the fire. There was also the Hôtel Dieu of Moulins. Perhaps the founder became interested in this new foundation in 1647 or earlier.[11] It was a long ten-day trip on horseback from La Flèche to Moulins on the Allier River in the Province of Bourbonnais.[12] How did he come to choose Moulins for what was to become one of his favorite foundations in France outside La Flèche?

A young priest, Fr. Gabriel Girault, a native of Moulins, noted for his devotion to St. Joseph, was the first link between his home town and Jérôme Le Royer.[13]

His father, a wealthy merchant, had given 100,000 livres to each of his five sons. Four of them took orders, one of them as a Jesuit, and all spent most of their income in behalf of the poor. When the founder of the Hospitallers first met Gabriel, he was about 27 years old.[14] The Royal College at La Flèche offered a theology course and he had registered for it, eventually carrying away his doctorate in divinity. During his studies in the Angevine city, he visited the prisons and the Hôtel Dieu. He was much impressed by what he found at the hospital—the orderliness and neatness, the competence and devotedness of the Daughters of St. Joseph.

The sharp contrast between the well staffed and well kept Hôtel Dieu before his eyes and the garret where a kindly soul called Julienne cared for a half dozen sick women in his own Moulins struck him forcefully. And— who knows?—maybe he was meant to remedy the situation!

Some time later, Jérôme Le Royer received the visit of a perturbed Girault. Since his first visit to the Hôtel Dieu of St. Joseph, the theology student had often toyed with the idea of a similar establishment on the Allier River; he then visualized the difficulties awaiting him along the way. He brooded upon them. But the urge grew more powerful each day. He turned to God for enlightenment and gave himself up to good works, especially at the Hôtel Dieu. There, as he helped out, he questioned the Daughters of St. Joseph and the inmates about the rules and regulations of the new congregation of Hospitallers and became more and more taken up with it. This was the story Gabriel Girault poured out to his host, the founder himself, whom he knew to be a prudent and saintly man.

Jérôme spoke to him kindly. No sanctimonious mouthing, but the quiet recommendation to pray and the promise to remember this important intention in his own prayers. If God intended this hospital to exist, he told his visitor, nothing in the world could stop it. And if God kept on pressing him with regard to a Hôtel Dieu in Moulins, Gabriel must disclose his aspirations to its notables, and do whatever he felt could bring about their achievement. But after having done his utmost, he must abandon the rest to Providence. On several other occasions, they discussed the project in detail. Finally Girault made up his mind to go on with it. To his everlasting credit, he never wavered despite stubborn opposition. On returning to Moulins, Fr. Girault began a vigorous one-man campaign in favor of the St. Joseph Hospitallers. The bigwigs in the City Council were reluctant to commit themselves. The priest's insistence and Jérôme Le Royer's prayers finally induced most of them to concur. The local authorities then agreed to broach the subject to Mother de la Ferre and to her assistants.

The founder, whom Fr. Girault had alerted, carefully studied the tentative request for St. Joseph Sisters, examined it with Mother de la Ferre and urged her, no matter what complications might follow, to accept it:

"God has given us, my Reverend Mother," he told her, "a perfect understanding of His holy Will. Let us follow it and surrender ourselves to his loving guidance. Great obstacles are to be overcome, but we will overcome them with his grace!"

Mother de la Ferre took his advice, and, in her prayers to the good Lord, told Him that if there must be trials and tribulations connected with the new venture, to send her to Moulins where she could bear the brunt of them alone.

However, before acknowledging the dispatch from Moulins, as Superior of the Institute, Bishop de Rueil had to be consulted. Mother de la Ferre soon had his authorization with his fatherly blessing and encouragement.[15] Then to Moulins went the answer with all the necessary information about hospitals and hospitallers. Mother de la Ferre also promised that Monsieur Le Royer would officially represent her and her community for the signing of the contract between the city officials of Moulins and the Daughters of St. Joseph.

On the afternoon of the nineteenth of September, Jérôme received his powers of attorney at the Hôtel Dieu and set off shortly after.[16] He was eager to see Fr. Girault through whom he had learned of the arrival in Moulins of the royal Letters Patent approving the establishment of a new Hôtel Dieu in that city. The priest was convinced Jérôme's presence might hasten the execution of the project and had written to him in this vein.

On reaching his destination, the collector of taxes from La Flèche immediately began a lively round of visits. Fr. Girault, who would have made an excellent publicity agent in our own 20th century, accompanied him on his calls to the influential people of the place: to the Lieutenant General of Moulins, to the Pastor, Fr. Sauldois, to the mayor and aldermen, to the future administrators of the Hôtel Dieu. He may even have accompanied him on his visit to Fr. de Lingendes,[17] rector of the Moulins college, today transformed into the district Court House. This Jesuit had been stationed at La Flèche during the early years of the Daughters of St. Joseph and had been consulted by Jérôme as he wrote the Constitutions for the new community. It was Lingendes who apparently introduced him to his illustrious penitent, Princess Marie Felicia Orsini, Duchesse de Montmorency, a niece of Pope Sistus V and a grandniece and godchild of Queen Marie de Médicis.[18]

Two months before, on the twenty-first of July, she had laid the cornerstone of a church in memory of her husband, Henri II, Duc de Montmorency and Maréchal de France. At first he had been loyal to Louis XIII in his fight against his brother Gaston d'Orléans. Unfortunately, for political reasons, Cardinal de Richelieu had refused to grant him the title of High Constable of France, which had always been held by someone of the elder branch of the House of Montmorency. Discouraged and disgusted, and aided and abetted by Princess Orsini, his wife, and by the Queen Mother, Marie de Médicis, he had sided with Gaston against the Crown. Wounded eighteen times and defeated at Castelnaudary by the royal troops under General Shomberg, the duke had been taken prisoner. With the utmost dispatch, at the age of 37 years, he was sentenced to death. On October 30, 1632, as he mounted the scaffold, his courage drew the tears of the soldiers. After his beheading, they drank of his blood and dipped their swords in it, hoping it would give them some of the qualities of the noble heart from which it flowed.

Marie de Médicis's punishment has already been mentioned; the Duchesse de Montmorency, her grandniece, was confined to the Château de Moulins for two years. Then, despite the solicitations of the boy King, of the queen, Anne of Austria, of the Duc d'Orléans, who wanted her back in Paris, and of her brother, the Duke of Bracciano, who insisted that she take up her abode in Rome, she retired to the hospitable Visitation monastery in Moulins. After her husband's execution, Jeanne de Chantal had written to her that her misfortune would serve to lead her to the summits of Christian perfection. She was not mistaken. The afflicted widow became a close friend of the foundress of the Visitation Order and was even present at her death in 1641.[19]

What came of the collector of taxes's meeting with the

Duchesse, whom Jeanne de Chantal considered a saint? No report exists of their first encounter. It did result in the founding of the Moulins Hôtel Dieu and in the coming to that locality of the Daughters of St. Joseph. Despite the apathy and the hesitation of the authorities, the hospital and its chapel, with four Daughters of St. Joseph to nurse the sick paupers, would slowly but surely pass from dream to reality thanks to the Duchesse's tenacity.

And so we find the city councillors and most of the prominent persons Jérôme had visited, among them Fr. de Lingendes, summoned to the parlor of the Visitation nuns on October 2, 1648. The agreement between Moulins and the St. Joseph Hospitallers of La Flèche was read and signed in the presence of the Duchesse de Montmorency.[20]

Two articles differed from the similar Hôtel Dieu contract at La Flèche: the Hospitallers agreed to buy the buildings needed to house the Community and to see to the repairs, without soliciting aid from the people of the city; they also accepted to take care of a certain number of orphan girls aged three to fourteen.[21]

Six days later Jérôme was still in Moulins. What was the cause of his delay? The Duchesse had donated 3,000 livres for the hospital chapel on condition it would be dedicated to the Immaculate Conception. Both Jérôme Le Royer and Fr. Girault suggested that it would be appropriate to name it after Our Lady's glorious spouse, St. Joseph. She willingly accepted their suggestion and, on the eighth of October, signed the necessary papers drawn up by her notary, to insure the change of name.[22]

Thus did Princess Orsini, Duchesse de Montmorency, supply the funds for the chapel and the city of Moulins pledge itself to build the Hôtel Dieu. But how was Jérôme to provide his Daughters of St. Joseph with a residence and all its furnishings?

The problem was settled in Paris a dozen days later.

Jérôme's position as collector of taxes for La Flèche opened several doors to him in the capital of the kingdom. Among them was that of Pierre Mérault, Farmer-General of the Treasury Department for the Province of Bourbonnais, who lived in the parish of St. Gervais.[23]

On the twentieth of October, Pierre Mérault and his wife, Anne Glue, vested Jérôme Le Royer with power of attorney to sign in their names a contract between the Sisters of La Flèche and themselves. This was exactly what Mother de la Ferre had done when he went to Moulins. Now, however, instead of representing the Superior of the Hôtel Dieu, he was to act for the Farmer General of Bourbonnais and his wife, who were ready to donate 4,800 livres for the construction of a convent for the Daughters of St. Joseph in Moulins.

On the ninth of November, in the familiar setting of the La Flèche Hôtel Dieu, Jérôme and his stand-by Notary Pierre de la Fousse, with an assistant in tow, met Mother Superior and her council. On the founder's advice, the Daughters of St. Joseph accepted the Méraults' generous gift and granted them the title of founders of the new community, which was to take effect as soon as the Hospitallers entered the future convent at Moulins.[24]

With the title went certain rights indicative of the original founder's gratitude. For the Méraults, two masses every year in perpetuity were to be offered. Before the *Introit* of these masses, the Hospitallers would chant the *Vexilla Regis* and afterwards receive Holy Communion for the two benefactors. At the death of each one of them, a Mass would be offered daily for an entire month at which, on the prescribed Communion days—in the 17th century, daily Communion was not permitted even in religious communities—the Daughters of St. Joseph would receive Communion for the repose of the soul of the deceased founder. Furthermore all the superiors of the Congregation were to be notified in order that their subjects commend to God's mercy the two honorary founders. Finally, as a special concession to Madame de Mérault, she was privileged along with two other ladies of her choice to enter the precincts of the convent whenever she pleased.

Ten days later, Jérôme was absent once again from La Flèche. His eldest son, Jérôme junior, for the first time in the capacity of lawyer, acted in his father's stead. By the second week of December, the collector of taxes was home once more. His son Ignace was then his main concern. Like Fr. Girault, this young man of twenty-five had studied for the priesthood at the Jesuit college of La Flèche and was about to receive the minor and major Orders. On Thursday, the ninth of December, with his wife, Jeanne de Baugé, Jérôme mortgaged his fief of Chantepie to assure the future priest sufficient security—in this case an annuity of 300 livres—as enjoined by the Council of Trent. Did the ordination take place on Saturday, the eighteenth of December, the last Ember Day of winter? Once again, we must regret the destruction of Jérôme's spiritual diary before his death; we can only surmise his great joy as well as his wife's when they received their first blessing from Fr. Ignace le Royer de Chantepie!

Fr. de Chantepré died in 1660,[25] but in the short span allotted to him, he proved a worthy son of Jérôme Le Royer. In 1650, consulted no doubt by Ignace and his father, the Jesuits advised them it would be an excellent idea to send the young priest for a year to the Seminary of St. Sulpice under Fr. Olier's direction. Often in those days, seminarians were day boarders only. This was the case for Fr. de Chantepie at the Royal College of La Flèche. The only clerical discipline he experienced was what he had imposed upon himself. In Paris, at St. Sulpice, he could acquire the theory and practice of Sulpician conduct. When he was named pastor of the 10th-century parish of Bazouges-sur-

Loir, he established an association for the clergy, "which was like an incipient seminary." [26] This was, of course, a source of legitimate pride and thankfulness for Jérôme and his wife.

Chapter XXI

Notes

1. *RPA*, Vol. 4, p. 304.

2. "Conventions, Pierre Chevrier et Louis d'Ailleboust" (March 17, 1648), in Mondoux, *L'Hôtel-Dieu, premier hôpital de Montréal*, p. 340.

3. *RPA*, Vol. 4, p. 315.

4. *Supra*, Chap. 7, p. 9.

5. *RPA*, Vol. 4, p. 316.

6. *Ibid.*, p. 319.

7. The Exempt were officers of the mounted constabulary.

8. *RPA*, Vol. 4, pp. 317, 319.

9. *Ibid.*, pp. 318-319.

10. *Ibid.*, Vol. 5, pp. 405-407.

11. *VJLD*, Vol. 2, p. 354, Note 1.

12. *RPA*, Vol. 4, p. 327.

13. *AM*, p. 59.

14. *RPA*, Vol. 4, p. 299.

15. *AM*, p. 63.

16. *RPA*, Vol. 4, pp. 327-328.

17. *NA*, p. 417.

18. (Louis-Emile) Bougaud, *Histoire de sainte Chantal et des origines de la Visitation*, 17th ed., Vol., 2, Paris, 1930, p. 513.

19. *Ibid.*, p. 515.

20. *RPA*, Vol. 4, pp. 328-330.

21. *NA*, pp. 418-419.

22. *AM*, p. 71.

23. *RPA*, Vol. 4, p. 332.

24. *Ibid.*, pp. 333-336.

25. Bertrand, *Monsieur de la Dauversière*, p. 178.

26. Faillon, *Vie de Monsieur Olier*, Vol. 3, p. 295.

Chapter XXII

A Very Sick Man

DURING THE WINTER OF 1648-1649, Jérôme Le Royer undertook another trip to Paris.[1] Eleven years later, his intimate friend, Baron Pierre de Fancamp, wrote to Fr. Pierre Chaumonot in Quebec that the tax collector scourged himself daily with a brass-wire discipline and wore a belt of more than 1,200 sharp barbs next to his body. In addition, his field gloves were lined with 2,000 of them. He also donned a hair-shirt which covered his infected shoulders.[2] At times he suffered so much he nearly fainted away. It was in this condition that he rode eastward.

What drew him to the capital? The problem of funds for Ville Marie constantly dogged him. About six months before, he had paid approximately one-ninth of the cost of the last shipment of supplies, using the monies given him by the Gentlemen of Montreal. In the latter half of 1648, he had had recourse to quite a few loans, which he paid off with the taxpayers's returns accumulated in his office, a total of at least 57,450 livres.[3] It appears that this practice was tolerated at the time, provided that money was on hand when the Farmer General demanded it.

Jérôme Le Royer's expenditures were always made in the name of the ladies and gentlemen of the Society of Montreal, who were supposed to reimburse him, even though their numbers had diminished alarmingly.

By the last days of the previous October, the Treaty of Westphalia had ended the Thirty Years's War. In continental Europe the Calvinists and Lutherans were permitted to practice their religion if their rulers were of the same persuasion. Politically Austria was defeated; Germany was broken and would remain so until Bismarck; France had the undisputed hegemony of the continent for three centuries. After all these years of fighting and carnage, enough bloodshed had drenched Europe for generations. True, talk of the Fronde—civil war between Parliament and Cardinal Mazarin—was on every tongue, but perhaps conditions would be better when Jérôme reached Paris.

Shortly after having dismounted in the capital, Jérôme found out the kingdom was embroiled in war—and not a comic-opera war. Forced to flee from the city on the sixth of January, Anne of Austria, the young King Louis XIV, Cardinal Mazarin and the Court had removed in haste to St. Germain, twenty miles to the west. This had been done with such dispatch that the child king and the queen mother came to an unfurnished palace and were compelled to sleep on mattresses strewn on the cold floor. The Cardinal Prime Minister thereupon ordered the royal troops to besiege Paris. The populace, the lawyers, and Parliament, with the support of the Princes de Conti, Beaufort, Longueville, and Elbeuf—having visions of the fat pensions that would accrue to them—resisted.[4]

In the countryside the life of the common people was anything but easy; within the walls of Paris attacked by Prince de Condé, it was worse. Assuredly this was not the time to beg for Montreal across the waters. To complicate matters, Jérôme then learned that Fr. Charles Rapine, Jeanne Mance's intermediary, had died during the second week of December.[5] Baron de Renty was busy taking care of the contagious patients in the slums. He thought little of the danger involved in carrying food and medication to the famished poor for whom he hurried through the dismal streets to the garrets where they lay dying.[6] Fr. Olier was desperately in need of provisions for his parishioners, since Condé's men had already begun to lay waste the approaches of the city. Some 1,500 families, his responsibility, were penniless and each day he distributed huge sums of money from his personal estate.[7]

Bitter cold weather gripped the city, resulting in added suffering. (Even today, in comparison with our North American standards, Paris is not too well equipped to meet the heating requirements of its population during the winter season.) The priest had great stores of wood and coal piled in different locations for distribution to the needy, particularly to those referred to as the "unworthy poor."

When the Princesse de Condé, the Duchesse d'Aiguillon, the Comtesse de Brienne and several other wealthy women fled the capital in order to avoid the rigors of the siege, Fr. Olier found himself without benefactors. With money and provisions having dwindled to nothing, in sad contrast to the ever increasing number of the poverty-stricken, he set out to seek help elsewhere. At the end of January or at the beginning of February,[8] Jérôme offered to accompany him to St. Germain, a locality quite out of bounds.

Prudently, they kept their plans to themselves. Had they been caught, or even suspected, it would have meant being branded as traitors and subjected to chastisement. Monsieur de Grandval, a friend of Fr. Olier's, quite willingly consented to transport them in the general direction of their destination, as far as the border of Saint-Germain-des-Prés. Having been left alone on the snow-covered road, with the city behind them, they proceeded on foot as rapidly as possible in the direction of the royal palace of Saint-Germain-en-Laye. The Seine had overflowed its banks and snow drifts blocked their passage. A cold biting wind tore at them. They often sank in the snow, which was hip-deep, leaving no trace of the road. In addition, the thought of the soldiers of the Fronde venting their fury on fugitives increased their apprehension. But as adroitly as the Three Musketeers—without cleaving anyone in twain—they crossed bridges, skirted body after body of troops without detection, and arrived at their destination worn-out but certainly pleased with themselves.

Their courageous feat caught the fancy of the Court. The Princesse de Condé, mother of the prince who commanded the royal army, gave the courageous priest a considerable sum of money for his poor and suffering charges. Others followed her example.

Can one suppose that Olier did not introduce his companion to at least a few courtiers? Making the most of the opportunity, Jérôme certainly recalled to them the little band of Frenchmen pinned down on an island of the St. Lawrence half-way round the world and the critical condition in which they were. The Iroquois seemed to be everywhere, concealed behind bushes and trees in readiness to assault, steal, and kill.[9] But the pioneers resisted bravely and built permanent structures, even a gristmill close to the fort.[10] Despite the hostile environment, they were there to stay.

Loaded down with contributions, the two beggars for Christ returned to the capital without being caught and Fr. Olier was able to take care of his parishioners until the end of the first Fronde during the month of March.

Had Jérôme Le Royer's visit to St. Germain benefited Ville Marie? Had his stay in Paris during these perilous weeks been of any help? There is no evidence one way or the other. Through his friend Olier, he may then have heard about a young Sulpician, Fr. Alexandre Le Ragois de Bretonvilliers, who later in the year was to prove a godsend to him.

Jérôme was in La Flèche by February 24, for on that day he had the Hospitallers ratify the contract signed on the second of October of the previous year concerning the new hospital at Moulins.[11] The collector of taxes then learned the sad news of the death of his beloved bishop, Claude de Rueil, at the beginning of 1649.[12] He would know the extent of his loss only when the time came to deal with the next

287

incumbent of the See of Angers.

In the early years of Rueil's episcopate, he had chosen two worthy priests and appointed them Vicars-General. He had convened many synods in line with the recommendations of the Council of Trent, proceeded firmly against abuses without enacting scores upon scores of regulations, convinced as he was that a froth of new ones would not be as effective as the enforcement of those already on the books.

Not satisfied with the suppression of abuses, Bishop de Rueil had bent his efforts to the improvement of the spiritual life of his flock. In this vein he had approved Jérôme's Confraternity of the Holy Family and the establishment of the Daughters of St. Joseph. He had been especially careful about safeguarding the Faith. No blemish of any sort tarnished his reputation; this being noteworthy in an age when so great a number of clerics proved to be unworthy of their calling. His kindness, which was extended not only to laymen but also to priests both diocesan and regular, endeared him to the entire diocese—a feat that most every bishop yearns to effect but does not always accomplish. Not surprisingly, the grief and love of the faithful of all classes of society far outshone the pomp and splendor of Claude de Rueil's funeral service.

This death may have been the event that finally brought Jérôme to a standstill, for Jeanne de Baugé soon discovered she had a very sick husband on her hands.[13] His condition deteriorated to the point that the end was expected at any moment. Prayers were offered for his recovery, not only by his devoted wife and children, by his spiritual family, the Daughters of St. Joseph, but also by the entire city.

This illness lasted several weeks. Then, amazingly, Mother de la Ferre, the woman who understood far better than anyone else how essential he was to the well-being of her community and to Montreal, was informed in prayer that he was to live for an additional ten years and that she herself would precede him in death.[14] In addition to this statement of private revelation pertaining to his future, Baron de Renty, from his residence in Paris during the first part of April, wrote to him: "My dear Brother, God has made known to me that you would not die of this illness and that He would keep you for your family and for the affairs concerning His glory and service..." [15]

Certainly, both of these messages gave comfort to Jérôme, and, as predicted, he recovered his health.

Then, strange to say, the roles were reversed, and his friend the Baron contracted a disease at the bedside of one of his patients.[16] On April 11, he did not feel well, but he continued to climb stairs to wretched lodgings, weighted down with food, medicine, and clothing for Christ's poor. On going to bed that night, he began to suffer excruciating pains. As the days elapsed, he grew worse.

It was the destitute, the hungry, the homeless, who were the concern of the Baron until the end of his life. He commended these children of God to his wife's loving care and assured her that regardless of what she gave them, she would never be left impoverished. Still acting as president of the Society of the Blessed Sacrament (his eleventh term in office), he ordered alms to be distributed to those who were in need as a result of the Fronde. Not only were the poor in the capital to be included but also those living in every province of the kingdom.

On April 13, he called for his confessor in order to settle his affairs with God, fearing that he might not remain lucid long enough to accomplish this important act in the manner that he wished. On the following day he went to confession, and this he did nearly every day until his death. On Thursday, two days before the end, he received the sacrament of Extreme Unction, and, at the priest's suggestion, gave his final blessing to his wife and children.

It was shortly before the Saturday noon Angelus that he asked for a picture of the Child Jesus and reverently kissed it. Then he kissed his crucifix and entered into a period of agony which was to last a quarter of an hour. During these last moments he constantly repeated the holy name of Jesus. The Baron Gaston de Renty gave up his soul to God on April 24, 1649, at the early age of 37.[17] Approximately ten years before, he had received the revelation that he was to play an important role in the establishment of the Church on the Island of Montreal.

The loss of his close friend and helper was keenly felt by Jérôme Le Royer. But life must go on and there was still much work to be done. During his convalescence, he no doubt informed Mother de la Ferre of his latest project: a new residence for the Hospitallers. As soon as he was up and about again, the "Father of the Poor" set to work at acquiring the nearby property, the largest lot being then occupied by Fr. Michel Hamelin's presbytery and several small buildings. It might have been that the years had temporarily subdued the pastor. At any rate, fire-breathing Hamelin came to a peaceful agreement with the Daughters of St. Joseph and sold them the entire estate on the nineteenth of July.

This transaction took place at the Hôtel Dieu of St. Joseph.[18] Many of the people already mentioned were present for the ceremony. These notables included presiding Notary Royal Pierre de la Fousse, Fr. Michel Hamelin, Jérôme Le Royer, Jérôme's brother, René Le Royer de Boistaillé, administrators for the poor of the hospital, Mother de la Ferre and her assistants, Mothers Anne de L'Espicier, Anne Aubert de Cléraunay, Marie Gyrot, and Renée Busson.

The pastor agreed to part with the presbytery and its appurtenances for 6,000 livres in order to avoid litigation— for his wall occupied a few feet of the Hôtel Dieu site—on condition that the Sisters find him "a decent and convenient house." Since the Community did not have this sum of money on hand, it was agreed that the Sisters would pay 300 livres by August 1 of each year, while being charged with an interest rate of five percent on the balance. Jérôme, with his brother and Notary de la Fousse, worked out the details of the contract and, with Fr. Hamelin's permission, had two masons and a carpenter inspect the premises.

Another transaction took place on the same day. A barn belonging to the pastor, bordering on the Hôtel Dieu in the direction of Port Luneau, was purchased for 2,400 livres. On the following day, July 20, a final acquisition was made by renting a nearby garden from a Monsieur des Pins, the agreed sum being an annual payment of 70 livres. Adequate provision was thus made for the future residence of the Sisters.

All of this responded to a definite need. Vocations, which had fallen off since 1647, were now on the uplift. From February to the end of May, seven young ladies had begged admittance to the Daughters of St. Joseph.[19]

And then on the twenty-fifth of June, there came from Laval a young lady, small in stature but long in name: Mademoiselle Lésine Scholastique Bérault des Essarts.[20] She skipped up the steps of the Hôtel Dieu drawing in tow Canon Arnoul, her uncle and tutor. The good priest was not over-enthusiastic about his niece's vocation. Upon arriving at La Flèche a queer idea popped into his mind: he would put his beloved Lésine to a final test of her vocation, truly an acid test.

"My niece," he began, "it is the custom of the community into which you are about to go, to chant a *Veni Creator* in church before the regular entry into the novitiate. And this is to be done while holding a large lighted candle in the hand, in front of all the Sisters. Now I want you to carry this large lighted candle along the street, from the inn to the hospital. It is on this condition that I shall leave you there and return in a year from now to receive your vows. What do you say to that?"

"Give me the candle, my kind uncle!"

To cross the city while holding a flaming light in one's hand required plenty of backbone, as the thoroughfares were swarming with students from the Royal College. The good Canon prudently kept his distance since he had no intention of being linked up with his young niece. Mother de la Ferre, however, having been quickly informed of the situation, hurried out of the Hôtel Dieu, extending open arms to the courageous sixteen-year-old girl.

Two weeks and a day following Lésine des Essarts's entry, a compatriot from Laval, Mademoiselle Jeanne Hérault de Grandmaison, aged nineteen years, asked to be received as a postulant at the La Flèche Hôtel Dieu. Both these girls stipulated, at the time of their entry, that once they had taken their vows they would return to their native city to work in the Hôtel Dieu, which would then have surely been completed.

Towards the end of August, Jérôme was again on his way to Moulins. Fr. Girault's enthusiasm for a hospital had not abated, and he seldom by-passed the chance to prod the slow-moving city officials. The mayor and aldermen finally sent a petition to their Bishop, Claude de la Magdelaine de Ragny of Autun, requesting his authorization to open a Hôtel Dieu within the limits of their fair city, with the understanding that the Daughters of St. Joseph of La Flèche would staff it.[21] The document was written out in Jérôme's hand.

Bishop de Ragny was a man of the world and something of a spendthrift. Yet he possessed good moral fiber. Sad to say, his priests were for the most part illiterate men. And even sadder to say, some were not reluctant to engage women as companions for the night. Ragny, however, was not the man to undertake the reform of his diocese single-handed. He appointed a saintly priest Vicar-General, enjoining him to run the diocese. He also welcomed new and fervent communities of men and women, among which, history was to note, were Jérôme's Daughters of St. Joseph.

On September 5, 1649, the Bishop issued a decree in favor of the mayor and aldermen of Moulins, granting them their request and wishing them the blessings of Heaven.[22]

About the same time, directly from Moulins, Jérôme Le Royer rode to Paris. There, at St. Sulpice, he met Fr. Alexandre Le Ragois de Bretonvilliers, who lived with Fr. Olier, and a little later, his two brothers, Jean and Bénigne, at their residence on the Place Royale in St. Paul's parish. On September 22, Jean, Bénigne and Fr. Alexandre generously contracted to pay the cost of the new residence for the Daughters of St. Joseph in La Flèche.[23] The only condition stipulated was that they be given the title of "founders" with the resulting privileges, which were like those granted to the Méraults de Corbeville.

These signal benefactors did not stint in the giving; the splendor of the edifice in general, the delicate carvings, the elegance of the chasing and staircases, the ornamentation of the bells, all this was ample proof and lasting evidence of their generosity. In this way nearly 40,000 livres were contributed to charity, profiting a province far removed from the heart of France.[24] No wonder Mother de la Ferre and her Sisters ratified the contract naming the benefactors "founders." [25]

This result alone would have amply compensated Jérôme's journey to Paris, yet it was still more rewarding. In the capital, he found two new candidates for his community, daughters of a Parisian lawyer.[26] They were warmly welcomed at the La Flèche Hôtel Dieu on November 8 by Mother de la Ferre.

On December 6, Jérôme Le Royer was still in Paris. As the agent for the Daughters of St. Joseph, he was then entrusted with the dowry of Sr. Marie Houzé, who had taken her vows on the seventeenth of August at La Flèche.[27] Still he did not return home, other business kept him where he was.

Chapter XXII

Notes

1. Bertrand, *Monsieur de la Dauversière*, p. 180.

2. Baron de Fancamp, "Copie fidelle de la lettre écrite au Reverand [sic] Père Chaumonot, Jésuitte, au Collège de Kebec, sur la mort de Monsieur de la Dauversière, en l'année 1660," in Morin, *Histoire Simple et Véritable*, p. 109.

3. *VJLD*, Vol. 2, p. 387.

4. Hilaire Belloc, Louis XIV, 3rd ed., New York, p. 49.

5. Daveluy, *Jeanne Mance, 1606-1673*, p. 117, Note 1.

6. Bessières, *Deux grands inconnus: Gaston de Renty et Henry Buch*, pp. 332-333.

7. Faillon, *Vie de Monsieur Olier*, Vol. 2, p. 491.

8. *Ibid.*, p. 495.

9. Dollier de Casson, *A History of Montreal*, p. 139.

10. *Ibid.*, p. 143.

11. *RPA*, Vol. 4, p. 339.

12. *NA*, pp. 421-423.

13. *AM*, pp. 78-79.

14. Le Royer de la Motte, *Le petit mémoire*, p. 29. See Chap. III, Note 20.

15. *Ibid.*

16. Bessières, *Deux grands inconnus: Gaston de Renty et Henry Buch*, p. 333.

17. *Ibid.*, p. 349.

18. *RPA*, Vol. 4, pp. 345-350.

19. On February 17, Marguerite Renard de la Groie, aged 22, related to the La Motte Le Royers, cousins of Jérôme's; on March 15, Anne and Claude Bidault de Ruigné, 15 and 14 years old respectively, related to Jérôme, to Mother de la Ferre, and Anne Foureau; on May 20, Marie Bérard des Loges, aged 15, followed shortly afterwards by her sister Madeleine, both being nieces of Canon Syette; on May 30, Jeanne Busson des Chaumières, joining her sister Renée, who had entered in 1641; on July 2, Jeanne Le Gras de Villette, sister of Renée, admitted in 1646. Both were nieces of Mother Anne Aubert de Cléraunay.

20. *NA*, pp. 441-442.

21. *RPA*, Vol. 4, pp. 351-352.

22. *Ibid.*, 352-354.

23. *Ibid.*, pp. 355-357.

24. *AM*, p. 77.

25. *RPA,* Vol. 4, pp. 357-358.

26. Catherine and Antoinette de Beaufort, respectively 18 and 15 years old.

27. *RPA*, Vol. 4, p. 366.

PART THREE

Achievement

Chapter XXIII

The Society of Montreal Lives Again

DURING HIS STAY in the French metropolis,[1] Jérôme met a traveller from Ville Marie. Conditions in New France and news from Old France had prompted Jeanne Mance to take the long, hazardous trip back to her native land. The sufferings and the wholesale destruction of the Hurons by the Iroquois[2] meant that Montreal would soon be the last outpost of the colony. To survive, it must be strongly fortified. Towards the end of July, she had learned that a few Indians had come up from Tadoussac to Quebec with the news that a ship was on its way, and she immediately went down to meet it.

By August 23, three ships had splashed anchor in the shadow of Cap Diamant, followed by another the next day, then still another in September, and finally the *Notre Dame* in October.[3] Jeanne quickly opened the letters addressed to her. Times were as bad in the motherland as in Canada.[4] She was informed of Fr. Charles Rapine's death, which posed a serious problem. In the future how was she to communicate with her benefactress, Madame de Bullion? The Society of the Ladies and Gentlemen of Montreal had melted down to a few members. Furthermore, because of the Fronde, the misery of the common people offered more immediate appeal to the charity of the wealthy than hyperborean Canada. To top it off, there were bad tidings about Jérôme Le Royer's health and the sorry state of his

297

affairs. All these misfortunes endangering the very existence of Ville Marie would have discouraged a weaker
woman than Jeanne Mance. She, however, instead of
returning to Montreal, decided to set sail for France to see
what could be done about this difficult situation and
boarded the *Notre Dame*,[5] which weighed anchor on the
twenty-second of October.

She reached France by early winter and thanked God
on finding Jérôme Le Royer in good health instead of on the
threshold of eternity. She informed him about the disastrous conditions in New France and together they planned
to aid Ville Marie as best they could by shoring up the
Society of Montreal in France.

Before leaving the capital, Jérôme informed his intrepid
associate he would soon be seeing her again. He reached
home about New Year's Day, 1650. On the tenth of January,
he attended a meeting of the people of La Flèche to elect a
mayor.[6] Pierre Jouye des Roches, an honest and capable
man, had exercised his charge of chief executive many
times and was well liked by the inhabitants of the city. He
was an old friend of Jérôme's. In 1634 he had endowed the
Hôtel Dieu with an annuity of twenty-two livres on condition
that each Holy Thursday loaves of the best whitened bread
be distributed to all the poor patients after they had
received Holy Communion.[7] The great majority of the
population wished him to continue as their chief magistrate despite an Order in Council to the contrary. A few violently opposed his reelection, among them bellicose Fr. Hamelin, who was hankering anew to pick a quarrel with someone.

Pierre Jouye, a peace-loving soul, proposed Jérôme Le
Royer for his successor. Though the natives of La Flèche
held him in high esteem, they did not abandon Jouye. The
virulent pastor took the case to the Presidial Court and
threatened to go to Parliament in Paris with it. Then the
Marquis de la Varenne, Governor of La Flèche, intervened,

and to practically everyone's satisfaction, in particular to Jérôme's, reinstated Pierre Jouye des Roches as mayor. The next day, January 11, the tax-collector was busy with paper work. He signed a promise to apprentice a young man named Gadois to an armorer of the city.[8] A priest stationed at Bailleul in northern France, Fr. François Cosnier, made over to Jérôme Le Royer the sum of three hundred livres for the Hôtel Dieu, with the stipulation that six low Masses be yearly offered for him in the hospital chapel.[9]

All the while Jérôme's mind must have wandered more than once. His daughter Marie was insisting that she wished to become a nun, and Mother Marie de la Ferre was nearing the end of her two terms as superior of the Daughters of St. Joseph. The rules of the new community expressly stated that the superior should not hold office for more than two three-year terms. Jérôme Le Royer could have obtained a dispensation. Who better than she was able to dispose the Bishop Elect favorably towards the La Flèche Hospitallers? The high calibre of her intellect, her tenacious energy, her wise conduct in difficult circumstances, her modesty and especially her extraordinary charity made her an ideal superior. But she as well as Jérôme decided not to deviate from the approved Constitutions.

Who then was to succeed Mother de la Ferre as head of the Congregation? Sr. Anne Foureau, the second to pronounce her vows, was dead; the third, Sr. Anne de L'Espicier was very ill, indeed close to death's door, and no other subject seemed to have a special title to the succession. Even so, Mother de la Ferre invited the Capitular Vicars-General of the diocese to delegate someone to preside at the election of the next superior. They commissioned Fr. Ignace Le Royer, Jérôme's son, to represent them.

On January 22, Sr. Anne Le Tendre was chosen superior and, four days later, her election was officially confirmed by the Capitular Vicars at Angers.[10] Mother Le Tendre was thirty-one years old and had devoted herself for nine years at the La Flèche Hôtel Dieu. Sr. de la Ferre was named assistant, Sr. Anne Aubert de Cléraunay replaced Sr. Renée Busson as instructress of novices—an unfortunate nomination as time would tell—, Sr. Marie Havard de la Tremblaye became head hospitaller, and Sr. Marie Gyrot, bursar.

No doubt Jérôme felt a pang of regret at seeing his saintly collaboratrix relegated to second place. The two had worked diligently together to establish the Daughters of St. Joseph. On Candlemas Father Le Royer presided at the renewal of vows of twenty-three Daughters of St. Joseph. If the two founders needed consolation, here it was for both of them.

The previous day, the first of February, had been bittersweet for Jérôme Le Royer. Marie, his child with the beautiful voice, and her cousin Renée Le Royer, adopted by the tax-collector in 1648, had entered the Visitation Convent at La Flèche.[11] His wife did not take her daughter's vocation easily. The unhappy mother used every means at her disposal—tears, caresses, and promises—to induce Sr. Marie Angélique to give up the religious life. All to no avail. The atmosphere at home must not have been too pleasant when, a few days later, Monsieur Jérôme Le Royer set out for Paris with his son Ignace, who was on his way to spend a year at St. Sulpice under the able guidance of Fr. Olier.[12]

More than ever, Jérôme was deeply concerned about Ville Marie. With Mademoiselle Mance and Fr. Olier, he discussed the ways and means of saving the island colony on the verge of succumbing to the Iroquois raids.

Their first objective consisted in rallying as many as possible of the initial associates of the Society of Montreal. Of the founding members two, Jérôme himself and Bertrand Drouart, were unable to contribute any financial help. On March 21, these devoted gentlemen gathered in Notary

Chaussière's study. Besides Jérôme Le Royer and Baron de Fancamp, were present Fr. Jean Jacques Olier, Fr. Alexandre Le Ragois de Bretonvilliers, Fr. Nicolas de Barrault, Roger du Plessis, Marquis de Liancourt and Duc de la Roche-Guyon, Henri Louis Haber de Montmor, King's Councillor and Master of the Court of Pleas, Bertrand Drouart, and Louis Séguier de Saint-Firmin. Until then Le Royer and Fancamp had been holding the Island of Montreal for the Company of the same name; on that day they turned it over to all the associates.[13] The entire group signed the new act, drawn up to implement that of March 25, 1644. They also voted 200 arpents—nearly as many acres— of land to the Montreal Hôtel Dieu.

The board of directors was reshuffled. Fr. Elie Laisné de la Marguerie felt he could no longer do justice to his role as head director of the Society since his nomination to the Privy Council. Heartily approved of by Jeanne Mance, Fr. Olier was elected to the post; Louis Séguier assumed the charge of secretary, and Jérôme Le Royer was maintained treasurer. At that same meeting or shortly afterwards, it was decided to have an official seal made for practical reasons: completed, it carried an engraving of Our Lady with the Infant Jesus in her arms standing on a knoll, with the inscription *Our Lady of Mount Royal.*[14]

Jérôme's faith in Our Lady's promise made to him at Notre Dame that she would always assist him never wavered. So he was not overly surprised when Mademoiselle Mance informed him that the "Unknown Benefactress," was as interested as ever in the distant colony. Indeed she made a generous donation to the Montreal hospital and assured Jeanne Mance that Fr. Rapine's death would not interrupt her contributions in any way.[15]

In the early summer of the year, when the time came for Jeanne Mance to return to New France, she could truthfully tell the Ville Marie settlers in the throes of constant attacks by the Iroquois that in their homeland influential people were once again concerned about the survival of the far-off island foundation.

As for Jérôme, his attention was soon drawn back to the Daughters of St. Joseph. On April 25, 1650, he signed an agreement with the city of Baugé, located some twelve miles from La Flèche, to supply it with enough of his Hospitallers to care for its penniless sick.[16]

Eight years before, on his death bed, a Monsieur de la Beauce had begged his daughter Marthe to found a hospital within the limits of Baugé. This she was to achieve empty-handed, for her father had no fortune to bequeath to her. She knew that Monsieur Le Royer had relatives in Baugé, Mother Marie de la Ferre, too, and that the late Anne Foureau was a native of Baugé. What they had accomplished at La Flèche, could not her people do in their own home town? By 1643, she saw the cornerstone of the long-desired hospital laid. Finally, after delegating one of the aldermen to look over the La Flèche Hôtel Dieu, presumably at Marthe's insistence, the city council resolved to invite the Hospitallers of St. Joseph to staff the new Hôtel Dieu as soon as they could be decently housed.

Before returning home, Jérôme Le Royer acquired a property called Champboisseau close by the Hôtel Dieu.[17] The price, 2,550 livres, was reasonable, even though it had to be paid up before July 1650. Since this land was sold "to oblige the Hospitallers who would be sent to care for the new institution," the proprietors, M. and Mme. Denays de Fontanelles, requested that they be buried in the hospital chapel as well as Madame's father, and that they be conceded the right to add Champboisseau to their name. Jérôme had no objections.

Scarcely had he hurried back to La Flèche and wit-nessed the signing of the contract by the Daughters of St. Joseph than the money for the Champboisseau land, even more than needed, was found. Then on April 27, two relatives of Mother de la Ferre, Anne and Claude Bidault de Ruigné, took their vows and presented the community with a substantial dowry.[18]

During June, Fr. Dubreuil, Jérôme's former spiritual guide, stopped at La Flèche and called upon Mothers de la Ferre and Anne Le Tendre. He proposed that they accept as lay volunteer a person whom he warmly recommended although he could not divulge her name and rank. This mysterious personage simply desired to be of service to the poor without pronouncing any vows. As the new superior and her predecessor had complete faith in the Jesuit, they consented to his proposal.

The newcomer arrived garbed in a coarse grey dress, with heavy shoes on her feet. Her brother, who accompanied her, was dressed as a peasant. The name she gave was Anne de la Haye, and her brother, who served as her valet, called himself M. de Baumé. He took lodgings with Fr. Gyrot.

The Daughters of St. Joseph, who had not completely divested themselves of their feminine curiosity, soon discovered that Anne de la Haye was of noble lineage. The fine linen in her trunk, her white hands, and her distinguished manners spoke louder than words. She quickly aroused the admiration of the community by her constant willingness to do the most humble tasks in the hospital wards.

About this time, Marthe de la Beauce began coming to La Flèche to prepare for her future role at the new Baugé Hôtel Dieu. She or one of her companions, having visited with Anne de la Haye who was ill abed, teasingly suggested that she might some day become the official foundress of the Baugé hospital, which, then "was not unlike the stable at Bethlehem."

"And why, my Sister," she replied, "would God not send a foundress to this poor hospital?" [19]

Anne de la Haye shortly assumed this office. Her true

name was Mlle. Anne de Melun, Princesse d'Epinoy, some-time canoness of the chapter of St. Gertrude at Mons in the Netherlands.[20] She was the daughter of Pierre de Melun, Prince d'Epinoy, Sovereign of Vernes, Grandee of Spain, hereditary Constable of Flanders, and Governor of Mons; and of Ernestine Claire-Eugénie d'Aremberg.[21] Her brother's veritable name was Guillaume Alexandre d'Epinoy. The princess and her brother could well afford to take on the foundation of the Hôtel Dieu.

On August 10, 1650, they were both at Baugé. She settled down in a garret near the walls of the unfinished hospital, and Guillaume roomed at the home of Marthe de Beauce's brother. Together they hired a considerable number of workmen. The brother spent himself as a laborer and the sister, not to be outdone, served the masons, carpenters, and plasterers their meals.

While the construction of the Hôtel Dieu of Baugé progressed, the new Bishop of Angers, Fr. Henri Arnauld, took possession of his See. This was the prelate who, for nearly a quarter of a century, was to do his utmost to undermine Jérôme Le Royer and Marie de la Ferre's foundation. Many years before, when Arnauld was still a child, St. Francis de Sales had foretold his elevation to the episcopate. This great saint should have revealed what sort of a prelate he would be.

Henri Arnauld was consecrated bishop of Angers on June 29, 1650, eight months after his nomination by the king.[22] Monsieur de Trie, as he was called, was the son of Antoine Arnauld, noted for his hatred of the Society of Jesus, which he had succeeded in 1594 in having tempo-rarily banished from France. This man with his wife and twenty children staunchly adhered to Jansenism, a heresy first taught by a Dutch bishop, Cornelius Jansens, in his book *Augustinus*, his peculiar interpretation of the Bishop of Hippo's doctrine. The youngest of the family, Antoine junior, known as "the great Arnauld," became the propagator of this heresy in his country. Henri, too, was a Jansenist to the core.

Jansenism denied the reality of free will in man and the universality of salvation through the death of Jesus Christ. It advocated a pessimistic view of predestination engendering great austerity and infiltrated the writings of Pascal, Racine, La Rochefoucauld, La Bruyère, Boileau, and even Molière! Its most vigilant adversary was the Society of Jesus, which taught that everyone was free to choose good or evil and that God gave one and all the means of saving themselves by granting *sufficient* grace to attain salvation.

For the time being, the Most Reverend Henri Arnauld dissimulated. Warped in mind and heart by this destructive doctrine, he would all too soon begin his attacks on the Daughters of St. Joseph.

During the summer months at the La Flèche Hôtel Dieu, three novices were received into the Congregation.[23] Jeanne Le Gras de Villette pronounced her vows on June 29, feast of St. Peter and St. Paul. (Her sister Renée had then been a professed religious for two years.) With her, Mademoiselle Bérault des Essarts, the young lady whose uncle, Canon Jean Arnoul, had obliged her to walk through the streets of La Flèche with a lighted candle in her hand, now had the satisfaction of seeing him offer the Holy Sacrifice and of receiving her vows in the name of the Church. A month later, on July 26, a compatriot of Sr. des Essarts, Jeanne Hérault de Grandmaison, also made profession as a Daughter of St. Joseph. The contract which she signed on the eve of her vows stipulated that she would eventually be attached to the future Laval Hôtel Dieu, if she so wished. For the first time, Bishop Henri Arnauld's name appeared on a document relating to the community founded by Jérôme Le Royer de la Dauversière.

On November 20, 1650, only a few days after having

officially taken possession of his See, at Jérôme's request, Bishop Arnauld authorized in writing the transfer of three Daughters of St. Joseph to Baugé: Sr. Renée Le Jumeau des Perrières as superior and Srs. Françoise Pilon and Renée Le Gras de Villette to work with her.[24] They were directed to go to the new Hôtel Dieu dedicated to St. Joseph at Baugé without stopping anywhere unless it were necessary. At the same time, the bishop also designated the sisters who were to staff the Laval foundation,[25] applying to them the same strictures concerning their transfer: along the way they were not to visit any shrine, monastery or residence of any sort. On November 22, the superior of the Laval group, Mother Anne Aubert de Cléraunay signed a document written in Jérôme's hand, promising obedience to the motherhouse and to the Constitutions as long as they were away from La Flèche.[26]

Four days later, after attending Mass and receiving Holy Communion, Mother Le Jumeau and Srs. Pilon and Le Gras signed a similar engagement on the morning of their departure for Baugé.[27] Dressed in riding habits, they were then accompanied to the doors of the enclosure by the other Hospitallers. Their chaplain, Fr. Gyrot, and most likely Mother de la Ferre[28] and Monsieur Le Royer[29] joined them for the trip. Their horses were ready, and the four ladies, having covered their faces with their black heart-shaped taffeta masks and drawn on their gloves, set off for their destination.

About half past five in the afternoon, the little troop reached Baugé. The pastor, Fr. Pierre Charbonnier, his curate, and several other clergymen with the hospital administrators had gathered at the Hôtel Dieu to welcome them.[30] As spokeswoman for her companions, the Superior, Mother Renée Le Jumeau, addressed Fr. Charbonnier. They had quit their residence at La Flèche, she said, at the request of the inhabitants of Baugé to serve God and His poor in their midst. She then handed him the episcopal decree and the authorization to change residence. Their official entry took place on the following morning, Saturday, November 26, between eight and nine o'clock, ending with Mass, the singing of the *Te Deum*, and the blessing of all the wards and rooms of the hospital.

Before returning to La Flèche, Mother de la Ferre inaugurated the novitiate by receiving the first novice, Marthe de la Beauce, who aspired to be a lay Sister. She had been instrumental in the founding of the Hôtel Dieu, she had realized her father's dying wish, and now she retreated into the background, happy to hand over to competent hands her heavy responsibilities.

Jérôme Le Royer and Marie de la Ferre did not forget to acknowledge their indebtedness to Mademoiselle de la Haye and to Monsieur de Baumé. They listened to the story of their lives at Baugé for the last four months. The couple sparked the curiosity of the people. Their fellow workers had not been long deceived by the peasant apparel of the two newcomers. Why were they spending their days in the little city of Baugé? Perhaps they were spies sent out to discover whether the population was for or against the Fronde, for or against the king, for or against the aristocracy. Even if the two claimed to be brother and sister, was it so? Didn't she call herself Anne de la Haye, he Guillaume de Baumé? Evil tongues began to wag. Then Anne became ill and to quiet the vicious gossiping had an aged invalid's bed placed next to hers. Under the inquisitive eye of the wizened old woman, simply by the example of her daily life, Anne de la Haye proved how groundless the accusations were.[31]

This was the first of the many foundations of Jérôme Le Royer's and of Mother Marie de la Ferre's Daughters of St. Joseph outside La Flèche. It served as a prelude to the Laval and Moulins Hôtels Dieu, and later on to the definitive establishment of the Montreal Hôtel Dieu, today the

307

motherhouse of the Sisters of St. Joseph of La Flèche throughout the world. Sr. Renée Le Jumeau des Perrières, it has already been noted, was assigned to the Hôtel Dieu at Baugé; years after, she would receive her appointment to Montreal.

On Thursday, December 1, the Laval nominees set out for their new hospital in the company of their chaplain, "the respectable Fr. Guillaume Troussard," and surely of Jérôme Le Royer.[32] Two days later, they came to the end of the road. At eight o'clock in the morning, on Monday, December 5, the official reception took place at Laval as it had at Baugé. This contingent of Daughters of St. Joseph was made up of the superior, Mother Anne Aubert de Cléraunay, of two subjects originally from Laval, Srs. Lésine Scholastique des Essarts and Jeanne Hérault de Grandmaison, followed by Marie Houzé, Marguerite Rénard de la Groie, Catherine Macé, Judith Mo-reau de Brésoles, and Marie Maillet. In 1659, the last three were to be the founding Sisters of the Montreal Hôtel Dieu.

Chapter XXIII

Notes

1. *RPA*, Vol. 4, p. 366.

2. Dollier de Casson, *A History of Montreal*, p. 149.

3. *Journal des Jésuites*, pp. 129-130.

4. Dollier de Casson, *A History of Montreal*, pp. 147, 149.

5. Daveluy, *Jeanne Mance*, p. 119. In *A History of Montreal*, Dollier de Casson asserts on p. 149 that she "decided to embark at the earliest possible moment." He does not tell us, however, when she left for Quebec.

6. *RPA*, Vol. 4, pp. 366-367.

7. *Ibid.*, Vol. 2, p. 151.

8. Gaudin, *Inventaire et extraits des papiers de famille de monsieur Le Royer de la Dauversière*, p. 20. Besides, on August 12, Jeanne de Baugé, Jérôme's wife, promises to pay the apprenticeship of Françoise Panier, an orphan, as tailor.

9. *RPA*, Vol. 4, p. 366, Note 1.

10. *Ibid.*, p. 369.

11. *Ibid.*, pp. 370-372.

12. Father de Chantepie registered at the seminary on February 11, 1650. See Mondoux, *L'Hôtel-Dieu, premier hôpital de Montréal*, p. 124, Note 5.

13. Faillon, *Vie de Mademoiselle Mance*, Vol. 1, pp. 54-55.

14. Daveluy, *La société Notre-Dame de Montréal*, p. 37.

15. Faillon, *Vie de Mademoiselle Mance*, Vol. 1, pp. 56-57.

16. *RPA*, Vol. 4, pp. 377-381.

17. *Ibid.*, p. 382.

18. *NA*, pp. 481-482.

19. *RPA*, Vol. 5, pp. 384-385.

20. Daveluy, *Jeanne Mance*, p. 164.

21. *RPA*, Vol. 5, p. 385.

22. T. Pletteau, *Henri Arnauld, sa participation à l'hérésie janséniste*, Angers, 1863, p. 7.

23. *NA*, p. 484.

24. *RPA*, Vol. 5, pp. 388-389.

25. *Ibid.*, p. 401.

26. *Ibid.*, p. 402.

27. *Ibid.*, p. 396, Note 1.

28. *AM*, p. 107.

29. *RPA*, Vol. 5, p. 396.

30. *Ibid.*, p. 397.

31. *NA*, pp. 508-509.

32. *RPA*, Vol. 5, p. 403.

Chapter XXIV

Back to Moulins

THE LA FLÈCHE HÔTEL DIEU had repeatedly opened its doors to newcomers who wished to join the Daughters of St. Joseph. Three young girls, Marie Giroust on April 23, 1650, and Marie and Marthe Bérard on November 30, begged for admission and were accepted as postulants.[1] More than ever before, the erection of a community building was imperative.

During December 1650, Sr. Catherine de Beaufort made ready to pronounce her first vows. On account of bad health during her year of novitiate, she had been dispensed from fasting and from arising at the prescribed hour each morning and, because of a sickly facial appearance, was not assigned to work in the wards. In Jérôme Le Royer's eyes, her attachment to her calling as a hospitaller and her hard work counterbalanced the above inconveniences. He had consequently written out in his hand a petition to Bishop Arnauld for a dispensation in order to have Sister de Beaufort serve the needy sick as a Daughter of St. Joseph. The dispensation was granted and Sister Catherine took her first vows on December 27th, 1650.[2]

During the second half of January 1651, an incident upset the quiet of Jérôme's household.[3] It is worth the telling, for it gives us as good an insight as any into the mentality of its people. During the previous August, for the sum of 36,000 livres, Jérôme Le Royer junior, according to the custom of the time, had bought the charge of lieutenant-general for the civil and criminal jurisdictions of La Flèche. As a result, there rested on his shoulders the responsibility of supervising public morals and of acting as judge of the public court. On January 18, 1651, the royal

311

prosecutor informed the new lieutenant-general that one of the bawds of the St. Jacques suburb had welcomed to her ill-famed establishment one Catherine Vallier, a girl originally from Angers, whose reputation was not of the best. The procuress had obtained this luxury prostitute for the young Baron de la Varenne, second son of the governor of La Flèche.

The lieutenant-general immediately ordered that the procuress be taken into custody. The next day with the royal procurator, with the clerk of the court and four bailiffs, he went to the house where Catherine Vallier had been put up. Just as he arrived, one of the baron's footmen, dressed in his master's green livery, handed him a message: on no account was he to jail her! The lieutenant-general ignored the order and had the girl discreetly taken to his father's home and placed under his mother's care.

During the late afternoon of the same day, the now thoroughly angry baron, with his features half concealed by his cloak, and accompanied by an unliveried lackey with a dark lantern, strode into the courtyard. Swearing and profaning the name of God and his saints, he came abreast of the lieutenant-general, "I sent a messenger to tell you not to bother with the girl; but you didn't obey; quite to the contrary, you did everything you could to displease me!"

Fearing for his life, the lieutenant-general invited him to enter the house where they could quietly discuss the affair. Once inside, he gave orders to the clerk of the court and several other men who were present to remain near the door and to keep their ears open. Later on they might be called upon as witnesses.

Lacing his words with more profanity, the young nobleman cried out, "You are trying to aggravate me by standing in the way of my enjoyment, but I shall smash through your opposition!"

The lieutenant-general quietly replied that it was his

duty to enforce the law.

This language did not exactly suit the irate visitor. He would pull his weight, he said, and, from cover, he was looking forward to shooting down every member of the household. Let the lieutenant-general send all the dispatches he wished to Paris, it would not stop him from taking care of the bailiffs who had thrown the procuress into prison. Young Jérôme Le Royer pointed out that the bailiffs were by duty bound to execute their order. With an oath, the baron cried out that he didn't care more about the lieutenant-general than about the devil himself, and that he would not hesitate to use his knife and musket since the former sought only to thwart all his designs. When Le Royer looked up, he was staring into the muzzle of the nobleman's pistol. He was ordered to reveal where the girl was hidden.

"She is with my mother, who put her under the care of her maids."

La Varenne retorted that he hadn't come to munch sweet chestnuts with him, and that he wanted to see Catherine Vallier at once.

He was quietly told that the house was royal property, and, that the lieutenant-general would allow no violence or disorder to take place within its confines.

Angrier than ever, La Varenne snapped that he didn't give a hang about the lieutenant-general and his responsibilities, adding that, if, within twenty-four hours, the girl had not been turned over to him, he would take the means to get her. He must, however, see her then and there.

As the baron was known to carry out his threats, the lieutenant-general excused himself and sought out his father's advice in the next room. Both returned to face the unwelcome visitor. Jérôme Le Royer had all the maids of the house called into the room with Catherine Vallier. He then politely questioned the baron who still held his pistol partially concealed in his cloak:

"So you wish to see a girl who came here this afternoon?" he asked.

"Yes," La Varenne replied, "but there are too many chandeliers alight in this apartment!"

"It's the custom in my home," Jérôme quietly said, "to light many chandeliers because nothing takes place here that is not for public consumption: that is why I have summoned all the young women of my household, for one does not engage in private conversation with them here!"

La Varenne fumed: "So you, too, are being obstinate! I'll get you yet; you have been an obstacle on my path for a long time. I know how to break both of you!"

With this threat, peppered with still more profanity, he stalked out as he had come in, accompanied by his lackey with the dark lantern.

The next day, the twentieth of January, one of the baron's retainers asked to be admitted into the presence of the lieutenant-general. The man was taken to him and he demanded that Catherine Vallier be turned over to him for the Baron de la Varenne intended to send her back to Angers. The answer was, of course, no!

Still another attempt was made to have her handed over to the young rake. But the lieutenant-general could take no more. "Tell your master," he said to the baron's messenger, "that if he doesn't understand my role here, I'm now defining it for him, and that as long as I have authority in this country, the king shall remain the master here. Tell him also that I have ways and means to exact obedience where it is due and these ways and means shall be applied to your lord and master first of all!"

This was the end of the story, except that the noble womanizer was murdered, later on, it is believed, by the guardsmen of the Comtesse de Lude.

More serious difficulties were in store for Jérôme Le

Royer and Mother de la Ferre. Although the foundations of Baugé, Laval, and Moulins had obtained the episcopal sanction in November 1650, only the first two of these hospitals were opened before the end of 1651. Why had the last one not been officially inaugurated? Was it the short days of December which made traveling difficult? The trip would take at least a week and the hospitallers, two of whom were still quite young, would have had to spend several nights in dingy inns, more ill-kept than usual because of the Fronde. But the delay lasted until the following May, and, consequently another explanation must be found.

Niggling Bishop Arnauld of Angers is to be held responsible for the procrastination.[4] After buying the La Flèche presbytery, Jérôme and Mother de la Ferre had found and acquired another residence for the pastor, Fr. Hamelin, into which the latter moved before the end of August 1649. Contracts were signed and all that was lacking was the Bishop's final approval. Nobody worried about it until Bishop de Rueil's death. Then the capitular vicars, Frs. Eveillon and Lasnier, who had been entrusted with the settling of the affair, after closely examining the proposed transaction, were favorable to it. But the new Bishop considered the dealings null and void as they had taken place before his nomination as Ordinary of Angers. He ordered that all details of the preliminary investigations, the subsequent formalities and contracts concerning selling of the presbytery and the buying of a decent residence for Fr. Hamelin be again taken up. The prelate, who later openly defied the Holy Father in favor of Jansenism, was extremely touchy about obedience to the Bishop of Angers!

Consequently, Mother de la Ferre, who had been appointed superior of the Moulins foundation, could not quit La Flèche until the Hamelin problem was resolved. With Jérôme Le Royer, she must again begin the wearisome proceedings.

On February 22, Lieutenant-General Le Royer called a city meeting to have the sale of the presbytery approved anew. Six days later the punctilious Bishop ordered an investigation into the advantages and disadvantages of the transactions, which took place on March 4, 1651. Clergymen, doctors, masons and carpenters all had their say in the matter. The minutes were drawn up describing the advantages of a separate dwelling for the community of the Daughters of St. Joseph, particularly in times of plague and other epidemics. It was noted that the city would also profit by the sale of the century-old presbytery since the Hôtel Dieu would provide Fr. Hamelin with a brand-new home without dipping into the public coffers. Better still, the community building for the hospitallers would not cost La Flèche anything.

All in all, the city, the parish, and the Hôtel Dieu would benefit by these transactions if the Bishop deigned to approve them. Even so, he had Jérôme Le Royer, Mother de la Ferre, and the Daughters of St. Joseph wait upon him until he felt they understood that he and only he made the decisions in the diocese.

On March 15, this shilly-shallying allowed Mother de la Ferre to close the eyes of Anne de L'Espicier de Chesteleux de Ribère, former maid of honor of the Princesse de Condé, at the relatively early age of fifty or so.[5] She had been Mother de la Ferre's first postulant; since 1644, she had served as the superior general's first assistant, and, along with her as well as with the late Anne Foureau, was considered one of the Institute's founding Mothers.

Meantime, far away from La Flèche, the actors on the political scene of France were changing, at least temporarily. After 11 months of captivity, the Princes de Condé triumphantly reentered Paris as Cardinal Mazarin fled into exile. The times were ripe to conquer the royal letters patent for the Moulins foundation, and Jérôme Le Royer and Gabriel Girault, now a Canon, improved the opportunity. Their petition was readily granted with the approval of the Queen Mother, and the act was "sealed with green wax, and knotted with red and green silk cords," on March 21, 1651.[6] About the same time, the letters patent for Baugé received the royal sanction with the stipulation that a Solemn Mass be offered yearly on the feast of St. Louis for the welfare of the King and the kingdom.

The letters patent were probably brought to La Flèche for Easter by Monsieur and Madame de Beaufort, who came to ratify the contract of their daughter Catherine, and also to sign that of their other daughter, Antoinette, who entered as a postulant of the Daughters of St. Joseph, on Easter Monday, April 13, at the early age of sixteen.[7]

In Moulins, Canon Girault, who had been busy urging the carpenters and masons on to work, now thought it was time to have the Daughters of St. Joseph take over the Hôtel Dieu, which was practically completed. As Moulins was in the diocese of Autun, he rode to the episcopal city and requested the authorization to bless the Hôtel Dieu and its chapel solemnly. The Vicar-General, Fr. Claude Saulnier, in lieu of the absent Bishop, Claude de la Magdelaine de Ragny, granted him all the testimonials he desired, not omitting high praise for the excellent Canon, and instructions to welcome the Hôtel Dieu hospitallers, with all the ceremony that was usual on such occasions, and with whatever else the circumstances might demand.[8] Having pocketed the precious documents, Canon Girault hastened to advise Jérôme Le Royer and Mother de la Ferre of the good news.

Not long afterwards, on April 24, Bishop Arnauld ratified the agreements concerning the sale of the La Flèche presbytery.[9] Orders were speedily given to demolish it and to set to work on the new community house. Mother de la Ferre had the consolation of seeing its walls

317

go up, though she did not see the finished building.

It was soon decided that May 8 would be the day of the foundress's departure for Moulins, with Srs. Claude Le Balleur de la Cousinière, Marie Bidault de la Barre, Anne Bidault de Ruigné, and Thérèse Havard de la Tremblaye.[10]

Mother de la Ferre had a sister, Madame de la Minotière, who resided at Luché-Pringé in the neighborhood of La Flèche.[11] The two were very close. Ten or eleven years earlier, the latter had obtained a separation from her husband, a ne'er-do-well, whose reputation for loose living was public property. With her two daughters, Sr. Marie Maillard, S.N.D., and Madame Louis de la Boulaye, she often visited Mother de la Ferre at the Hôtel Dieu. Now they must bid farewell to one another, knowing they would perhaps never meet again. There were other farewells in the offing, most of them equally painful. The time had come for Mother de la Ferre to quit the Hôtel Dieu she had founded with Jérôme Le Royer, the Daughters of St. Joseph whom she had affectionately introduced to community life, and, of course, the founder himself.

Jérôme, too, had his own crosses to bear. Besides the departure of Mother de la Ferre, whom he had first seen in a vision many years before, and who had enthusiastically collaborated with him over the years, his daughter Marie, under the name of Sr. Marie Angélique, had made her profession as a religious of the Visitation on about the third of May,[12] in the monastery that served until shortly before as the community house of the La Flèche Sisters of St. Joseph. He rejoiced spiritually at the thought that his daughter had consecrated herself to God, but his heart was heavy with longing for her presence at home. On the eve of her vows, Jérôme received a receipt in full for the 5,000 livres he had gladly contributed as his daughter's dowry, though he was by no means a millionaire.

The pensions of the five departing Daughters of St.

Joseph were settled on May 6 and Mother de la Ferre signed, in her companions' names, a promise of fidelity to the motherhouse and to the Rules and Constitutions[13] as the Baugé and Laval Sisters had done.

On the morning of May 8, after attending Mass, and receiving Holy Communion, accompanied by their chaplain Fr. Jean Gyrot, Mother de la Ferre and the four other Daughters of St. Joseph set out for Moulins, some 224 miles distant.[14]

The little group seems to have reached its destination by May 18, the fifteenth anniversary of Mother de la Ferre's and Sister Foureau's entry into the dilapidated building of what had then been the La Flèche hospital. Canon Girault, who had been instrumental in their coming to Moulins, went out to meet them. It was a bleak welcome: because of misunderstandings among the aldermen of the city, no lodgings had been prepared for the tired hospitallers, but the kind priest comforted them by opening wide the door of his own home to them.

Naturally the Daughters of St. Joseph were somewhat upset by the unseemly attitude of the civil authorities until their superior spoke up:

"We are here only because it is the will of God. I'm most confident that His goodness will crown this undertaking with success. The differences of opinion concerning us are a proof that our efforts are bound to succeed; we must however contribute to their success by our patience and by our submission to God's good pleasure. The manner in which we glorify Him matters little so long as He is glorified. We await whatever He pleases to do with us; He is our Father and we are His children. May His name be blessed forever!" [15]

Mother de la Ferre knew that prayer was not enough. Accordingly, being an intelligent woman, she carefully planned her strategy with the approval of Canon Girault and of Fr. Gyrot. They would not officially notify City Hall of their arrival, much less hold the civil authorities to their contract despite the royal and episcopal assents, which rendered it binding on all parties. Neither would they have a notary list their complaints nor testify to their truthfulness according to the custom of those bygone days. She decided that the Daughters of St. Joseph would only be seen as they went to Mass in the nearest church; that they would knock at no other door for help than that of the tabernacle. In short they would remain in Moulins, and they would pray, and they would wait. At Mother de la Ferre's suggestion, Fr. Gyrot returned to La Flèche and reported to Jérôme Le Royer and to Mother Anne Le Tendre. It was soon repeated in the influential circles of Moulins that the newcomers no longer had need of the priest's backing since they had resolved to stay on with or without the aldermen's consent.

Thanks to their kind host, Canon Girault, and to their effective ally, Father Claude de Lingendes, S.J.,[16] the former's home immediately became the haunt of the Moulins notabilities. Mother de la Ferre, by her warm and friendly conversation, her innate tact, and exquisite distinction, charmed them all. One of the visitors, Monsieur Dubuisson de Beauregard, treasurer of France for the Province of Bourbonnais, was so impressed by the Daughters of St. Joseph that he offered them a suite of rooms in his own residence where they could live a normal religious life. The superior gratefully accepted the offer, and after sincerely thanking Canon Girault for his hospitality, moved with her sisters to the more convenient home of Monsieur and Madame Dubuisson.

Another highborn personage, the widowed Duchesse de Montmorency, after having learned of their arrival, expressed the desire to meet them.[17] On the other hand the Daughters of St. Joseph felt in duty bound to call upon her at the monastery of the Visitation since the contract regarding the establishment of the La Flèche Daughters of St. Joseph in Moulins, had been signed with her encouragement in the convent parlor of that institution on October 2, 1648. The Duchess responded favorably to her visitors, and promised to do her utmost to see them installed as soon as possible in the new Hôtel Dieu.

Mother de la Ferre's point at issue was as simple to understand as it was difficult to solve. Without any funds, it consisted in finding and buying a sufficiently large site to build a convent for her community in the neighborhood of the hospital. At the sight of the long faces her companions pulled when they became aware of this new problem, she suggested that they place their trust in God, and in all the simplicity of her heart turned to Him in prayer. She had barely finished when her host, Monsieur Dubuisson, knocked at her door and announced that she had callers, Monsieur and Madame Mérault de Corbeville, who had donated 4,100 livres for the Sisters's residence as early as 1648. At Canon Girault's suggestion, they generously promised 20,000 livres more.

A fortnight after they had set foot in Moulins, on June 4, 1651, Feast of the Blessed Trinity, the five Daughters of St. Joseph thanked the Dubuissons for their warm hospitality and unofficially took possession of the Hôtel Dieu.[18] It was the eleventh anniversary to the day of the founding of the Congregation of the Daughters of St. Joseph. Their quarters were small and uncomfortable, their furniture strictly functional, but they made little of it. Mother de la Ferre turned to her little community, "Here, Sisters," she said, "I shall rest for eternity," and recited the *Nunc Dimittis*.[19] Later on, the four hospitallers would recall these words.

At nine o'clock, on the morning of June 24, the canonical erection of the Hôtel Dieu dedicated to St. Joseph took place with all the pomp and circumstance that befitted the occasion.[20] The Duchesse de Montmorency had offered altar linen, and Madame Girault, the zealous Canon's mother, had contributed 3,000 livres for the pulpit and ornamentation of the church, while the Canon himself, out of his own pocket, had completely furnished the sacristy with everything that was needed, even a chalice and ciborium. The place was packed. The Lieutenant-General of Moulins, the royal procurator, the mayor and aldermen, various other members of the administration, numerous friends and notables had gathered together to honor Mother de la Ferre and the Daughters of St. Joseph, who had come to serve Christ in the needy sick of the district.

Canon Girault, accompanied by his secretary and two other Canons, betook himself processionally to the Hôtel Dieu Chapel. In the sanctuary, awaiting the red-robed canons, was Mother de la Ferre with her associates. She requested Canon Girault to publish and execute the Bishop of Autun's decree with regard to his acceptance of this new Congregation in his diocese and to its taking over of the new hospital.

After the solemn reading of the decree, Canon Girault vested for Mass, intoned the *Veni Creator*, blessed the chapel, and offered the Holy Sacrifice. After the hospitallers had received Communion, he deposited the Blessed Sacrament in the tabernacle and concluded the ceremony with a triumphant *Te Deum*.

One of the priests attached to St. Pierre's parish in Moulins, Fr. Pierre Oyseau, in a diocese where many clerics lived a worldly if not disorderly life, enjoyed a reputation for piety and holiness. It was assumed that he was favored with celestial communications. To show his esteem for the hospitallers he was present that morning at the liturgy. During the procession, as the formal blessing of this new temple was under way, while Jérôme Le Royer's spiritual daughters headed by Mother de la Ferre entered the sanctuary, the good priest distinctly saw Jesus, Mary, and Joseph, who raised their hands to bless them.[21] The dear man often had visions, perhaps a result of his advanced age. At any rate, when this apparition was retold, it helped gain complete acceptance of the new Congregation by the people of Moulins.

Chapter XXIV

Notes

1. *RPA*, Vol. 5, p. 407. Marie Giroust was 13 years old but of course could not pronounce her vows until she had reached the canonical age of 16 years. Marie Bérard was 23 years old, her sister Marthe, 17.

2. *Ibid.*, pp. 408-409.

3. *Ibid.*, pp. 410-416.

4. *NA*, pp. 526-527, 535-538, 543.

5. *Ibid.*, p. 539.

6. *RPA*, Vol. 5, pp. 425-427.

7. *NA*, p. 543.

8. *RPA*, Vol. 5, pp. 425-428.

9. *NA*, p. 543.

10. *Ibid.*, pp. 545-546.

11. *RPA*, Vol. 5, p. 431.

12. *Ibid.*, p. 430.

13. *Cenomanen*, p. 23.

14. *RPA*, Vol. 5, p. 431.

15. *AM*, pp. 113-115.

16. *NA*, p. 563.

17. *Ibid.*, pp. 116-117.

18. *RPA*, Vol. 5, pp. 434-435.

19. *AM*, p. 128.

20. *Ibid.*, pp. 127-130.

21. *Ibid.*, p. 131.

Chapter XXV

The Patients Were Inconsolable

WHEN MOTHER DE LA FERRE and her Daughters first set foot in the Moulins Hôtel Dieu, they were met by Julienne, an elderly widow, who until then, practically alone, had cared for the needy patients and a few orphan girls, with the modest means at her disposal.[1] With the advent of the Daughters of St. Joseph, the poor woman felt unsure about herself, wondering what the future held in store for her. She need not have worried. Mother de la Ferre, who had a heart of gold, instantly assured her that she did not have to quit the establishment and that she could live happily there for the rest of her days. Though Julienne stayed on, she did not join the Hospitallers.

The novitiate was immediately inaugurated with the admittance of two girls from Moulins: twenty-one year old Elisabeth Harel and twenty-seven year old Marie Venuat, who requested to be received as a lay member of the Institute. Then the regular life of the nursing Sisters began. The community chose a confessor, Fr. Albert Fournier, and Mother de la Ferre informed Bishop de Ragny of its choice and requested that this priest be officially assigned to the house. The request posed no problem for the Bishop and he approved it.[2]

The superior placed great value on the prompt accomplishment of the humble tasks of everyday life. Since her arrival, the place had already taken on a new look; soon the entire hospital was to have a face-lifting. Punctuality, which the French call "the politeness of Bishops," was practised by the Daughters of St. Joseph, though the thought of ordination never even remotely entered their minds. Cleanliness, vigilance, proper care of the patients also concurred in making the Hôtel Dieu into a viable institution. The comfort that both the sick and the orphans experienced within its walls drew them to the Daughters and by rebound to God. More and more of the poor asked to be cared for, and more and more financial assistance poured in to provide for their maintenance.

Many young ladies wished to become Daughters of St. Joseph, and Mother de la Ferre promised most of them that after the community house was erected during the autumn of the following year, they would be accepted as postulants. She did, however, immediately open the doors of the overcrowded Hôtel Dieu to Reine Marguerite Menudet, who was not 16 years old, and to Marguerite de Laval, both daughters of gentlemen of Moulins.[3]

Mother de la Ferre's main preoccupation was to wield together her sisters in love. In her eyes the best short cut to achieve her aim consisted in fidelity to the Rules and Constitutions of the Institute—not a cold, juridical fidelity, but an intelligent warm-hearted adhesion to them. To this end, according to the La Flèche custom, she had Sister Baillif's admonitions read monthly at the Moulins Hôtel Dieu.

The aging foundress was always the first at the bedside of the most repulsive patients. She ministered tenderly to their needs, often kissing their sores as if they were the sacred wounds of Christ upon the Cross[4] (a practice nobody would approve of nowadays). Although she worked diligently, her heart often soared to the heights of contemplation. During these moments, quite unknown to herself, the profound peace and untroubled serenity of her countenance struck the patients and the volunteer aids alike. By the beginning of 1652, the Superior of the Daughters of St. Joseph at Moulins was considered a saint by all who knew her, a very practical and human saint!

This new year was of special significance to the entire Congregation. On January 22, 1644 the first twelve members had pronounced their temporary vows. During the following eight years, five of them died. The time had come for the survivors either to make their perpetual profession or to renew their temporary vows for three years and, if they so wished at every subsequent triennium. On January 23, 1652, Feast of the Espousals of Our Lady, the six Daughters of St. Joseph took their final vows at La Flèche.[5]

Mother Marie de la Ferre prepared for this complete gift of self to God by an eight-day retreat and by special penances. On the twenty-second of February, at Moulins, she took her perpetual vows in the presence of Fr. Nicolas Feydeau, superior of all the feminine religious of the city, of Canon Girault, and of the community confessor, Fr. Albert Fournier.[6] At the end of Mass, Fr. Feydeau blessed a silver ring on which were engraved the names of Jesus, Mary, and Joseph, and slipped it on the annulary finger of the foundress—as the Child Jesus had done with Jérôme Le Royer at Notre Dame de Paris, during 1635.

Despite her delicate constitution, Mother de la Ferre never hesitated to practise austerity and, since her coming to Moulins, she had never refused any task, light or heavy as it might be.[7] With Ash Wednesday, ignoring her impaired health, she began to observe the Lenten prescriptions to the letter, notably fasting, which was highly rigid in those early post-Tridentine years. As usual, she added her customary mortifications, whose harshness she may have overstressed at the sight of the somber clouds piling up on the horizon.

The year 1652 was already revealing itself for what it was—a death's-head. The Fronde civil war, after an all too brief respite, broke out once again, more vicious than ever. At La Flèche, Jérôme Le Royer was worried. Since Angers sided with Parliament and the princes in revolt against the Crown and Cardinal Mazarin, who had returned from exile, Anjou fell prey to devastation and calamity, the lot of any land transformed into a battle-field.

During that Lent, as Marshal d'Hocquincourt and his royal troops overran La Flèche and advanced towards Angers, the friends of the Visitation nuns, in particular the Jesuits of the Royal College, urged them to abandon their monastery temporarily and seek refuge elsewhere.

Jérôme graciously offered them the hospitality of his home.[8] His reputation for virtue, for cool-headedness, and for many other qualities was so well known that his invitation was immediately accepted. He set apart half of his residence for the nuns, among them his daughter, Sr. Marie Angélique. They were thus able to continue living in accordance with the Rules of their Order as if they had been in their own monastery. The Jesuit Fathers regularly officiated at Lenten devotions for them and preached to them in the house on Hail Mary Street. Relatives and friends of the community were admitted; these guests were also present when their "very pious and learned host," Monsieur Le Royer, gave stirring talks to the Visitation Sisters. The superior noted that "his house was a refuge for the poor and the afflicted, who were always sure they would find a cure there for all their sufferings."

Conditions reached the proportions of a catastrophe during early spring when the rivers of France overflowed. Moulins and Le Bourbonnais were as hard hit as Paris and as many other provinces of the kingdom. The Allier river on the banks of which the Hôtel Dieu was located, flooded the lower quarters of the city, including the basement of the hospital and the ground floor. Worse was to come. When the waters finally receded, in their wake they left the walls and the floors of the riverside buildings caked with foul slime. The inevitable happened: a violent contagion, perhaps typhoid, hit the proud capital of Bourbonnais, and the Hôtel Dieu, still reeking with the stink of the fetid river mud, was soon crammed with the sick and the dying.

The Daughters of St. Joseph, their three postulants, and old Julienne had more than they could cope with. Mother de la Ferre took care that the patients lacked for nothing. She also saw to it that her Sisters did not overtax themselves.[9] Nonetheless, one after the other they contracted the dread disease, and the superior found herself practically alone to care for them and for the bedridden in the crowded wards.

More than ever before, the patients considered her a saint and cried out for her to come to them. Better than potions and powders, her kind and efficient hands soothed and comforted them. The dying called out for her to assist them in their agony, for she had the gift of calming their fears and of easing their passage into eternity.

The outbreak held Moulins in its grip throughout the entire month of May until the end of June. Despite a fatigue beyond words, Mother de la Ferre found little time to rest and when she did, she fell into a fitful, stuporous sleep. To her satisfaction, however, her little band of Hospitallers wan and pale though they were, began to recuperate; the three postulants, who had shared their work and their illness with the Sisters, remained true to their calling. Although the superior's courage was as staunch as ever, she was completely worn out. Canon Girault and other friends recruited volunteers to help her, but she was obliged to instruct them in their new work and to provide for every living soul in the Hôtel Dieu. So she still found no time to rest properly, and slowly but surely her last reserves of strength gave out.

In the second half of July, she awoke one morning a prey to the terrible illness.[10] She tried to hide her condition from her beloved Daughters, but finally was forced to take to bed. Every means was used to relieve her from the burning fever which was consuming her, but in vain. She felt she would never leave her room alive and prayed to be the last victim of the dread disease.

On her second day of sick-bed, she made ready for death by receiving the sacraments of Penance and of the Eucharist. During the last days of her life, she had the following advice for her Daughters, which is here lumped into one paragraph:

"God is our Father and He will always be so as long as you are faithful to Him... Put all your trust in Him... Often recall to mind the countless blessings and never ending graces He granted to each one of you. Love your holy calling; love your Rules: they are from God—about this you can have no doubt, so love and practise them punctually... May humility, charity, and the union of hearts with all the other virtues befitting your holy state of life be the main concern of your existence. I am leaving you in the hands of God. In His goodness, He will see to all your needs; this favor I ask of Him with all my Heart." [11]

As the state of her health deteriorated with repeated attacks of colic and raging fever, on the twelfth day of her illness, the foundress requested the Holy Viaticum and Extreme Unction. Fr. Fournier assisted by Canon Girault complied immediately with her request. She thanked her confessor and asked him one more favor: that he continue to see to the spiritual needs of the little community. The priest immediately promised to do so.

After adoring the Lord whom she was about to see face to face, she begged pardon for the bad example she may have given to her Daughters and then turned her thoughts to Our Lord in the Blessed Sacrament before receiving Him. Her prayers during this solemn hour of her life were carefully noted:

"You are calling me to Yourself, oh, my Beloved! It is right for me to obey you... My trust in your mercy, the tender marks you gave me of your goodness by the Passion and death of your most lovable Son won't allow me to doubt that you will be merciful to my poor soul. Save it, Lord, through your precious Blood, for it is on your infinite merits that I base all my hope. I ask you for this grace through the intercession of the Most Blessed Virgin and of St. Joseph."

When the pains became excruciating, Mother de la Ferre cried out, "Don't spare me, my God! Destroy this sinful body of mine!"

Most of the time she lay silent and recollected, her mind at peace and her thoughts constantly with Him whom she had so faithfully served in the sick and poor over the years.

The patients of the Hôtel Dieu were inconsolable on learning that the superior's death was imminent. They joined the Daughters of St. Joseph, the orphans, and those who had been cured through the care of the dying woman in praying for a miracle. Even the religious of the other institutions of the city entreated God to spare her. It was not to be.

After seventeen days of illness, on the night of July 27, 1652, shortly before midnight, in the presence of Canon Girault, of Fr. Fournier, and of all the Sisters in tears, her soul went forth to her Lord as she joyfully cried out, "I rely on you, oh, my Savior! What bliss for me, poor miserable creature that I am, to be able to enjoy you for all eternity!"[12]

Mother Marie de la Ferre was sixty-three years old, sixteen of which she had devoted herself as a hospitaller including the sixteen months at Moulins.

Before the sobbing of the Sisters subsided, an extraordinary change occured, one which is verified in the lives of certain saints like Blessed Kateri Tekakwitha, the Iroquis Maiden, who died in Canada in 1680. Sweetness, devotion, and gravity marked her features. The Sisters were so impressed that they had an artist come in to capture on

331

canvas the expression of peace on the face of their foundress.*

Dressed in her severe black habit with its white wimple she was laid out in the Hôtel Dieu chapel. The public who wished to see and venerate her came running. The poor wept unashamedly. The throng grew so quickly that it took time and energy to approach the coffin. Those who managed to reach it, touched their rosaries and articles of piety to Marie de la Ferre's remains; many kissed her hands, several snipped off pieces of her habit as relics while others requested personal articles of hers. Quite a few stated they obtained extraordinary favors through her intercession.[14]

On the twenty-ninth of July, when the time came for her burial, the mourners were as numerous as ever despite the torrid heat of the dog days. After the funeral Mass, in a solemn ceremony, with Canon Girault and several other priests as well as the Daughters of St. Joseph, Mother de la Ferre's remains were carried to their final resting place in the crypt beneath the chapel.

Mother Claude Le Balleur, as the superior's assistant, should normally have conveyed the sad news of her death to the Hôtel Dieu at La Flèche. Upset as she was, she was

---

* This painting was honoured at Moulins until the Revolution of 1793.[13] When the religious were expelled from the Hôtel Dieu, one of them, Sister Philippine Tardy, carefully preserved it at home. After the Revolution, seeing there was no hope of the Moulins Hôtel Dieu being reopened, she asked to be admitted at La Flèche as a Daughter of St. Joseph. She was affectionately welcomed and brought along with her the precious painting of Mother de la Ferre and other objects such as the altar linen thought to have been donated to the Hôtel Dieu by the Duchesse de Montmorency. The painting was in a very bad condition. Fortunately the lines of the face were still intact. During the last century the painting was photographed with astounding results. The Religious Hospitallers of St. Joseph throughout the world now have an authentic likeness of their saintly Mother.

unable to do so. Canon Girault notified Monsieur Le Royer, Mother Anne Le Tendre and her staff, relating in detail the saintly death of Mother de la Ferre.[15] At the same time he requested that the founder's daughter, Sr. Jeanne, be appointed superior of the Moulins Hôtel Dieu. She was only twenty-four years old and held the important charge of mistress of novices. Although she already had to her credit the eight years of religious life required by the Council of Trent for the post of Superior, she had not yet attained the age to assume this responsibility. A dispensation was certainly obtained, and she was assigned to Moulins.

Jérôme Le Royer was intensely grieved by the unexpected death of his long time collaboratrix Mother Marie de la Ferre. He summoned up his courage and wrote a comforting, deeply spiritual letter to the Moulins community, promising he would be in the capital of Bourbonnais as soon as possible. On September 5, commissioned by the Bishop of Angers, he set out with his daughter, Sr. Jeanne Le Royer, Sr. Renée Olivier de la Guittière, and Sr. Jeanne Pillet, a lay Sister. Jérôme was furthermore entrusted with the important mission of bringing the remains of Mother de la Ferre back.[16] The tired travellers rode into Moulins on September 16, six weeks after the death of the foundress.

An early tradition of the Congregation asserts that almost immediately on arriving, Sr. Jeanne Le Royer descended to the crypt to pray at the tomb of the late superior. The other Sisters accompanied her and all together they gave way to their grief. It took some doing on the part of Jérôme and the priests who were with him to calm them. Although he contained himself, the founder's feelings were no doubt akin to theirs.

Ten days later, on September 26, the Daughters of St. Joseph of Moulins assembled together and voted to confirm Jeanne Le Royer's nomination as their superior. On October

1, this election was ratified by the religious authorities. Then Mother Le Royer set to work, assigning the Sisters, who were all convalescing, with the exception of the newcomers, to the chores they were strong enough to undertake. Her aim was to comfort and strengthen the afflicted community and to lead it back to the effective nursing and to the fervent religious life it had practised before the death of Mother de la Ferre. Her father proved invaluable with his advice and assistance.[17]

It may be assumed that in the course of their conversations, Jérôme mentioned the new postulant who had been welcomed at La Flèche on June 5, Anne de la Barre de Hautepierre, from Villiers in Anjou. In turn his daughter confided to him that Mother de la Ferre had put off receiving several young ladies as postulants, and that they had steadfastly kept coming to the Hôtel Dieu to assist the sisters in caring for the sick, with the idea, of course, that they would eventually be admitted. Was it Jérôme who advised Mother Jeanne Le Royer to postpone receiving them still longer? At any rate, she resolved to follow this line of conduct, but she did decide to admit to their vows the first two novices whom the former superior had opened the doors of the community to.[18]

The founder remained in Moulins for the occasion and, on October13, he was present when Canon Feydeau, assisted by Canon Girault and Fr. Fournier, presided as Sr. Elisabeth Harel took her simple vows as Hospitaller, and Sr. Marie Venuat as lay Sister.

Notwithstanding the written permission of Bishop Arnauld of Angers and of Vicar-General Saulnier of Autun, and the clearly expressed wish of the La Flèche Daughters of St. Joseph, Jérôme finally took it upon himself not to bring the relics of Mother de la Ferre back with him.[19] Although quicklime had been thrown into the coffin, the body of the foundress was probably in no condition to be removed; moreover, the intense sorrow of the Moulins Hôtel Dieu Daughters of St. Joseph may have influenced him at the time in deferring the transfer of the precious remains to a later date. . Three days later, on October 16, following an affectionate good-bye to his daughter and to the other Hospitallers, he quit Moulins with sickly Sr. Claude Le Balleur, who felt she could no longer live in the Hôtel Dieu where Mother de la Ferre had died.[20] Sorrow and gladness rode along with him: sorrow under the guise of Mother de la Ferre's death and of his farewell to Mother Le Royer, gladness under that of the Hôtel Dieu of Moulins staffed with Daughters of St. Joseph, and once again in full operation. Until the Revolution, 110 years later, the needy sick of the district would knock at its door, knowing that it would always open to welcome them.

Chapter XXV

Notes

1. *AM,* p. 132.

2. *Ibid.,* p. 134.

3. *Ibid.,* p. 144.

4. *Ibid.,* p. 136.

5. *RPA,* Vol. 5, pp. 439-440.

6. *AM,* p. 143.

7. *NA,* pp. 617-618.

8. *La famille Le Royer et la Visitation de La Flèche*, Extrait des documents de notre Monastère de La Flèche et des Vies de nos Soeurs Le Royer. MS (typescript copy) 1886? (Dossier La Dauversière). ARHSJ, Montreal.

9. *AM*, p. 144.

10. *Ibid.*, p. 145.

11. *Ibid.*, p. 146.

12. *Ibid.*, p. 147.

13. *RPA*, Vol. 5, p. 443.

14. *NA*, p. 631.

15. *AM,* p. 149.

16. *RPA*, Vol. 5, pp. 444-445.

17. *AM*, p. 150.

18. *Ibid.*

19. *RPA*, Vol. 5, pp. 447-448.

20. *AM*, p. 150.

Chapter XXVI

"The Second Foundation...."

AT THE END OF 1651, Governor Paul de Chomedey de Maisonneuve had returned from New France with alarming news. Despite his personal problems, especially a tragic death in the family, his main concern was the sorry state of Ville Marie. During her stay in France, Jeanne Mance had already informed Jérôme about the destruction of Huronia by the Iroquois. In 1650 the Huron survivors, fleeing before the onslaught, passed by Ville Marie on their way to safety at Quebec—a sinister omen of things to come.

On May 6, 1651, pioneer Jean Boudart and his wife were set upon by a band of about fifty Indians.[1] After a terrible struggle he was struck down, and she was taken prisoner and later burnt at the stake. The enemy also tried to seize Jean Chicot, but, as the French were coming to rescue, "they took off his scalp and some of his skull." The man survived. The first three who ran out to help him, Charles Le Moyne, Denis Archambault, and an unnamed settler, found themselves in the midst of war-painted Iroquois. The only solution was flight, and cut and run they did in the direction of the hospital. Luckily the door was ajar. Before Le Moyne reached it, a ball pierced his hat. He ducked and vanished into the building with his two companions. In all haste they barred the door. As Maisonneuve explained to the founder of Montreal, "Had the Iroquois passed by the hospital before these men found refuge in it, they would have plundered, burnt it, and captured Mademoiselle Mance."

Four days later, at two o'clock in the morning, a band of forty Iroquois surrounded the brewery and tried to set fire to it as well as to a few other houses.[2] They would have succeeded had not the four guards posted within vigorously repulsed them. At the same time, others were burning the homes of Urbain Tessier, known as Lavigne, and of Michel Chauvin nicknamed Sainte-Suzanne after the town he came from.

On Sunday, the eighteenth of June, a large party of Indians fell upon four settlers on their way home from Mass. Eluding the assailants, they took cover in a sorry hovel, called a redoubt, and there resolved to sell their lives as dearly as possible. Urbain Tessier managed to pass through the enemy ranks and join them despite the sixty to eighty shots aimed at him.

The uproar attracted the attention of the men in the fort. On Governor de Maisonneuve's order, Charles Le Moyne led a relief party to reinforce their countrymen. The Iroquois fired all their ammunition imprudently. Not so the French, who then laid low twenty-five to thirty of them, not counting the wounded who escaped. Four settlers were hurt, one of them, Léonard Lucault, died two days later.

From that time on, the French were constantly harassed by the Iroquois and they no longer dared venture more than a few feet from their log-houses without their muskets, their pistols, and swords. At night-time, nobody opened the door of his home to anyone.

Governor de Maisonneuve's handling of the situation was the only reasonable one under the circumstances. He called a meeting of all the Ville Marie colonists and ordered them to repair to the fort with their families.[3] Jeanne Mance took possession of the rooms in which she had lived ten years earlier. By sending a few armed men to garrison the Hôtel Dieu and a few other strategic spots, the governor succeeded in saving the whole settlement.

Other similar engagements occurred. "Finally," wrote Dollier de Casson, "as we grew weaker daily whilst the enemy grew bolder, on account of their great number, everyone saw quite plainly that unless powerful aid appeared very shortly from France, all would be lost." [4]

Paul de Maisonneuve discussed the plight they were in with Jeanne Mance. Should he return to France to explain conditions in Ville Marie to the Montreal Associates? Bad news about his family may have been the occasion though not the motive of his departure during 1651. A close relative, Guillaume de Rouxel, had recently murdered Paul's brother-in-law, François de Chevilly.[5]

Before sailing, Governor de Maisonneuve met with Jean de Lauson, the new governor-general, who was unsympathetic to Ville Marie, even though he may have been a member of the Society of Montreal. He was to prove his antipathy to its settlers in more ways than one. Dollier de Casson wryly notes that he made known "the goodwill he had towards them and the generous treatment they might expect therefrom," by deducting 1,000 livres from the 4,000 allotted to Maisonneuve for himself and for his men. At the time he upped his own salary to the tune of 2,000 livres.[6]

In 1647, the King had considerably raised the governor-general's and the governor of Montreal's salaries—to 25,000 livres for the former and to 10,000 for the latter. But in 1648, His Majesty reduced them by 19,000 livres, the which he applied to the creation of a flying column for the defense of the colony including Ville Marie. Later on, to the benefit of Trois-Rivières, Governor de Lauson would suppress the flying column so useful to the protection of Montreal.[7]

Still, Maisonneuve obtained the governor-general's promise to dispatch ten soldiers to Montreal to reinforce its decimated garrison. Although the governor of Ville Marie agreed to shoulder the cost, Lauson was faithful only to the word but not to the spirit of the agreement. This, Paul de Maisonneuve was to learn during the following autumn. In a shallop, Governor de Lauson had sent these men off, unarmed and so ill-provided with food and clothing for the Canadian winter that they nearly died of exposure before disembarking at the island settlement on December 10, 1651.[8]

On the fifth of November, Maisonneuve embarked for his homeland on the *Hollandois*,[9] after naming as his substitute a good soldier, Charles Joseph d'Ailleboust des Muceaux, the nephew of the former governor-general of New France.

On arriving in his country torn by civil war, did the Governor of Ville Marie make for La Flèche, for Paris or for Troyes? We do not know, but it is likely that he stopped at La Flèche on his way to the capital. He owed it to the founder of Ville Marie.

Jérôme Le Royer would appreciate any first-hand information about his island foundation. After welcoming his friend and collaborator, he carefully listened to his report on life at Ville Marie during 1651. Paul de Maisonneuve summed up the predicament of the Montreal settlers without glossing over the deaths inflicted by the belligerent Iroquois. The population of Ville Marie was constantly decreasing, for there remained barely fifty French colonists with only seventeen able to bear arms.[10] Conditions were not better than in 1642.

Jérôme's heart grew heavy with him. Humanly speaking, he wondered what the future held for the distant habitation. Either it was doomed to destruction or the pioneers would abandon it before falling prey to the enemy. Many of these men, who really had no close ties with the land, were already talking of repatriation. This was no problem for them since the Ladies and Gentlemen of the Society of Montreal had obligated themselves to pay the would-have-been colonists's passage home, should they so demand. The governor had come for help. What could possibly be done?

Maisonneuve answered the unasked question. In reality, the answer was Jeanne Mance's. She had urged him to return to France for assistance. But who would cover the expenses? Jeanne Mance suggested a solution to the difficulty of raising a shipload of settlers—a solution that might work. The 22,000 livres donated to the Hôtel Dieu by the Duchesse de Bullion, which the late Baron de Renty had invested on an annuity basis, were about to be recalled. This respectable sum destined to the upkeep of the Montreal Hôtel Dieu could be used instead to defray the expenses of engaging and transporting sufficient manpower to the New World in order to save the beleaguered island settlement. Now Jeanne Mance could not dispose of this money, so a plan of sorts was drawn up: in exchange for this financing, in the capacity of the governor, Paul de Maisonneuve would transfer to the poor of the Hôtel Dieu one hundred arpents of farmhold with the live-stock, the implements, and the barn, in the hope that the "Unknown Benefactress" and the Montreal Associates in Paris, who had the power to do so, would authorize the transaction.

How was Governor de Maisonneuve to reach Duchesse de Bullion, who was supposed to be unknown? Paul de Maisonneuve played his part well. Quite adroitly, he managed to enter into Madame de Bullion's presence.[11] At the time, his sister, Madame de Chevilly, was engaged in a lawsuit with the powerful aristocrat, and he offered to be her escort while she discussed the affair with her. Jeanne Mance had warned him that to divulge any knowledge of the great lady's generosity to Ville Marie "would be to lose all." So he had himself announced at her private hôtel, knowing full well that she had heard about him.

"God blessed my wiles," he said, "for when we greeted her, and after my sister had discussed her business with her, she inquired of me whether I was governor of Montreal, which was said to be in New France. I answered that I was and that I had recently come from there."

Following on her questions, Paul de Maisonneuve explained the dire straits in which the island foundation was caught.

"That, madam," he continued, "is how things stand. Indeed we are so pressed for help that Mademoiselle Mance, realizing that the aims of her foundress are like to be frustrated, gave me authority to take 22,000 livres belonging to the foundation, which are in Paris in exchange for 100 arpents of land granted her by the Company of Montreal, with the words, 'Take this money, for it is better that part of the foundation should perish than the whole; use the money to hire men, to secure the whole country by saving Montreal..' "

Pleased with the governor and his work, Madame de Bullion invited him to call on her again. This he did on several occasions. Finally, she entrusted Guillaume de Lamoignon with 20,000 livres for the island colony. This nobleman was closely connected with many Montreal Associates if not already one of them.[12]

During 1652, Maisonneuve did not return to Canada. Jeanne Mance, who had travelled to Quebec to welcome him, was disappointed. On the other hand, she was comforted by his letter, "in which he wrote that he hoped to return the following year with more than 100 men..." [13] Until then, she had been quite doubtful about seeing him again at Ville Marie, for before his departure, he had said to her and to Charles d'Ailleboust de Muceaux, "I will try to bring back 200 men, which we badly need for the defence of this place; if, however, I cannot get at least 100, I will not return and the whole enterprise must be abandoned, for certainly the place will be untenable."

Towards the end of the summer, Duplessis-Kerbodot, governor of Trois-Rivières, and 15 of his men were massacred and seven taken prisoners. At Ville Marie, the attacks had in no way diminished but they were repulsed with the loss of three men.[14]

In France Jérôme Le Royer and Paul de Maisonneuve had come to the conclusion that the recruits should not be hired for less than five years and that they should be encouraged to settle permanently in Montreal by means of substantial subsidies.[15] Since Quebec and Trois-Rivières as well as Ville Marie suffered from a shortage of men, the two friends concluded that every precaution must be taken to foil any attempt on the part of Lauson to retain some of their colonists in Quebec.

One wonders where Jérôme found the time to take care of his personal responsibilities besides those of the Montreal venture. How did he and Paul de Maisonneuve manage to knock at enough doors to find 100 settlers for Ville Marie and the means to sustain them? These two dedicated men continued to work hard well through the winter of 1652-1653 as it mercilessly pounded the kingdom with its icy fist and the shivering war-racked Frenchmen sought the warmth of their hearths and fireplaces—if these existed.

In early 1653, Maisonneuve found an unexpected recruit, a woman who was to exercise a far-reaching influence in the New World and whom the Church was to elevate to the altars in the 20th century: Marguerite Bourgeoys. It happened during a visit to his two sisters at Troyes. When they were not living in Paris, his widowed sister, Jacqueline de Chevilly, and her two daughters resided at the Hôtel du Chaudron.[16] His elder sister, Louise de Sainte-Marie, belonged to the French Congregation of Notre-Dame founded by St. Pierre Fourier. These nuns hoped to emulate the example of the Ursulines in Quebec by sending members of their monastery to Ville Marie. Governor de Maisonneuve, who had agreed to make use of these Sisters, was obliged to inform them that the hour had

343

not yet come for a cloistered monastery in the island foundation. Sr. Louise thereupon suggested that a good candidate for Ville Marie would be Mademoiselle Marguerite Bourgeoys, a woman of thirty-three years of age, who was then living with their sister, Madame de Chevilly. She belonged to a pious association under the direction of the Sisters of the Congregation and was well known to them.

As Marguerite happened to be at the convent, a meeting with the governor was immediately arranged. He questioned her courteously but unsparingly: Was she ready to leave Troyes and cross the sea? Was she prepared to live in a rough settlement among soldiers, working men, and peasants? Would she consent eventually to teach their children and the Indian youngsters born in the wild-wood? She would, yes, she would, she told him.

"Sisters importuned him," she wrote, "but he accepted me alone."

Curiously enough, in a dream. she had seen a handsome youth, St. Francis of Assisi, and a bald man dressed in brown like a country pastor, with an air of authority about him though he was not an elderly man.[17] Marguerite mentioned this dream to her entourage. How surprised she must have been to discover that the bald man was none other than Paul de Maisonneuve. She did have, nevertheless, qualms about putting herself under the care of a complete stranger, and consulted her spiritual advisor.

"Fear not," the priest replied, "put yourself in his hands as into those of one of the first knights of the Queen of Angels. Go quite confidently to Ville Marie!"

Another vision totally dissipated her apprehensions:

"One morning, being wide-awake," she later noted, "I saw a great Lady, dressed in white serge, who said to me: 'Go, I will not abandon you,' and I knew she was the Blessed Virgin, though I did not see her features. These words reassured me and gave me plenty of courage. I no longer found anything difficult, despite my fear of illusions."

Before setting out on the return trip to Paris, towards the end of 1652, Maisonneuve learned that his sister Jacqueline planned to bid him a final farewell in the capital. He suggested that she invite Marguerite Bourgeoys as her travelling companion. She did and on the sixth or eighth of February, Mme. de Chevilly, Mlle. Bourgeoys, and Uncle Cossard took the stagecoach for Paris. Marguerite carried a little bundle of indispensable linen but not a sou or penny to bless herself with. Her relatives and friends were under the impression that she was simply off for a few days' vacation. As the coach jogged along the desolate countryside, where windowless houses stared at them and rotting corpses filled the air with their nauseating stench, Marguerite revealed to Madame de Chevilly and to her uncle her plans concerning Canada. They thought she was trying to distract them from the depressing vistas of the Fronde.

In plague-stricken Paris, they found Paul de Chomedey quickly, probably with Jérôme Le Royer. Marguerite was asked to take the governor's personal effects to Nantes. First, Marguerite must convince her Uncle Cossard that she truly intended to sail across the sea, so she led him to a notary's study and asked him to witness the bequest of all her possessions to her younger sister and brother, Madeleine and Pierre.[18] She did not reap much gratitude, for when they heard of her decision, they accused her bitterly of abandoning them.

During March, on the day before she was to leave for Nantes, more opposition beset her in the form of the Provincial of the Paris Carmelites, who invited her to enter Carmel wherever she pleased.[19] As she had given serious thought to becoming a Carmelite, and had even been turned down by one of the two Carmels of Troyes, the Provincial's letter upset her. A Jesuit, who had laboured in

Canada, quickly calmed her, and she set out.

The journey from Paris as far as Orleans lasted only a few days. During that time Marguerite found herself in more than one embarrassing situation since it was not customary in those days for a woman of good breeding to travel unattended. From Orleans to Nantes, which she covered in a river barge, Marguerite Bourgeoys succeeded in having the other passengers join her in prayer; she even had the rivermen put on more speed in order to hear Mass on Sunday. By the end of March, Marguerite had set foot in Nantes. Once again, to put it mildly, she was taken for an undesirable. She was finally identified and welcomed into the house of Monsieur Lecoq de la Beausonnière, ship owner of the *Saint Nicolas de Nantes* on which she was to sail.

Meantime, in Notary Chaussière's Parisian study, on March 4, 1653, an agreement was reached by the Montreal Associates. The signers were men of piety and determination: Frs Jean Jacques Olier, Alexandre de Bretonvillers, and Nicolas de Barrault, along with Duc Roger du Plessis de Liancourt, Louis Haber de Montmor, Fr. Pierre Chevrier, Baron de Fancamp, ordained a priest in 1652, Bertrand Drouart, Jérôme Le Royer de la Dauversière, and Paul de Chomedey de Maisonneuve, the last two signing for Jeanne Mance and Louis d'Ailleboust.

Mention is made in this document of Ville Marie's perilous position and of the difficult times which discouraged charitable people from helping "this establishment so useful to the glory of God and to the propagation of the Faith." [20]

In harmony with the intentions of the "Unknown Benefactress," the Associates redeemed an annuity of 1,100 livres, whose capital of 22,000 livres added to other charitable contributions would be used by Jérôme to send reinforcements to Montreal "to protect the said island from the violence of the enemies of the country, to bring the land under cultivation, and to draw the Indians hither." In the minds of the signers, the venture still remained a missionary enterprise.

Did this contract entail loss of the annuity for the Ville Marie Hôtel Dieu in favour of the island foundation? Not at all. The hospital would continue to benefit from the 1,100 livres which would normally have accrued to it from the 22,000 livres had they been reinvested. Who then would provide the annuity? None other than the Montreal Associates, by mortgaging their property on the Island of Montreal.

As the spring of 1653 advanced, preparations for the journey back to Canada were speeded up. Because of Governor-General de Lauson's attitude, unfavourable to the Montreal settlement, steps were taken to transport the recruits from Quebec to Ville Marie when the time came. During April, a document under the King's private seal was drawn up maintaining Paul de Maisonneuve as governor of Ville Marie and granting him the needed authority to act independently of Lauson.[21]

A tentative date, the last day of April, already set for the departure of the ship that was to carry the recruits to Canada, was delayed, no doubt to recruit more settlers. Le Royer and Maisonneuve did not waste their time. The weeks following the signing of the agreement on March 4, 1653 were crammed with meetings of prospective colonists, many of whom had been contacted during 1652. The two friends acted hand and glove, and incredible as it may seem, at La Flèche from the twenty-third of March to the twelfth of May, they obtained the signatures of 120 men. They quickly increased to 152, 103 of whom effectively departed for Canada.[22] They came from Champagne, Picardy, Ile de France, Normandy, Burgundy, Touraine, Maine, and Anjou, especially from the vicinity of La Flèche.

All were meticulously screened. According to Atherton in his *Montreal, 1535-1914,* "there were three surgeons, three millers, two bakers, a brewer, a cooper, a copper-smith, a pastry cook, four weavers, a tailor, a hatter, three shoemakers, a maker of sabots, a cutler, two armourers, three masons, a stonecutter, four tilers, nine carpenters, two joiners, an edge-tool maker, a nail maker, a saw maker, a paviour, two gardeners, a farrier, sixty tillers or labourers for cultivating the soil, of whom several were sawyers, etc." [23]

To be sure, Jérôme Le Royer and Paul de Chomedey de Maisonneuve warned them of the dangers to which they would be exposed in the New World, but they were hardy men and probably thought that conditions at Ville Marie could not be much worse than in Fronde-ridden France.

Worthy of note is the motivation that inspired these recruits, as indicated at the beginning of each individual contract: the conversion of the Indians of Canada. Fifteen years later, the Mission of St. Francis Xavier for Christian Indians would be founded across the St. Lawrence River from Montreal, and after a dozen more, Blessed Kateri Tekakwitha would there achieve holiness—all of which would have been impossible at the time had it not been for the efforts of Jérôme Le Royer and his friends and associates.

Even a summary examination of the contracts signed by these men in 1653 furnishes us with a good idea of the annual cost the Ladies and Gentlemen of Montreal would have to meet to cover the salaries and the upkeep of the emigrants. No less than 8,720 livres in yearly wages alone,[24] plus the expenses incurred for transportation, housing, farming implements, food, arms, and ammunition.

On the seventeenth of May at the latest, Jérôme de la Dauversière and Paul de Maisonnevue were at Nantes, where they oversaw the immediate preparations for the Canadian voyage. Some thirty miles from sea, the city proudly reared its towers and steeples at the junction of the Loire with the Sèvre, Erdre, Chézine and Sail rivers.

This ancient town etched itself in the memories of the departing recruits: a final image of their homeland with its château, a splendid Gothic fortress, St. Pierre's cathedral, its storehouses, wharves, and medieval houses.

For about two months, Mademoiselle Bourgeoys had been busy at Nantes completing the purchase of provisions for the relief force at the cost of 75,000 livres.[25] How grateful she was when two couples and several girls joined the emigrants. In particular, the founder of Ville Marie confided to her care twelve-year old Marie Dumesnil from La Flèche,[26] who, in the years to come, was to give four of her daughters to Marguerite Bourgeoys' Congregation of Notre-Dame.

At last, in the third week of June, Paul de Chomedey de Maisonneuve, Marguerite Bourgeoys, and the lot of colonists boarded the waiting craft. Captain Pierre Le Besson commanded his sailors to unfurl the sails and to lift anchor and the stretch of water widened between the ship and the wharf until the *Saint Nicolas de Nantes* was swallowed up by the river traffic. On the twentieth of June, at Saint Nazaire, an unpretentious place of call at the mouth of the Loire estuary, with Notary Beliotte several more men boarded the *Saint Nicolas* when the river pilot went ashore. A last formality had to be concluded: those who had shipped under Governor de Maisonneuve were invited to sign a receipt for the advance payment on their wages and hand it over to the notary. After he had disembarked with all the papers, the ship slowly sailed out of the roadstead and steered its course to the high sea.

The signed receipts were soon in Jérôme's hands. Quite unexpectedly, a month later he received another communication from Saint Nazaire. Maisonneuve wrote that 350 leagues from land, the vessel had sprung a leak and Captain Le Besson had ordered her back to port. The recruits were terrified and would just as soon have returned home as gone to New France. The governor prudently landed them on a little island in the Loire from which they could not escape.

The *Saint Nicolas* was repaired and it definitively quit France on July 20, 1653. Eight men died during the crossing. On the sixteenth of November, approximately 95 recruits[27] entered the gates of the fort at Ville Marie. With Jérôme Le Royer de la Dauversière, Paul de Chomedey de Maisonneuve, and above all, Jeanne Mance, they were responsible for what was truly "the second foundation of Montreal."

Chapter XXVI

Notes

1. Dollier de Casson, *A History of Montreal*, pp. 155, 157.

2. *Journal des Jésuites*, p. 153.

3. Jeanne Mance, quoted by Daveluy in *Jeanne Mance*, p.130.

4. Dollier de Casson, *A History of Montreal*, p. 159.

5. Desrosiers, *Paul de Chomedey, sieur de Maisonneuve*, p.137.

6. Faillon, *Histoire de la Colonie Française en Canada*, Vol. 2, p. 135.

7. Lucien Campeau, *Les finances publiques de la Nouvelle-France sous les Cent-Associés*, 1632-1665, Montreal, 1975, p. 89.

8. Dollier de Casson, *A History of Montreal*, p. 163.

9. *Journal de Jésuites*, p. 164.

10. Trudel, *Montréal, la foundation d'une société*, pp. 20-21.

11. Dollier de Casson, *A History of Montreal*, pp. 185, 187, 189.

12. Daveluy, *La société de Notre-Dame de Montréal*, p. 323.

13. Dollier de Casson, *A History of Montreal*, p. 167.

14. Trudel, *Montréal, la foundation d'une société*, p. 30.

15. Desrosiers, *Paul de Chomedey, sieur de Maisonneuve*, p. 140.

16. *Ibid.*, p. 145

17. Jamet, *Marguerite Bourgeoys*, Vol. 1, p. 48.

18. Montgolfier, *La vie de Marguerite Bourgeois*, pp. 53-54.

19. Jamet, *Marguerite Bourgeoys*, Vol.1, p. 67.

20. Mondous, *L'Hôtel-Dieu, premier hôpital de Montréal*, p. 352.

21. Faillon, *Histoire de la Colonie Française en Canada*, Vol. 2, p. 182.

22. Trudel, *Montréal, la formation d'une société*, p. 21.

23. Atherton, *Montreal*, Vol.1, p. 116.

24. *RPA*, Vol. 6, p. 471.

25. Morin, *Histoire Simple et Véritable*, p. 63.

26. Marguerite Bourgeoys, *Les écrits de Mère Bourgeoys, autographie et testament spirituel*, Montreal, 1924, p. 45.

27. Trudel, *Montréal, la formation d'une société*, p. 21.

Chapter XXVII

Faith It Was

ON JUNE 30th, 1653, 28-year-old Marie Grasset, from the parish of Vieille-Ville in the diocese of Nantes, solicited her admission to the Daughters of St. Joseph.[1] She was apparently drawn to the Hospital Sisters by Jérôme Le Royer during his brief stay at the seaport on the Loire in order to wish God-speed to his latest contingent of colonists sailing for Montreal. She was the last postulant to be admitted to the Daughters of St. Joseph in La Flèche during his lifetime.

Why was this so? Jansenist Henri Arnauld was at the root of the trouble. Since coming to the Diocese of Angers, he had taken upon himself to "reform" the convents and religious communities under his jurisdiction. At Angers, for instance, he had already invaded the Visitation monastery. Jansenistic Sr. Marie Constance was to abet the prelate in his misguided zeal.[2] Later on during two terms of office (1660-1666, 1669-1675), this clever woman tightly grasped the reins of power and ran the Visitandines, the Bishop, and the diocese to boot. She soon rather disrespectfully became known as the "Bishop's Pea Shooter." *

Henri Arnauld was quick to ferret out a kindred soul

---

* In 1661, during the Pea Shooter's first triennium as superior, "two young professed Sisters wrote and staged a play in her honor with comic interludes, in which Jesuits were lampooned, Arnauld and his friends extolled. One of the tableaux represented the Bishop in his coach drawn by two Jesuits instead of horses, with the community pall serving as tester... When the prelate's brother, the "great Arnauld," came to Angers in 1671, the play was read to him and to Madame Angran, who thought she would die of laughter." Claude Cochin, *Henry Arnauld, Bishop of Angers, 1599-1692*, Paris, 1921, p. 305.

among the Daughters of St. Joseph at La Flèche: Mother Anne Aubert de Cléraunay.[3] She sided with him in his aim to transform them into a religious order with solemn vows, an old ambition of hers. As early as 1649, during her tenure as instructress or mistress of novices, she tried to implant her views skillfully among the postulants and novices entrusted to her care. Highborn and endowed with a remarkable mind, sparkling with wit, she rapidly gained ascendancy over them. At Laval, in 1650, with the young Sisters whom she had trained at La Flèche and with a few older ones who had followed her from the start, she felt much more at ease to promote her mistaken ideals of the monastic life and solemn vows for a sisterhood dedicated to the care of the destitute sick. In La Flèche, Mother de Cléraunay had left behind five or six sympathizers who surreptitiously propagated, with little enough success it must be admitted, the acceptance of her standards for the Hospitallers. Among the other Daughters of St. Joseph, however, opposition to the change was brewing; soon it would boil over into open hostility.

In the course of the summer and early autumn of 1653, Arnauld stopped three times at La Flèche. The struggle between the prelate and the Sisters was certainly carried on from one visit to the other, each party determined not to give in. On August 11, 1653, in the company of an impressive retinue of clergy, the Bishop passed through La Flèche on his way to the Abbey of St. Jean, founded in the forest of Mélinais[4] by its first abbot, St. Reginald, in 1196. Thereafter authenticating the 900-year-old relics of the saint canonically, he pontificated at a Solemn Mass and Vespers. It could have been on his way home that he clearly revealed to the Hospitallers his plans to modify their Constitutions, which his predecessor, Bishop de Rueil had approved. The Daughters of St. Joseph were to become a great order of nuns with solemn vows.

Or perhaps he put his arbitrary demand to them on the fourth of September, on the same day that he consecrated four altars at the nearby Jesuit college.[5] Ever gracious in manner, but grim as a somber granite wall in outlook, he presented the Hôtel Dieu Sisters with a relic of St. Reginald[6] and, if he had not done so before, communicated his design to "reform" them.

On the eighth of November, once again at the Hôtel Dieu, "Henri, by the mercy of God and the grace of the Apostolic See Bishop of Angers," authorized Srs. Anne Aubert de Cléraunay, Judith Moreau, Catherine Macé, Marguerite Rénard, and Marie Maillet to remain at Laval for a second triennium.[7] At the same time, he ordered Sr. Marie Houzé back to La Flèche as soon as she could come conveniently.During this visit, it is likely that he brought up the subject of solemn vows anew. Of the thirty-one Sisters who then made up the personnel of the La Flèche Hôtel-Dieu, twenty-five or more preferred the simple vows as more appropriate to their calling and opposed any sort of change with regard to this essential point of their Constitutions.[8]After Arnauld's first visit in August, Mother Le Tendre consulted with Jérôme Le Royer, who found himself on the sharp horns of a dilemma: should he hold to the original Constitutions revealed to him by God, approved by the late Bishop de Rueil, by his spiritual guides and other saintly men or comply with his Bishop's wishes? What was he to advise the Sisters if autocratic Bishop Henri Arnauld, in the capacity of superior of the Daughters of St. Joseph, commanded them to take solemn vows? He could recall to the Sisters Mother de la Ferre's impassioned plea on her deathbed that they always remain faithful to their rules, for "they are from God." But there was no need for that; her dying recommendations were written in their hearts.

The history of the Church is not lacking in what, at first

glance, may seem to be instances of disobedience in canonized saints. Founders of religious orders, in particular, were sometimes blessed with the gift of prophecy, speaking out against legitimate authority. St. Francis de Sales taught that the Holy Spirit could lead certain great saints "to actions contrary to the laws, regulations and customs of the Holy Mother Church." [9] These cases, he warned, are not ordinarily imitable.

Fortunately, at this time, Bishop Arnauld issued no formal order on the subject of solemn vows. Still, then or shortly afterwards, to express his displeasure at what he considered their negative attitude, he forbade the La Flèche Daughters of St. Joseph to admit new candidates to the religious life with simple vows.[10]

In compliance with Arnauld's interdiction, for seventeen years the Hôtel Dieu Sisters at La Flèche no longer opened the doors of their novitiate to candidates seeking admission.[11]

With this stranglehold on Jérôme's Daughters of St. Joseph, did the Bishop grasp that if he kept on strangling, their very existence would be compromised? Was he convinced that it was better for the needy sick to be deprived of care rather than to be attended by Sisters bound only by simple vows? *

For Jérôme, to this menace to the very existence of the Daughters of St. Joseph was added the worry entailed by the persistent ailments of his friend Fr. Olier, who, most of the time, was in no condition to help him.

Owing to a violent siege of fever, the priest had resigned

---

* In 1694, when most of the opposing Sisters formed by Jérôme Le Royer and Marie de la Ferre had died, another generation of Daughters of St. Joseph, under the leadership of Mother Lésine Scholastique des Essarts, accepted the solemn vows.[12] In our times, even before Vatican II, on this point, the Sisters of St. Joseph's *ressourcement* providentially led them to dispense with the solemn vows.

his pastorate of St. Sulpice in Paris and given up his priory of Bazainville on June 20, 1652.[13] As soon as he felt better, he intended to dedicate himself to what he considered his prime responsibility in life—the founding and maintaining of seminaries to prepare a worthy diocesan clergy for the Church.

Fr. Olier was hardly up and about when he found himself once again prostrate with excruciating pain from calculi and piles, aggravated by vicious toothaches.[14] After recuperating somewhat, without laying aside forever his plans for well-run seminaries, the valetudinarian turned his attention once again to the foreign missions, which had haunted him since 1636. In 1647, he had accepted to become a Bishop of Babylon in order to evangelize Persia (today known as Iran) but was persuaded to desist.[15] Later, after preparing Charles II of England to abjure Anglican Protestantism secretly, Olier longed to work in Great Britain, but had to content himself with praying for the return of the British Isles to the old faith.[16] When, after many years of labor in what we now call Viet Nam, the noted Jesuit Alexandre of Rhodes visited Paris in 1653, the abbé begged of him to be accepted as an associate for the missions of the Far East.[17] Sincere though the offer was, the missionary rejected it, for the volunteer was in no condition to sail to the other side of the world. Not long after, Fr. Olier suffered a stroke leaving him with his left side paralysed.

About the end of November, Jérôme was informed that, during the voyage across the Atlantic, some fatal malady had carried off nine of the recruits he and Maisonneuve had so painstakingly assembled for Montreal. The *Saint Nicolas de Nantes* with its load of emigrants had reached Quebec on September 22, 1653.[18]

As the Montreal leader had anticipated, Governor-General de Lauson tried to detain as many of the Ville

Marie men as he could. But the order of the previous April under the king's private seal, forced him to give in. After lengthy bickering, Paul de Maisonneuve obtained two pinnaces[19] and transported the imposing contingent of about 95 colonists up-river to Ville Marie, where they put ashore on the sixteenth of November.[20]

Although it is pure fabrication,[21] the following story, which Dollier de Casson included in his *History of Montreal*, illustrates how critical the conditions were at the time. During that same spring, Lauson is said to have sent a pinnace to Ville Marie with the strict orders for the commander not to land "unless he saw signs there were still Frenchmen there; if he saw none, he was to return to Quebec, for fear that the Iroquois, after capturing the place, should use it as an ambush to catch them." [22] The vessel is supposed to have approached the island and dropped anchor. As fog shrouded the entire settlement, without attempting to penetrate into the phantom-like fortifications, faithful to his order, the commander sailed back to Quebec with news that Ville Marie had been blotted out!

During 1654, one of the points that caught Jérôme's eye and made him nod his head in approval was an event that had taken place a few weeks after the recruits' arrival in Montreal. In December 1653, Governor de Maisonneuve had called to his quarters those who planned to stay at Ville Marie for good and all. Dressed in their grey serge suits and wrapped in their heavy greatcoats they made their way, one after the other, to their leader's house. The Montreal Associates, he told them, were willing to cancel their debts so they could buy the clothing and the tools they needed. Better still, the Company of Montreal would grant each one of the men who really intended to strike root in Ville Marie two plots of land, the first, of an arpent within the limits of the settlement, the second, of thirty others, beyond its outskirts. Finally everyone would receive the substantial sum of 400 or more livres provided that it be refunded if the would-have-been Montrealer quit the island.[23] Jérôme considered this measure an important step ahead in consolidating his dream city of nearly two decades earlier. The governor had also enlarged the hospital[24] and later on added to it a fifty-foot chapel with its proud little steeple and two bells.[25] When the snow disappeared and the first white blood-roots and wake-robins bloomed, Jeanne Mance and her patients quit the fort and moved to the newly enlarged Hôtel Dieu.

On August 8, 1654, Paul de Maisonneuve registered a transfer of property, which was later to be ratified by the Society of Montreal.[26] In its name, he surrendered a large farm, well cleared and stocked, to the Hôtel Dieu of which it became a fief, in exchange for its annuity, a benefaction of the "Unknown Benefactress," which had served, certainly with her approval, to recruit new men.

For twelve years now, close by the fort, the triangle formed by the junction of the St. Lawrence river and the St. Pierre streamlet served as cemetery, though the ice build-ups of spring flooded it nearly every year. A new cemetery was on the agenda and Maisonneuve offered for this purpose a piece of land next to the hospital, in part occupied today by Place d'Armes.[27] Fortunately, the number of burial was not excessive—less than six per cent of the population yearly—during the two score years following the foundation of Ville Marie.[28]

So all was not centered in gloom. A few months later, Jérôme could indeed see the sun's rays strafing the clouds above the island habitation. Besides, although the Jesuit missionaries had blessed only thirteen marriages up to 1654, in that year alone they celebrated the Holy Sacrifice at fifteen weddings, a promise for the future.

This does not mean that the Iroquois had completely

faded away into the darkness of the forest. During Maisonneuve's absence, the Onondagas had carefully hatched their strategy. On June 26, 1653, a delegation of sixty of their warriors appeared before the walls of the Ville Marie fort and invited the French to bury the war-axe with them.[29] Ailleboust des Muceaux, Maisonneuve's temporary replacement, had hesitantly agreed. Later on, with the same idea in mind, the Oneidas, taking pattern on the Onondagas, sent a body of their braves on special embassy to Ville Marie. As proof of their good faith they informed the French of an imminent attack of six hundred Iroquois on Trois-Rivières, a valuable tidbit of information.

At the time, the French leaders sought to fathom this sudden desire for peace on the part of their enemies. They would soon find out and relay the news to Jérôme Le Royer, who was always attentive, as usual, to anything dealing with the Island of Montreal. One must bear in mind that two Huron villages had merged with the westmost Senecas, thus strongly reinforcing them as a nation. The Onondagas had no intention of being outdone in this play for manpower and decided to incorporate into their nation the six hundred Huron refugees established at the Island of Orleans, and, in this matter, they counted on Governor-General de Lauson's assistance.[30] He could either protect the Hurons or allow them to depart. Hence the Onondagas's desire to negotiate. The Mohawks, who were warring at Trois-Rivières, did not take long to seize the Onondagas's purpose and immediately manoeuvred to lead the Hurons to their own canton. Lauson was vastly inferior to the Iroquois strategists and did not comprehend their calculations nor grasp their estimation of the Hurons as a reservoir of fighting men.

Since the aging and indolent governor-general inspired no fear in his copper-skinned opponents, they fiddle-faddled with him, even talking in February 1654 of a symbolic treaty-pole at Quebec.[31] He finally postponed the departure of the Hurons for at least another year and, at wit's end, transferred the treaty pole to Ville Marie, thus designating the island habitation as the official place for future parleys.[32] In reality, this decision was a tacit acknowledgment of Maisonneuve's role as "liberator of Canada," and could be interpreted as a delegation of authority to him. It could also be construed as the move of a weak man to embarrass a potential rival with the difficult problems of ulterior negotiations with a wily foe.

Working, negotiating, and fighting, Paul de Maisonneuve was ready for them. After more trouble with the Onondagas and Oneidas, he managed to achieve a period of mutual concord with them. The Mohawks, however, were refractory, for they were determined, by all means, to take back to their country the reluctant Hurons of the Island of Orleans. They were partially successful, but tenacious and adroit, Maisonneuve was able to bring the eastern Iroquois to heel. Thanks to his paramount qualities of leadership, he was able to offer to Ville Marie and also to all France, not a lasting peace but a full year of quiet, which guaranteed the settlers time to reinforce their positions.[33]

What probably hurt the Montreal leader most was the governor-general's constant opposition to Ville Marie. No matter what Maisonneuve said or did, he was unable to win Jean de Lauson over to a favourable view of Ville Marie. Extremely fussy about his prerogatives as governor-general, one by one he sought to peel Governor de Maisonneuve's powers off when he found it expedient to do so. He declared that the Company of Montreal was obliged not only to people Ville Marie but also New France in its entirety, that it should in addition see not only to the clearing of the land at Montreal but also at Quebec, and not only that it should fortify Ville Marie but even the capital of the country. He bitterly blamed the Montreal Associates for not sending more colonists and imposed duties on the food and munitions destined to Ville Marie. He took over the plot in Quebec where the Company of Montreal had erected a storehouse. To make matters worse, he declared that Ville Marie had no right to a store of its own, and added that Montrealers must henceforth buy whatever needed in Quebec.

Did Maisonneuve report Lauson's obstructionist tactics to Le Royer? It is inconceivable that he acted otherwise. The founder immediately grasped the need for action and called for assistance upon the most prominent of the remaining members of the Company of Montreal, in particular Fr. Olier, who, despite his ailments, was still acting president of the association. With their cooperation, Governor-General de Lauson's obnoxious conduct was brought to the king's attention. His Majesty decided to take the matter in hand. Communications were slow in those days and many months would pass before the Governor of Ville Marie was advised that Lauson's hold on the Island of Montreal was broken.[34]

About this time, Paul de Maisonneuve, who had remained single, was advised to wed by his confessor.[35] The suggestion upset him and, as he did not feel called to marital bliss, he talked the matter over with Marguerite Bourgeoys. She suggested that he take the vow of perpetual chastity, and this he did after having obtained permission from Fr. Jérôme Lalemant, a Jesuit, whom he consulted twice yearly in Quebec about his spiritual life.

Of course, Jérôme Le Royer knew little enough concerning his friend's interior struggles and victories. He did know, however, that Paul de Chomedey de Maisonneuve was deeply religious and completely detached from filthy lucre. From any lucre indeed, for he could easily and honestly have accumulated a fortune of 200,000 livres or more by engaging in the fur trade.[36] Out of love for evangelical poverty, Maisonneuve shut his heart to the blandishments of wealth.

Jérôme, too, forged ahead in the service of His Maker. In the course of 1654, at prayer, he was inspired to request some special gift from God. His choice fell on the virtue of faith.[37] No doubt about it, he would need and need until the hour of his death, a faith as strong as the enormous dikes he had seen in Holland. To his spiritual adviser, who thought that he should have asked for the grace never to sin again, he quietly countered that this was not the state in which the Creator had placed mankind. His admirable frankness and humility led him to rely on faith to help him overcome whatever difficulties might lie in store for him, all the violent storms which were to beat relentlessly down upon him, each one more shattering than its predecessor.

One of his pressing worries sprang from the many loans that he and his wife, Jeanne—always ready to stand by him—contracted in 1654 to keep Ville Marie alive. On the twelfth of January, he borrowed 2,000 livres from a La Flèche draper; on the thirtieth of August, 4,000 livres from the Laval Daughters of St. Joseph; on the same day, so great was the need, 1,800 more from the Visitandines of La Flèche. By the middle of 1655, he would be in debt to the pretty sum of 17,500 livres.[38] He saw his wife's security and his own dwindling away, but the faithful servant firmly trusted that God, who was leading him, would eventually extricate him from the quagmire of debt.

As in the lives of most holy men, an uprush of happiness now and then broke through the dark shroud of Jérôme's anxiety. Towards the end of July 1654,[39] he attended the wedding of his eldest son, the only one of his children to marry, Lieutenant-General Jérôme Le Royer, to Mademoiselle Louise Brochard des Bourdaines. About this time, to his youngest son, Joseph, who then felt not the slightest attraction for the clerical state, LeRoyer predicted that some day he would become a priest.[40]

The Hôtel Dieu of Moulins, dear to the founder of the Daughters of St. Joseph, was a source of comfort to him. There Mother Marie de la Ferre had died; there his daughter Jeanne was superior. To the initial band of six Sisters from La Flèche, the foundress of Moulins Hôtel Dieu had added four novices; her successor, five. The love of Christ that he found in the fifteen Sisters, and their joyful service of the needy patients made him lift up his heart in thanksgiving to God. Many other young women were begging to be admitted to the novitiate. In 1654 on a visit to Moulins, Jérôme Le Royer met them individually and indicated to Mother Le Royer those he considered truly called to the Institute.[41]

Because of the threat to the Constitutions, in all likelihood, it was during this visit, in his talks to the community or in his private conversations, that in order to strenghthen the Sisters in their vocations, Jérôme revealed the message he had received in 1635 at Notre Dame of Paris.[42] It is one of the rare confidences of this sort that he is known to have made, for he was extremely reticent about the special graces and revelations with which he had been favoured. Before returning to La Flèche, he proposed to the Sisters and to their chaplain that they let him take the precious remains of Mother de la Ferre back with him, but once again the translation of her relics was deferred.

364

Chapter XXVII

Notes

1. *RPA*, Vol. 6, p. 472.

2. Claude Chochin, *Henry Arnauld, évêque d'Angers, 1599-1692*, Paris, 1921, p. 309; *RPA*, Vol. 6, p. 474, Note 1.

3. Bertrand, *Monsieur de la Dauversière*, p. 205.

4. *RPA*, Vol. 2, p. 73.

5. Rochemonteix, *Le collège Henri IV*, Vol. 4. p. 227.

6. *RPA*, Vol.2, pp. 73-74.

7. *Ibid.*, Vol. 6, p. 475 (suite).

8. Bertrand, *Monsieur de la Dauversière*, p. 205.

9. Andre de Bovis, "Obéissance et liberté," in *Nouvelle Revue Théologique*, Vol. 77, No. 3, (Namur, March, 1955), p. 295.

10. *RPA*, Vol. 6, p. 475.

11. *Ibid.*, pp. 472-473.

12. *Ibid.*, pp. 292-293.

13. Faillon, *Vie de Monsieur Olier*, Vol. 2, p. 610.

14. *Ibid.*, Vol. 3, pp. 433-444.

15. *Ibid.*, p. 378.

16. *Ibid.*, Vol. 2, p. 320.

17. Albert Jamet, "Jérôme Le Royer de la Dauversière et les commencements de Montréal," *Revue de l'Université d'Ottawa*, (Oct.-Dec. 1936), p. 413.

18. Marguerite Bourgeoys, *Les écrits de Mère Bourgeoys*, p. 45.

19. Dollier de Casson, *A History of Montreal*, p. 193.

20. Mondoux, *L'Hôtel-Dieu, premier hôpital de Montréal*, p. 132.

21. *Journal des Jésuites*, pp. 179-180.

22. Dollier de Casson, *A History of Montreal*, p. 177.

23. Desrosiers, *Paul de Chomedey, sieur de Maisonneuve*, p. 162.

24. Dollier de Casson, *A History of Montreal*, p. 195.

25. Robert Lahaise, *L'Hôtel-Dieu de Montréal*, p. 20.

26. "Concession, Paul de Chomedey à Jeanne Mance," in *Mondoux, L'Hôtel-Dieu, premier hôpital de Montréal*, Appendix, pp. 355-357.

27. Desrosiers, *Paul de Chomedey, sieur de Maisonneuve*, p. 165.

28. One hundred and twenty-two deaths from 1642-1663: See Trudel, *Montréal, la formation d'une société*, p. 30.

29. *JR*, Vol. XL pp. 163, 165.

30. Desrosiers, *Paul de Chomedey, sieur de Maisonneuve*, p. 172.

31. *JR*, Vol. XLI, pp. 51, 53.

32. *Ibid.*, p. 63.

33. Dollier de Casson, *A History of Montreal*, p. 205.

34. "Lettre du roi pour faire cesser les prétentions de Monsieur de Lauson à l'égard des associés et des colons de Montréal," in Faillon, *Histoire de la Colonie Française en Canada*, Vol. 2, pp. 245-246.

35. Morin, *Histoire Simple et Véritable*, p. 72.

36. *Ibid.*, p. 68.

37. *RPA*, Vol. 6, p. 479.

38. *Ibid.*, p. 480.

39. Gaudin, *Inventaire et extraits des papiers de famille de monsieur Jérôme Le Royer de la Dauversière*, p. 27.

40. *AM*, p. 164.

41. *Ibid.*, p. 161.

42. *Ibid.*, p. 12, Note.

Chapter XXVIII

Father Olier Keeps His Promise

AT THE BEGINNING of March, generally a month of mild weather in France, Jérôme was once again in Paris, where he rented a room at his customary pension on rue St. Christophe, in the parish of St. Geneviève des Ardens. Montreal affairs had propelled him to the capital.

On the fourth of the month, he made his way to Notary Chaussière's study at the *Châtelet*.[1] With Fr. Olier, Fr. Alexandre Le Ragois de Bretonvilliers, the latter's successor as pastor of St. Sulpice, and Baron Louis Séguier de St. Firmin, Provost of Paris, he listened to the reading of the two deeds drawn up and signed in Ville Marie during the previous August by Paul de Maisonneuve and Jeanne Mance, "administratrix of the hospital of St. Joseph of Ville Marie." The first one was for a transfer of land and livestock to the Hôtel Dieu for the 22,000 livres of the "Unknown Benefactress" endowment; the second one was its acceptance. The four men as Montreal Associates and in the name of the others, then appended their signatures in approval of Maisonneuve's transaction. They would obviously never have done so had they suspected any opposition on the wealthy helper's part.

Jérôme was undoubtedly home in La Flèche two months later when a significant if somewhat laconic entry was made in the register reserved to the Daughters of St. Joseph who took or renewed their vows: "The said Sister Le Balleur took her departure on 19 May 1655. [signed] Anne Le Tendre." [2]

A surprising departure at first glance. Sr. Le Balleur had entered the community in 1646, one of the first to do so. Later she had accompanied Mother de la Ferre to

Moulins, but "for reasons of health" returned to La Flèche after the latter's death. A manuscript life of Jérôme Le Royer intimates that the discussions concerning solemn vows may have been the underlying cause of Sr. Le Balleur's break with the Daughters of St. Joseph. Arnauld's attitude was stirring up plenty of uneasiness and apprehension.

A decision of his about another foundation did nothing to calm the current agitation. Château Gontier on the Mayenne was on the boundary line of the former provinces of Lower Maine and Anjou. Even in Jérôme Le Royer's day, it was considered an old town, having grown under the protection of a fortified castle erected in 1037 by one of the first counts of Anjou. As it was not very far from La Flèche, Monsieur de la Dauversière mounted his horse and rode off towards the northwest. On the twenty-third of July during the afternoon, in Château Gontier a contract was prepared and signed by Ysabel Marie Malier, dowager marquise of Château Gontier and Jérôme Le Royer, representing Mother Anne Le Tendre, superior of the Daughters of St. Joseph at La Flèche and her council.[3] The buildings and lands that the marquise was willing to donate to the future Hôtel Dieu as well as the constructions to be erected were carefully indicated; the remaining clauses were the same as in the contracts of the Moulins, Laval, and Baugé foundations.

On the eighth of August, fifteen days after Jérôme's trip to Château Gontier, the beneficent marquise was received at La Flèche by Mother Le Tendre and by Srs. Renée Busson, Marie Gyrot, Jeanne Busson, and Jeanne Le Gras. She ratified the agreement, and so did Mother Le Tendre and her council. After Notary La Fousse and his assistants had added their signatures and the scratching of the quills was silenced, all that was needed to take it into the realm of reality was Bishop Arnauld's blessing since he was the religious superior of the Daughters of St. Joseph.

369

The Hôtel Dieu of Château Gontier later opened its doors according to the marquise's wishes, but the Daughters of St. Joseph were not present to welcome the patients: another community of nuns had taken their place. Henri Arnauld, who had forbidden Mother Le Tendre to receive postulants at La Flèche, did not favor another hospital run by her Sisters.[4] He put his episcopal foot down and thus came to naught the founder's fond hopes and diligent efforts for the Château Gontier foundation.

Jérôme's faith sustained him in the melancholy days that followed.[5] The future seemed to hold no promise for any further development of the Daughters of St. Joseph in France. The falling through of the promising Château Gontier establishment coupled with the Bishop's interdiction to accept new subjects would have deterred a lesser man than Jérôme Le Royer from still trying to carry out the heaven-sent orders he had received some twenty years before.

In his disappointment, Jérôme found some comfort at the thought of Mademoiselle de Melun at the Baugé Hôtel Dieu. Her interest in the hospital never flagged. As the narrow dimensions of the building restricted the Sisters' activity in favor of the sick, the enterprising princess decided to remedy the situation. Furthermore, as the Hôtel Dieu had no assured revenue, she gave much thought to the endowing of the entire organization. Before so doing, however, she bought several plots of land, part of which she levelled at considerable expense, and walled them in. She aimed to build up an estate for the community, with yards and gardens. On her brother's advice, she then offered the Sisters a choice: she was willing to buy a large property to provide them with a settled income or, instead, to erect a bigger and more convenient building than the one they occupied, built as it was to accomodate only five or six Daughters of St. Joseph. Mother Anne de la Haye and the rest of the Sisters preferred the latter, and before long the main portion of the building with its halls and living quarters began to take shape.[6]

While the workmen were still sawing and hammering, Princesse de Melun fell ill. At her urgent request, it was in the poor women's ward that she was put to bed, but, as she grew worse, the Sisters carried her to their own infirmary where she recovered her health sufficiently to take charge of the building operations once again.

As soon as the ships once again plowed their way through the heavy Atlantic seas, Jérôme Le Royer resumed the correspondence interrupted by the winter gales. One of the first ships to put in an appearance at Quebec carried a letter from Louis XIV to the governor-general.[7] Who would doubt that Jérôme's influence was not alien to it? The king sharply reprimanded Lauson for his conduct with regard to Ville Marie, and curtly reminded him that it had been founded for purely apostolic motives, informed him also that its inhabitants had the right to have a store of their own in Quebec and on their island without interference from any quarter, and that the Montreal Associates were not bound to send more emigrants to New France than they judged necessary. Thus was Ville Marie's autonomy guaranteed; so was its right to unrestrained navigation, to tax exemptions and to the ownership of a storehouse in Quebec. Governor de Lauson's attempt to subject the Island of Montreal to his authority had miserably failed and for him it must have been a bitter pill to swallow.

Reports from Paul de Maisonneuve spoke of more trouble with the Iroquois, especially with the Mohawks, and then of his decision to return to France to discuss important affairs concerning the welfare of Ville Marie.

Even before Fr. Olier's attack of paralysis, in 1654, Monsieur de Maisonneuve, spurred on by Jeanne Mance, often mulled over the idea of explaining to the founder of the Sulpicians Ville Marie's need of priests. To be sure, the

371

Jesuits were caring for the spiritual needs of the inhabitants since the foundation of Ville Marie. However, as missionaries, they considered the conversion and instruction of the Indians their first responsibility. Nearly every year one Jesuit after another was assigned to the missions and replaced by a new man.*

Late that autumn, after the Canadian maples shed their gorgeous crimsons and safrans, Paul de Chomedey de Maisonneuve knocked at Jérôme Le Royer's door in La Flèche on Hail Mary Street and the two friends fell into each other's arms.

When exactly? We know that on the twenty-fifth of August in Ville Marie, the governor authorized the settlers to break new land on the seigneurial domain close by the fort.[8] The men were guaranteed in writing the right to use and enjoy the benefits of the cleared properties until the Company of Montreal reclaimed them: in exchange, a plot of land equally large and well grubbed would be allotted to each individual. The fighting had simmered down, too, into a peace of sorts, and thanks to Maisonneuve's foresight, in case of another explosion of terror, the fortifications stood strong and sturdy.

A proclamation in September 1654 of a general order issued by the Duc de Vendôme, Superintendant of Navigation, had forbidden ship captains to take aboard any Frenchman interested in returning to the fatherland without a passport signed by the governor-general himself. Thus Paul de Maisonneuve felt that he could leave the

---

* Among these devoted religious specially worthy of mention were St. Isaac Jogues (1645), Gabriel Druillettes (1643-45), "the Apostle of Maine," Jacques Buteux, (1645), who died riddled with balls, Charles Albanel (1650), described as "a little old man of English parentage," taken captive and sent to England, and Paul Le Jeune (1645-46), known as the "Father of the Canadian missions."

country for a while without fear that the population of Ville Marie would dwindle away. On the same day that he opened the seigneurial lands to the colonists, he appointed Major Lambert Closse as his substitute, and, accompanied by Louis d'Ailleboust and Charles d'Ailleboust des Muceaux, sailed for Quebec and finally for France in the middle of October.[9]

When did the governor, after disembarking from his ship, learn of the great misfortune awaiting him? Was it as he stopped at La Flèche on his way to Paris, that Jérôme gently revealed to him the terrible tragedy which had swooped down upon his sister Jacqueline, Madame François Bouvat de Chevilly, scarcely a few days after his departure from Ville Marie?

Between four and five o'clock in the afternoon of August 29, 1655, at Neuville-sur-Vanne, as she made her way to Vespers, a horseman rode up and point-blank fired his musket at her.[10] She recognized her assailant and cried out: "This time, you won't escape a criminal's death!" Again and again he pulled the trigger, and she collapsed. The assassin, who had also murdered her husband, was her cousin Guillaume de Rouxel, Sieur du Deffand and de Médavi, in collusion with Abraham d'Aulquoy, his father-in-law.

Paul de Maisonneuve felt the full impact of the blow. Until his brother-in-law's death, he had acted as his proxy promising fealty and service and settling any number of minor affairs for him.[11] Then Jacqueline was his last link with Neuville-sur-Vanne, and that link no longer existed. His domain and belongings were placed under distraint. Although little enough is known about his comings and goings during these unhappy months, there is no doubt that he spent quite some time with the notaries and magistrates of Neuville and Troyes reclaiming his property and protecting the rights of his two orphaned nieces.

Despite his grief, Paul de Maisonneuve did not neglect

373

his purpose in returning to France. To Jérôme, he detailed the growth of Ville Marie since his last visit in 1653. He spoke of the new hospital, of grants to the settlers, of the marriage contracts that he had drawn up for many of them, of the land cleared, of the houses built, of the trouble with Lauson, of the Iroquois raids, and in particular of the violent death on the thirty-first of May, of Julien Daubigeon, one of the recent newcomers to Ville Marie.[12]

With all the ups and downs, the settlement was taking root. The time was ripe for the Daughters of St. Joseph to go to Montreal and take over the little hospital. There was also a strong demand for the Sulpicians to cross the ocean and organize a regular parish at Ville Marie: hadn't Fr. Olier promised that he would send some of his men to New France when conditions were suitable? Finally, more than ever, Canada, and preferably Ville Marie, needed a Bishop. Fr. Thomas Le Gauffre had been chosen bishop of the French colony in 1645, but died inopportunely before coming to a decision about his nomination.

Maisonneuve was probably in Paris some time in late December. Did Jérôme Le Royer accompany him to the capital or join him on his return from Neuville-sur-Vanne? Probably the latter. The two friends called upon the associates who were still faithful to the Company of Montreal. The governor, no doubt with the founder of Ville Marie, also made their way to St. Sulpice, where they were welcomed by failing Fr. Olier.

Despite his successive bouts with sickness and despite his interest in other missions than those of Canada, the St. Lawrence island foundation always remained close to Olier's heart. This great priest was ever alert to the finger of God beckoning him on in the events of daily life, but for many years it had not beckoned in the direction of Montreal. Now it did.

Maisonneuve laid his case before him, inviting him to

374

remember a letter he had received during the previous year from Mlle Mance in which "she advised him that the time had come to fulfil the lofty designs he had always had for Montreal, and that he ought to delay no longer in sending out some priests from his seminary." [13]

Olier was moved. His one regret was that his health would not allow him to take his place among the Canadian missionaries. He saw things in better perspective now. Hadn't he offered himself for the missions of the Orient and been refused? True, some of his Sulpicians were already at work in the field afar. In 1636, Our Lady had revealed to him that "he would be a light which would give revelation to the Gentiles." That light, he finally understood, would shine through the holy clerics whom he had formed and instilled with love for the Blessed Virgin Mary. So he agreed to designate four or five of his Sulpicians to accompany the governor of Montreal on his return trip to the New World.

It is difficult to imagine that the question of a Bishop for Canada did not then arise; equally difficult to suppose that Jérôme Le Royer and Paul de Chomedey avoided mentioning the staffing of the Ville Marie hospital with Daughters of St. Joseph.

On his long journey homeward, as Jérôme's mind grappled with a hundred and one problems, he had the satisfaction of reflecting that his "foolish enterprise" was by way of shedding its qualifier.

In January 1656, Mother Le Tendre's second term of office was up, and, since the Constitutions allowed the superior no third term, elections were held in La Flèche on the twenty-second day of the month. Sr. Renée Busson was chosen to guide the little ship of the St. Joseph Hôtel Dieu in a troubled period of its history.[14] Mother Busson, who had entered in 1641, eighteen days after Mother Le Tendre, knew that she could rely on the latter's close collaboration in her new post as "instructress" of novices. Together with Sr. Marie Gyrot as assistant, with Sr. Jeanne Busson des Chaumières as depository or bursar, and Sr. Marthe Berard as head nurse, Jérôme felt that they would adhere completely to the original Constitutions and would prove adequate to the important dealings that lay ahead.

At the La Flèche Hôtel Dieu, on March 13, 1656, Mother Renée Busson had Notary Pierre de la Fousse draw up a delegation of powers for Monsieur Pierre Blondel, one of Jérôme's Parisian acquaintances, as procurator for the Daughters of St. Joseph.[15] To avoid a conflict of interests, the founder of the Sisters, who held the post until then, abandoned it, for, in the capital at the end of the month, a highly important business transaction was to take place between the Sister and Ville Marie's Hôtel Dieu. Since he was one of its administrators, he could not act for Mother Busson and her community.

On the afternoon of the thirty-first of March, in Notary Chaussière's Parisian office, a group of gentlemen, administrators of the Ville Marie Hôtel Dieu and associates for the conversion of the native population of New France, met to sign an important deed between the Daughters of St. Joseph, represented as agreed by Monsieur Blondel, and the Montreal Company.[16] Jérôme let his eyes wander over the nine distinguished priests and laymen present: his two faithful standbys, Frs. Olier and Le Ragois; his faithful friend Fr. Pierre Chevrier, Baron de Fancamp; Roger du Plessis, Marquis de Liancourt, Duc de la Roche-Guyon and Pair de France; Antoine Barillon, Seigneur de Morangis and director of the king's finances, "a gentleman of profound learning and of never-failing faith and charity, an eminent and saintly personage," Christophe du Plessis, Baron de Montbard, one of the best-known parliamentary lawyers of the time; Bertrand Drouart, Master of Sommelan, an intimate acquaintance of St. Vincent de

Paul; Louis Séguier, Baron de St. Firmin, secretary of the Company of Notre Dame of Montreal; and, finally, Governor Paul de Chomedey de Maisonneuve.

A good part of the afternoon must have gone by before the deed was signed by the Associates in the names of the Company of Notre Dame of Montreal and of the highly appreciated "Unknown Benefactress." This document shows Jérôme's prudence and discernment clearly. The principal motive that bound the Montreal Associates together was recalled once again: the conversion of the Indians. With His Majesty's consent and the subsequent approval of the Bishop of Angers, the Daughters of St. Joseph agreed to maintain three or four sisters at the Ville Marie Hôtel Dieu and others in the future to care for the needy sick "in accordance with their Institute and their vows."

The Administrators, in return, gave the Daughters of St. Joseph the site of the transoceanic Hôtel Dieu with its "houses, yards, gardens, property, fields and woods, appurtenances and outbuildings," for them to exploit. They also added the buildings already built and to be built upon land chosen by Governor de Maisonneuve and Mademoiselle Mance. The community of Sisters, however, must provide its own furniture and guarantee each one of its members an annual pension of not less than 150 livres. A final clause stipulated that should the Daughters of St. Joseph be obliged to quit Canada, the La Flèche Hôtel Dieu would have the right to claim the estate.

On the evening of that eventful day, Jérôme Le Royer could have cast a white pebble into the urn of history. He had taken a giant step forward in the realization of one of the paramount missions with which he had been charged in 1634. Seven months later, Mother Busson and her assistants ratified the agreement.[17]

Both the founder of Montreal and its governor felt that a body of wealthy and influential ecclesiastics should be given the unrestricted ownership as well as the spiritual and temporal conduct of the Island of Montreal. Otherwise who would assure the survival of Ville Marie after their death? The effective transfer of the land was to take place in 1663, when Jérôme Le Royer and Fr. Olier were no more.[18]

As 1656 wore on, in conformity with the plans of the Associates, the prospect of obtaining a Sulpician Bishop for Canada seemed more and more a possibility. Already in the previous year, at their suggestion, a Sulpician had submitted the case to the Lords Spiritual of the country, or more simply the Assembly of the Clergy. On August 10, 1656, Bishop Godeau of Vence pleaded in favor of a Canadian Bishop.[19] The Assembly approved the proposition unanimously, without, however, knowing the name of the priest to be designated for the first Episcopal See of New France. It requested that the Bishop of Vence solicit the approbation of Pope Alexander VII. The prelate and his assistants pursued their purpose actively in Rome, and, in January 1657, it looked as if all that remained to be done was to obtain the royal consent.

The Company of Montreal commented enthusiastically on the good news and offered to take care of the expenses the erection of a bishopric would entail. They were even ready to endow it with the gift of half the Island of Montreal with its cleared land, plus all the ensuing seigneurial rights.

On January 10, 1657, at the meeting of the hierarchy of the realm, presided over by Cardinal Mazarin, Bishop Godeau arose and named the Associates' choice as incumbent of the future Canadian See: Gabriel de Tubières de Levy de Queylus, Abbé of Loc-Dieu, and priest of St. Sulpice. Then the prelate overreached himself. Well aware that neither Louis XIV nor Cardinal Mazarin would accept a Bishop whom the Jesuits would not sponsor, he stated on his own, and perhaps at the suggestion of the Company of Montreal, that Fr. de Queylus would be agreeable to the

Society of Jesus.

The sons of St. Ignatius, who had not been consulted, preferred another candidate, the future Blessed François de Laval de Montigny, whose nomination was approved by the king before the last day of January[20] thereby eliminating Queylus as the first Canadian Bishop.

This miscarriage of the Company of Montreal's design with regard to Sulpician prelate for New France, preferably stationed at Montreal, did not deter Fr. Olier from designating four of his men for Ville Marie as he had promised Jérôme Le Royer and Paul de Chomedey two years earlier. At the first suggestion that he needed volunteers for the New World, each and every Sulpician offered himself spontaneously. Fr. Jacques Lemaître declared enthusiastically that he would gladly seek out the Indians in their own homes and villages to instruct them in the Faith.

"It won't be necessary;" retorted Fr. Olier looking into the future, "they themselves will come to get you, and you will be so entrapped that you will not be able to break free." On August 29, 1661, Fr. Lemaître was tomahawked and beheaded as his superior had predicted.[21]

For the time being, Fr. Lemaître remained in France, and Fr. Olier named Fr. de Queylus superior, Fr. Gabriel Souart pastor of Ville Marie, and Fr. Dominique Galinier as his assistant.

Olier's interest in Ville Marie once again began to inspire sympathetic benefactors to cooperate financially. On April 19, 1657, Fr. Pierre Chevrier, Baron de Fancamp, donated to the future parish on the Island of Montreal 2,000 livres, which guaranteed it 100 livres annual income.[22] Some time later, the two Frs. de Bretonvilliers, P.S.S., added 18,000 livres, and Fr. de Queylus 6,000 livres more.

On Easter Sunday, April 2, 1657, in the arms of St. Vincent de Paul, Fr. Jean Jacques Olier died at the early age of forty-eight years and a half.[23] Waiting to sail at

Nantes, Governor de Maisonneuve and the four Sulpicians were notified of his death. Undaunted, the four priests, knowing that they were carrying out their beloved founder's dying wish, boarded their ship, which finally unfurled its sails at Saint Nazaire on the seventeenth of May.[24] Jeanne Mance, Paul de Maisonneuve, and Jérôme Le Royer saw God's Providence at work in the institution of Ville Marie's first parish at the time it took place. Had the founder of the St. Sulpice seminary died sooner, or had he procrastinated about Ville Marie's first diocesan priests, would the Sulpicians have ever come to Montreal?

Notably absent from the ship on its way to Canada were the three of four Daughters of St. Joseph, who should have accompanied Governor de Maisonneuve, Fr. de Queylus and his clerics. When authorization to send them to the New World was requested by Jérôme, Bishop Henri Arnauld, good Jansenist that he was, lifted an elegant hand and dismissed him with a gesture of disdain.

Chapter XXVIII

Notes

1. Mondoux, *L'Hôtel-Dieu, premier hôpital de Montréal*, p. 358.

2. *RPA*, Vol. 6, p. 480.

3. *Ibid.*, p. 481.

4. *Ibid.*, p. 482.

5. Bertrand, *Monsieur de la Dauversière*, p. 212.

6. *AM*, pp. 165-166.

7. Desrosiers, *Paul de Chomedey, sieur de Maisonneuve*, pp. 182-183, where the king's letter is given in extenso.

8. *Ibid.*, p. 185.

9. *Ibid.*

10. *Ibid.*, p. 186.

11. *Ibid.*, p. 187.

12. Faillon, *Histoire de la Colonie Française en Canada*, Vol. 2, p. 234.

13. Dollier de Casson, *A History of Montreal*, p. 213.

14. *RPA*, Vol. 6, p. 484.

15. Mondoux, *L'Hôtel-Dieu, premier hôpital de Montréal*, p. 363.

16. *Ibid.*, pp. 358-362.

17. *RPA*, Vol. 6, pp. 490-491.

18. Atherton, *Montreal*, Vol. 1, p. 183, quoting Edicts and Ordinances of the Province of Quebec.

19. Faillon, *Vie de Monsieur Olier*, Vol. 3, p. 408.

20. Atherton, *Montreal*, Vol. 1, p. 138.

21. *Journal des Jésuites*, p. 303.

22. Daveluy, *La société de Notre-Dame de Montréal*, p. 106.

23. Faillon, *Vie de Monsieur Olier*, Vol. 3, p. 475.

24. Desrosiers, *Paul de Chomedey, sieur de Maisonneuve*, p. 203.

Chapter XXIX

I'll Huff and I'll Puff...

DURING 1658, did Jérôme Le Royer allow his thoughts to wander back to Mother de Ferre's prediction of 1649: He was to live ten years more? Time was running out on him and his work; the work Our Lord had given him to do had not been completed.

The founder of the Daughters of St. Joseph could take some comfort in turning over in his mind the progress of the Baugé Hôtel Dieu. Ever generous Anne de Melun, after having seen to its building, now furnished it with the goods and chattels essential to the well being of the Sisters and of their poverty-stricken patients.[1] Seeing her happily immersed in charitable activities, her brother, Prince Guillaume Alexandre d'Epinoy, decided to remove to Paris for good and all. The princess consented reluctantly to his departure, and continued to devote herself unstintingly to the ailing poor.

An unprecedented occurrence strengthened her resolve to do so until the end of her days. It also convinced Jérôme, if he needed convincing, that God approved of the Baugé hospital and, indirectly, of the Sisters of St. Joseph. It took the form of lightning, quickly attributed to the light and smoke devices of the devil. Weird though it may seem, it should not appear too strange to us in the era of ambient Satanism that is ours.

A La Flèche girl, thought to be possessed by an evil spirit, was exorcized with book, bell, and candle during July.[2] In the course of one of the ceremonies, after spells of furious contortions, she refused to answer the questions put to her by the priest. Half an hour later, she fell into convulsions. Then she was asked why she had been silent for so long.

"I certainly didn't speak, for I wasn't here!" a strange voice replied distinctly.

"Where were you?" probed the exorcist. "I was at the hospital in Baugé."

Thereupon the priest questioned the voice about its owner's doings in that town.

"We went there, seven of us in all, to overthrow the Hôtel Dieu, but we weren't allowed to do any other harm than to give the people a good scare!"

Here they berated St. Joseph violently for protecting the hospital from their fury, and mentioned the thunder and lightning that struck the building. The description given by the voice was so muddled that ten days later, obviously with Jérôme Le Royer's consent, the good Father Exorcist made for Baugé to get to the root of the matter. He saw for himself the mess caused by the thunderbolt as he listened to the story of its impact.

The summer day had dawned calm and comfortable. Several hours after, a wild rain and thunderstorm suddenly developed and in a flash, lightning fell upon the Hôtel Dieu. It entered the building through a closed window of the men's ward. Two convalescents, as they sauntered back and forth, were chatting about one thing and another. One of them, with the reputation of a hardened sinner, felt his night-cap being torn from his head and flung to the floor at his feet. He frantically called for a priest to make his peace with God.

The ball of fire whizzed round the room, split the posts of the bed closest to the chapel, pierced a hole in the wall of the pharmacy and slipped in through it, raining all the while chips of stone on the tables and cupboards. A Sister, having opened the door, with her hand still on the key, saw coming in her direction the ball of fire trailing heavy fumes of noisome smoke. Feeling that she would be crushed by the flying fragments, she cried out to God for help and

384

ducked instinctively before the lightning passed at the spot occupied by her head a few seconds before.

The thunder-bolt had not finished its visit. Monkey-like it jumped to the upper story into the Sisters' rooms, broke several windows, ripped off the eaves of the building and, without harming anyone, carried away a rafter of the roof to a distant suburb of the city. Two Daughters of St. Joseph, working in the attic, were sent sprawling and thought that they had broken their legs for the pain of it. The visitation, infernal or otherwise, lasted no longer than the time it takes to say the Lord's Prayer. Mademoiselle de Melun, meditating in her room, was alarmed by the commotion and acrid smell of burnt cannon powder. She descended to the ground floor and, finding no one injured, gave thanks to St. Joseph for having saved the Hôtel Dieu, the Sisters, and the patients.

Whereupon the exorcist, after listening attentively to the story of the event, examined with a magnifying glass the windowpane through which the bolt had entered. There he discovered what he considered to be the signature of the forces of evil—seven minute but well-formed holes in the glass that had given entrance to the seven devils! Pure imagination? Perhaps. Be that as it may, all the witnesses including Anne de Melun, and later, Jérôme Le Royer, saw in this happening a manifestation of satanic hatred for the works of mercy accomplished at the Baugé Hôtel Dieu and, too, of God's tender love for the Daughters of St. Joseph who staffed it. *

The next four months hurtled by. During the last days of December, word came to Jérôme Le Royer from Montréal

---

* Compare with Blessed André Bessette's encounters with the Evil One from 1911 to 1937 as told in Etienne Catta's *Le Frère André 1845-1937 à l'Oratoire Saint-Joseph du Mont-Royal*, Montreal, 1964, pp. 852-861.

that hospital Sisters from Quebec were in Ville Marie at the Hôtel Dieu, presumably to take over the care of the sick.[3] The founder of the pioneer town had not been consulted and he staggered under the blow.

The truth of the matter was that Fr. Gabriel de Queylus, after planning the coming to Ville Marie of Mother Jeanne Thomas Agnès de Saint-Paul and of Mother Renée Bouillé de la Nativité, who was recuperating from a "providential ailment," had them deposited at the door of the Hôtel Dieu. His pretext for sending them up the river was that Mother Renée needed a change of air. His true intention, however, we do know: once the good Mothers found their way into the Ville Marie hospital, it would be easy enough, he thought, to have them take it over little by little. Jérôme Le Royer's plans to entrust the Hôtel Dieu to the Daughters of St. Joseph would thus come to naught. By this time, Jeanne Mance had decided to sail for France with Marguerite Bourgeoys. During the previous year, she had broken her arm, which still pained her acutely. She could no longer bear the full responsibility of the upkeep of the Montreal Hôtel Dieu and hoped to obtain funds and Daughters of St. Joseph for it. She welcomed the Quebec Hospitallers, "You are come," she told them, "and I am going." [4]

Having given orders that they must be treated with the utmost consideration befitting their rank and condition, perspicacious as she was, Mademoiselle Mance handed over to Marie de la Bardillière, a god-child of Queen Marie de Médicis and of Cardinal de Richelieu, the care and responsibility of the Hôtel Dieu. Under no account was any unwarranted interference in the administration of the hospital by the Quebec nuns to be tolerated.

For the two travellers, the voyage across the Atlantic was extremely difficult. From La Rochelle to La Flèche, first by coach, which proved to be pure torture for Jeanne

Mance, and then slowly, very slowly, by litter, they made their way to Jérôme Le Royer's home on the Street of the Ave at La Flèche, where they arrived for the Feast of the Epiphany, 1659.[5]

He received them with frigid politeness, for he was convinced that Jeanne Mance with her arm in a sling, had come to notify him of her resignation as a member of the Company of Montreal and to obtain official approval for a community of Hospital Sisters other than the Daughters of St. Joseph to staff the Ville Marie Hôtel Dieu.

Jeanne soon set him aright: she had returned to France in order to take back to Canada the Daughters of St. Joseph, whom he himself had promised so long ago to send to the Island of Montreal. However, she candidly informed him about the pressure which the Abbé de Queylus had brought to bear upon her. Even though he, too, was a member of the Company of Montreal, the contrary Sulpician had insisted that she defend his viewpoint at a meeting of the association in Paris. She must also solicit the aid needed to establish the Quebec nuns in Ville Marie. As Queylus's insistence had been like a knife in her ribs, she agreed to do so reluctantly.

"Let Father de Queylus bestir himself as much as he wishes; he won't stop our Daughters from going to Montreal nor God from realizing his designs!" [6]

These were Jérôme's final words on the subject to his two visitors. After this brief but complete explanation of her presence in France, Jeanne Mance, at the request of her host, now wholly reassured, related the story of her accident. Nearly a year before, at eight o'clock in the morning of January 28, 1657,[7] she had slipped and fallen on the ice—of which there was plenty in Canada—breaking two bones of her right forearm and throwing her wrist out of joint. Hastily summoned, the town surgeon, Etienne Bouchard, found her unconscious. When she came round, he quickly set her forearm. The broken bones mended, but, somehow, Jeanne Mance was still a cripple. Her condition went from bad to worse. The governor-general of New France and other high-ranking officials concerned themselves about her. Jean Madry, the surgeon-general of the colony, sailed up from Quebec to examine her. His diagnosis was the same as Etienne Bouchard's. Six months later it was discovered that her wrist was disjointed, and it was too late to reset it.

Jeanne Mance described the unsatisfactory state of her emaciated arm and left hand:

"I remained completely bereft of the use of my hand, and furthermore, I suffered a good deal from it, and was always forced to carry my arm in a sling, unable as I was to hold it up without some sort of support; since the moment I fractured it... I could not take care of myself nor use my hand in any way nor enjoy any freedom of movement with it so that it became necessary to dress and serve me as a child..." [8]

For eight days Mademoiselle Mance and Marguerite Bourgeoys were the guests of the Hôtel Dieu Sisters.[9] During their stay, Jérôme Le Royer met with them several times. Of course, he carefully read the reports from Governor de Maisonneuve; still he wanted their version of the last two years' events on the Island of Montreal. They told him of their deep satisfaction caused by the return of Governor de Maisonneuve to Ville Marie in August 1657. Accompanying him were Frs. de Queylus, the new Vicar-General of Canada,[10] Gabriel Souart, P.S.S., Dominique Galinier, P.S.S., and Antoine d'Allet, a young deacon, who hoped to be ordained priest in the New World.

The importance of these Sulpicians should not be underrated; their presence was the accomplishment of the prophetic words uttered many years before to Father Olier: "A light of revelation to the Gentiles." It was also the realization of part of the plan about which Jérôme Le Royer and Jeanne Mance had dreamt—a parish in New France set up and run as in Old France.

The election of the first three church wardens during the following November may seem of little or no account to us, three centuries removed from the event. For Jérôme, it was another sign of the steady growth of the island foundation. The men elected to the post were Louis Prud'homme, Jean Gervais, and Gilbert Barbier,[11] three of the older and most deserving settlers.

All was not silver lining, there were dark clouds, too. Jeanne Mance told him of the killing of Nicolas Godé, father of the first Ville Marie family, of his son-in-law, Jean de Saint-Père, first notary of the frontier town, and of their servant, Jacques Noël, by a party of thirty Oneidas, on October 25, 1657.[12]

Godé, a native of Normandy, was one of the emigrants of the initial 1641 contingent. This was the end of the peace lasting since 1653.

Neither the founder of Ville Marie nor later historians until recently were conscious that long years of war could have been averted had there existed between the Indians and the French a better understanding of one another's customs. Among the Amerinds, when blood was spilt, through negotiations, wampum or something equivalent was generally agreed upon to be turned over to the nearest of kin. On acceptance, justice was considered done. Europeans proceeded differently. The death of the killer seemed to be the only solution. These hardly reconcilable attitudes resulted in more hostility between the red and white men, which was to last till 1666, several years after Jérôme Le Royer's death.

Before setting out for Paris, Jeanne Mance and Marguerite Bourgeoys probably met Father Pierre Le Gouvello de Kériolet, a member of the Company of Montreal since

389

1642.[13] This nobleman from Brittany had been a guest at Jérôme's home since the middle of December. Though doubtless impressed by the austere clergyman, as far as we know, they had no second thoughts about him. Kériolet was known in many circles as "the penitent baron." Until the age of thirty-five this Breton aristocrat had led a wild life even to the point of invading the sanctity of the cloisters to rape a defenceless nun![14]

From 1633 to the end of 1634, throughout France and even beyond its furthest frontier, swept interest in the Loudun affair, in which Ursuline nuns of the city, claiming to be possessed by a rout of devils, stirred up a furor far greater than the witch hunts of the same century in Salem, Massachusetts. The Baron de Kériolet decided to attend one of the public exorcisms of the religious. Were these women truly possessed or were they simply sucked down into the whirlpool of mass hysteria? It is still a moot question.[15] Be that as it may, the young nobleman was in for the surprise of his life. One of the so-called possessed, in the grip of terrible convulsions, led him down the murky corridors of his past, which no one else could have known.

From that day on, the change in Pierre Le Gouvello de Kériolet was complete. After the general confession of his sins, in true Celtic style, he practised the most hair-raising penances. This patrician, accustomed to fine clothes, choice meals and vintage wines, distributed his fortune to the poor and went on a pilgrimage to Rome. He walked to the Holy City barefoot, bare-headed and poorly dressed, all the while begging alms as if he belonged to the brotherhood of paupers. In atonement for his misdeeds, he generally kept his eyes on the ground, prayed from eight to ten hours a day and ate little food from Thursday noon till Sunday at the same time. In the wake of this transformation, with some reluctance on his part, he was ordained a priest. Now a clergyman of twenty-five years' standing, what was Fr. de

Kériolet doing at La Flèche?

Close upon his conversion, "the penitent baron" had turned his residence into a hospital of sorts. At the beginning of 1659, four women patients, in a fit of diabolical rage, howled that they would overthrow heaven and hell, if needs be, to destroy Jérôme Le Royer, his family, and the Hôtel Dieu.[16] Father de Kériolet considered it his duty to warn the collector of taxes, who had become the founder of the Hospitallers of St. Joseph and of a pioneer town on the edge of nowhere.

What the devil was trying to say, had he spoken in English, was:

"I'll huff and I'll puff and I'll blow your house in!"

Jérôme was not perturbed. Years ago, had not Our Lord promised that He would clothe him with strength and wisdom, and that he would always have his Guardian Angel at his side to guide and protect him?

Chapter XXIX

Notes

1. *AM*, p. 171. After more than thirty years of service as lay benefactress of the Hôtel Dieu, at her death, the Princess had spent more than 50,000 crowns, leaving behind one of the most solidly built and commodious hospitals of Anjou.

2. *Ibid.*, p. 174.

3. Morin, *Histoire Simple et Véritable*, p. 79.

4. Dollier de Casson, *A History of Montreal*, p. 227.

5. Bourgeoys, *Les écrits de Mère Bourgeoys*, p. 50; Daveluy, *Jeanne Mance*, p. 164.

6. Faillon, *Vie de Mademoiselle Mance*, Vol. 1, p. 102.

7. Daveluy, *Jeanne Mance*, p. 173. Dollier de Casson mistakenly gives January 27 as the day the accident happened in his *History of Montreal*, p. 213.

8. Morin, *Histoire Simple et Véritable*, p. 81.

9. *Ibid.*, p. 78, Note 2.

10. Desrosiers, *Paul de Chomedey, sieur de Maisonneuve*, pp. 205-206.

11. Dollier de Casson, *A History of Montreal*, p. 221.

12. Daveluy, *La société de Notre-Dame de Montréal*, pp. 210-216.

13. Hippolyte Le Gouvello, *Le pénitent breton, Pierre de Kériolet, [1602-1660]*, Paris, 1878, p. 45.

14. Michel de Certeau, *La possession de Loudun*, Paris, 1970, a close scrutiny of the problem; Jean Vinchon, "Diabolic possession: the devils of Loudun," in *Soundings in Satanism*, assembled by F. J. Sheed, New York, 1972, pp. 1-12.

15. Le Royer de La Motte, *Le petit mémoire* ou *Ecrit autographe*, p. 29. See Chap. III, note 20.

Chapter XXX

Without the Community's Consent!

DESPITE THE RUMBLINGS from hell, the first months of 1659 were better than middling. At Christmastide Mother Renée Busson had completed her three years' spell of office at the Hôtel Dieu. In her place, on the twenty-second of January, Sr. Marie Grasset, whom Jérôme Le Royer had brought back from Nantes in 1653, was elected superior and "instructress" of novices,[1] a sure sign of the faith the community had in her. She was firmly opposed to any change of the Constitutions. The former superior, Mother Busson, became assistant superior, Sr. Marie Giroust head nurse, and Sr. Marie Gyrot was maintained as bursar. The founder himself would have been hard put to pick a more reliable staff.

Towards the end of the next month, news from Paris elated Jérôme. Jeanne Mance, whom he had seen with her bandaged arm in a sling, and worn out nearly to exhaustion, was totally cured! What had happened? On arriving in the capital, she wisely rested a few days at the congenial home of her cousin, Madame de Bellevue on Férou Street in the parish of St. Sulpice. Faithful to her promise to Fr. de Queylus, she then called on the Duchesse d'Aiguillon, foundress of the Quebec Hôtel Dieu. For this distinguished niece of Cardinal de Richelieu, the transatlantic visitor drew a word-picture of Ville Marie, stressing conscientiously how very useful a few hospital nuns from Quebec would be in the frontier town. This great lady, whose reputation of never hesitating to help a charitable enterprise was well known, shook her head in refusal.[2] As Jeanne Mance withdrew from her presence, Jérôme Le Royer's words echoed in her ears: "Fr. de Queylus will not stop God

393

from realizing His designs!"Advised of her arrival in Paris, the Company of Montreal assembled. The group of notables was well disposed and eagerly awaited Mademoiselle's report on Ville Marie. She candidly depicted conditions as they were in the island settlement, called to the members' attention that because of her age—she was then fifty-three years old—and broken arm, she would no longer be able to take charge of the distant hospital. She then paused before making her main point: It was high time that the La Flèche Daughters of St. Joseph devoted themselves to the sick and wounded of Ville Marie. Clearly and calmly Mademoiselle Mance recalled that she was speaking about the very young ladies to whom, not so many years before, the late Fr. Olier and all the ladies and gentlemen of the Company of Montreal had shown consideration. What were they going to do about them? To induce the Company of Montreal to comply with her request, she promised that she would ask the "Unknown Benefactress" for another endowment, which would enable the Daughters of St. Joseph to live in Ville Marie without outside help.

After her final remarks, Mademoiselle Mance was surrounded by the members of the Company, admirers all, who congratulated her on her spirit of dedication to Ville Marie and its Hôtel Dieu. They were touched by her infirmity and suggested that she consult Paris's eminent general practitioners. Baron Christophe du Plessis de Montbard even offered to have his sister Madame Cahüe accompany her by coach to the best of them. She did consult them. One and all, however, averred the case was hopeless; some even went so far as to predict that in time her entire right side would be half-paralysed.

Nothing remained to be done, she felt, except to persuade the "Unknown Benefactress" that she should accept the responsibility of setting up the Daughters of St. Joseph in Ville Marie. In the midst of her visits to the duchess, to the doctors and surgeons, dawned the second of February, feast of what was called until recently the Purification of the Blessed Virgin Mary and Candlemas. Now it is called the feast of the Presentation of the Lord. Remembering Fr. Olier's devotion to this feast of Our Lady, without any thought of self, she visited the Seminary of St. Sulpice to pray at his tomb. As she meditated on the mystery of the Purification, an inspiration came to her: she would ask Fr. Olier to cure her! After attending Mass and receiving Holy Communion, she requested the superior, Fr. de Bretonvilliers, to place within reach the heart of the founder of the Sulpicians, contained in a leaden case. As she took the heavy reliquary in her left hand and placed it upon her right hand resting in its sling, life surged through her right arm and down to her finger tips. Although her wrist remained dislocated, she was able to use her arm and hand freely without the least trace of pain for the first time in years.[3]

When the Duchesse De Bullion heard about this spectacular cure, she saw in it a blessing upon Ville Marie and, under the seal of continued secrecy, gladly donated 20,000 livres to establish the Daughters of St. Joseph at Ville Marie. This generous lady added 2,000 livres more for Mademoiselle Mance's passage to France and back to Montreal, furnished her with a fine supply of liturgical vestments and precious gems for the altar and chapel of the Hôtel Dieu, and topped off her munificence with extra money for the poorest of the struggling settlers.

These particulars on Jeanne Mance and the convening of two meetings by the Company of Montreal, which Bishop de Laval would attend, set Jérôme Le Royer on his way to the capital, his heart filled with happy anticipation. In the afternoon of the twenty-ninth of March, we find him at the Châtelet with Mademoiselle Mance and Notary Marreau. A historic day it was, as the La Flèche collector of taxes, in the capacity as procurator for the Daughters of St. Joseph, and Jeanne Mance as the administratrix of the Ville Marie Hôtel Dieu in her role as proxy for the "Unknown Benefactress" concluded an agreement of the utmost significance for the Island of Montreal foundation.[4]

After more than fifteen years of procrastination, it was stipulated that a few Daughters of St. Joseph and one lay Sister were to be sent to New France in the near future to take charge gratuitously of the Ville Marie Hôtel Dieu and its indigent patients. This free service was to be made possible through the donation of the "Unknown Benefactress." It was expected that the 20,000 livres would produce an annual income of 1,000 livres for the first Sisters to emigrate and later for their successors in Canada. At the same time, Jeanne Mance was maintained for life as the administratrix of the "property of the poor"—the Hôtel Dieu. Following her death, the seigneurs of Montreal were to name two administrators, after which, at every triennium, they were to replace the first one of the two who had been appointed.

Before affixing their signatures to this document of capital importance, Jeanne Mance remitted the lovely sum of 20,000 livres in gleaming Spanish gold pistoles, louis d'or and silver to the procurator of the Daughters, Jérôme Le Royer. He agreed to invest it within three months.

Precisely when the going seemed the smoothest for Jérôme, things began to break down. Two days before the signing of the contract, March 29, 1659, in the name of Louis XIV, the Queen Regent issued Letters Patent in which she ordered that François de Laval, Bishop of Petrea, be recognized as the Ordinary of New France.[5] The young prelate had secretly been consecrated bishop by the Papal Nuncio to Paris in the course of the previous December. From Canada, Fr. de Queylus had written him a letter detailing his plans to install the Quebec Augustinian hospital nuns in Ville Marie. He also informed the Bishop that two of them were already in residence at the Montreal Hôtel Dieu. Consequently there was no need to send Daughters of St. Joseph from La Flèche to the New World. Furthermore, one community of nursing Sisters was amply sufficient to run the two hospitals of New France. Why complicate the Bishop's administration of his vast Canadian diocese?

At a meeting of the Company of Montreal, Bishop de Laval was informed of the 1656 agreement between its members and the Daughters of St. Joseph, three of whom were to cross the blue sea that same year. He asked for a delay. At another gathering of the Company, the prelate persisted in his inclination to hold back the embarcation of the Sisters until 1660. Respectfully but firmly, the Company of Montreal reiterated its stand: It would be disadvantageous for Ville Marie to postpone the boarding of an outward-bound ship by the La Flèche Daughters of St. Joseph.[6]

With the intention of hastening as much as possible the sailing of at least three Sisters for Ville Marie, Jérôme left Paris not long after his daughter Mother Jeanne Le Royer, elected to head the Laval Hôtel Dieu, took leave of Moulins on the first of April, having completed her second triennium as superior. With two other Sisters, Renée Olivier de la Guittière and Thérèse Havard, Mother Le Royer and Fr. Jean Girault, in a small coffer of fir planks, carried to La Flèche the skull and half the remains of their beloved foundress, Mother Marie de la Ferre, leaving the rest to Moulins.[7] Time and time again, the motherhouse had claimed them, and now they were on their way. At Orléans, Jérôme met his daughter, greeted her companions, and thanked Fr. Girault[8] for having escorted them on the trip. Bidding him farewell, the little band with the relics of the saintly foundress converged on La Flèche, which it reached on the tenth of April. The Sisters of the Hôtel Dieu, many of whom owed their admission to the religious life to Mother de la Ferre, welcomed the precious relics prayerfully.

On the twenty-first of April, a stroke of good news was relayed to the Montreal Associates. To the Baron de Fancamp, the Company of New France retroceded the 500 arpents of land on Mt. Royal which it had reserved to build a fort. In exchange, he was to do homage for them and pay the seigneurial dues according to the Custom of Paris.[9]

During May, tenacious Bishop Arnauld convoked a general assembly of the Daughters of St. Joseph in order to induce them to accept his "reform." The minutes of the assembly, if they ever existed, are lost. The gist of it, however, we do know: Solemn vows for all with the strictly cloistered life they implied. The majority of the Sisters, as they had always done, opposed his demands consistently.[10] Six or less, headed by cross-grained Anne de Cléraunay, favored the radical change of the Institute, which the prelate was more determined than ever to impose.

It was about this time that letters from Paris, signed by Jeanne Mance, urged Jérôme and Mother Grasset to designate several Sisters for Ville Marie.[11] Many had been praying long and ardently to know God's Will concerning their future as missionaries. Mother Pilon, superior of the Baugé Hôtel Dieu, had been fasting on bread and water, with other corporal penances, so as to be among the chosen ones. Quite a few begged the Most High to send them to Canada, and also pleaded with their superiors to be assigned to the Island of Montreal.

On no consideration did Mother Grasset and her Council intend to commission anybody for Ville Marie who supported Arnauld's monastic ideas. On the other hand both she and Jérôme Le Royer were well aware that the Bishop of Angers would never confirm the appointment of active opponents like Mother Françoise Pilon and Sr.

Havard de la Tremblaye. Finally Jérôme picked three other capable Sisters, Catherine Macé, Marie Maillet, and Judith Moreau de Brésoles, though in the community's estimation they were perhaps the least satisfactory of all.[12] For several years they had worked under Mother Anne Aubert de Cléraunay, leader of the cabal for solemn vows. It was a shrewd choice and calculated to gain the Bishop's consent. Even so, since the attitude of the community at large had indisposed Arnauld, any suggestion with regard to Ville Marie was bound to exasperate him. It did. He refused the authorization requested by the founder and it seemed as if nothing in heaven or on earth could budge him.[13]

For Jérôme, completely at the end of his tether, the anxiety this refusal bred brought about an excruciating attack of gout.[14] It was so violent that he could not bear any bed-clothes on his feet. He was all nerve ends and raw flesh and cried out in pain continuously. He worsened so quickly that the doctors abandoned all hope of saving him.

His condition had been building up for months. To begin with, his austere style of life already mentioned did not help him healthwise. It would have been a mark of mental derangement had he not been taken up in the whirl-blast of divine folly. Not a way for us to follow unless, like Jérôme, we are favored with the visible presence of the Sacred Humanity of Christ for six weeks of stupendous bliss.

Simultaneously, for more than a year and a half, he was stricken with various complaints, every one of which would have driven all others to the brink of despair. An ulcer, a monstrous stone, acute inflammation of the kidneys, gravel and calculi, which he could not pass,[15] lowered him into the depths of suffering. He had been seen in the streets so convulsed with pain that he fainted away.

Far more torturous than all the rest, another circle of horrors closed in upon him. Despite himself the founder of the Daughters of St Joseph stirred up the resentment of their relatives as well as of his own.[16] Bishop Arnauld, as I have noted, was set on solemn vows and the strictly enforced monastic enclosure. This meant that no Sister would be allowed to sail for New France unless Jérôme Le Royer abided by the prelate's wishes, thus fixing him on the horns of a dilemma. The community could not forget its earlier teaching: the rules of the Congregation were from God Almighty Himself and had been approved by Bishop de Rueil. Even if it further delayed the St. Joseph foundation in Ville Marie, they felt that they should not support what they regarded as their founder's caving in to their Jansenistic Bishop. Bitter comments falsely attributed to the Sisters were noised about and Jérôme found them as distressing as the cruel stack of all his other afflictions. Even the common people loaded him with abuse, convinced as they were that he was doing a profitable business selling girls from the Province of Anjou to his preposterous island outpost across the water.

As he floundered in the troughs of pain, Jérôme reread the letters from Paris which reached him on the twenty-third of May. The Company of Montreal insisted that he conduct the Hospital Sisters assigned to Ville Marie as far as La Rochelle, where Jeanne Mance and Marguerite Bourgeoys would await them. His friend Fr. de Fancamp and several others were of the same mind: "The time the Lord has chosen is approaching," the Baron wrote.[17] Sick to death, the one and only recourse the organizer of the Montreal enterprise had was prayer. He poured out his heart before the Lord and begged for the strength to carry out the mission with which he had been entrusted. Two days later, on May 25, he was up and about though by no means a well man.[18]

On the same day, unbelievable as it may seem, all episcopal opposition vanished. For no sooner had Jérôme made his way to the Hôtel Dieu to inform Mother Grasset that he was in good enough condition to accompany the three Sisters to La Rochelle whenever they obtained permission to depart than Bishop Arnauld knocked at the door. When the names of the designees for Canada were submitted to him anew, he did not let his feelings override his better judgment. Here surely was the fulcrum he was seeking for. With a deceptively bland countenance, Arnauld refused to approve the list of candidates unless, of course, the founder agreed to impose enclosure on the Daughters of St. Joseph once they reached their destination.

What was Jérôme to do? Somehow he realized that the vanguard of his hospitaller Sisters must find their way to New France in the following months. And if they were to cross the ocean that year, by stress of circumstances, he must bow to the inevitable; he must comply with the Bishop's demands.

Srs. Macé, Maillet, and de Brésoles were informed that in Ville Marie they would be strictly cloistered. Before bidding farewell to their homeland, they must renounce the articles of their Constitutions allowing them to pass in and out of the Hôtel Dieu without written episcopal consent. Future candidates for the Ville Marie hospital, including subjects from outside the diocese of Angers, must also be advised of these changes.

Who would be the superior of the little band? Arnauld decided on the spot that it would be Sr. Catherine Macé.[19] As this Sister was frail in health and naturally retiring, she threw herself at the prelate's feet and entreated him not to lay this heavy burden upon her. He helped her to arise and looked questioningly at the founder. Jérôme answered by indicating Sr. Moreau de Brésoles, who was instantly appointed first superior of the Montreal Hôtel Dieu.

On the twenty-fifth of May, in writing, Bishop Arnauld authorized the establishment of the Daughters of St. Joseph on the Island of Montreal. Two Sulpicians, Jacques

Le Maître and Guillaume Vignal, had already made their appearance in La Flèche to join the Sisters for their long and perilous journey. The latter, the Bishop of Angers named their spiritual director. Suzanne de Gabriel and her husband, Claude Robutel de Saint-André,[20] were to accompany them to the New World.

Henri Arnauld was now all smiles and good cheer. Had he not achieved his goal of "reform", at least for the Canadian Daughters of St. Joseph? So there he stood, the image of Caiaphas, Mother Grasset must have thought, even to the point of making predictions: In God's plans, the Ville Marie Hôtel Dieu would in time become the ornament of the entire St. Joseph Institute![21] Like the High Priest's, his prediction came about. He did not, however, lift the ban to admit candidates to the La Flèche Hôtel Dieu until eleven years later.

On the morning of the first of June, Mother de Brésoles, Srs. Macé and Maillet, surrounded by the entire community, read the formal declaration enjoined on the Daughters of St. Joseph when they received a new assignment. They solemnly promised that they would always faithfully observe their Rules and Constitutions inasmuch as conditions allowed and would never permit any change in them without the agreement of the different houses of the Congregation.

A final hitch somewhat delayed the departing Sisters' farewell. For months, Jérôme Le Royer's role as founder of Ville Marie and as its colonizing agent was giving rise to opposition, which now broke out into open hostility. The growing number of recruits whom he had signed up over the years as colonists for the Island of Montreal was far from acceptable to the relatives of many of the emigrants. Ville Marie's advantage was working to the disadvantage of Anjou. Then again, certain individuals strongly resented the disappearance from La Flèche and its vicinity of what they called "the flower of feminine virtue"—the Daughters of St Joseph, who were leaving France for a cold, barbarous land where they would be in danger of being massacred by the bellicose Indians. It was also bruited about that these saintly persons were forced to go to New France. No doubt, were they free to choose, they would much prefer to remain in France. Weren't there enough abandoned and sick people in their own country to keep busy thousands of Daughters of St. Joseph?

During the night, a bitter, sullen crowd filled the streets of Port Luneau and of the Recollects in the neighborhood of the Hôtel Dieu. Some imagined that they could hear the Sisters moaning and groaning into the late hours of the night; others fancied that they could hear them sighing and crying out to have pity on them. The throng resolved to deliver them in the morning as they rode out of the gates of the Hôtel Dieu.

At ten o'clock, when the Sisters mounted their horses and quit the place, the mob made such a disturbance that Claude Robutel de Saint-André and the other cavaliers who were to accompany them, drew their swords and hurried forward to open up a passage. Without harming anyone, they scattered the scowling faces that pressed in on them, through the fear that they stirred up, "not a difficult thing," wrote 17th-century Dollier de Casson, "in country towns which are not on the frontier." [22] Within her little room, Mother Grasset, having opened the register containing the roll of the Sisters who had taken their simple vows, put on record the position of the La Flèche Daughters of St. Joseph as to Mother de Brésoles and Srs. Macé and Maillet: "On the first day of June 1659, the said Sister...left for the Montreal establishment without the consent of the community." (signed) Marie Grasset. [23] Two times more the above statement was repeated, varying only with the names of the Sisters.

Chapter XXX

Notes

1. *RPA*, Vol. 6, p. 505.

2. Daveluy, *Jeanne Mance*, p. 168.

3. *Ibid.*, pp. 172-174.

4. "Contrat de fondation des filles hospitalières de Saint-Joseph de Montréal, 29 mars 1659-9 juin 1659," in Mondoux, *L'Hôtel-Dieu, premier hôpital de Montréal*, pp. 364-365. It is important to notice that the word "fondation" means endowment. Bertrand, *Monsieur de la Dauversière*, p. 223.

5. Mondoux, p. 152.

6. Daveluy, *Jeanne Mance*, pp. 181-182.

7. Florence Moreau, *Présente à notre temps*, p. 148.

8. *RPA*, Vol. 6, p. 504.

9. Desrosiers, *Paul de Chomedey, sieur de Maisonneuve*, pp. 219-220.

10. *RPA*, Vol. 6. pp. 507-509.

11. Dollier de Casson, *A History of Montreal*, p. 245; Mondoux, *L'Hôtel-Dieu, premier hôpital de Montréal*, pp. 153-154.

12. *RPA*, Vol. 6, pp. 509-510.

13. Dollier de Casson, *A History of Montreal*, p. 245.

14. Morin, *Histoire Simple et Véritable*, p. 110.

15. Faillon, *Vie de Mademoiselle Mance*, Vol. 1, p. 166.

16. Morin, *Histoire Simple et Véritable*, p. 110.

17. Faillon, *Vie de Mademoiselle Mance*, Vol. 1, p. 143.

18. *RPA*, Vol. 6, p. 510.

19. Daveluy, *Jeanne Mance*, p. 187.

20. Morin, *Histoire Simple et Véritable*, p. 86, Note 2.

21. *Ibid.*, p. 189.

22. Dollier de Casson, *A History of Montreal*, p. 247.

23. *RPA*, Vol. 6, p. 509.

Chapter XXXI

"Master, Let Your Servant Go..."

WITH THE THREE SISTERS, the two Sulpicians, Monsieur de St. André and his wife, Madame Suzanne de Gabriel, went Monsieur Le Royer and a few horsemen.[1] Once out of La Flèche, they joyfully pressed ahead to La Rochelle, stopping on the way at the Baugé Hôtel Dieu, where they were welcomed by Mother Le Jumeau, her companions, and Princesse de Melun.

Somewhere along the road, Jérôme seems to have parted company with his fellow travellers to go to meet four female emigrants to Ville Marie: Magdeleine Fabrecque, Isabelle Camus, Marguerite Rebours, and Marguerite Martin.[2] He would rejoin the Sisters at La Rochelle.

Towards the end of the first week of June, on Pentecost or the eve of Pentecost, as the little cavalcade led by Monsieur de St. André approached the brisk, lively seaport with its smell of brine and fish, a large coach jogged into view, carrying Mademoiselle Mance. When it drew up to the travellers, she had the coachman halt, alighted to help the Daughters of St. Joseph dismount from their horses and invited the voyagers as well as Madame Suzanne de Gabriel to take places in her cumbersome vehicle.

The Sisters, who had heard about Jeanne Mance's cure, were interested in her telling of it. So she related the story in detail and also her accident on the way from Paris to La Rochelle.[3] The barking and yapping of dogs had scared the skittish mount on which she rode and it leapt over a ditch, throwing her violently on her recently cured hand. Luckily she suffered only a few scratches. In a letter to a Jesuit in La Rochelle, some flippant Parisian commented sarcastically that her miracle had been "unmiracled!" The religious, who was something of a practitioner, saw for himself that this was not the case.

Mademoiselle Mance then dwelt upon other subjects: How happy she and her friends had been with the information Monsieur Le Royer's messenger gave them as to the forthcoming arrival of the Daughters of St. Joseph at La Rochelle! They in turn would rejoice to learn that she had found "nine companions who were to take employment at the Ville Marie Hôtel Dieu or as her domestics, which amounted to the same thing." [4] Better still, to sail with them as candidates-to-be for the community, was a brace of very young ladies, Mesdemoiselles Perrine Picoté de Bellestre, aged sixteen, and Catherine Gauchet de Belleville, aged eleven, a niece of Sulpician Fr. Souart. Years later, after having lost her husband and brought up her family, Catherine eventually became a Daughter of St. Joseph.

For the time being, the Sisters put up at the lodging provided by a Monsieur Le Meunier, from whose place they set out every morning to attend Mass and help the sick and poor at the city refuge. The rest of the day they kept to themselves.

On the afternoon of June 9, 1659, the trio signed a declaration drawn up by Royal Notary A. Demontreau of La Rochelle, in which they adhered to the terms of the March 1656 Ville Marie foundation of the Daughters of St. Joseph.[5] Three days later, the Sisters appended their signatures to another document promising to meet Bishop Arnauld's stringent requirements with regard to the monastic cloister[6]—the bone of contention at the General Assembly of the previous month.

Still feeling under the weather, Jérôme Le Royer at last found himself in La Rochelle with the four girls his powers of persuasion had won over to the Montreal habitation. To Marguerite Bourgeoys, who had shepherded twenty or more to emigrate from Paris to the western seaport, he entrusted his four volunteers. As he talked with her, he discovered that another piece of the Ville Marie puzzle was falling into place. This outstanding lady from Troyes had attracted three hardy, intrepid women, Marie Raisin, daughter of a wealthy merchant tailor, Edmée Chastel, daughter of a lay notary apostolic, and Catherine Crolo, for six years now an aspirant after the Canadian mission.[7] They were ready to join together with Sr. Bourgeoys, as she was already called, in teaching the children of the white settlers and later of the Indian children, whose parents would not object to European learning.

As the number of recruits had already swelled to respectable proportions and as the price of their bed and board increased with each passing day, Jérôme was acutely aware that they must sail as quickly as possible. Obstacles delayed sailing, obstacles higher than the dike built by Cardinal de Richelieu when he besieged La Rochelle in 1627.

At this stage, the fleet of the Company of One Hundred Associates was ready to weigh anchor. The founder of Montreal pleaded with its commanding officers to await the *Saint André*, which was to carry the Ville Marie passengers to New France. They turned a deaf ear to his request and he quietly said, "Then God will be the master." Scarcely had the Great Company's vessels put out some three miles to sea when the flagship opened up and sank.[8]

Before his departure for Canada on Easter Sunday, Bishop de Laval had instructed his agents to do their best to dissuade Monsieur Le Royer from sending his Daughters of St. Joseph to Ville Marie. Like flies these men swarmed round the founder, harrying him so that he would change his mind. The Sisters had no chance, they insisted, of a warm welcome in a cold country such as Canada. Whether they objected to it or not, the three Sisters of St. Joseph would be back in France before the year was over. Why spend so much money, time, and energy to no avail? At least they should postpone their taking ship for another year or so. The argument of these well-intentioned but meddling intermediaries did not deter Monsieur Le Royer from hurrying the Sisters' departure. To those who belabored him with questions concerning his haste, he peremptorily answered: "If they don't go this year, they will never go."

It was probably the same men who awakened the suspicions and fears of Jacques Mousnier, the ship owner. The emigrants, he was told, were purchasing so many supplies that they might well be unable to pay their way for lack of funds. He thereupon refused to allow them on board his ship, the *Saint André*, until the charge was settled. To make it worse, he hoisted the score from approximately 50 to 175 livres for each passenger. What was to be done? For Sr. Bourgeoys succinctly wrote, "We had no money." [9] Most of the travellers were in the same predicament.

Did Sr. Bourgeoys then regret having refused 700 of the 1,000 livres offered her by Marie Raisin's father during her stay in Paris out of love for holy poverty? The suggestion which presented itself to her was to make out two promissory notes, one to be paid in Ville Marie and the other, if provisions proved insufficient in Canada, to be covered in Paris by Monsieur Raisin. After considerable discussions, Mousnier accepted them. [10]

While Monsieur de la Dauversière was doing his utmost to persuade the proprietor of the *Saint André* to order her to sail at once, Mademoiselle Mance sought and found an adequate substitute for empty purses. And there were many of them. Three more settlers had been added to the lot: for the Hospitallers of the Hôtel Dieu, Mother de Brésoles had hired Marie Polo, a La Rochelle girl, as maidservant; René Cullerier as landgrubber and Jean Celier as landgrubber and baker, all to be paid out of Madame de Bullion's bounty. Jeanne Mance, able woman that she was, sprung from a family of lawyers and magis-

409

trates, did the right thing at the right time. She negotiated an important loan from some merchant or other and on June 5, 1659 lent to married couples and their children the price of their passage across the Atlantic along with their baggage on condition it be reimbursed in two years.[11]

Fr. Dollier de Casson, a Sulpician well acquainted with Mademoiselle Mance and Sr. Bourgeoys, describes the morass of pecuniary trouble into which this shipload of Montrealers plunged Jérôme Le Royer and his associates: "As there were 110 (sic) persons to provide for, you may imagine how great their disappointment was. For, to pass on, consider, in view of all that had to be purchased for Canada, the expense involved, especially by the delay at La Rochelle, which was of three months' duration that year; consider how large a sum it cost the members of the company of Montreal, the Seminary of St. Sulpice, and the hospital, which three bodies bore the expenses of this voyage..." [12]

As a result of these business entanglements, the Bursar of the Daughters of St. Joseph, Sr. Marie Maillet, began to worry about the investing of the Hôtel Dieu endowment. To whom, she asked the founder, must she write to claim the annual income issuing out of the "Unknown Benefactress's" generosity? Plainly speaking, she wanted to know what Monsieur Le Royer had done with the 20,000 livres. The gold and silver pieces were lying dormant at his home in La Flèche. Since the signing of the contract on March 29th at Paris, illness and the trip to La Rochelle had prevented him from putting the money out to interest. So he answered evasively: "My daughter, God will provide; put your trust in Him." [13]

On Sunday, June 29th, Feast of St. Peter and St. Paul, with 90 or more other passengers, the Montreal contingent was finally allowed to embark. Some of the voyagers, for instance, Sr. Bourgeoys and her group, had been cooling their heels for weeks and weeks at the seaport. The final count of the Ville Marie colonists was impressive. Of the 107 who clambered aboard, 39 were married women and girls, 60 were men, among them, priests, soldiers, laborers, and 8 were children. [14]

There on the upper deck of the vessel with sails still unfurled, stood Jérôme Le Royer surrounded by friends and collaborators, whom he never was to see again. He was successfully bringing his mission to a close despite his many adversaries—some of them well-meaning such as François de Laval; others, not so well-disposed such as Bishop Henri Arnauld. For nearly three decades, Jérôme had striven with might and main to accomplish his purpose. Since 1642, with the cooperation of sensible, energetic Mlle Mance, of his lieutenant, Governor Paul de Chomedey de Maisonneuve, and of Fr. Olier, he had managed to transform the "Foolish Enterprise" into a sound one destined to become the metropolis of Canada.

He had founded a hospital institute, the Daughters of St. Joseph, to care for its sick and wounded, and now three of them were on the verge of saying a last good-bye to France. He had supplied Ville Marie with a diocesan clergy, and, just a few yards away, two more of his late friend Fr. Olier's Sulpicians, were trying to estimate how soon they would join their colleagues on the Island of Montreal. He had also made due provision for the education of the French and Indian children, and the future St. Marguerite Bourgeoys was returning to Canada with her first adherents. Perhaps Jérôme Le Royer, for whom, quite often, time to come obligingly spread out its vistas before him, foresaw them as the nucleus of the first teaching community founded in the New World, expressly for the New World. And then, of course, there were the all-important settlers with their families, whom he placed under the protection of his beloved St. Joseph, head of the Holy Family.

Slowly lifting up his hands, he gave a last blessing, his heart filled with the words of Simeon's hymn, the *Nunc Dimittis*: "Now, Master, You can let Your servant go in peace..."

This peace, which was so desirable, would most certainly come, but not for some time. With shoulders bent under the load of a fatigue seemingly without limit, he disembarked and disappeared quietly from sight in one of the little streets converging on the waterfront.

Two days later, on Wednesday, the second of July, Feast of the Visitation of the Blessed Virgin Mary, with every stitch of canvass spread, "most worthy Captain Jean Poulet," steered his vessel out of the La Rochelle roadstead.[15] Nobody knew it, but sickness and death were fellow passengers on this voyage. The *Saint André* had served as a hospital ship during the previous two years and was crawling with pestilential bacteria. During July, far out to sea, practically everyone was stricken with high fever. The majority survived, while at La Flèche, Jérôme Le Royer battled for his life.

Chapter XXXI

Notes

1. Mondoux, *L'Hôtel-Dieu, premier hôpital de Montréal*, pp. 158-159.

2. Jamet, *Marguerite Bourgeoys*, Vol. 1, p. 215; Daveluy, *Jeanne Mance*, p. 262.

3. Dollier de Casson, *A History of Montreal*, p. 243.

4. Daveluy, *Jeanne Mance*, p. 188.

5. "Contrat de fondation des filles hospitalières de Saint-Joseph de Montréal, 29 mars 1659—9 juin 1659," in Mondoux, *L'Hôtel-Dieu, premier hôpital de Montréal*, pp. 364-366. See also Chapter XXX, Note 4.

6. "Protestation ou acte fait par nos trois premières mères durant leur séjour à La Rochelle," 12 juin 1659, in Mondoux, *l'Hôtel-Dieu, premier hôpital de Montréal*, p. 367.

7. Bourgeoys, *Les écrits de Mère Bourgeoys*, pp. 51-52.

8. Le Royer de la Motte, *Le petit mémoire*, p. 29, see Chap. III, Note 20. 9. Bourgeoys, *Les écrits de Mère Bourgeoys*, p. 61.

10. Mondoux, *L'Hôtel-Dieu, premier hôpital de Montréal*, p.160.

11. "Contrat entre Mademoiselle Mance et divers colons," in *The Canadian Antiquarian and Numismatic Journal*, (Montreal, April, 1913), pp. 90-95.

12. Dollier de Casson, *A History of Montreal*, p. 247. As a matter of fact, 109 persons had their passage paid for, but two of them, Jean Condart and André Bouvier, went into hiding before the ship sailed. See E.-Z. Massicotte, "Une recrue de colons pour Montréal, en 1659," in *The Canadian Antiquarian and Numismatic Journal*, 4th series, Vol. X, (Montreal, April, 1913), p. 71.

13. Morin, *Histoire Simple et Véritable*, p. 89.

14. Daveluy, *Jeanne Mance*, p. 190.

15. Bourgeoys, *Les écrits de Mère Bourgeoys*, p. 53.

Chapter XXXII

"What Time Is It?"

AFTER THE SAINT ANDRÉ sailed out to sea, Jérôme Le Royer struck homewards. At a day's distance from La Flèche, as he approached Saumur, high above the Loire river, stood out the alabaster-white castle made famous by an illumination from the Duc de Berry's *Très Riches Heures*.[1] A glimpse of fairyland, the miniature masterpiece depicts the castle as originally built by Louis I of Anjou, pure harmony in stone, crowned with one hundred turrets on top of which twirled as many golden weather-vanes. The way-worn rider, however, did not go to the princely habitation. Instead he stopped at the nearby shrine of Notre Dame des Ardilliers.[2]

As he prayed within the chapel dedicated to the Mother of Christ, his strength failed him. Calculi and other complications racked him unmercifully. The next day, deathly sick, he went on to La Flèche. As the sun sank below the western horizon, he reached the outskirts of his little city, crossed the bridge over the Loire, bypassed the Carmelite Fathers' convent, breathed a prayer to Our Lady of the Head of the Bridge and drove his tired mount down Ave Maria Street. He was home at last. For good and all.

Fr. de Fancamp welcomed the pale, bone-weary man and, as he embraced him, noticed that he was still wearing his hair shirt. Another friend, Fr. de Kériolet, "the penitent baron,w" came to Jérôme with devastating news. His resources, some 100,000 livres, had disappeared in a day.[3] It was believed that a ship, whose cargo would have covered Jérôme Le Royer's debts, had foundered, leaving him penniless and the butt of his disgruntled relatives.[4] Unperturbed, he accepted the disastrous tidings.

414

Not long after his return, the home-comer was forced to take to his room and bed. In the first week of October, he painfully gathered his spiritual diaries together and destroyed them. Later on, Fr. de Fancamp discovered three of them, which had been overlooked. During the three months they covered, not a single day had gone by without Jérôme's being favoured with mystical graces. At times, one wishes that God's saints were not quite so humble. In throwing his notebooks into the blazing hearth, he deprived the world of what may have been a treasure of spiritual experiences unheard of until then in a married man.

On October 18th, Jérôme and Jeanne de Baugé, his wife, signed a declaration to the effect that their eldest son, Jérôme Le Royer junior, Lieutenant-General of La Flèche, was standing as surety for them with regard to the score and more of their creditors.[5] How distasteful the need of such a guarantee must have been!

Meanwhile, the dark night of the soul into which Our Lord had seen fit to plunge his servant years before did not let up. Like Job, he was entirely bereft of consolation. A deeply spiritual person became mysteriously aware of his condition and was so broken up with compassion that, with tear-stained face, she begged of God to relieve him. The austere answer was that He would hunt him down more and more.

So Jérôme pushed on in stark faith, his one and only remaining benefit. The unimaginable increase in this virtue, which he had obtained from Christ in preference to any other divine gift, was to uphold him to the end. In the near past, it had strengthened him in difficult circumstances such as in the somewhat strained relations between himself and his former teachers, the Jesuits, since they had been replaced by the Sulpicians in Montreal.[6] It had strengthened him in the face of the determined opposition offered him by the community he had founded, when Bishop

415

Arnauld obliged him to cloister the Ville Marie Daughters of St. Joseph.

He was not even sure that the Hôtel Dieu was as a matter of fact established in Montreal. Faith was his only answer.

He was distressed by the thought of his bankruptcy, not because of himself but because he would be leaving his wife and children in straitened circumstances. So here again, faith was his only recourse. "O my God," he prayed, "must my means be inadequate to all my obligations? Don't allow this, O Lord; let me be the only victim. You are not unaware of the motives that made me act. You know I didn't incur expenses that were incompatible with your law... You are the one, my Beloved, who did me out: Thy Will be done! I commend my children to your care; be their Father in all things." [7]

He was convinced his Bishop would try more than ever to undermine the spirit of the Institute he had founded under divine guidance. What could he do? Faith was the only solution. He must needs muster up every drop of his stupendous faith.

"God has abandoned me," he confided to Fr. de Fancamp. "The heavenly Father, who used to be so good, so endearing, is now but a cold and severe master. Yet the more He forsakes me, the more I want to be His. I wish to love Him in His rigor even though I don't feel I love Him." [8]

To his previous ailments, a double hernia added its torture, his gout worsened, pneumonia and fever jumped him, gripes developed and hemorrhoids, which had been tormenting him for years, burgeoned into vicious ulcers. His doctors were at wits' end to explain his survival and concluded that he was fated to suffer. When they gave him medicine for the complaint that oppressed him most of the time, it was sure to aggravate the others. In an entire month he slept no more than an hour. By the middle of

October, he was only skin and bones. Night and day he cried out in anguish. Whenever he was granted a few minutes' respite, his gentleness and peace brought tears to the eyes of the onlookers. If he spoke, it was to complain about his faintheartedness, when exposed to pain. The final blow fell in the form of dysentery. The consultants were convinced that he suffered as much as if he had been stretched out on a white hot grill.

Eight days before his death, Jérôme told Fr. de Fancamp that he was unable to pray. The priest recalled to his mind words he had proffered years before—that suffering was the most beautiful of all prayers.

Four days later, Fr. de Fancamp was again at his bedside.

"Behold," Jérôme murmured, "the man of sorrows." But instantly he pulled himself together, saying that only Our Lord had the right to that title, whereas he was too pusillanimous to endure anything.

As he was then in the throes of a bad attack of the hiccups, Fancamp advised him that it would bring about his death and that he should be well aware of this. The priest thereupon inquired if the news surprised him. Opening his arms to his friends, Jérôme gaily replied, "Oh, what a joy it is to be reunited with God!"

Seeing that they had been so close for years, the Abbé questioned the dying man: Was there anything which he would like to be reminded about before drifting off into unconsciousness?

"You know me intimately," Jérôme quietly said. "God is our Master."

On the following day, he received the Holy Viaticum with "angelic devotion," and when he was asked how he felt interiorly, softly came the answer, "A little better, thank God."

Years before, a saintly woman, perhaps the very one who wept at the thought of Jérôme Le Royer's sufferings, had revealed to Fr. de Fancamp that the La Flèche collector of taxes would be flooded with peace and consolation. And so he was.

After receiving the Viaticum, the dying man repeatedly asked what hour it was. And why did he want to know the time, he was questioned. No answer was forthcoming.

After the bedcurtains were drawn, Fr. de Fancamp heard Jérôme sighing, "How wearisome it is for me not to be with my God!"

The good priest was convinced that his old comrade knew the hour of his death. A little later he inquired about the whereabouts of his friend's diaries, written in obedience to his spiritual director. At death's door, the patient acknowledged that he had burned them, for he did not want to be talked about after his death.

The next day brought terrible convulsions. The household thought the time had come to ring the church bell for the dying, a local custom.

"The time has not yet come," Jérôme demurred.

In the course of the evening, Fr. de Fancamp had another priest, his confessor no doubt, administer the sacrament of the Sick, or Extreme Unction, as it was then called, to Jérôme. Afterwards Fancamp asked him how he felt.

"In peace, thank God," whispered Jérôme.

On Thursday, November 6, 1659, the last day of his life, he was extremely restless and constantly asked to be moved from one side of the bed to the other. His confessor, made of sterner stuff than those of the 20th century, rebuked him, "Jesus died nailed to a cross; imitate Him."

From that moment on, the pain-racked man did not budge, though he now and then moaned piteously. At noon he seemed to be resting peacefully when suddenly he lifted his joined hands towards heaven, stared for a moment in the same direction and called out, "Mercy!" He fell back, to all appearances dead. A quarter of an hour later, he regained consciousness, and his confessor probed him about his outcry.

"God showed Himself to me," he said, "in the rigor of his justice and made me suffer more in one moment than I have ever suffered in all my life. Afterwards, though, his mercy manifested itself so abundantly that I thought I was in paradise."

The physician in attendance then declared to Fr. de Fancamp that Jérôme Le Royer would survive the night. Now the priest would have sat up with Jérôme, but reassured, he slipped quietly away.

This authentic but uncanonized saint lived four hours more in a strange purgatory of love. The *élans* or mystical impetuses were so violent that, in comparison all his past bodily and mental suffering took on the semblance of a wisp of mist in the autumn air. The love which he felt for His Maker exploded, "I can't stand it any longer!" he cried out.

His confessor and the members of his family thought that he was referring to his many ailments and the priest urged him to practise greater love of God. The mere mention of divine love fired his heart with an agony of longing, "You are setting me ablaze, you are burning me up, I can't take it any longer!"

These extraordinary favors continued until four o'clock in the afternoon. Once again he lifted up his arms heavenwards, and gazed intently upwards, his features serene as at the sight of something eminently gratifying, then folded his arms on his chest and died without the least sigh or commotion.

Later Fr. de Fancamp wrote to Fr. Pierre Marie Joseph Chaumonot in Quebec, that Jérôme Le Royer died as he had lived—as a saint. His death, he declared, was one of the most beautiful of the 17th century.

Although the Abbé had attended Jérôme during the last six weeks of his life, he was not present at the final moment. In obedience to his Bishop, the priest was exorcizing a possessed woman. Was this poor creature simply hysterical, was she gifted with parapsychological powers or was she truly possessed? All that can be said is that Bishop Arnauld and Fr. de Fancamp were convinced that she had *le diable au corps*, the devil in her. After seven or eight minutes, the evil spirit became sarcastic, "Aren't you going to take part in the victory? You do have the right to share in the celebration!"

The exorcist did not grasp the meaning of the possessed woman's words until a messenger informed him that the Servant of God had just died. As soon as he could, he hurried to Ave Maria Street, and that night he attended the autopsy performed on his bosom friend. Fancamp mentions the prodigy of patience that Jérôme performed. The rough and abrasive stone discovered in his bladder was as big as the bladder itself and had been one of the main causes of his sufferings.

On the following day, Father de Fancamp returned to his exorcism. The evil one was never known for his genteel manners. "My, you stink! I have plenty to say to you, but at present, I'm too heavy-hearted to talk. Strike out as much as you want; you'll get it only by laying about me with hammer and tongs!"

The priest asked who he was.

"We're all here to stop you from continuing."

Fancamp insisted, but to no avail, and the thought came to him that the stone he had in his pocket, unknown to those about him, might be the source of this particular aggressiveness. As he had a cold, he casually took out his handkerchief containing the enormous calculus and placed it on the possessed woman's head. She uttered a frightful cry and flew into a greater fury than ever before. In his capacity as exorcist, Father de Fancamp asked her why she was horn-mad.

"When dogs feel the stones thrown at them, they bark," was the answer.

"But a stone is only a stone," Fancamp argued.

"You're right," the fallen angel rejoined, "in your hand it's simply a stone, but it's a palm of victory in the hand of the one who carried it!"

Imprudently, perhaps, the Abbé again laid the stone on the demoniac's head. The latter instantly flew into so towering a rage that she tore his surplice into shreds, bashed him and the two other priests in attendance and just about twisted the three clergymen around her little finger, something that had never happened previously, not even in the presence of the Blessed Sacrament.

A few more words passed between them, followed by a short discussion on purgatory until Fr. de Fancamp bluntly stated that Jérôme had not passed through its flames because of what he had endured. The evil one partially agreed, saying that the founder's purgatory was a suffering of love—the élans—and nothing more.

Despite the estrangement between Jérôme and his family, they claimed his heart, which was embalmed and placed in a heart-shaped leaden container, to be preserved as a precious relic. The remains of Jérôme Le Royer were laid to rest in a leaden tomb, in the burial vault he had built in 1634 beneath the chapel dedicated to St. Joseph at the La Flèche Hôtel Dieu.[9]

A few days after her husband's death, Jeanne de Baugé quit the Le Royer residence, which was no longer hers.[10] A servant accompanied her, carrying a bundle, probably house linen and clothes, wrapped up in a piece of tapestry. They made for the monastery of the Ave Maria. Her niece, Mother Jeanne Lamé, superior of the convent, welcomed her as a boarder. There is reason to believe that her son, Fr. Ignace Le Royer, pastor of nearby Bazouges, provided for her maintenance. Six months and a day later he died at the early age of 36 years. Another priest, a nephew, Fr. Michel Lamé, prior of Clermont and pastor of Yvré le Polin in the neighboring diocese of Le Mans, took it upon himself to pay for her bed and board since the wife of the founder of Montreal was poverty-stricken.

Thereafter her youngest child, Joseph, was her standby. For a while he had successfully practised law and then gone into business administration. After the death of his brother Fr. Ignace, he decided to receive Holy Orders according to his father's prediction, and to be a priest worthy of his calling.[11] (At his death in 1692, he left a reputation of sacerdotal zeal not only in his own parish but throughout the diocese.)

Through all this storm and strife, what was the attitude of the eldest son, Jérôme Le Royer Jr., lieutenant-general for the king at La Flèche? It seems that he did not show due consideration for his father's memory and for his mother's welfare. In a notarized act, he refused to acknowledge the fees for his father's funeral Mass as well as for the burial expense.[12] From the start, he had favored Bishop Arnauld's transformation of the Daughters of St. Joseph into an order with solemn vows, and continued to do so all his life, even to the point of interfering with the Hôtel Dieu administration. On the other hand, he worked hard at establishing the Daughters of St. Joseph at Beaufort and was always quite devoted to the Montreal foundation.

His father's estate was indeed in a sorry condition. A debt far exceeding his assets had his lenders clamoring for reimbursement.[13] It is necessary here to stress that most of the liabilities incurred by Jérôme Le Royer were the result of loans he had contracted for Ville Marie. This narrows the problem down to its essentials. Although Le Royer obtained these loans under his own signature, he had always acted as agent for the Society of Montreal and was recognized by its members in this capacity; furthermore, the monies he obtained always served either to send recruits to the island colony or for its upkeep.

In 1650, it will be recalled, Jérôme Le Royer and Pierre de Fancamp had made over to the Montreal Associates the proprietary title of the Island of Montreal. The joint responsibility of the Ladies and Gentlemen of Montreal is well attested. It is beyond question that they were perfectly aware of the legal and financial obligations assumed in their names by the two procurators, especially when one takes into consideration some 200 contracts agreed on with the Ville Marie pioneers. Jérôme Le Royer discharged more than his share of the loans made for the distant foundation, since his estate furnished over twenty-five per cent of the total debt. The balance should have been settled by the other Associates: Jérôme is not to be held responsible.

What upset the apple-cart was his role as head tax-collector at La Flèche. The administration of the Royal Treasury immediately took in hand Jérôme's assets, and his creditors resolved to fight back. Despite his innocence, the fourteen principal creditors whose names are known to us—five religious houses, two clergymen and seven laymen—made every effort to be compensated. Even the Hôtel Dieu pressed its claim. Father Pierre Filaleau in the name of Jérôme Le Royer's brother, René de Boistaillé, quickly levied a distress on the estate. This gesture, however, may simply be interpreted as a measure of security until its eventual apportionment.

Although the new superior of St. Sulpice, Fr. Alexandre de Bretonvilliers, whose confrères were at work in Ville Marie, sued for 23,000 livres,[14] he showed himself somewhat more considerate. Thanks to his diligent intervention, the creditors came to an amicable arrangement and were accommodating with regard to Jeanne de Baugé and her family. She was allowed to keep her furniture and her husband's papers, for the levy of distress was maintained on the property only.

Six years later, in 1666, proceedings were still going on in the High Court of Justice in Paris. That year found Jeanne de Baugé in the capital for the winding up of the estate. There this heroic lady, always faithful to her husband's memory, died, on the sixteenth of August, assisted by her two sons, Fr. Joseph and Jérôme, the La Flèche lieutenant-general.[15]

One of the saddest aspects of the situation was its effect on the Montreal foundation. Madame de Bullion's 20,000 livres were swallowed up by the Royal Treasury. The Ville Marie Hôtel Dieu was ruined and Fr. de Fancamp, Jérôme's successor as procurator for the Society of Notre Dame of Montreal, urged the three Daughters of St. Joseph to return to France.[16] They decided to stay on, confident that Divine Providence would see to their needs as their founder had assured them at La Rochelle.

On the Island of Montreal, the Hôtel Dieu struggled for its life, then slowly revitalized, grew and prospered. Today, three centuries later, the motherhouse of the Institute has its headquarters at Montreal, and the Hospitallers of St. Joseph care for Christ in the sick not only in France and Canada but also in the United States, Africa, Central and South America. To their great satisfaction and to that of their friends, the diocesan informative processes on the reputation of sanctity of Jérôme Le Royer and of Mother Marie de la Ferre were completed in 1936 and the results sent to Rome. May the two founders of Montreal and of the Hôtel Dieu Sisters of St. Joseph soon be elevated to the glory of the altars!

Chapter XXXII

Notes

1. "The very handsome Book of Hours of Duc de Berry," preserved at the Condé Museum, Chantilly, France.

2. Pierre Chevrier, baron de Fancamp, "Copie fidelle de la lettre écrite au Reverand [sic] Père Chaumonot, Jésuite, au Collège de Kebec, sur la mort de Monsieur de la Dauversière, en l'année 1660," see Chap. 1, No. 27. Faillon, *Vie de Mademoiselle Mance*, Vol. 1, p. 166. The material contained in this chapter is taken from the aforesaid letter unless otherwise indicated.

3. F.-C. Uzureau, "Un mystique du XVIIe siècle, Jérôme Le Royer de la Dauversière (1597-1659)," *Vie spirituelle, supplément*, Vol. XIX (Paris, Octobre 1928), p. 33.

4. *AM*, p. 189.

5. Gaudin, *Inventaire et extraits des papiers de famille de Monsieur Jérôme Le Royer de la Dauversière*, p. 29.

6. Faillon, *Vie de Mademoiselle Mance*, Vol. 1, p. 164.

7. *Cenomanen*, p. 28.

8. *Ibid.*

9. Faillon, *Vie de Mademoiselle Mance*, Vol. 1, pp. 168-169. In 1718, a grandson of Jérôme's had a chapel erected in honour of St. Joseph at the chateau of La Motte-Lubin near Crosnières, in which he placed his grandfather's heart

beneath a plaque of black marble, inscribed in letters of gold. In 1838, Monsieur André-Louis Le Royer de la Motte and his wife, with Monsieur Henri-Gustave Le Royer, descendants of the founder of Montreal, returned the heart to the Sisters of Saint Joseph in La Flèche.

10. *RPA*, Vol. 6, p. 535.

11. *Ibid.*, p. 536.

12. *Ibid.*, p. 539.

13. Bertrand, *Monsieur de la Dauversière*, pp. 245-250.

14. *RPA*, Vol. 6, p. 534.

15. *Ibid.*, p. 536.

16. Faillon, *Vie de Mademoiselle Mance*, Vol. 1, pp. 171-172.

Appendix I

Marie-Claire Daveluy, in *Jeanne Mance, 1606-1673,* Montreal, 1962, p.73, note 4, asserts that Jeanne Mance, Paul de Maisonneuve, and Father Le Jeune were at Tadoussac on September 20, 1641, and took part in the baptism of an Indian child. In a letter of September 19, 1952, to Sr. Mondoux, author of *L'Hôtel-Dieu, premier hôpital de Montréal,* historian Fr. Adrien Pouliot, S.J., conclusively sets the place of this baptism at Sillery in the neighborhood of Quebec and not at Tadoussac. Consequently, Jeanne Mance and the leader of the Montrealers were in Quebec on September 20, 1641.

I

After a careful study of the original baptismal records of Sillery, he writes:

1. The word Tadoussac [Tadousac], in the margin, is to be found in the first 30 pages whenever the sacrament of baptism was administered to one or many Tadoussac Indians, and even to Papinachois Indians (from farther down the St. Lawrence), who belonged to the Tadoussac mission, begun in 1641.

2. The word Tadoussac is neither in Fr. Le Jeune's nor in Fr. Duperron's hand, but in that of Fr. de Quen. For proof, take the same word Tadoussac written in the same way in the body of Fr. de Quen's baptismal acts.

3. The ink (paler in the original and yellowish) is always the same whenever it is found in the margin: it is the same ink used by Fr. de Quen on p.32, in *1645* and *never before.* Seeing the happiness of the Christians at Sillery, in 1640, the Montagnais begged Fr. Le Jeune to send them a missionary for Tadoussac, as the *Jesuit Relations* of 1641 and the following years bear witness. Inaugurated rather

than founded in 1641, the Tadoussac mission was only visited by missionaries in 1641-1642. Nothing more. There was no chapel nor house for the missionary, but in 1643, "a poor hut—built by the French, who unlade the ships in Tadoussac—serves as chapel." (JR, Vol. XXIV, p.127) There were no separate registers either, since the Fathers spent only the summer months there and since the mission was still in embryo. Where were the Tadoussac baptisms inscribed? In the Sillery register even when the baptisms were administered at Tadoussac.

The day came when the Tadoussac mission took on importance to the point of nearly becoming autonomous. Fr. de Quen decided to indicate in the margins of the Sillery register the Tadoussac Indians so as to find them easily when needed. As already noted, the faded ink is the same as that of Fr. de Quen's baptismal acts of 1645.

Other proofs based on Fr. Le Jeune's inscriptions:

In concluding Chapter XII of the *Relation of 1641*, concerning a mission established at Tadoussac, Fr. Le Jeune writes, "The Father (himself) arrived at Tadoussac on the second day of June, and was recalled thence on the twenty-ninth. He baptized fourteen or fifteen Indians, principally children and aged persons; he would have baptized many more, if these poor people had been in a place where they could have been kept in the faith; all that will come in its own time." (JR, Vol. XXI, p.105) This excerpt alone should suffice to prove that the baptism of September 20th was not administered at Tadoussac, but the manner in which were afterwards inscribed in the Sillery register the acts of baptism mentioned above and surely administered at Tadoussac makes the evidence even more manifest.

1) *Anno Domini 1641, die 29 junii, Ego Paulus Le*

Jeune, Societatis Jesu sacerdos, baptizavi sine caeremoniis defectu Sacrarum Unctionum in loco vulgo Tadoussac nuncupatur sequentes personas (about 20)... i.e. On June 29, 1641, I baptized without the [solemn] ceremonies, not having the holy oils, in the place ordinarily called Tadoussac, the following persons (about 20)... Godfathers [Nicolas] Marsolet, Daniel Lebrun, Pierre Boquet, Nicolas Aulart.

2) Between the acts of the baptisms of May 5 (Fr. André Richard) and June 5 (Fr. Vimont), administered at Sillery, Fr. Le Jeune inscribed at the end, because of the limited space he had at his disposal, the following act: *Ego Paulus Le Jeune baptizavi die 2 junii Tadoussaci* (at Tadoussac) *Mariam...Espiravit paulo post baptismum sine caeremoniis collatum ob necessitatem*, i.e., I baptized at *Tadoussac* Marie, who died shortly after her baptism, administered of necessity without the [solemn] ceremonies (even if he had the holy oils). Finally here are a few samples of baptismal acts in the margins of which one finds in Fr. de Quen's handwriting and with the 1645 ink, the word *Tadoussac*, though the baptism was surely administered at Quebec or Sillery:

1) On September 25, 1641, Fr. Joseph Duperron baptized a child of about six years of age, born of Tadoussac parents. Godfather: Thomas Harenc of the city of Rouen.

2) On October 15, the same priest baptized at Sillery (*in nostro sacello sancti Joseph*, i.e., in our chapel of St. Joseph) Ambrose, Papinachois Indian.

3) On October 17, Fr. de Quen, pastor of the Quebec church, baptized in said church (that is to say in the mission of One Hundred Associates, transformed partially into a church after the fire of June 14, 1640) two boys from Tadoussac, who were sufficiently prepared. Godfathers: Thomas Harenc and Nicolas Marsolet, residents of Quebec.

4) On November 27, Fr. de Quen solemnly baptized at the hospital (i.e., at Sillery) two young men of twenty

years, the first of whom comes from Tadoussac.

Conclusion: It is in no way permissible to infer from their quality of *inhabitants of Tadoussac* attributed to the baptized persons mentioned in the body of the baptismal act of September 20, 1641, nor from the word *Tadoussac* in the margin of this act, that this baptism was administered at Tadoussac. It is even clear, taking into account the return of Fr. Le Jeune to Sillery two months earlier, and also the express mention of *Tadoussac* in the acts of the baptisms indubitably administered there from June 2 to June 29, that the baptism of the twentieth was administered at Sillery.

II

In 1981, the problem was again put before Fr. Pouliot. To his previous comments, in his answer of June 5, he added:

The Le Jeune-Maisonneuve-Mance meeting set by Mademoiselle Daveluy at Tadoussac on September 20, 1641, because of the word Tadoussac inscribed in the margin of the act of baptism on that day, could not have possibly taken place at that spot. Since Fr. Le Jeune wrote this baptismal act himself at its proper date, and also at its proper date the next one of September 24, this time of a person who did not come from Tadoussac, but for whom Jeanne Mance acted also as godmother, it would have been necessary for Fr. Le Jeune to carry with him to Tadoussac the Sillery register for the baptism of September 20, then carry it back to Sillery for the baptism of September 24, after which Fr. Joseph Imbert Duperron would have had to return it to Tadoussac for the baptism of a Tadoussac Indian on September 25. It was not the custom to carry back and forth the *Liber Baptizorum* from one "reduction" to another.

Finally, it must be taken into account that, when the wind and the tides were not propitious, the voyage could be very long; there are examples of it having lasted several weeks. See *Véritables Motifs*, published in the *Mémoires de la Société Historique de Montréal*, edited by Verreau, Montreal, 1880, Vol. IX, Note 1, p. 79.

Appendix II

The True Motives

Divided into two parts, the first one put forward four motives—the real incentives of these dedicated men and women—in favor of the evangelization of the native population of Canada. The initial motive is a clarion call to all Christians, including the laity, to cooperate in the conversion of souls. The reader is then reminded that God is agreeable to those who labor to make His name known and preach the merits of His Precious Blood among pagans. He is told that alms-giving for the conversion of souls is of greater value before the Most High than for all other motives and, finally that of all nations of the Americas, none more than those of New France, are in need of spiritual assistance.

In the second part, nine current objections are refuted:

1. The first one thrown at Jérôme Le Royer and the Associates is borrowed from Holy Scripture: *The left hand should not know what the right hand is doing. Good works should be hidden. In giving alms to the Company of Montreal, the charitable action would be revealed.* The answer, of course, is that all depends on the intention of the benefactor and the aim he has in mind.

2. *The Montreal enterprise is foolhardy; for anyone but a king, the expenses are prohibitive, in addition to which the perils of the sea and shipwreck must be taken into account.* But the King of kings, whom the wind and waves obey, is interested in the venture! "What we are unable to do in a year," declare the Associates, "we will do in ten; if we are unable to do anything in ten, we will do it in a hundred

3. *Paupers are so numerous in France that the alms collected for them are insufficient to take care of their needs.*

432

Why send to unknown people in far-away lands what could be used at home? This question is met with a spirited retort: "Will the 15,000 or 20,000 livres sent to Montreal each year truly hurt the needy of the kingdom? In Paris alone over 4,000,000 livres are annually distributed among them, not to mention the many endowments in their behalf.

4. *Since the inhabitants of Canada are invincibly ignorant of the Gospel, they can obtain salvation by observing the natural law written in their hearts.* This difficulty is quickly resolved: So could the pagans to whom the Apostles preached, and still they preached!

5. *Bread should not be taken away from the children of the poverty-stricken Christians of France for unbelievers who are impossible to convert.* The riposte is to the point: Bread for the poor of France, certainly; but at least crumbs for the infidels!

6. *The work of the Jesuits in New France suffices. They receive help from the well-to-do and from the gentlemen of the Company of New France, who are disturbed by the Montreal settlement.* The author or authors of the *True Motives* calmly reply that neither the Jesuits nor the members of the Company of New France have complained about the Montreal enterprise: quite to the contrary, both groups favor it!

7. *Indians are lazy and lascivious, adverse to cultivating the land, and unteachable, as experience has shown.* Not so! Many Indians are sedentary and do cultivate the land. With regard to the nomads, if nothing can be gained with the old folk, the children will respond more readily; besides, numerous families have already agreed to settle down on reclaimed land.

8. *The Island of Montreal is close to the Iroquois, a cruel and ferocious people, who hinder other Indians from using the St. Lawrence River. The latter, in turn, would not dare live in Montreal, where even the French are exposed to*

433

surprise attacks... Too optimistically, perhaps, the Associates assert that the Iroquois shall be subdued or converted, and then bravely add, "If, however, we are massacred, others will replace us!"

9. *It is a loss of time to labour in New France, a cold land on account of the icy waters surrounding it, where the French are able to subsist only with what is brought from France with peril and little profit. They will finally tire of it and lose patience as is their wont. The Company of Montreal being established on charity alone, will not last, since God no longer performs miracles. On the other hand, the missions of Central America are less costly, are richer in good lands, fertile and so temperate that one never suffers from cold weather.* This final objection is thus rebutted: More good has been done in Canada than St. James did in Spain, since he did not succeed in converting more than five or six persons. Does an establishment raised by God for a particular design need to be everlasting? We know that someday it will be dissolved and we offer our prayers to God for this, so that the French and the Indians who live there may, by their labor and industry, get along without us. Even if God did do away with it sooner, it is not in the least out of order that those who begin a task are not those who finish it.

Bibliography

I. *Unpublished sources*

BOUCHÉ, Baron de Trétaigne, Letter addressed to Lieutenant de Trétaigne, Paris, July 16, 1953, MS.

BURON, Edmond, *Extrait des notes sur M. de la Dauversière.* Addressed to Sister Maria Mondoux of the Hôtel Dieu of Montreal, on December 28, 1939, MS (Typescript), ARHSJ, Montreal.

[Contract between René Le Royer de Boistaillé and Florimond Le Royer, concerning a salt storehouse, October 7, 1634, at La Flèche.] MS, ARHSJ, Montreal.

DE LA MOTTE, Joseph Jérôme Le Royer, *Le Petit Mémoire ou Écrit Autographe.* A five page copy of the *Petit Mémoire* was made at La Flèche, May 1938, by Sister Marie-Marthe Dupuis, R.H.S.J. This manuscript is lost.

[Deed of acceptance of a salt storehouse by the Adjudicator General of the Salt Taxes in La Flèche, December 22, 1634.] MS, ARHSJ, Montreal.

[Deed of sale of a property to the Hôtel Dieu Hospital in La Flèche, November 2, 1634.] MS, ARHSJ, Montreal.

Document concernant l'établissement des Hospitalières de Saint-Joseph à Montréal, March 13, 1656. MS, ARHSJ, Montreal.

DU BREIL, Isaïe, O.F.M., CAP., (Jules Boussard), *Famille Le Royer*, MS (typescript), ARHSJ, Montreal. Written about

1935 and transcribed by Sister Maria Mondoux, R.H.S.J., at the Hôtel Dieu of La Flèche, on June 6, 1938.

DU BREIL, Isaïe, O.F.M., CAP., *Vie de Jérôme Le Royer de la Dauversière*, Vol. 1, MS (typescript), ARHSJ, Montreal, written in Paris in 1952.

GAUDIN, Adolphine, R.H.S.J., *Inventaire et extraits des papiers de famille de Monsieur Jérôme Le Royer de la Dauversière*. Collected by Mother Adolphine Gaudin of La Flèche. MS, ARHSJ, Montreal, circa 1875.

[GAUDIN, Adolphine, R.H.S.J.], *Recueil des pièces authentiques de l'histoire de l'Institut des Réligieuses Hospitalières de St-Joseph, fondé à La Flèche en 1636*, MS (photostat), 6 vols., ARHSJ, Montreal. This manuscript has been compiled and annotated at La Flèche by Sr. Adolphine Gaudin, between 1870 and 1880. The Montreal copy is a photostat of the original.

La famille Le Royer et la Visitation de La Flèche. Extrait de documents de notre Monastère de La Flèche et des Vies de nos Soeurs Le Royer. MS (typescript), ARHSJ, Montreal, 1886? (Dossier La Dauversière).

[MELANÇON, Arthur, S.J.] *Jérôme Le Royer de la Dauversière et Marie de la Ferre: leurs vies, leurs oeuvres, leur temps*. MS, ASJCF, St. Jérôme, Quebec.

MENNETRIER, Charles, Letter to Sister Maria Mondoux, April 20, 1953, MS, ARHSJ, Montreal.

MENNETRIER, Charles, Letter to Sister Maria Mondoux, May 10, 1946. MS, ARHSJ, Montreal.

MONDOUX, Maria, R.H.S.J., Letter to Henri Béchard, Montreal, July 19, 1954. MS.

MONDOUX, Maria, R.H.S.J., Letter to Mr. Buron, April 12, 1940, MS, ARHSJ, Montreal.

OLIER, Jean-Jacques, P.S.S., *Mémoires autographes*, 6 vols., MS, ASS, Paris. These memoirs were begun in 1642.

PÉRET, Elisabeth, R.H.S.J. *Histoire de l'institution de la Congrégation des Réligieuses Hospitalières de Saint Joseph; ou sont compris les événements avantageux qui ont donné naissance à cet institut en l'année 1630.* Also known as *Annales de Moulins.* Manuscript written about 1740 by Mother Péret who was superior at the Hôtel Dieu of Moulins in France, according to the testimonies of the Sisters who had known the foundresses of that residence. MS (photostat), ARHSJ, Montreal.

TRONSON, Louis, *L'esprit de M. Olier, d'après les notes de M. de Bretonvilliers*, 3 vols. MS, ASS, Paris.

II. *Printed sources*

A) Books

Les Annales de l'Hôtel-Dieu de Quebec, 1636-1716. Composées par les révérendes Mères Jeanne-Françoise Juchereau de St-Ignace et Marie Andrée Duplessis de Ste. Hélène, anciennes réligieuses de ce monastère, editée dans leur texte original avec une introduction et des notes par Dom Albert Jamet de l'abbaye de Solesme. [Quebec] 1939.

ATHERTON, William Henry, *Montreal, 1535-1914*, Montreal, 1914, 3 vols.

ATHERTON, William Henry, *The Saintly Life of Jeanne Mance, first lay nurse in North America*, St. Louis, MO., 1945.

Beatificationis et canonizationis servae Dei Catharinae, Tekakwitha virginis Indianae (1680) Positio super introductione causae et super virtutibus ex officio compilata. Publication of the Sacred Congregation of Rites, Historical Section, No. 38, Vatican City, 1938.

BÉCHARD, Henri, S.J., *The Original Caughnawaga Indians*, Montreal, 1976.

BELLOC, Hilaire, *Richelieu: A Study*, Philadelphia, 1929.

BERRY, Jean de France, Duke of, *The Tres Riches Heures of Jean, Duke of Berry*. Musée Condé, Chantilly. Introduction and legends by Jean Longnon and Raymond Cazelles. Preface by Millard Meiss. [Translated from the French by Victoria Benedict] New York, 1969.

BERTRAND, Camille, *Monsieur de la Dauversière, fondateur de Montréal et des religieuses de S. Joseph, 1597-1659*, Montreal, 1947.

BESSIÈRES, Albert, *Deux grands inconnus, précurseurs de l'Action catholique et sociale, Gaston de Renty et Henry Buch*. Au temps de saint Vincent de Paul, Paris, 1931.

BOUCHARD, Jean, S.J., *Le R.P. Paul Le Jeune, S.J., et la fondation des missions des Jésuites en Nouvelle-France, 1632-1642*. Étude des méthodes missionnaires. Excerpta ex dissertatione ad Lauream in Facultate Missiologica Pontificiae Universitatis Gregorianae, Romae, 1958.

BOUGAUD, [Louis-Marie] *Histoire de sainte Chantal et des origines de la Visitation*, 17e ed. 2 vols., Paris, 1930.

BOURGEOYS, Marguerite, Saint, *Les écrits de Mère Bourgeoys*. Autobiographie et testament spirituel, Montreal, 1964.

BUTTERFIELD, Herbert, *Christianity in history*, London, 1960.

CAMPEAU, Lucien, S.J., *Les finances publiques de la Nouvelle-France sous les Cent-Associés, 1632-1665*, Montreal, 1975.

CANITROT, Étienne, *Le plus familier des saints, Vincent de Paul*, Paris, 1947.

CARMONA, Michel, *Marie de Médicis*, Paris, 1981.

CATTA, Étienne, *Le Frère André, 1845-1937, à l'Oratoire Saint-Joseph du Mont-Royal*, Montreal, 1964.

CERTEAU, Michel de, *La possession de Loudun*, Paris, 1970.

CHAMPLAIN, Samuel de, *Les voyages de Samuel de Champlain* selectionnés, mis en orthographe moderne et annotés par Jean Dumont, *La découverte du Canada*, Vol. 2, Montreal, 1969.

CHAMPLAIN, Samuel de, *The works of Samuel de Champlain*. In six volumes. Reprinted, translated and annotated by six Canadian scholars under the General Editorship of H.P. Biggar, Vol. 2, 1608-1613, Toronto, 1925.

439

COCHIN, Claude, *Henry Arnauld, évêque d'Angers, 1599-1692*, Paris, 1921.

COMPAGNIE DES ASSOCIÉS AMIS DE MONTREAL, *La Flèche et Montréal, ou l'extraordinaire entreprise canadienne du fléchois, Jérôme Le Royer de la Dauversière*, La Flèche [1947]; 1986. *Constitutions [primitives] des Filles Hospitalières de Sainct Ioseph*, [Angers?, 1643].

DAVELUY, Marie-Claire, *Jeanne Mance, 1606-1673*, suivie d'un essai généalogique sur les De Mance, par M. Jacques Laurent, 2e ed. rev. et mise à jour, Montreal, 1962.

DAVELUY, Marie-Claire, *La société de Notre-Dame de Montréal, 1639-1663. Son histoire, ses membres, son manifeste*, Montreal, 1965.

DENAIS, Joseph-Rémi, *Armorial général de l'Anjou d'après les titres et les manuscrits de la Bibliothèque Nationale, des bibliothèques d'Angers, d'Orléans, de La Flèche, etc.* 3 vols., Angers, 1885.

DESROSIERS, Léo-Paul, *Iroquoisie (1534-1646)*, Montreal, 1947.

DESROSIERS, Léo-Paul, *Paul de Chomedey, sieur de Maisonneuve*, Montreal, 1967.

DOLLIER DE CASSON [François], *A History of Montreal, 1640-1672*. From the French of Dollier de Casson, translated and edited, with a life of the author, by Ralph Flenley, Toronto, 1928.

ESTIENNE, Yvonne, *Undaunted*, Dorval-Montreal, 1973.

(FAILLON, Étienne-Michel), *Histoire de la Colonie Française en Canada*, 3 vols., Ville Marie, 1865-1866.

[FAILLON, Étienne-Michel], *Vie de M. Olier, fondateur du séminaire de Saint-Sulpice*, 4e éd., revisée et compléteé par l'auteur, 3 vols., Paris, 1873.

[FAILLON, Étienne-Michel], *Vie de Mlle. Mance et histoire de l'Hôtel-Dieu de Ville Marie dans l'Ile de Montréal en Canada*, 2 vols., Ville Marie, 1854.

FERRIER, Gustave Dupont, *Du collège de Clermont au Lycée Louis-Le-Grand (1563-1920)*, La vie quotidienne d'un collège français pendant plus de trois cent cinquante ans, 3 vols., Paris, 1921-1925.

GAGNON, Ernest, *Louis d'Ailleboust*, 2e ed. revisée, Montreal, 1931.

GEORGES, André, *L'Oratoire*, Paris, 1928.

GÉRIN, Léon, *Aux sources de notre histoire*. Les conditions économiques et sociales de la colonisation en Nouvelle-France, Montreal, 1946.

GOYAU, Georges, *Une épopée mystique, les origines réligieuses du Canada*, Paris, 1925.

[GROSJEAN, Adele-Josephine, R.H.S.J.] *Notions abrégées sur Jérôme Le Royer et Marie de la Ferre: Leur mission et les interventions surnaturelles qui s'y rattachent.* (Laval, France, 1887) Reprography.

GUILHERMY, Elesban de, *Ménologe de la Compagnie de Jésus*, Assistance de France, 2 vols., Paris, 1892.

HARNEY, Martin P., S.J., *The Jesuits in history: the Society of Jesus through four centuries*, Chicago, 1962.

IGNATIUS OF LOYOLA, *The Spiritual Exercises*. Translated by Thomas B. Moore, S.J., from the original Spanish in the "autograph," New York, 1948.

JAMET, Albert, O.S.B., *Marguerite Bourgeoys*, 2 vols., Montreal, 1942.

The Jesuit Relations and Allied Documents, Travels, and Explorations of the Jesuit Missionaries in New France, 1610-1791, edited by Reuben Gold Thwaites, Cleveland, 1896-1901, 73 vols., reprint New York, 36 vols., 1959.

Le Journal des Jésuites publié d'après le manuscrit original conservé aux archives du Séminaire de Québec, par MM. les abbés Laverdière et Casgrain, 3e éd. exactement conforme à la première (1871), Montreal, 1973.

LACROIX, Yvon, *Les origines de Laprairie (1667-1697)*, Montreal, 1981.

LADAME, Jean and Richard Duvin, *Les prodiges eucharistiques*, Paris, 1981.

LAHAISE, Robert, *L'Hôtel-Dieu de Montréal (1642-1973)*, Montreal, 1973.

LALLEMANT, Louis, S.J., *The Spiritual Doctrine of Father Louis Lallemant of the Society of Jesus*. Preceded by an account of his life by Father Pierre Campion, S.J. Edited by Alan G. McDougall, Westminster, Maryland, 1946.

LANCTOT, Gustave, *Montréal sous Maisonneuve, 1642-1665*, Montreal, 1966.

[LA TOUR, Louis-Bertrand de] *Mémoires sur la vie de M. de Laval, premier évêque de Québec*, Cologne [Montauban], 1761.

LECLERCQ, Chrestien, *The First Establishment of Faith in New France*. Now first translated, with notes by John Gilmary Shea, 2 vols., New York, 1881.

LEFEBVRE, Esther, *Marie Morin, premier historien canadien de Villemarie*, Montreal, 1959.

LE GOUVELLO, Hippolyte, *Le pénitent breton, Pierre de Kériolet [1602-1660]* Paris, 1878.

LEMOYNE, Giovanni Battista, *Memorie biographice di Don Giovanni Bosco*, recolta dal sac. Salesiano Giovanni Battista Le Moyne, San Benigno, Canavese, Italy, 1898.

LESAGE, Germain, *L'accession des congrégations à l'état religieux canonique*, Ottawa, 1952.

LÉVESQUE, E[ugène], *Lettres de M. Olier, curé de la paroisse et fondateur du séminaire de Saint-Sulpice*, Paris, 1935.

MARIE DE L'INCARNATION, *Correspondance*. Nouv. éd. par Dom Guy Oury, moine de Solesmes. Préf. de S. E. le cardinal Charles Journet, Solesmes, 1971.

MARQUET, Alphonsus, *Cenomanen beatificationis et canonizationis servorum Dei Hieronymi Le Royer de la Dauversière necnon sororis Mariae de la Ferre, fundatorum instituti sororum hospitalarium a S. Joseph in oppido "La*

Flèche" [La Flèche, 1934].

MÉNARD, Jacques-E., *Les dons du Saint-Esprit chez monsieur Olier*, Montreal, 1951.

[MONDOUX, Maria, R.H.S.J.], *L'Hôtel-Dieu, premier hôpital de Montréal*. D'après les Annales manuscrites, les documents originaux de l'Institut des Religieuses Hospitalières de Saint-Joseph et autres sources, 1642-1763, Montreal, 1942.

[MONGOLFIER, Étienne de] *La vie de la vénérable Marguerite Bourgeois dite du Saint-Sacrement...* A Ville-Marie, 1818.

MONIER, Frédéric, *Vie de Jean-Jacques Olier, curé de la paroisse et fondateur du séminaire de Saint-Sulpice*, Paris, 1914.

MOREAU, Florence, R.H.S.J., *Présente à notre temps, Mère Marie de la Ferre, 1592-1652, fondatrice de la congrégation des religieuses de Saint-Joseph*, Montreal, 1964.

MORERI, Louis, *Le Grand Dictionnaire Historique ou Le Mélange Curieux de l'Histoire Sacrée et Profane...* Nouvelle édition dans laquelle on à refondu les suppléments de M. l'abbé Goujet, le tout revu, corrigé et augmenté par M. Drouet, Paris, 1795, 10 vols.

MORIN, Marie, R.H.S.J., *Histoire Simple et Véritable: Les Annales de l'Hôtel-Dieu de Montréal, 1659-1725*, édition critiqué par Ghislaine Legendre, Montreal, 1979.

OURY, Guy-Marie, O.S.B., *Madame de la Peltrie et ses fondations canadiennes*, Solesmes, 1974.

PARKMAN, Francis, *The Jesuits in North America in the Seventeenth Century. France and England in North America*, 2 vols., Boston.

PLETTEAU, Abbé T., *Henri Arnauld, sa participation à l'hérésie janséniste*, Angers, 1863.

POULIOT, Léon, S.J., *Aventurier de l'Évangile: Le Père Énémond Massé, premier missionnaire jésuite au Canada.* Montreal, 1961.

POULIOT, Léon, S.J., *Étude sur les Relations des Jésuites de la Nouvelle-France (1632-1672)*, Montreal, 1940.

POURRAT, Pierre, *Jean-Jacques Olier, fondateur de Saint-Sulpice*, Paris, 1932.

Premier registre de l'Église Notre-Dame de Montréal, Montreal, 1961. Photostatic reproduction of the original manuscript.

ROBERTS, Leslie, *Montreal, from mission colony to world city.* Toronto, 1969.

ROCHEMONTEIX, Camille de, S.J., *Un collège de Jésuites aux XVIIe et XVIIIe siècles. Le Collège Henri IV de La Flèche.* 4 vols., Le Mans, 1889.

ROY, J.-Edmond, *Histoire de la Seigneurie de Lauzon*, 6 vols., Levis, 1897.

TANQUERAY, Adolphe, *The Spiritual Life, a treatise on Ascetical and Mystical Theology.* Second and revised edition, translated by Herman Branderis, Tournai, 1932.

DUFAY, Pierre, "Réponses: La compagnie du Saint-Sacrament," in *Intermédiaire des chercheurs et curieux*, (Paris, January 15, 1938) Col. 14.

ESMONIN, Edmond, "Les Intendants du Dauphiné des origines à la Revolution," in *Études sur la France des XVIIe et XVIIIe siècles*, Paris, 1964, pp. 71-112.

GODBOUT, Archange, O.F.M., Review of "Mondoux, Sister Maria, l'Hôtel-Dieu, premier hôpital de Montréal, 1642-1763," in *Culture*, Vol. 3, No. 3 (Quebec, Sept. 1942), pp. 417-419.

JAMET, Albert, "Jérôme Le Royer de la Dauversière et les commencements de Montréal," in *Revue de l'Université d'Ottawa* (Oct.-Dec. 1936), pp. [387]-419.

LABERGE, Damase, "Le père Charles Rapine, récollet," in *Les Récollets et Montréal*, Montreal, 1955, pp. [137]-149.

[Le Royer de La Motte, Joseph-Jérôme] "Jérôme de la Dauversière. Mémoire de quelques particularités arrivées à l'établissement des filles de Saint-Joseph de La Flèche," in *La Semaine religieuse. La Semaine du fidèle.* (Le Mans, France, December 15, 1946) No. 3, pp. [28]-29.

La Semaine religieuse, Semaine du fidèle, Diocèse du Mans, 85, 3 (15 décembre 1946), pp. [27]-29.

LÉVESQUE, Eugène, art., "Compagnie du Saint-Sacrement," in *Dictionnaire de spiritualité ascétique et mystique, doctrine, et histoire*, Vol. 2, Paris, 1953, Part 2, Cols. 1301-1305.

MASSICOTTE, E[douard]-Z[otique], Ed., "Contrat entre Mlle. Mance et divers colons," in *The Canadian Antiquarian and Numismatic Journal*, 4th series, Vol. X (Montreal, April 1913), pp. 90-96.

MASSICOTTE, E[douard]-Z[otique], Ed., "Une recrue de colons pour Montréal en 1659," in *The Canadian Antiquarian and Numismatic Journal*, 4th series, Vol. X (Montreal, April 1913), pp. [63]-78.

MAURAULT, Olivier, "Question de mesure," in *Les Cahiers des Dix*, Montreal, 1946, pp. [9]-24.

NOYE, Irénée and Michel Dupuy, art., "Olier, Jean-Jacques," in *Dictionnaire de spiritualité ascétique et mystique, doctrine et histoire*, Vol. XI, Paris, 1982, cols. 738-751.

OLPHÉ-GALLIARD [Michel] art., "Bernier (Claude)," in *Dictionnaire de spiritualité ascétique et mystique, doctrine et histoire*, Vol. 1, Paris, 1937, cols. 1521-1522.

PERRIER, Philippe, "Jérôme Le Royer de la Dauversière," in *Les Récollets et Montréal*, huit manifestations commémorant le 250e anniversaire de l'établissement des Récollets à Ville-Marie: 1692-1942. [Textes édités par le Père Ferdinand Coiteux, O.F.M.] Montreal, 1955, pp. 175-207.

PINARD DE LA BOULLAYE, Henri, art., "Conversions," in *Dictionnaire de spiritualité ascétique et mystique, doctrine et histoire*, Vol. 2, Paris, 1953, Part 2, Cols. 2224-2265.

POULIOT, Adrien, S.J., "La dévotion à la Sainte Famille en Nouvelle-France au XVIIe siècle," in *Cahiers de Joséphologie*, Vol. XXIX (Montreal, 1981), pp. [1000]-1033.

POULIOT, Léon, S.J., art., "Lallemant, Charles," in *DCB*, Vol.

1, (Toronto, 1966) pp. 411-414.

POULIOT, Léon, S.J., art., "Le Jeune, Paul," in *DCB*, Vol. 1, (Toronto, 1966) pp. 453-458.

POULIOT, Léon, S.J., "Premières pages du journal des Jésuites de Québec, 1632-1645." Reconstituées et présentées par le Père Léon Pouliot, S.J., in *Archives du Québec, Rapport 1963*, Vol. 41, Quebec, pp. 1-119.

PROVOST, Honorius, art., "Vimont, Barthélemy," in *DCB*, Vol. 1, (Toronto, 1966) p. 665.

RENAUDIN, Paul, "Une voyante parisienne: Marie Rousseau," in *La vie spirituelle*, Vol. LVIII, No. 234, (Paris, March 1, 1939) pp. [263]-280.

RENAUDIN, Paul, "Une voyante parisienne: Marie Rousseau," in *La vie spirituelle*, Vol. LIX, No. 235, (Paris, April 1, 1939) pp. [44]-67; No. 236, (Paris, May 1, 1939) pp. [161]-185.

TESSIER, Albert, "La compagnie du Saint-Sacrement, 1627-1665," in *Les Cahiers des Dix*, Montreal, 1972, No. 7, pp. [27]-43.

UZUREAU, François-Constant, "Un mystique du XVIIe siècle, Jérôme Le Royer de la Dauversière (1597-1659)," in *La vie spirituelle*, supplement, Vol. XIX, (Paris, October 1928) pp. 29-41.

VINCHON, Jean, "Diabolic Possession: The Devils of Loudun," in F.J. Sheed, Ed., *Soundings in Satanism*, New York, 1972, pp. 1-12.

Glossary

Almonry - A place where alms or material necessities such as money, food and clothing are given to the needy.

Arquebus - An early type of rifle.

Bell, book and candle - These are used within the context of a variety of Church services such as exorcism, excommunication and Holy Communion for the sick. The bell signaled the presence of a priest and his attendants. The book was the service book containing the rite to be performed. The candle lit the way through the corridors from the entrance of the building to the place where the rite was to take place.

Benefice - An endowed income attached to a Church office such as (that of) pastor, chaplain, etc.

Calvinists - Followers of the Protestant Reformer John Calvin; for example, Presbyterians and members of the Dutch Reformed Church.

Canon - A clergyman belonging to a cathedral or collegiate church, such as Westminster Abbey in London. It is also used as an honorary title for clergy who are not attached to a cathedral or collegiate church. The title is not used in the Catholic Church in the United States.

Churchwarden - A layman responsible for assisting a pastor with the material or temporal needs of a parish. Now largely confined to the Anglican Communion.

Circumvallation - An encirclement of a city or town consisting of trenches, ramparts and walls.

Council of Trent - The Ecumenical Council of the Sixteenth Century which dealt with the problems surrounding the Protestant Reformation.

Crozier - A staff shaped like a shepherd's crook, often carried in procession by bishops and abbots, symbolizing their office as spiritual shepherds of their flocks.

Distraint - Property is placed under distraint when it is seized and kept as indemnity or security for a debt.

Ember Day - One of three days set apart four times a year for prayer, fasting and abstinence. They are now observed in the Church at the discretion of the National Conferences of Bishops.

Escutcheon - Shield

Esquire - A member of the gentry holding the rank just below that of knight.

Étienne - The French equivalent of Stephen.

Extreme Unction - The Sacrament of the Anointing of the Sick, which is to be administered when recovery from an illness seems doubtful and death probable.

Hair shirt - An undershirt made of goat's hair or other coarse fabric. It is worn as a means of mortification.

Hôtel Dieu - A hospital

Hyperborean - Far northern

Jesuit Relations - Collections of letters written by missionary Jesuits to their superiors and confrères in Europe. They contain accounts of the day-to-day hardships and struggles experienced in establishing the Faith in foreign missions.

Lady altar - An altar dedicated to Our Lady and normally placed to the right or Gospel side of the main altar in a church.

Master of Arts degree - In France, in the seventeenth century, the Master of Arts degree was the equivalent of a contemporary Ph.D. in the United States.

Mitre - The shield-shaped liturgical head-dress worn by bishops.

Paraph - A flourish added to a person's signature. It was orginally used to help avoid forgery.

Perrier - A short shipboard mortar used for firing stones and light shot.

Pinnace - A small sailing ship.

Pension - A boarding house (see chapter 28).

Presbytery - A priest's house or rectory.

Recollects - A reformed branch of the Franciscan Order which sought to observe with exactitude the primitive Rule of St. Francis of Assisi.

Richelieu, Cardinal - Armand Jean du Plessis Richelieu (1585-1642) was a French Cardinal and politician, who beginning in 1629 was the virtual ruler of France. Though orthodox, he favored the separation of the Catholic Church in France from the control of the Church of Rome.

Santa Casa of Loreto - The Holy House of Loreto (Italy), thought to be the house in which Our Lady received the Annunciation. It is said to have been miraculously transported to Macedonia from the Holy Land and from Macedonia to Loreto.

Scrutineer - An examiner of votes.

Seigneur - A nobleman; literally, a lord.

Seigneurie - A domain.

Seneschal - A powerful representative of a lord or a king.

Shallop - A shallop can be either a small rowboat or a small sailboat.

Sieur - A French title of respect for a man, meaning lord or sir.

Straw man - A stand-in or representative of someone else.

Tattoo - A continuous rapping.

Te Deum - *The Te Deum Laudamus (We Praise Thee O God)*. A majestic hymn of praise and thanksgiving sung or recited at the Office of Readings in the Liturgy of the Hours on solemnities, and also at special ceremonies such as the consecration of a bishop and religious professions.

Tercentenary - A three hundredth anniversary.

Viaticum, holy - Holy Communion given to the dying.

About the Author

Rev. Henri Béchard, S.J., was, during his lifetime, very instrumental to the cause of Blessed Kateri Tekakwitha. In 1948, he founded the periodical *KATERI;* this account of his life was written by Fr. Maurice Ruest, S.J, and was published in the Summer 1990 issue of *KATERI.*

REV. HENRI BÉCHARD, S.J. (1909-1990)

The death of Father Béchard

On March 19, 1990, on the feast of St. Joseph, a great ordeal awaited all those who have taken to heart the Cause of Kateri Tekakwitha: Father Henri Béchard died of cardiac arrest.

For several days all those who approached Father Béchard brought to his attention how tired he looked. But as always, he answered that all was well and that he knew how to take a rest. Nevertheless we could not foresee such a sudden end.

At supper, Monday night, he chatted happily with his

companions seated around the commmunity table at Immaculate Conception Parish. We mention his happiness because he always looked happy. His well-known phrases were referred to as "béchardisms."

As usual he watched the news on television with his brother companions. He was the only one who remained at his place after the news was over. About 15 or 20 minutes later we found him stretched out on the floor, seemingly lifeless. We administered the anointing of the sick to him. The doctor and three technicians from the Emergency Ambulance Service tried in vain to revive him. Worn threadbare, his heart could no longer react. He had celebrated his 80th birthday last December.

The funeral

The funeral was celebrated in Kahnawake as he would have wished. Mgr. Bernard Hubert, bishop of the diocese of St-Jean-Longueuil, where the Kahnawake reserve is situated, presided the ceremony. About 30 priests from various parts of Canada and the U.S. concelebrated. The liturgical service was certainly enhanced by the exceptional performance of the Mohawk choir. The population of Kahnawake and numerous relatives and friends rendered vibrant homage to a life consecrated to the Cause of Blessed Kateri.

The first years

Father Béchard was born December 16, 1909, in Lewiston. He was baptized 3 days later by his uncle Fr. Arthur Hamel, in Ste Marie Parish and received the name of Henri Arthur Rosario. Lewiston is part of the diocese of Portland, Maine, U.S.A. His parents were Advocate Philippe Béchard and Rose-Marie Hamel. He was still quite young when his father died. With his mother, he went to live with his grand-parents in Quincy, Mass. He finished grade eight in a public school in that city. Like many Franco-Americans he oriented himself towards the seminary in Sherbrooke. He studied there for ten years, finished two years in the Business course, one of Junior High and seven in Classic Arts. He received his Bachelor of Arts degree in June 1932.

With the Jesuits

It was on September 7 of the same year that he was admitted to the Jesuit novitiate in Sault-au-Récollet. He then followed the long formation of the times for all Jesuits, in spiritual, academic, philosophical and theological studies. At the end of his philosophical studies, he was named professor of Methodology, the equivalent of a tenth grade in secondary schooling, at Jean-de-Brébeuf College.

After three years Fr. Béchard returned to studies in theology. At the end of the three first years in this discipline he was ordained a priest by Mgr. Joseph Charbonneau, Archbishop of Montreal, on August 13, 1944. After completing a final year of theology and a third year of probation, he served for two years as director of scholastics, philosophers and theologians, at Immaculate Conception College.

With the Amerindians

At the very end of his theological studies Fr. Béchard requested of his Fr. Provincial to minister to the Amerindians of Caughnawaga, now Kahnawake. The parish, named St. Francis Xavier Mission, was founded in 1668. In addition to the apostolate with the aboriginals, Fr. Béchard felt drawn to the historical context of the mission.

His wish was granted in 1948. A new Catholic school

was built the following year under the jurisdiction of the Federal Government. Fr. Béchard became its first director, a post he held for six years.

On September 25, 1949, he received his nomination as Vice-Postulator for the Cause of Kateri Tekakwitha. From then on we can say that his whole life was consecrated to this gently unassuming Lily.

In 1948 he started the Kateri periodical which was published only in English until 1958. From then on there would be two editions, one in French and one in English. Fr. Béchard single-handedly edited each pamphlet, translating each text according to need either in one or the other language. From 1959, Fr. Béchard founded and directed the Kateri Center in Montreal. He resided at Immaculate Conception College and at Antoine Daniel Residence where he was Superior from 1968 to 1984. Since the closing of this house he was part of the community of Immaculate Conception Parish until the time of his death.

In addition to the articles in his magazine, Fr. Béchard published a few works in French and English, one of which was the life of Kateri. At the time of his death, two manuscripts were almost ready to be sent to the publishers, a new biography of Kateri in French and the life of Jérôme le Royer de la Dauversière in English. Fr. Béchard had already foreseen the task of translating these two works. It was not going to be his. Others would undertake the task.

We can say that Fr. Béchard's entire active life was centered on the Cause of Blessed Kateri Tekakwitha. A man of intense spiritual life, he created a great movement of prayer in favor of the Cause. It is this dedication, without a doubt, that led to the beatification of this Iroquois virgin in 1980. To all those who recommended themselves to Kateri, Fr. Béchard promised to confide their intentions to her, himself. Here is the text of a very meaningful prayer,

457

written by him, that we found on his bedside table on the same evening of his death:

O Blessed Kateri Tekakwitha
I beg you
watch over all those
whose problems I confide to you
spiritual as well as temporal.
They believe in you
because they know
that you loved the Lord Jesus
and His gentle Mother
during your stay here on earth
and that you served them
in love and in purity.
Take these friends by the hand
and lead them
through the difficulties of life
to the throne of Mother and Son.
Amen.

Well known by all who assisted at the Amerindian gatherings in Canada and the U.S., Fr. Béchard left the legacy of a man who was gentle and meek like those of the gospel who conquer the earth. He did it with graciousness and a smile.

In heaven, he will certainly not stop working for the canonization of Kateri. More than ever we can hope in the near future for the success of the Cause, which was his whole life. Thank you, Fr. Béchard.

Maurice Ruest, S.J.

THE RELIGIOUS HOSPITALLERS
OF SAINT JOSEPH

The Religious Hospitallers of Saint Joseph, founded by Jérôme LeRoyer de la Dauversière and Marie de la Ferre, continue today. As in 1636, they desire to be "entirely consecrated to God to serve Him piously in the exercise of the spiritual life and in the practice of perfect charity towards their neighbour, especially the poor, the sick and the most needy."

The life and work of the Hospitallers in France have been marked from the beginning by poverty, sickness and contradictions. Revolutions and wars expelled them from their hospitals but in spite of these ordeals they carried on their apostolic service.

The three Hospitallers sent by Mr. LeRoyer in 1659 cared for the sick at the Hotel Dieu of Montreal. Thanks to them, the work undertaken by Jeanne Mance was continued. They have remained faithful to their mission in situations of extreme poverty, privations, fires and wars.

From the Montreal foundation and its daughter houses the work of the Religious Hospitallers spread so that today they number more than 500 and work on four continents, that is, in France, Canada, the United States, Peru, the Dominican Republic (West Indies) and Benin (East Africa).

Their work includes ministry in the fields of health, education, care of the aged, the handicapped, various social services and parish ministry.

For more than two and one-half centuries, the Religious

459

Hospitallers of Saint Joseph lived a cloistered life in autonomous houses. In 1953, the houses of America united, and with the entry of the communities of France in 1965, all the houses of the Institute have now become part of one Generalate.

From the visions of one man and one woman came a Congregation of Sisters, the foundation of a city as a Christian community and an outreach to the poor and the sick on four continents.

The causes of Jérôme LeRoyer de la Dauversière, Marie de la Ferre and Jeanne Mance have been introduced in Rome. May they soon be officially recognized as saints and models to encourage others to follow their example of dedication to the work of the Lord.

Apostolate for Family Consecration
John Paul II Holy Family Center, Box 151
Bloomindgale, OH 43910
614-765-4301 or 414-652-2600

WHAT IS THE APOSTOLATE FOR FAMILY CONSECRATION?

The Apostolate for Family Consecration is an international community of families seeking to rebuild family life. How? By transforming neighborhoods into God-centered communities. Our spirituality is that of Pope John Paul II, and may be described precisely as being joyful, Marian and, of course, family-centered. This apostolate of family sanctification and renewal is exercised through a variety of ministries and evangelization programs, as follows:

SACRED HEART
FAMILY CONSECRATION/HOME VISITATION
VIDEO PROGRAM

Jesus told Saint Margaret Mary Aloquoque that those who promote devotion to His Sacred Heart "will have their names written in My heart, never to be blotted out." Consecration to the Sacred Heart will richly bless you in the next life. And on this side of Paradise it can start to transform your family life and plant the seeds of positive change in your neighborhood. When a family is conse-

461

crated to the Sacred Heart, graces begin to flow in abundance. Our enthronement of the Sacred Heart program, featuring Mother Teresa of Calcutta and Father Ken Roberts, is a good place to start for those who want to become involved in the work of the AFC.

REPARATION PROGRAMS
FOR PARISH CHURCHES

Be Not Afraid Weekly Holy Hours and **First Saturday Light of the World Cenacles** bring families into the Eucharistic Presence of Our Lord —to go to Confession, to make reparation for sin, to pray for an end to abortion, and to learn the Truths of our Faith from videotapes featuring some of the best teachers the Church has to offer. Pope John Paul II and Mother Teresa are featured on each program.

BE NOT AFRAID WEEKLY HOLY HOURS:
Mother Teresa said that we can win the fight for life and stop the scourge of abortion if we bring families into the Eucharistic Presence of Jesus for an hour every week. These weekly Holy Hour programs on videotape are our way of doing this. They make that hour with Jesus very special — for the entire family. Many of these programs include the Rosary with Scripturally based meditations and pictures, changing with each Hail Mary, to hold children's attention and enhance meditation for adults.

FIRST SATURDAY
LIGHT OF THE WORLD CENACLES:

Our Lady of Fatima told us that one of the factors for world peace is whether or not we come to Church on the First Saturday of the month, to pray and make reparation for the sins that offend her Immaculate Heart. Jesus said He wants us to place devotion to the Heart of His precious Mother alongside devotion to His own Sacred Heart. Pope John Paul himself sets the pace for First Saturday devotion by leading the Rosary on Vatican Radio on the First

Saturday of every month. Our First Saturday "Light of the World Cenacle" programs on videotape include the Rosary with 15 minutes of Scripturally based meditations, as requested by Our Lady.

T.V. MINISTRY

Sanctifying the airwaves by using them for God. Our daily **Family Covenant** and weekly **Healing Our Families** series reach millions in America and Canada, challenging them with the Truth and giving them practical helps for Christian living in today's world.

Our shows air on Mother Angelica's EWTN Catholic cable network at the following times. They can also be picked up from satellite Galaxy 3, Transponder 10:

every Friday: 1:00 a.m.
Monday through Friday: 5:30 a.m., 1:00 p.m., 11:30 p.m.
every Saturday and Sunday: 12:30 p.m.
every First Saturday: 1:00 p.m.
every Saturday: 5:00 p.m.
every Tuesday: 7:30 p.m.

plus . . . periodic one-hour specials.

Consult EWTN schedule or your local listing for current airing times.

NEIGHBORHOOD PEACE OF HEART FORUMS:

AFC members set aside time every day for quiet prayer, spiritual reading and reflection. Then once a week these families and individuals meet in private homes to be formed in the Faith through videotapes featuring some of the most knowledgeable and loyal sons and daughters of the Church. These Cardinals, Bishops, priests, religious and lay people share their expertise and insights on subjects ranging from the Holy Eucharist, Mary, saints, angels, heaven, hell and purgatory to papal documents, philosophy and theology.

Committed members then go out to evangelize their neighborhood, creating a growing nucleus of God-centeredness as more and more families come to know the Truth through use of the AFC's evangelization/formation video programs.

The Apostolate's FAMILY CATECHISM and FAMILY CATECHISM CHAPTERS:

The 1980 World Synod of Bishops expressed the hope that "a suitable catechism for families would be prepared, one that would be clear, brief and easily assimilated by all." (*Familiaris Consortio*, 39).

The Apostolate's Family Catechism is our answer to this call. Intended to help parents teach their children of all ages the Faith, it is divided into 7 volumes, with 21 chapters in each volume. Each daily lesson has two or three short questions and answers. Parents are supplied references to several more detailed adult catechisms. **The Apostolate's Family Catechism** is enriched by references to Scripture and the Vatican II teachings. A daily prayer summarizes each day's lesson.

The Catechism is designed for family use at dinnertime each night. Each week is backed up with two half-hour video programs featuring Sister John Vianney. The videos are to be viewed each week in a neighborhood setting by both parents and children. Thus use of the Catechism creates a community of families focused on tbe Truth that will truly set them free.

Cardinal Edouard Gagnon, President of the Pontifical Council for the Family, wrote: *"I particularly encourage the use of* **The Apostolate's Family Catechism** *by parents as a helpful means for fulfilling their solemn duty to impart* *adequate knowledge of the faith to their children and to prepare them properly for receiving the sacraments."* Mother Teresa of Calcutta has also encouraged **The Apostolate's Family Catechism**, saying *"The Apostolate's Family Catechism" will now enable parents to fulfill their primary obligation in teaching their children. I pray that every parent will join the Apostolate for Family Consecration and use The Apostolate's catechetical programme in their neighborhood."*

RETREAT MINISTRY:

Nestled in the rolling hills of rural Ohio, the AFC's "John Paul II Holy Family Center" invites individuals and entire families to come and be formed in Pope John Paul's Marian spirituality, while growing closer to God and each other. The Center is located on 800 acres of countryside, 13 miles from the Franciscan University of Steubenville, forming an ideal setting for retreats and family gatherings. Retreats center on Pope John Paul II's spirituality and our methods for evangelization. The following programs are available:

September through May:

• Chartered retreats: organize 20 or more to participate in a retreat that will not only renew you spiritually, but will also give you the formula and tools to go back and transform your neighborhood and parish into a God-centered community.

• Marriage and Family Life retreats
• Cursillo weekends
• Priests' retreats
• Businessmen's retreats
• Businesswomen's retreats

June through Labor Day (September):

• Weeklong Holy Family Fests — the entire family will experience the joy of a vibrant Christian community life, close to God and close to His creation in this beautiful country setting. Lots of clean-cut fun, practical spiritual formation and support. Whether your family is united or not, you and your children will be deeply touched. You'll want to come back.

Other organizations are also welcome to use the retreat facilities available at the John Paul II Holy Family Center. Write AFC, Box 151, Bloomingdale, Ohio 43910 or call 614-765-4301 or 414-652-2600 for more information.

Attend the inspiring Immaculate Conception "Be Not Afraid Eucharistic Holy Hours™" *for true family renewal. They are on videotape for weekly Parish Church gatherings.*

See Pope John Paul II, Bishop John Magee and Mother Teresa every night of the Novena series, plus these themes and other spiritual personalities.

Day 1   He is JOHN PAUL !
Cardinal Bernard Law

Day 2   *Totus Tuus:* The Marian Spirituality of Pope John Paul II
Cardinal Francis Arinze and Loretta Young

Day 3   Vatican II, Pope John Paul II, and the Laity: a Renewed World
Cardinal John O'Connor, Cardinal Joseph Bernardin and Sister John Vianney

Day 4   The Immaculate Conception: A Challenge to the U.S.
Cardinal Bernard Law, Cardinal John Krol, Cardinal Luigi Ciappi, Father Brian Harrison, Father Randall Paine and Loretta Young

Day 5 Mary Mother of God and Mother of the Church
Father Patrick Peyton and Loretta Young

Day 6 The Priesthood and the Holy Eucharist
Cardinal John Krol, Archbishop John Foley, Father Gene Jakubek and Sister John Vianney

Day 7 Confidence and God's Mercy through Mary's Intercession and Respect for Life
Cardinal John O'Connor, Monsignor John Woolsey, Father Michael Scanlan and Father John Bertolucci

Day 8 Youth, Hope of Mankind and the Church— Catholic Corps
Cardinal Francis Arinze, Cardinal Edouard Gagnon, Father Lawrence Lovasik, Mother Angelica, Mother Immaculata, Sr. John Vianney and The Catholic Corps

Day 9 Fatima: A Message of Hope—Our Destiny
Cardinal O'Connor, Bishop Donoghue, Sr. John Vianney and Loretta Young

Miraculous Medal Investiture on Day 4
Brown Scapular Enrollment on Day 7

Apostolate for Family Consecration®
John Paul II Holy Family Center, Box 151
Bloomingdale, OH 43910
Telephone 614-765-4301 or 414-652-2600

The "Be Not Afraid Eucharistic Holy Hours™" offer nine weekly gatherings of profound spiritual insights for the entire family in getting to know the depth of Pope John Paul II's mind and heart.

Dedicated to the Immaculate Conception, Patroness of the United States

• Pope John Paul II's motto is "Totus Tuus": "All Yours, Mary!" He has given all that he is and has to God through Mary, so that she, who never sinned, can "present him" to her Divine Son, Jesus.

• He's made the spiritual regeneration of families and peoples a primary crusade of his papacy.

• That's why the Apostolate for Family Consecration® (a lay Catholic organization that has adopted the spirituality of Karol Wojtyla, now Pope John Paul II) has launched the Papally blessed "Marian Era of Evangelization Campaign™."

• And why this spiritual learning event, the **"Be Not Afraid Eucharistic Holy Hours™" Program**, is dedicated to the Immaculate Conception, and is in support of the intentions of Pope John Paul II, who is the advocate of Christ-centered families and nations.

• The destiny of our families and entire nations are linked to her, the Immaculate Conception.

• The Mother of God is a channel of God's Mercy and Pope John Paul II assures us that **God wants to forgive us** and enable us to start again.

• That's why guests on the nine videotaped programs (who include those listed on the previous pages) talk so fervently and urgently about Mary's role in bringing us into the fullness of life promised by Jesus, her Son. "Total consecration," dedicating ourselves completely to God through God's most perfect creature, Mary, is the chosen spiritual path of Pope John Paul II.

Purpose of these "Be Not Afraid Eucharistic Holy Hours™"

1. Renewed esteem for the value of human life.

2. Consecration of our families, parishes, dioceses and nations to the Immaculate Conception.

3. Greater love of Our Holy Father, Pope John Paul II.

4. Invocation of God's Mercy upon all in attendance and all those who helped to promote the Holy Hours.

*The "Be Not Afraid Eucharistic Holy Hours™" Can Be a Source of **Powerful Spiritual Renewal for Families, the Whole Christian Community, and our world!***

"Be Not Afraid Eucharistic Holy Hours™"

1. *"Be Not Afraid Eucharistic Holy Hours™"* introductory videotape (item #133-322)

includes excerpts from the Divine Mercy Novena

2. Immaculate Conception Novena (item #171-72K)

(set of 9 programs plus 2 promo and preview tapes)

features Pope John Paul II...Mother Teresa...Bishop John Magee...Cardinal Luigi Ciappi, O.P. ...Cardinal Francis Arinze...Cardinal Edouard Gagnon...Cardinal John O'Connor...Cardinal Bernard Law...Cardinal John Krol...Cardinal Joseph Bernardin...Archbishop Pio Laghi...Archbishop Anthony Bevilacqua...Archbishop John Foley...Bishop John Donoghue...Msgr. John Woolsey...Fr. Michael Scanlan...Fr. Randall Paine...Fr. Brian Harrison...Fr. Patrick Peyton...Fr. John Bertolucci...Fr. Lawrence Lovasik...Sister John Vianney, S.S.N.D. ...Mother Immaculata, H.M.C. ...Mother M. Angelica...Mrs. Loretta Lewis Young...Jerry and Gwen Coniker.

3. 28¹/₂ minute T.V. promo, for Immaculate Conception Novena (item #171-74MD)

³/₄" broadcast quality tape

Includes 30- and 60-second promo spots.

4. Divine Mercy Novena (item #133-310K)

(set of 10 programs plus 2 promo and preview tapes)

features Pope John Paul II...Mother Teresa...Fr. George Kosicki, C.S.B. ...Cardinal Francis Arinze...Cardinal Edouard Gagnon...Archbishop Anthony Bevilacqua...Archbishop John Foley...Archbishop Pio Laghi...Bishop John Magee...Bishop Peter Van Lierde...Fr. John Bertolucci...Fr. Richard Drabik...Fr. Albert Krapiec...Fr. Seraphim Michalenko...Fr. Patrick Peyton...Fr. Michael Scanlan...Fr. Andrej Szostek...Richard Dumont, Ph.D. ...Helen Hayes...Rabbi Harold Kushner...Anthony Paruta, Ph.D. ...Burns K. Seeley, Ph.D. ...Jerry Coniker

5. 28¹/₂ minute T.V. promo, for Divine Mercy Novena (item #133-320MD)

³/₄" broadcast quality tape

Includes 30- and 60-second promo spots.

6. Planning meeting tape (item #133-321)

for developing a parish Holy Hour committee
(delegation forms included) 1-hour tape

Suggested ordering:

7. Pre-Novena Rosary videotapes (item #133-221K)

Rosary video with organ concert and pictorial meditations, to be played/
prayed before Novena. Set of three half-hour tapes includes Joyful,
Sorrowful, and Glorious Mysteries.

May 20, 1989

Jerome and Gwen Coniker
Founders
Apostolate for Family Consecration
John Paul II Holy Family Center
Box 151
Bloomingdale, OH 43910 USA

Dear Jerome and Gwen,

I want to encourage you and all of your members and friends to faithfully support Our Blessed Mother's request to come together in the churches on the First Saturday of the month, to receive Our Lord in Holy Communion, pray the Rosary and meditate for fifteen minutes and go to confession if at all possible, all in reparation for the sins that offend the Immaculate Heart of Mary and the sin of abortion in our world.

Your videotaped presentations are excellent; they hold the interest of the entire family and focus them on the Holy Eucharist, Our Blessed Mother, and the teachings of the Holy Father, the Pope.

It is so important that we be loyal to the Holy Father during these confusing times. On the First Saturday is a very sperial time for the parish communities to come together to honor and thank Our Lady.

I assure you of my continued prayers for your family and for all the members and co-workers of your Apostolate for Family Consecration.

Keep the joy of loving Jesus in each other and share this joy with all you meet.

God bless you.

God bless you
lu Teresa m

M. Teresa, M.C.

473

Letter from Pope John Paul II through his Secretary of State's Office

SECRETARIAT OF STATE — FIRST SECTION - GENERAL AFFAIRS

From the Vatican November 18, 1989

No. 250.418

Dear Mr. Coniker,

The Holy Father was pleased to learn about the "Marian Era of Evangelization Committee" of the Apostolate for Family Consecration, and he wishes me to convey his cordial greetings and good wishes to you and to all those associated in this worthy initiative.

His Holiness hopes that as a result of the Committee's activities, many Catholics will be led to a deeper appreciation of their faith and to a renewed commitment to Christ and his Church. The wise use of the communications media in the service of teaching and pastoral guidance creates new possibilities for evangelization. By focusing on family life in the home, neighborhood and parish, the Committee's efforts strengthen the very foundations of Christian living for the benefit of the Church and all of society.

As the Apostolate for Family Consecration works for a spiritual and moral transformation of society, the Holy Father commends all of you to God's loving care. In particular, he joins you in asking the intercession of the Blessed Virgin Mary so that all you do may be inspired by her shining example of faith and trust. With confidence in her powerful protection, he willingly imparts the requested Apostolic Blessing.

With every good wish, I am

Sincerely yours,

+ E. Cassidy

+E. Cassidy
Under-Secretary of State

Mr. Jerome F. Coniker
President/Founder
Apostolate for Family Consecration
John Paul II Holy Family Center
Box 151
Bloomingdale, OH 43910   U.S.A.

474

If Jerome Le Royer lived today, his spirituality would be in total harmony with that of Pope John Paul II, who is totally consecrated to the Sacred Heart of Jesus through the Immaculate Heart of Mary.

The above picture is the logo for the papally blessed *"Marian Era of Evangelization Campaign"* of the Apostolate for Family Consecration, which is focused on the Holy Eucharist, Mary, and the Papacy, with Mother Teresa as the symbol of fidelity to all three.

Pope John Paul II on the meaning of Consecration

On the cross, Christ said, "Woman, behold your son!" With these words, He opened His Mother's heart in a new way. A little later, *the Roman soldier's spear pierced the side of the Cricified One.* That pierced heart became a sign of the redemption, achieved through the death of the Lamb of God.

The Immaculate Heart of Mary, *opened with the words,* "*Woman, behold your son!*" is spiritually united with the heart of her Son opened by the soldier's spear. Mary's heart was opened by the same love for man and for the world with which Christ loved man and the world, offering Himself for them on the cross, until the soldier's spear struck that blow.

Consecrating the world to the Immaculate Heart of Mary means drawing near, through the Mother's intercession, to the very Fountain of life that sprang from Golgotha. This Fountain unceasingly pours forth redemption and grace. In it, reparation is continually made for the sins of the world. It is a ceaseless source of new life and holiness.

Consecrating the world to the Immaculate Heart of the Mother means returning beneath the cross of the Son. It means consecrating this world to the pierced heart of the Savior, bringing it back to the very source of its redemption. Redemption is always greater than man's sin and the "sin of the world." The power of the redemption is infinitely superior to the whole range of evil in man and the world.

The heart of the Mother is aware of this, more than any other heart in the whole universe, visible and invisible.

And so she calls us.

She not only calls us to be converted, she calls us to accept her motherly help to return to the source of redemption.

Taken from Pope John Paul II's homily, which he delivered at the shrine of Our Lady of Fatima on May 13, 1982. On the 65th anniversary of the first apparitions at Fatima, His Holiness went to Fatima to consecrate the world to the Immaculate Heart of Mary, and to thank Our Lady for her intercessory help in the saving of his life exactly one year earlier. On May 13, 1981, an attempt was made on the Holy Father's life in St. Peter's Square, Vatican City.

This illustration depicts St. Dominic, the first papal theologian, followed by St. Thomas Aquinas, the fourth papal theologian, and finally, Mario Luigi Cardinal Ciappi, O.P., the eighty-fifty papal theologian, primary theological advisor for the Apostolate for Family Consecration, and one of the greatest theologians of our time.

On the following page, you will find a letter from Cardinal Ciappi to the Apostolate's founder, Jerome F. Coniker, describing the essence of consecration. Please read it carefully and prayerfully. It describes the positive power of consecration which Jerome Le Royer certainly discovered and lived in his time.

Il Pio Teologo della Casa Pontificia
00120 Citta del Vaticano, Vatican City

August 24, 1989

Mr. and Mrs. Jerome F. Coniker
Apostolate for Family Consecration
PO Box 220
Kenosha, WISC. 53141
U.S.A.

Dear Jerry and Gwen Coniker and all the families of The Apostolate,

I wish to encourage your continued stress on total consecration to Jesus through Mary.

Paragraph 4 of Pope Paul VI's Apostolic Constitution on the Revision of Indulgences states:

"By the hidden and kindly mystery of God's will a Supernatural solidarity reigns among men. A consequence of this is that the sin of one person harms other people just as one person's holiness helps others."

If this is true, how true it is that when we give all our merits to Mary, She multiplies them by Her own incalculable merits. This puts into motion positive spiritual forces to repair the damage due to sin and significantly change the course of history, if enough make this commitment.

Mary's merits can multiply the effects of one person's holiness and help countless souls. Only Heaven knows the depth of holiness a soul must achieve to tip the scales for world peace.

I agree that this apostolate of family consecration is the best way to defeat the scourge of abortion and renew family life.

The spiritual offensive must always be in the vanguard, presupposing all other activities.

The "Marian Era of Evangelization Campaign" can put into motion a chain of events to bring about that era of peace promised at Fatima. With His Holiness Pope John Paul, we look expectantly and prayerfully for this era to begin with the dawn of the third millennium, the year 2001.

Praying for the success of your most needed apostolate, I remain,

Yours in the Hearts of Jesus and Mary,

Mario Luigi Card. Ciappi, O. P.

Mario Luigi Cardinal Ciappi, O.P.
Pro-Theologian of the Pontifical Household